THE PROFESSIONAL PRACTICE SERIES

The Professional Practice Series is sponsored by the Society for Industrial and Organizational Psychology (SIOP). The series was launched in 1988 to provide industrial/organizational psychologists, organizational scientists and practitioners, human resource professionals, managers, executives, and those interested in organizational behavior and performance with volumes that are insightful, current, informative, and relevant to organizational practice. The volumes in the Professional Practice Series are guided by five tenets designed to enhance future organizational practice:

1. Focus on practice, but grounded in science
2. Translate organizational science into practice by generating guidelines, principles, and lessons learned that can shape and guide practice
3. Showcase the application of industrial/organizational psychology to solve problems
4. Document and demonstrate best industrial and organizational-based practices
5. Stimulate research needed to guide future organizational practice

The volumes seek to inform those interested in practice with guidance, insights, and advice on how to apply the concepts, findings, methods, and tools derived from industrial/organizational psychology to solve human-related organizational problems.

Previous Professional Practice Series volumes include:

Published by Jossey-Bass

The 21st Century Executive
Rob Silzer, Editor

Managing Selection in Changing Organizations
Jerard F. Kehoe, Editor

Evolving Practices in Human Resource Management
Allen I. Kraut, Abraham K. Korman, Editors

Individual Psychological Assessment
Richard Jeanneret, Rob Silzer, Editors

Performance Appraisal
James W. Smither, Editor

Organizational Surveys
Allen I. Kraut, Editor

Employees, Careers, and Job Creation
Manuel London, Editor

Published by Guilford Press

Diagnosis for Organizational Change
Ann Howard and Associates

Human Dilemmas in Work Organizations
Abraham K. Korman and Associates

Diversity in the Workplace
Susan E. Jackson and Associates

Working with Organizations and Their People
Douglas W. Bray and Associates

Creating, Implementing, and Managing Effective Training and Development

Creating, Implementing, and Managing Effective Training and Development

State-of-the-Art Lessons for Practice

Kurt Kraiger

Editor

Foreword by Eduardo Salas

JOSSEY-BASS
A Wiley Company
www.josseybass.com

Published by

JOSSEY-BASS
A Wiley Company
989 Market Street
San Francisco, CA 94103-1741

www.josseybass.com

Jossey-Bass books and products are available through most bookstores. To contact Jossey-Bass directly, call (888) 378-2537, fax to (800) 605-2665, or visit our website at www.josseybass.com.

Substantial discounts on bulk quantities of Jossey-Bass books are available to corporations, professional associations, and other organizations. For details and discount information, contact the special sales department at Jossey-Bass.

We at Jossey-Bass strive to use the most environmentally sensitive paper stocks available to us. Our publications are printed on acid-free recycled stock whenever possible, and our paper always meets or exceeds minimum GPO and EPA requirements.

Library of Congress Cataloging-in-Publication Data

Creating, implementing, and managing effective training and development: state-of-the-art lessons for practice / Kurt Kraiger, Editor.
     p. cm.—(The professional practice series)
   Includes bibliographical references and index.
   ISBN 0-7879-5396-2 (alk. paper)
     1. Employees—Training of.   I. Kraiger, Kurt, 1957–
HF5549.5.T7 C74 2002
658.3'12404—dc21

2001004584

FIRST EDITION
HB Printing   10 9 8 7 6 5 4 3 2 1

Contents

Part Three: Evaluating and Institutionalizing Training

Foreword

None of us can avoid it: we all go through some form of training during our professional (and personal) lives. It may be formal or informal, short or long, computer-based or instructor-led, in-house or in a nice resort outside the workplace, self-paced or locked-space, mandatory or voluntary, and focused on technical or "soft" skills. And we all experience variations of these. We have all been to some good training and to some not-so-good training. We have all been to training that is very relevant to our jobs and some that makes us think, "Why am I here?"

Why are there such inconsistencies in the quality and delivery of training? Why indeed—when we have had seen an explosion in training research in recent years and seem to know a lot about how to design, deliver, and evaluate training systems. Although the science of training has not answered all the questions, progress has been made. We have more principles, guidelines, and tips derived from the research at our disposal than we care to admit or document. This book is just an illustration of what we know and what works.

But this is not enough. We need, at least in my opinion, to do a better job of translating the findings and conclusions from our numerous studies, especially because industrial/organizational psychologists have been at the forefront of the science of training. We need to provide those in practice with useful, relevant, and practical information about how to design, deliver, and evaluate training. This book is also an illustration of how the research findings can be translated to serve those that need it.

Kurt Kraiger and associates have compiled a set of refreshing yet practical (and challenging) chapters that clearly show how the science of training can contribute to enhancing training effectiveness in organizations. When designed and delivered systematically, training can lead to significant performance improvements—just follow the advice provided by the authors in this volume. The editorial board of the Professional Practice Series hopes this book (and others to come) will help those interested in accelerating expertise in their organizations and improving individual as well as team competencies. We hope it provides HR practitioners, instructional developers, chief learning officers, and all those who promote learning in organizations with some useful answers to their training challenges.

I thank and congratulate Kurt Kraiger and the other authors in this volume for putting together this much-needed work on training.

September 2001

EDUARDO SALAS
University of Central Florida
Series Editor

Preface

What a difference a decade makes! From the early 1960s until the late 1980s, training research lay largely dormant. Reviewers for the *Annual Review of Psychology* habitually characterized the research as atheoretical, uninspiring, or virtually nonexistent (for example, Goldstein, 1980; Campbell, 1971; Latham, 1988; Wexley, 1984). Latham (1988) summarized the state of the art in the late 1980s as follows: "It may become a tradition in this journal for the authors of the chapter on training and development to lament . . . the lack of attention to theory and the lack of research influencing practice evident in the practitioner literature on this topic" (pp. 545–546). Early on, Campbell also noted that research tended to compare new and old training methods, rather than attempt to advance our knowledge of how learning needs should be diagnosed, addressed through training, or evaluated. Goldstein and Sorcher's (1974) and Decker's research (Decker & Nathan, 1985) on behavioral modeling might well represent the best in theory development and research during the 1970s and 1980s.

In contrast, the past decade has seen an unprecedented level of activity. There have been new theories or models of training evaluation and transfer of training, broader systems thinking with respect to training effectiveness, and at the close of the decade, a transition from traditional instructor-led models to exciting new applications of e-learning such as Web-based training and virtual reality training. Indeed, in their *Annual Review* chapter, Salas and Cannon-Bowers (2001) refer to the 1990s as the decade of progress and pronounce the training research patient healthy. It is interesting to consider what might have accounted for the decade long surge in interest in training theory and application.

I believe that much of the credit goes to three influential papers appearing between 1985 and 1989. First, as part of his dissertation, Ray Noe developed a general model of training effectiveness

(Noe, 1986). Because of their emphasis on measurement and evaluation, industrial/organizational (I/O) psychologists have been naturally interested in pretraining needs assessment and post-training evaluation. For example, Hinrichs's (1976) chapter in the first I/O handbook devoted as much space to needs analysis as to learning theory. Topics of training design and effective instruction were left to other disciplines. Noe's paper made two important points. The first is that the quality and effectiveness of training are not merely a function of how well the training is designed and delivered but also of the attitudes and motivational states of trainees before, during, and after training. The second is that there is a direct, predictable relationship between organizational level factors (climate or supervisory support, for example) and the attitudes or motivation of trainees. By linking training effectiveness to individual differences and organizational variables, Noe made training appear psychological and encouraged research on subjects linking both organizational factors and individual attributes to training outcomes. In this volume, Noe and Colquitt contribute a chapter that summarizes fifteen years of training effectiveness and embellishes on Noe's initial model.

Second, Tim Baldwin and Kevin Ford (1988) wrote a review and conceptual paper on transfer of training. Transfer deals with how much of what is learned in training is applied to the job. Through their examination of transfer, Baldwin and Ford redirected training researchers toward a focus on learning (in part by suggesting that learning and transfer are two ends of the same continuum). That is, the critical question focused not on how to *train* employees but how to encourage *learning* in a way that generalizes across situations and can be maintained over time. The shift in focus is important because it began to move training research away from the evaluation of teaching tools or training methods and toward a science of how and when individuals learn. In addition, like Noe (1986), Baldwin and Ford recognized the importance of organizational factors that could facilitate or hamper learning and transfer. Baldwin and Ford's thinking about transfer is reflected in Machin's chapter on transfer of training in this volume.

Third, in a volume published in 1989, Bill Howell and Nancy Cooke contributed a chapter on training and information processing theories. Their intention was to introduce the training researcher to the cognitive scientist, but not necessarily to marry them. That is, Howell and Cooke presented few original examples of how the integration of training models and cognitive research on learning might result in new methods of needs assessment, training design, training, or evaluation. In contrast, for many training researchers, their chapter was the first to suggest that information processing models from cognitive psychology could be relevant to training processes. Like Baldwin and Ford (1988), Howell and Cooke helped to shift the predominant paradigm from one centered on how to instruct toward one centered on how individuals learn. Training research slowly became less parochial, and following Kraiger, Ford, and Salas's (1993) monograph on learning outcomes and Ford and Kraiger's (1995) chapter applying cognitive models to needs assessment, design, and transfer, training researchers began to integrate modern learning theories into training research questions. Advances rooted in Howell and Cooke's work can be seen in this volume in the chapters by DuBois; Brown and Ford; Salas, Burke, and Cannon-Bowers; and Kraiger.

Training research has never been healthier, more active, or more conceptually well-founded than it is today. The question that remains is whether this accumulated knowledge can be applied successfully to training practice. The training industry itself has evolved rapidly over the past five to ten years. Evidence suggests that organizations are investing more in employee training and development (Van Buren, 2001), the form of instructional delivery is changing as e-learning explodes (for example, Scribner, 2000), and chief learning officers are finding their ways into executive boardrooms in organizations such as American Airlines, Sprint, Ford, and the Internal Revenue Service. The healthy state of training research and the dynamic state of the field suggests that this is an opportune time for this volume in the SIOP Practice Series.

Purpose and Audience

The purpose of the current volume is to provide guidelines for implementing and maintaining effective training and development programs in organizations. The intent is to capture theoretical advances made in training over the last ten years and apply insights from this work as a foundation for grounding processes such as strategic planning and needs assessment, training design and media selection, training delivery, transfer of training and training evaluation, and long-term maintenance of learning programs in organizations. The intended audience is practitioners in the field of employee training and development. They may be internal or external consultants and are likely to hold such job titles as consultant, chief learning officer, training manager, director of management development, instructional designer, performance technologist, and manager of human resources. In many larger organizations, responsibilities for employee training and management development are differentiated. Although the principles in this book should apply to both, to the extent that employee training is more likely to be concerned with fundamental practices such as needs assessment, informal or formal instruction, transfer, and evaluation, this volume will prove more helpful to individuals working in that domain.

Why This Book?

As noted earlier, training research has progressed rapidly in the past ten years. Where can I/O practitioners look for guidance on training decisions? The primary textbooks (Goldstein & Ford, 2001; Noe, 1999; Wexley & Latham, 2000) necessarily lack the depth to address in detail specific issues such as planning a diversity training program, establishing a coaching program, or maintaining a learning organization. There have been several very good edited books, but these are either now dated (Goldstein & Associates, 1989), espouse a single (rather than multidisciplinary) perspective (Robinson & Robinson, 1998), or are focused on research rather than practice (Ford, Kozlowski, Kraiger, Salas, & Teachout, 1997; Quiñones & Ehrenstein, 1997). Accordingly, there is a need for a book that is founded on current theory and research and applies this work to training decisions in organizations. This volume presents contributions from practitioners and researchers who provide state-of-the-art, multidisciplinary principles and guidelines for training practice. Brief summaries of the chapters follow.

Overview of the Volume

To open the volume, Colleen Petersen and Linda Rogers of Cisco Systems provide a practitioner's perspective on the actual and potential impact of the science of training on planning and managing the training function. Petersen and Rogers were given a set of questions on the research-practice interface. They collected responses from their colleagues in the training industry. The question-and-answer format of the chapter allows for a quick overview of the historical limits of training research as well as suggestions for optimizing the impact of this research in the future.

Chapters Two through Four discuss how to position training and development in the organization and plan for effective training interventions. In Chapter Two, Scott Tannenbaum describes a strategic view of organizational training and learning. He proposes a set of strategic learning imperatives to address five broad challenges facing today's organizations. Strategic learning imperatives are high-level, learning-related actions necessary to ensure continued organizational success. The broad challenges are intensified competition, rapid change, a power shift to the customer, collaborations across organizational and geographic boundaries, and the need to maintain high levels of talent in organizations. Tannenbaum identifies seven lessons from the past decade of research, including these: even well-designed training does not necessarily transfer to on-the-job performance; employees must perceive value in their learning experiences to benefit from them; what happens in the broader organizational system has a big impact on training effectiveness; and formal training is not the primary source of learning. Considering both today's business challenges and the lessons from training research, Tannenbaum offers eight strategic learning imperatives and suggests that human resource and training managers adapt and integrate them into their own strategic plans. The strategic learning imperatives include diversifying employees' learning portfolios, accelerating the pace at which employees learn, ensuring ample opportunities for employees to learn and grow, and diagnosing and modifying the work environment to support transfer and learning.

In Chapter Three, which updates Noe's (1986) model of training effectiveness, Ray Noe and Jason Colquitt continue the theme that successful training and development is a systemwide phenomenon. *Training effectiveness* refers to the processes before, during, and after training that collectively enhance the potential for impact. This chapter should be relevant to virtually anyone involved in any aspect of training planning, design, delivery, or evaluation. Noe and Colquitt note that for training to be effective, trainees must meet four conditions: they must be ready to learn, they must be motivated (to learn and apply their learning), they must learn the training content, and they must transfer or apply their training back on the job. The third and fourth conditions have been the traditional focus of both training researchers and training practitioners. Therefore, it is clear that the greatest added value of the training effectiveness model is to delineate conditions that influence trainee readiness and motivation. Noe and Colquitt review the literature on influences on all four training conditions and present practical guidelines for positively affecting them through systems-level, interpersonal, and training-level interventions.

Chapter Four presents a specific methodology to be used during the training needs assessment process. David DuBois discusses why, when, and how to use cognitive task analysis (CTA). CTA is a method for analyzing job tasks and requirements that places special emphasis on eliciting mental processes. Cognitive task analyses can supplement traditional needs assessment strategies by describing important, unobservable cognitive activities such as decision making, problem solving, and situational assessment. CTA is especially useful with jobs that are complex, have high-stakes outcomes, and require adaptive knowledge. DuBois seeks to clarify why, when, and how cognitive task analysis can be used to improve individual and organizational effectiveness. The chapter is divided into three sections. The first explains what CTA is. The second identifies the need and potential drivers for it. Finally, the third section provides tips and guidelines for implementation, including suggestions on how to integrate cognitive task analysis into routine organizational processes.

Chapters Five through Eight provide detailed discussions of specific training and development methods—best practices in various content areas. In Chapter Five, Donna Chrobot-Mason and Mickey Quiñones talk about training in a diverse workplace. The authors note that although the number of diversity training programs implemented in the United States continues to accelerate, research suggests that they may do more harm than good. They argue that more attention must be paid to the development and evaluation of effective diversity training if organizations are to achieve the benefits of a diverse workforce. The chapter integrates research findings from the training literature with diversity training practices and offers suggestions for improving diversity training practices. Following traditional instructional models, Chrobot-Mason and Quiñones walk the reader through a systematic approach to developing diversity training, including performing needs assessment and developing clear objectives, developing content based on a three-phase approach to learning (awareness, skill building, and action planning), gaining management buy-in, and evaluating and maintaining the intervention.

In Chapter Six, David Peterson writes about leadership development through coaching and mentoring programs. This chapter provides a practical framework for accelerating learning and development through coaching, examines best practices in coaching, and provides specific recommendations on designing individual coaching programs, organizational programs for coaching multiple individuals, and companywide mentoring programs. As Peterson notes, strategies for effective coaching programs are in many ways the same as those for any effective training program: an environment of trust, understanding, and supportiveness; committed participants; and a focus on skills. In addition, successful coaching and mentoring allow for customization and just-in-time learning. Peterson's chapter should be of interest to any training practitioner—not only those involved in coaching and mentoring programs.

In Chapter Seven, Ken Brown and Kevin Ford discuss facilitating the use of computer technology in training by building an infrastructure for active learning. They discuss the trend away from instructor-led, classroom training toward technology-mediated training. Research to date on computer-based learning has focused more on the technology itself (for example, navigation, screen design) than on the learning process. Brown and Ford argue that we need to understand *how* individuals learn in technology-mediated environments and then translate that understanding into design principles. Poorly designed training will not result in learning no matter the cost or appeal of the technology. This chapter offers design principles for technology-based training that results in active learning. When learners are active they want to master the subject and are motivated. The design principles presented are organized around four themes: information structure and presentation, learner control and guidance, learning activities and feedback, and metacognitive monitoring and control. Although the principles offered are specific to computer-mediated environments, any training practitioner involved in the design or delivery of training will want to review them.

In Chapter Eight, Eduardo Salas, Shawn Burke, and Jan Cannon-Bowers offer tips and guidelines for designing and delivering team training. Just as Noe and Colquitt's chapter summarizes and applies nearly twenty years of research on training effectiveness, Salas, Burke, and Cannon-Bowers's chapter summarizes research over a similar time frame that focuses on understanding how to promote, train, and measure effective teams and teamwork. The authors offer tips and guidelines to help practitioners understand the requirements for effective teamwork and for designing and delivering an effective team training system. Among other things, they suggest conducting a systematic team-oriented training needs analysis (a team-based cognitive task analysis), embedding both task and teamwork skills in the team training system, attending to prepractice training conditions that may affect the benefit of guided team practice, and combining traditional individual training methods with research-based team training strategies such as team coordination training, guided self-correction, cross-training, and event-based training. Just as Peterson's chapter offers useful advice that is applicable to most training efforts, many of Salas, Burke, and Cannon-Bowers's tips for effective team training apply equally well to programs for individuals.

The final three chapters discuss issues of ensuring, maintaining, and measuring training impact. In Chapter Nine, Tony Machin discusses planning, managing, and optimizing transfer of training. Machin first reviews several important theoretical models of the transfer process; these models highlight the importance of variables such as transfer climate and transfer-enhancing activities during training, and individual characteristics such as ability, self-efficacy, previous knowledge, and skill. These models suggest that events before, during, and after training affect learning during training and subsequent transfer afterwards. They also form the theoretical basis for planned interventions to enhance transfer. Pretraining interventions focus on improving motivation and self-efficacy. Interventions during training target improving learning, improving transfer intentions, and improving reactions to the training.

Posttraining interventions focus on improving the transfer climate and the vertical transfer of training. For each set of interventions, Machin offers researched-based strategies for improving transfer.

In Chapter Ten, John Jeppesen contributes his thoughts on creating and maintaining the learning organization. Learning organizations are defined as those that deliberately (and continuously) plan for employee development and support continuous learning systems; as a result their operational environments remain competitive and ready to move into the future. As discussed throughout the book, but particularly in the chapters by Tannenbaum, Noe and Colquitt, and Machin, the success of specific training programs can be affected by broader systems-level factors. Training and development programs are most successful when learning outcomes are aligned with corporate strategic initiatives. When an organization makes a commitment to build a learning organization it addresses such issues. Jeppesen notes that as research on learning organizations has grown, it has become clear that leaders and organizational change agents benefit from viewing training and learning as part of larger systems that influence training transfer. Jeppesen makes the business case for learning organizations, reviews key characteristics of effective learning organizations, and offers evidence of desired outcomes in learning organizations. Finally, he proposes a new tool for designing and measuring learning systems and offers practical guidelines for developing and maintaining a learning organization.

In Chapter Eleven, Kurt Kraiger discusses decision-based evaluation. Kraiger begins by noting somewhat pessimistically that state-of-the-art training evaluation measures today seem virtually unchanged from the well-accepted measures of four decades ago. He discusses the widespread acceptance of the forty-year-old four-levels model, despite recent criticisms of it. He asserts that progress in evaluation has (and will) come not so much from thinking about what or how to evaluate (the content and measures) but from making better decisions about why (the purpose) and when (the design). Kraiger proposes an approach to evaluation that begins with delineation of the purpose for the evaluation, and then bases on it decisions about what, how, and when to evaluate training programs. He proposes a new model for evaluation that targets training content and delivery, changes in the learner, and organizational payoffs. A series of tables help readers choose the most appropriate evaluation measures given the purpose of evaluation and content of training.

Lessons Learned

It is sometimes customary to end volumes such as this with a chapter on lessons learned across the various contributions. Here, I offer these lessons at the outset, hoping they will whet the reader's appetite for the full chapters rather than satiate their hunger. In no particular order, here are the lessons.

Training Outcomes Are Affected by the Broader Organizational System

This was one of the messages given by both Noe (1986) and Baldwin and Ford (1988), and that message is reinforced here in the chapters by Tannenbaum, Jeppesen, Noe and Colquitt, Chrobot-Mason and Quiñones, Petersen and Rogers, and Machin. Organizational level variables (for example, emphasis on performance or continuous learning climate) have an impact on the pretraining motivation of trainees, their focus and efforts to learn during training, and their motivation and success in transferring training to the job. Organizational attitudes *do* make a difference. For example, I was once involved in a cognitive task analysis of air traffic controllers. We asked controllers in Daytona Beach which factors affected their pretraining perceptions of an upcoming program. One told us that if the training was being held there, it was probably not important. If it was held in Orlando, it probably was important. And if they had to go to Orlando and spend the night (at a nice hotel), it was probably very important. Managers' behavior—particularly the behaviors of direct supervisors of trainees—toward training also make a difference. Supervisors who take the time to learn (about) the training content, reduce trainee workloads during training, and show support for newly learned behaviors will find that their trainees benefit the most from interventions.

In its annual state-of-the-industry reports, the American Society of Training and Development differentiates "training investment leaders" from other organizations participating in its bench-marking studies. Training investment leaders are organizations that have made a dedicated commitment to training that is evident in statistics on training expenditures, training hours per employee, percentage of eligible employees receiving training, and applica-tion of learning technologies. The best practices cited in this volume suggest that in addition to these numerical indicators, organiza-tions that get the most out of training successfully align it with or-ganizational practices (or perhaps align organizational practices with training).

Support and Buy-In from Upper Managment Are Essential

In their chapters, Tannenbaum and Jeppesen most directly address the importance of getting management on the training band-wagon, but similar ideas are offered by Noe and Colquitt, Chrobot-Mason and Quiñones, Peterson, Brown and Ford, Machin, and Kraiger. Training and development efforts must be consistent with key strategic organizational initiatives and those linkages must be clear to organizational stakeholders, training designers, and the trainees themselves. Tannenbaum's chapter in particular offers suggestions on how to gauge the winds of change and align the training with new organizational directions. Obviously, upper man-agement support during the planning stages offers clear benefits. With a champion onboard, both the financial and human re-sources necessary to make training happen are more likely to be there. However, it is equally clear from many chapters in this vol-ume that good things happen at other stages of the instructional process if top management support is there. At the outset of train-ing, the link between intended learning outcomes and organiza-tional processes is evident to trainees, enhancing their motivation. Chrobot-Mason and Quiñones provide a good example of the sym-bolic power and impact on learning of top management partici-pation during the training process. Finally, when trainees get back on the job, upper management support will encourage supervisory support for transfer and that, in turn, will enhance trainee moti-vation to transfer.

Employees Must Perceive Value in Their Experiences to Benefit from Them

Ensuring the relevance and realism of training is stressed in several chapters, including those by Noe and Colquitt, DuBois, Chrobot-Mason and Quiñones, Peterson, Brown and Ford, Salas, Burke, and Cannon-Bowers, and Kraiger. The importance of the fidelity of the training environment has long been accepted as an important characteristic of successful training, and the importance of the relevance of the training material has emerged as a tenet of the adult learning literature. One of the messages that emerges from these chapters is that given all the information now available to workers, training content must appear more relevant, more useful, and more important than other available information. The relevance of training content can be established during the needs assessment process or by evaluating prior training programs. Ideally, the training content is packaged so that trainees can see the relationship between the content and the demands of their jobs. The authors in this volume make it clear that for training to be most effective, participants must see, for example, how they may become better managers by learning how to resolve diversity-related conflict or by completing a difficult assignment.

Training Measurement Is Valuable But Should Fit the Training System

The role of measurement is highlighted to some extent in all chapters, but particularly in those of Noe and Colquitt, DuBois, Chrobot-Mason and Quiñones, Machin, and Kraiger. No author advocates measuring simply for the sake of measuring, but each indicates how purposeful measurement can improve the efficiency or effectiveness of a training system. For example, Noe and Colquitt and Machin discuss using measurement to diagnose pre- and post-training environments to improve training effectiveness, Chrobot-Mason and Quiñones discuss the importance of needs assessment to ensure that diversity training is aligned with corporate strategic initiatives and target meaningful on-the-job skills, and Kraiger discusses how posttraining evaluations can be useful in making decisions about training or marketing training to other organizational units or future trainees. In all, the authors recognize the additional costs and threats that come with measurement, but associate these negative outcomes with routine, reflexive assessment rather than measurement systems designed for specific purposes. By being aware of the nature of the resistance to training and assessment, training practitioners can design and use measurements that make more effective use of resources and optimize training impact.

Training Is About Learning

Understanding how individuals learn and building that learning into training programs is another central theme that runs through virtually all chapters, but in particular those of DuBois, Peterson, Brown and Ford, Machin, and Kraiger. All the processes of planning, design, delivery, evaluation, and positioning of the training function discussed are important and advance training practice. But to paraphrase St. Paul, if we have all these things but do not have learning, we have nothing. Thus, the single most important attribute of successful training programs is the creation of a true learning environment—setting the spark that flames up into learning.

In the beginning of this Preface, I noted that one of the biggest influences on training research before 1990 was a shift from thinking about training as instruction to thinking about training as learning. That is, as training researchers began to consider how individuals learn, they began to think more broadly about how to plan for, influence, and evaluate that learning. A little over a decade later, this paradigm shift is evident in many of the chapters in this volume. For example, DuBois emphasizes the cognitive aspects of job performance and discusses ways to elicit expert models and problem-solving methods from job incumbents, Peterson discusses how conditions of learning can be designed into coaching and mentoring relationships, and Brown and Ford provide tips for designing technology-based training based on active learning principles. According to Brown and Ford, active learning occurs when learners are mastery oriented, mindful, and motivated. As we should all keep in mind, active learning is not simply a preferred state for technology-mediated training but an important, even necessary, condition for any learning to occur. Parents who have not yet formed a strong visual image of what active learning looks like may recall the fierce determination, attentiveness, and single-mindedness of a three-year-old who wants to learn to do something that an adult can do—be it cooking, shaving, or drinking from an open glass. Anyone who has ever taught a course or conducted a training program would admit there is too often a huge gulf between the active learning of that three-year-old and that of our students or trainees. Both as a parent and as a researcher interested in training and learning, I have become increasingly convinced that, ultimately, learning is magic. Of course there are biological and cognitive explanations for what happens in our brains when we learn, but these are not necessarily more useful than simply characterizing it as magic. The magic comes from insights, connections, or ideas that weren't there before. Yet we all understand that the illusion we see as magic is the result of considerable preparation and careful accomplishment. This book is about how to prepare for and accomplish successful training.

Denver, Colorado   Kurt Kraiger
September 2001

References

Baldwin, T. T., & Ford, J. K. (1988). Transfer of training: A review and directions for future research. *Personnel Psychology, 41,* 63–105.

Campbell, J. P. (1971). Personnel training and development. *Annual Review of Psychology, 22,* 565–602.

Decker, P. J., & Nathan, B. R. (1985). *Behavior modeling training: Principles and applications.* New York: Praeger.

Ford, J. K., Kozlowski, S.W.J., Kraiger, K., Salas, E., & Teachout, M. S. (Eds.). (1997). *Improving training effectiveness in work organizations.* Hillsdale, NJ: Erlbaum.

Goldstein, I. L. (1980). Training in work organizations. *Annual Review of Psychology, 31,* 229–272.

Goldstein, I. L., & Associates. (Eds.). (1989). *Training and development in organizations.* San Francisco: Jossey-Bass.

Goldstein, I. L., & Ford, J. K. (2001). *Training in organizations* (4th ed.). Pacific Grove, CA: Wadsworth.

Goldstein, A. P., & Sorcher, M. (1974). *Changing supervisor behavior.* New York: Pergamon Press.

Hinrichs, J. R. (1976). Personnel training. In M. D. Dunnette (Ed.), *Handbook of industrial and organizational psychology* (pp. 829–860). Skokie, IL: Rand-McNally.

Howell, W. C., & Cooke, N. J. (1989). Training the human information processor: A review of cognitive models. In I. L. Goldstein & Associates (Eds.), *Training and development in organizations* (pp. 121–182). San Francisco: Jossey-Bass.

Kraiger, K., Ford, J. K., & Salas, E. (1993). Application of cognitive, skill-based, and affective theories of learning outcomes to new methods of training evaluation (Monograph). *Journal of Applied Psychology, 78,* 311–328.

Latham, G. P. (1988). Human resource training and development. *Annual Review of Psychology, 39,* 545–582.

Noe, R. A. (1986). Trainees' attributes and attitudes: Neglected influences on training effectiveness. *Academy of Management Review, 11,* 736–749.

Noe, R. A. (1999). *Employee training and development.* Burr Ridge, IL: Irwin.

Quiñones, M. A., & Ehrenstein, A. (1997). *Training for a rapidly changing workplace: Applications of psychological research.* Washington, DC: American Psychological Association.

Robinson, D. G., & Robinson, J. C. (1998). *Moving from training to performance: A practical guidebook.* San Francisco: Berrett-Koehler.

Salas, E., & Cannon-Bowers, J. A. (2001). The science of training: A decade of progress. *Annual Review of Psychology, 52,* 471–499.

Scribner, S. A. (2000, November 20). Take the e-train. *Business 2.0 Newsletter* [http://www.business2.com/magazine/2000/11/23486.htm].

Van Buren, M. E. (2001). *State of the industry: Report 2001.* Washington, DC: American Society for Training and Development.

Wexley, K. N. (1984). Personnel training. *Annual Review of Psychology, 35,* 519–551.

Wexley, K. N., & Latham G. P. (2000). *Developing and training human resources in organizations* (3rd ed.). Englewood Cliffs, NJ: Prentice-Hall.

The Authors

KURT KRAIGER is professor of psychology at the University of Colorado at Denver. His major research interests include training theory, training evaluation, cognitive assessment, and performance appraisal. Kraiger has published or presented over 120 scientific articles, chapters, and technical reports and is currently on the editorial board of *Human Factors*. He coedited one training book, *Improving Training Effectiveness in Work Organizations* and is the editor of *Creating, Implementing, and Managing Effective Training and Development: State-of-the-Art Lessons for Practice*. He has consulted in training, selection, and organizational effectiveness at a number of organizations, including McDonald's, Miller Brewing, Warner Lambert, US WEST, the National Institute of Occupational Safety and Health, and Global Crossings. Kraiger received his B.A. in psychology from the University of Cincinnati in 1979 and his Ph.D. in I/O psychology from The Ohio State University in 1983. He is a fellow of the Society of Industrial and Organizational Psychology.

KENNETH G. BROWN received a B.S. in psychology from the University of Maryland in 1993 and a Ph.D. in industrial and organizational psychology from Michigan State University in 1999. He is now assistant professor of management and organizations at the Henry B. Tippie College of Business at the University of Iowa. Brown's research interests center around the role of learner choice and activity in determining training effectiveness, particularly in learner-controlled and technology-mediated environments. He has published or presented over twenty papers and articles, including articles in *Journal of Applied Psychology, Organizational Behavior and Human Decision Processes, Personnel Psychology,* and *Human Resource Planning,* and written chapters in edited volumes. His work also includes design and evaluation projects for Ford Motor Company and the National Center for Manufacturing Sciences, and needs assessment projects at Tenneco Automotive, Aegon USA, Toyota Financial Services, and the Iowa Health Care System. Brown is currently evaluating Web-based learning interventions at the Stead New Media Center and Information Technology Services, both at the University of Iowa.

C. SHAWN BURKE is a research associate at the Institute for Simulation and Training (IST) at the University of Central Florida. Burke earned her doctorate in industrial and organizational psychology in 2000 at George Mason University. Her primary research interests include teams, team training, team performance, shared mental models, leadership, and team performance measurement, and she now uses this expertise in work for law enforcement agencies, fire services, medical teams, navy helicopter crews, and private organizations. Previously, Burke was a consortium fellow at the U.S. Army Research Institute in Alexandria, Virginia, for six years. She has presented at numerous conferences and is a member of the Society for Industrial and Organizational Psychology and the American Psychological Association.

JANIS A. CANNON-BOWERS is a senior research psychologist in the Science and Technology Division of the Naval Air Warfare Center Training Systems Division. In 1988, she received her Ph.D. in industrial and organizational psychology from the University of South Florida. Her research interests include team training and performance, crew coordination training, training effectiveness, and tactical decision making.

DONNA CHROBOT-MASON is assistant professor of psychology at the University of Colorado at Denver, where she teaches organizational psychology and statistics and mentors industrial/organizational graduate students. She earned her B.S. in psychology from Miami University in 1991 and her M.S. (1994) and Ph.D. (1997) in industrial/organizational applied psychology from the University of Georgia. She has researched ethnic identity development, cross-race dyadic work relationships, leaders of diversity, and organizational diversity initiatives. Previously, at Xerox Corporation, she was involved in diversity training and leadership development programs.

More recently she developed a diversity training program for the Office of Veterans' Affairs and is now partnering with the City of Colorado Springs to create a diversity climate survey and evaluate a comprehensive diversity training initiative.

JASON A. COLQUITT is assistant professor of management at the University of Florida's Warrington College of Business. He earned his Ph.D. in business administration at Michigan State University's Eli Broad Graduate School of Management. Colquitt's research interests include organizational justice, team effectiveness, and personality influences on learning and task performance. He has published articles on these and other topics in the *Academy of Management Journal, Journal of Applied Psychology,* and *Personnel Psychology.*

DAVID A. DUBOIS is the senior research scientist at Psychological Systems and Research, Inc. (PSRI). As principal investigator on contracts with the Office of Naval Research, his recent work focuses on the nature of job expertise and designing technologies to support workplace learning. He has designed software systems to support instructional design and to design cognitive tests. He has published and presented work in training design, cognitive task analysis, expertise, test design, and performance measurement. DuBois founded PSRI in 1994 to use basic and applied science for the design of innovative solutions to organizational and societal problems. He is a member of the Society for Industrial and Organizational Psychology (SIOP), American Psychological Society (APS), and the American Psychological Association (APA).

J. KEVIN FORD is professor of psychology at Michigan State University. His major research interests include improving training effectiveness through efforts to advance our understanding of training needs assessment, design, evaluation, and transfer. Ford also concentrates on building continuous learning and improvement orientations in organizations. He has published over fifty articles, chapters, and technical reports and serves on the editorial board of *Human Performance.* He was the lead editor of the book *Improving Training Effectiveness in Work Organizations* and is coauthor with Dr. Irwin Goldstein on the fourth edition of *Training in Organizations.* He is an active consultant with private industry and the public sector on training, leadership, and organizational development issues. He is a fellow of the American Psychological Association and the Society of Industrial and Organizational Psychology. He received his B.S. in psychology from the University of Maryland and his M.A. and Ph.D. in psychology from The Ohio State University.

JOHN C. JEPPESEN, senior consultant with Intellinex, a leading provider of e-learning solutions, earned his B.S. in psychology in 1974 at the University of Nebraska, Lincoln, and both his M.S. (1978) and Ph.D. (1985) in applied psychology, with an emphasis on research use in organizations, at Michigan State University. Before entering the training and human performance field, he consulted in the energy and market research industries. Jeppesen's primary research interests include performance consulting, knowledge management, training transfer, and integrated performance solutions. He has extensive experience in competency-based training systems and is skilled in future-readiness and learning competencies. He has conducted benchmark research and written about competencies, leadership, employee turnover, and knowledge management.

M. ANTHONY MACHIN, senior lecturer in organizational psychology at the University of Southern Queensland, Toowoomba, Australia, received his Ph.D. in 1999 from the University of Southern Queensland. A registered psychologist in the state of Queensland, he is a member of the Australian Psychological Society (APS), the APS College of Organisational Psychologists, the International Association for Applied Psychology (IAAP), and an international affiliate of the American Psychological Association (APA) and the Society for Industrial and Organizational Psychology (SIOP). Before entering USQ, he was a practitioner consulting with both private and public organizations. He is editor of *Interface,* the newsletter of the APS College of Organisational Psychologists. His research interests include interventions that enhance the transfer of training and benefits resulting from them, assessment of occupational well-being and insecurity, and management of driver fatigue.

RAYMOND A. NOE, the Robert and Anne Hoyt Designated Professor of Management in the Department of Management and Human Resources at The Ohio State University, has taught for over fifteen years at Big Ten universities. Before joining Ohio State he taught in the Department of Management, Michigan State University, and the Industrial Relations Center of the Carlson School of Management, University of Minnesota. He received his B.S. in psychology from The Ohio State University and his M.A. and Ph.D. in psychology from Michigan State University. Noe conducts research and teaches students—from undergraduates to executives—in human resource management, managerial skills, quantitative methods, human resource information systems, training and development, and organizational behavior. He has published in the *Academy of Management Journal, Academy of Management Review, Journal of Applied Psychology, Journal of Vocational Behavior,* and *Personnel Psychology,* is on the editorial boards of *Personnel Psychology, Academy of Management Learning and Education, Journal of Business and Psychology, Journal of Training Research,* and *Journal of Organizational Behavior,* and has authored three popular textbooks: *Human Resource Management: Gaining a Competitive Advantage, Employee Training and Development,* and *Organizational Behavior.* He received the Herbert G. Heneman Distinguished Teaching Award in 1991 and the Ernest J. McCormick Award for Distinguished Early Career Contribution from the Society for Industrial and Organizational Psychology in 1993. He is a fellow of the Society for Industrial and Organizational Psychology.

COLLEEN W. PETERSEN has twenty years of training and development experience, specifically in leadership and workforce development. She also served as a consultant to lines of business at Cisco Systems, Lam Research, and Zenger Miller.

As a manager of training and development for Cisco systems, Colleen led the new manager integration efforts, leader-led global leadership facilitation, and the initial e-learning leadership portal. Colleen is the recipient of ASTD's "New Guard" award, given to eight people around the world for innovative efforts in learning and development. She was also awarded "Cisco Citizen of the Year 2000" for implementing a project in a computer lab and training in a Russian orphanage near Moscow.

Colleen serves on the 2002 ASTD advisory committee for e-learning and is a reviewer for the American Council on Education PONSI programs for business.

DAVID B. PETERSON is senior vice president and global practice leader for coaching services at Personnel Decisions International. He received his Ph.D. from the University of Minnesota, specializing in industrial/organizational and counseling psychology. His B.A. in linguistics and anthropology is from Bethel College in St. Paul. An expert on coaching, executive development, and how organizations can create strategic advantage through learning and development, he has been quoted in *The Wall Street Journal, Fortune, Business Week, Sloan Management Review, Working Woman, Training, Human Resources Executive, HR Magazine, Washington Post,* and *USA Today.* He is a frequent speaker at conferences on leadership development, coaching, organizational learning, and knowledge management. With his colleague Mary Dee Hicks, Peterson has authored two best-selling books that offer practical advice to help people develop themselves and coach others: *Development FIRST: Strategies for Self-Development* (1995) and *Leader As Coach: Strategies for Coaching and Developing Others* (1996). He is currently working on a book about how organizations can build a culture of learning.

MIGUEL A. QUIÑONES received his B.S. in psychology from Texas A&M University in 1987 and his M.A. (1990) and Ph.D. (1993) in industrial and organizational psychology from Michigan State University. As associate professor of psychology and management at Rice University, he teaches statistics, psychometrics, psychological testing, personnel selection, training, and motivation. He has published in journals such as *Personnel Psychology, Journal of Applied* Psychology, and *Training Research Journal,* has presented numerous papers at professional conferences, and is coeditor of *Training in a Rapidly Changing Workplace: Applications of Psychological Research.* He is associate editor of the *International Journal of Selection and Assessment* and on the editorial boards of the *Journal of Applied Psychology, Personnel Psychology, Journal of Management,* and *Human Factors.* A consultant to public and private organizations on training issues, executive development, and coaching, he is a member of the Society for Industrial and Organizational Psychology, the American Psychological Association, and the Academy of Management.

LINDA L. ROGERS has twenty-plus years of business consulting and training experience with organizations of all sizes and industry types—including Hewlett-Packard, IBM, Tomy Toys, The Stanford

Business Group, Addison Wesley Publishing, Times Mirror, Cisco Systems, and others. She was founder and president of Compass Training Resources, a provider of organizational development and training services to Silicon Valley companies. Her background includes training strategy and plan development, curriculum design and delivery, internal communications training, and change management consulting. As a manager of training and development for Cisco Systems, Linda led the development of their on-line leadership development Web site; Leadership Express, their Web-based performance review tool; and the companywide executive integration process.

Linda is also a speaker and workshop facilitator whose presentations include, "Rattling the Organizational Cage: Why, When, and How to Challenge the Status Quo," "Managing the Horizon: A Comprehensive Approach to Change Management," and "The Mother of All Processes: Developing an Organizational Development Plan."

EDUARDO SALAS is professor of psychology at the University of Central Florida, where he is also project director of the Department of Human Systems Integration Research at the Institute for Simulation and Training. Previously, he was a senior research psychologist and head of the training technology development branch of the Naval Air Warfare Center Training Systems Division for fifteen years. During that time, he was principal investigator for numerous R&D programs on teamwork, team training, and performance assessment. He is an expert in helping organizations to foster teamwork, implement team training strategies, facilitate training effectiveness, manage decision making under stress, develop performance measurement tools, and design learning environments. He also designs tools and techniques to minimize human errors in aviation, law enforcement, and medicine. He has coauthored over 150 journal articles and book chapters, has coedited eight books, has two books in preparation, and is on the editorial boards of several top-tier journals. A fellow of the American Psychological Association and the Human Factors and Ergonomics Society, and a recipient of the Meritorious Civil Service Award from the Department of the Navy, he received his Ph.D. in 1984 in industrial and organizational psychology from Old Dominion University.

SCOTT TANNENBAUM, founder and president of the Group for Organizational Effectiveness (gOE), has served as consultant and adviser to many Fortune 1000 organizations, including Johnson & Johnson, Tiffany & Co., BP Amoco, Whirlpool, The St. Paul Companies, Bank One, UBS Warburg, USAA, PSEG, GE Capital, American Express, First USA, the U.S. Navy and Air Force, Citicorp, Progressive Insurance, and NASA. Tannenbaum has also been an active researcher in training and development, for which work he has received awards from the National Academy of Management and the American Society for Training and Development. He has served as principal investigator or research scientist on many navy and air force contracts related to training effectiveness and team performance. He has over seventy-five publications and professional presentations on related topics, coauthored the 1992 *Annual Review of Psychology* chapter on training in organizations, and has written books on HR technology and knowledge management. He is on the editorial boards of *Training Research Journal* and *IHRIM Journal*. With a doctorate in industrial and organizational psychology from Old Dominion University, he maintains a consulting professor position in the business school at the State University of New York at Albany, where he has been awarded for excellence in graduate-level teaching.

Creating, Implementing, and Managing Effective Training and Development

PART 1

Designing and Positioning Training and Development

CHAPTER 1

Beg, Borrow, and Steal
How the Best Training Professionals Keep Up
Linda L. Rogers, Colleen W. Petersen

Editor's Note: In planning this volume, Eduardo Salas, editor of the Practice Series, thought it would be informative to begin with the perspective of practitioners who are selling, implementing, and evaluating training systems on a regular basis in the field. As we planned the contents of this volume to fit the needs of practitioners, we wondered what, exactly, those needs are. Where do they look for information on new methods, new tools? How do they see us? What types of knowledge or information are they looking for? In thinking of people we could get this perspective from, I came across a profile of Colleen Petersen, a training and development manager for Cisco Systems, in a training trade magazine. Consistent with this volume's title, Petersen's views seemed very much on the cutting edge, and with Cisco at the center of the burgeoning e-learning phenomenon, one of that company's training leaders seemed a good candidate.

As the project took shape, Petersen invited a peer at Cisco, Linda Rogers, to collaborate with her. Eduardo Salas and I drafted a set of questions and sent them to Petersen. Petersen and Rogers forwarded them to a number of their colleagues in Northern California, all working as internal or external consultants either in training or in performance consulting. The two then compiled the responses to each question into one coherent answer. Thus, as you read the following questions, what you will see in response are the joint opinions of several training professionals, not one (although admittedly sampled from a single geographic region). Following these answers, Rogers adds her own commentaries; the "I" in the following paragraphs is Rogers speaking.

As you read the responses, ask yourself to what extent the respondents' perspectives and needs match your own. Then, as you read the rest of the volume, judge how well our authors anticipated and responded to their needs for information on tools, methods, and strategies for training. In general, you will have to read the volume for yourself to see how well the chapters address the practitioner issues raised here. But I have added parenthetical mention in a few places of chapters that address concerns and issues raised here.

Question: What are the primary sources of information you look to when investigating new methods or trends in training and development?

Answer: Although respondents named a number of different sources, the two sources for which there was the strongest consensus were other professionals in the field, including coworkers and peers in professional organizations, and trade publications such as *Training and Development Journal.*

Question: Do you rely on the science of training to make decisions about new training systems, tools, or methods? If so, in what ways? If not, why not? Why has the body of knowledge generated by the science of training not had a bigger impact on your practice?

Answer: Most respondents make decisions about training based on their own experience—in other words, trial and error—or on the experience of others in the field whom they respect. Those who said they use the science of training indicated that the primary value of this body of knowledge was with respect to evaluating the effectiveness of a new training offering or methodology and ensuring its instructional validity.

This was a difficult question for many respondents because they were not clear about what the phrase "the science of training" actually meant. I am not sure I know either. Lacking a clear definition, I took it to mean the (published) body of knowledge on subjects like training metrics, methodology, psychology, and so on, which has been developed from such scientific methods as formal research, surveys, planned assessment, theoretical papers, and so on.

Frankly, the training professionals I know—unless they are Ph.D.'s with limited exposure to an actual training and development environment—use this type of research to stay up to date on the discipline of training and development, but they are pretty down to earth when it comes to implementing new techniques and methodologies. The overriding question for them is "Does it work?"—meaning, "Is it short, to the point, relevant, and compelling enough to keep participants' attention, and can people apply what they learned immediately back on the job?" These questions can be addressed through formal research, but they can be answered from direct experience as well.

From my experience in the real world, the body of knowledge generated by the science of training probably most often appears in the form of footnotes to training investment proposals and presentation slides at operations reviews; thus, the value of this information is to support preconceived training notions and plans or to justify training investments proposed or already made. In most cases the decisions of what to do have already been made based on "gut feelings" or personal experience.

> *Question:* In your opinion, why has the body of knowledge generated by the science of training not had a bigger impact on your practice?
>
> *Answer:* The training professionals surveyed indicated that a change in training methods is often costly and hard to sell internally; thus, they tend to stick with methods and practices with which they are already comfortable. Furthermore, corporations are generally satisfied with so-called smile sheets as a primary evaluation tool, eliminating the need for more extensive evaluations of alternative delivery methods.

I am convinced that the reason corporations are satisfied with smile sheets as a primary evaluation tool is because they have no idea and no expectation that training can solve real business problems. (See

Chapter Two, this volume, by Scott Tannenbaum, on connecting the training function to business challenges.) Furthermore, the reason they have no expectations of training impact is because we as training professionals have fallen into the "I've got a hammer, so everything looks like a nail" syndrome. Every training organization I have ever been involved with has dealt with the same fundamental challenge—"How do we tie or link our training solutions to the customer's business problems?"—after the fact. Basically, the training organization leads with its training "hammer," then identifies leadership or management or interpersonal skill "nails," and starts pounding away while explaining to whoever will listen that if the company addresses skills in collaboration, teamwork, coaching, and so on, its "real problems" will go away. Unfortunately, there is no way to prove that connection, even if it does exist. As a business development consultant, my clients were primarily CEOs or equivalents, vice presidents of business units, and other managers with profit and loss responsibility. Over time, it became clear to me that many of the business solutions or recommendations I presented to them had significant organization development (OD) implications requiring training and development products and services. An example of the relationships between common business issues, typical business solutions, and implied OD or training interventions are shown in Exhibit 1.1.

For this reason, I built a training component into my business (a strategic partnership with multiple training professionals), and used my business consulting work to "pull through" additional revenue from training. It was fairly simple for my clients to see the link between the business issues I was helping them address and the OD training issues that were raised as a result. I do not believe that they would have made the same connection if I had led with training products and services. In addition, during times of economic downturn, my clients' demand for real business solutions remained the same or increased, but many postponed buying my pull-through training and development services. My business did not suffer significantly, however, because my value to clients was primarily as a provider of business solutions, not training solutions.

So what is the implication for corporate training professionals? Perhaps that leading with an assessment of the business problems up front, providing training and consulting (even if outsourced)

Exhibit 1.1. Sample Links Among Business Issues, Business Solutions, and OD-Training Implications.

Business Issues	Business Solutions or Recommendations	OD Implications
Reduction in revenue	Revise sales or marketing strategy	Leadership or strategic direction
		Strategy facilitation
	Increase market penetration	Performance management
	Reorganize or reduce head count	Change management
		Conflict management
		Motivation
Declining profit margins	Reconstruct pricing model	Communication
	Reduce expenses	Finance training
		Collaboration
	Eliminate or expand product line	Communication
	Add or change distribution channels	
Intensified competition	Revise competitive strategy	Strategy facilitation

to address them, and then following through with training to address the organizational and personal development implications is a more effective way of linking what they do to real business issues. Why? Because the science of training will never come up with a metric that will show how a collaboration training course solved a revenue or profit problem.

Question: Which training tools, methods, strategies, guidelines, and principles do you need and why?

Answer: The tools, guidelines, and principles most commonly cited by respondents reflect fundamentally the key objectives or processes for training managers and consultants. They include the following:

1. Evidence that the training works (for example, method A changes or enhances behavior, attitude, or performance as measured by ___) as well as strategies for showing that training works, strategies for showing that its value outweighs its cost, and ways to convince management that training works and is cost-effective.

The key here is what we mean by the word *works*. If it means "solves a business problem," then it seems to me it would be fairly simple to show that its value outweighs its cost and to convince management that it works and is cost-effective.

2. On-line tools to conduct needs assessments or training evaluation, or authoring tools to create the measurement (assessment-evaluation) instruments.
3. Tools to measure training outcomes and training effectiveness, and to aid decision making around training. (See Chapter Eleven of this volume, by Kurt Kraiger, for an explicit discussion linking evaluation to decision making on training.)
4. Return on investment (ROI) measurement tools: strategies to link business needs and objectives with appropriate training content, methodology, and resources (and needed competencies).
5. Strategies to motivate and facilitate self-directed learning over the employee life cycle. (Chapter Three

of this volume, by Noe & Colquitt, deals extensively with trainee motivation; Chapter Seven by Brown & Ford addresses enhancing motivation in learner-centered computer-based applications.)

6. Customization—proven tools that relate to *my* company, business, and training clients.

Question: What is the best forum for researchers to communicate new findings, tools, guidelines, or principles to training professionals such as yourself?

Answer: Training Web sites, conferences or seminars, or trade publications.

Personally, I liked your questions on research, its limitations, and the types of research training professionals would really like to see done. I've been involved in various aspects of the training and development industry for more than twenty-five years, and if I ruled the research world I would ask the following questions:

- Who actually uses the Internet to access training and development resources? Can this be broken down by age group, industry, function, role (individual contributor, manager, executive), geography, and gender in terms of usage patterns, why they are using the Internet, and when in the decision-making process they are accessing this information?
- What is the profile of the self-directed learner? Self-directed learners appear to be the key to the future of training and development, particularly with the growing influence of the Internet. Therefore, it would be interesting and helpful to know more about them. Who are they? What makes them self-directed? How can training professionals encourage or facilitate self-directedness among employees?

As noted above, we as training practitioners often rely on trial and error when adopting new techniques and look to training research to validate or support new initiatives. Perhaps our comments here can stimulate more research, more communication on methods, tools, and techniques that really work.

CHAPTER 2

A Strategic View of Organizational Training and Learning

Scott Tannenbaum

How organizations develop their employees can be a competitive advantage or disadvantage for them. To enhance organizational competitiveness, human resource and training leaders must think strategically about the ways in which their company develops its employees' capabilities (Jackson & Schuler, 1990). As part of the planning process, leaders should clarify their company's core set of strategic learning imperatives.

Strategic learning imperatives are high-level, learning-related actions that an organization must take to ensure continued success. They should be based on an understanding of the business environment, an awareness of company aspirations, and insights about various training and learning options. Collectively, they can provide a sense of direction and serve as a high-level road map to guide an organization's learning and training efforts.

This chapter provides a strategic view of organizational training and learning. It has four main parts. First, it describes five significant business challenges, selected because they currently affect a wide range of organizations and the way we should think about training and learning in organizations. Second, the chapter highlights seven lessons learned from the training research literature. There has been an explosion of empirical training research in the last several years; the findings discussed here were selected because they may influence strategic thinking about training. Third, with the business challenges and training research findings in mind, the chapter identifies eight strategic learning imperatives. Although each organization should identify its own strategic learning imperatives, many will find the eight imperatives discussed here relevant. At a minimum, they can be used to stimulate thinking about company-specific imperatives. Finally, two sets of strategic questions are presented for each of the strategic learning initiatives. One set should be answered when a company establishes its overall training and learning plan; answering these questions can help clarify learning imperatives and guide action to ensure strategic alignment. The second set can be used when planning a specific training initiative; these questions can help ensure that each training program aligns with the strategic learning imperatives.

Exhibit 2.1 summarizes the framework for the chapter.

Business Challenges

Organizations face numerous challenges, some with serious implications for the way their employee capabilities should be developed. Five important business challenges are discussed in this chapter: intensified competition, incessant change, a power shift to the customer, collaborations across organizational and geographical boundaries, and the need to maintain high levels of talent.

Intensified Competition

Organizations the world over are operating in an environment of growing competitive pressures. Globalization means that we live in what feels like an increasingly small world. Trade agreements are making international commerce easier. The global marketplace presents companies with opportunities to sell their goods and services across national borders, but it also increases international competition. Competitors are now as likely to come from another continent as another town.

Technology, and in particular the Internet, have intensified competition too. The Internet facilitates commerce at a distance and also reduces barriers to entry. Companies no longer need to

Exhibit 2.1. Chapter Overview.

Business Challenges

1. Intensified competition
2. Incessant change
3. A power shift to the customer
4. Collaborations across organizational and geographical boundaries
5. The need for high levels of talent

Lessons from Training Research

1. Transfer rates for traditional training programs are low
2. The role of the training function has changed
3. Trainee motivation matters
4. Trained skills decline over time
5. Poor alignment between individual and organizational needs hinders transfer
6. Work environment matters
7. Formal training is not the primary source of learning

Strategic Learning Imperatives

1. Diversify the learning portfolio
2. Expand the view of whom to train
3. Accelerate the pace of employee learning
4. Prepare employees to deal with customers better
5. Make sure employees believe they have opportunities to learn and grow
6. Capture and share knowledge more effectively
7. Ensure that training and learning efforts support the strategic direction
8. Diagnose and modify the work environment to support transfer and learning

invest in physical infrastructures in all locations, making it easier and less expensive for them to enter new markets and become competitors.

This intensified competition makes it increasingly difficult to develop and sustain any kind of competitive advantage. New products are quickly reverse-engineered, copied, and produced less expensively. When new services are launched, competing services soon follow. Promising industries grow, and then consolidate when sufficient competition leads to an industry shakeout. The ability to adjust continually is a prerequisite for success.

Implication: There is continual pressure to innovate and stay ahead of the competition.

Incessant Change

The business environment is changing at an incredibly rapid pace, which means that organizations must respond in kind. Because products and services can be copied more quickly than ever before, there is pressure on organizations to stay ahead or to respond rapidly to the competition. The result is that organizations are undergoing constant internal change.

Some companies attempt to compete through continual innovation, reducing product development time and accelerating speed to market. Others attempt to compete by continually improving their efficiency through changes in work flow or new technology. Organizational and unit-structuring efforts are increasingly common. Change initiatives are ubiquitous. A study by Kepner-Tregoe, Inc. (as cited in Spitzer & Evans, 1997) reported that nearly half the companies surveyed had implemented eleven or more change initiatives in a three-year period.

Regardless of the strategy selected, the result is that many companies are in a constant state of reinvention. Connor (1995) reports that the percent of managers who describe their environment as one of continuous, overlapping change has increased from 5 percent in the 1970s to 75 percent in the 1990s.

Implication: Employees are being asked to adapt continually to new demands.

A Power Shift to the Customer

Historically, organizations have had an advantage over customers. Why? Because, as Sir Francis Bacon noted in 1597, knowledge is power, and organizations have traditionally possessed more knowledge than consumers. In the past, if a consumer wanted to purchase a car, a home mortgage, or an insurance policy, or even choose a hospital, she would have little information with which to make an informed decision. She would know little about the actual cost of the car or about the price of competing loans or insurance policies. She would have little or no information about the quality of treatment at different hospitals. And she would be at a disadvantage. A well-developed marketing campaign might convince her that a weak or overpriced package was a good value.

But today the trend is to more knowledgeable consumers. This is due in part to the Internet, which allows consumers to access information in ways they never could before. This is also attributable to the adoption of new business models that capitalize on this capability (Boulton, Libert, & Samek, 2000; Slywotzky & Morrison, 1997). As a result, consumers can compare prices, examine product reviews, and access databases with relative ease. The balance of power is shifting.

Implication: Organizations need to prepare better the employees who interact with customers, providing them with better information, better skills, and greater autonomy to address customer requests and concerns.

Collaborations Across Organizational and Geographical Boundaries

In the past, organizations could be clearly classified: our competitors, our suppliers, our customers, ourselves. Now, the distinctions are often less clear. Strategic alliances, joint ventures, and partnerships are common. For example, Corning participates in about forty joint ventures around the world (Lipnack & Stamps, 1993). Today you can find suppliers who are co-located with manufacturers and share access to information about inventory levels. Companies may invest directly in some of their suppliers—in essence becoming both customer and shareholder simultaneously.

Competitors in one arena are seen collaborating in another. For example, IBM and Apple formed a strategic alliance for the Taligent project. British Telecom and AT&T formed Concert as part of a joint venture. In the oil industry it is not uncommon to see project teams that include members from various external entities, including perhaps suppliers, consultants, partners, regulators, or even competitors.

To complicate matters further, many organizations operate across geographic borders. For example, Nestle operates in over 100 countries (Rapoport, 1994) and ABB manufactures and sells products in 140 countries through thirteen hundred companies (Peters, 1992). Multinational corporations rely heavily on multinational teams. Intercultural and language issues can create additional challenges for learning and performance.

Managing these complex, boundary-spanning interrelationships is an organizational challenge. People need to share information and ideas with members of their external network, but some information may still be proprietary. Team members and collaborators need to possess the requisite skills and knowledge to work together effectively, but the best ways to build those capabilities are not always clear.

Implication: Many organizations need to build knowledge and skills that allow them to work across traditional boundaries.

The Need to Maintain High Levels of Talent

Perhaps the most compelling challenge with implications for a company's training strategy is the war for talent. Labor shortages exist in many markets, and particularly in knowledge-intensive industries. Heightened competition exacerbates this problem. If products and services can be copied, then competencies—for example, to innovate, to refine processes, to solve problems, to form relationships—become an organization's only sustainable advantage. Attracting, retaining, and developing people with critical competencies becomes paramount.

The talent challenge is exacerbated by a shift in the type of work people perform. An increasing percentage of people in the workforce can now be thought of as knowledge workers—they work with information and ideas or solve problems and carry out creative tasks. As one indication, in the early to mid 1990s, companies employing a large base of knowledge workers accounted for 43 percent of new employment growth in the United States (Stewart, 1997). Not surprisingly, we have also seen a decrease in the number of jobs that involve routine production tasks or services (Barley, 1994).

What are the challenges of employing knowledge workers? First, they are harder to develop and replace than people who carry out routine or repetitive tasks. Second, it is harder for them to avoid obsolescence. The Department of Labor estimates that on average, 50 percent of an employee's knowledge and skills become outdated every thirty to thirty-six months, compared to an estimated twelve to fifteen years in the 1970s (Harris & Brannick, 1999). Thus, knowledge workers must continually update their skills.

Knowledge workers tend to feel affiliated more with their profession and their projects than with the company for which they work. Employees who feel that they are not growing and enhancing their skills are more likely to look for alternative employment opportunities. A recent Gallup survey of over a hundred thousand employees from twenty-five hundred business units showed that those who believe someone from their company is encouraging their development are less likely to switch companies (Buckingham & Coffman, 1999). Research also reveals that organizations differ significantly in the extent to which they provide developmental opportunities for their employees (Carnevale, Gainer, & Villet, 1990).

Implication: Organizations need talented people to succeed and must compete in part on their ability to attract, develop, and retain them.

Lessons from Training Research

There has been a tremendous amount of research conducted on training issues in the last decade or so. A few research findings have particular relevance for the way companies need to think about their training and learning strategy.

Transfer Rates for Traditional Training Programs Are Low

The instructional design process is a well-established approach for applying some rigor to the development of training programs (Gagne & Briggs, 1979). Yet several researchers have suggested that no more than 20 percent of the dollars spent on training result in transfer to the job (Baldwin & Ford, 1988; Newstrom, 1986). In some cases, trainees did not acquire what they needed to learn during training. In other cases they did not maintain what they learned or did not apply what they learned on the job. For example, in a study of 120 restaurant units, Pfeffer and Sutton (2000) showed a consistent gap between what people knew they should be doing and what they actually did. There are a number of reasons why people do not apply what they learn in training, including a few that are highlighted in the following paragraphs.

Lesson learned: Traditional training, even if it is instructionally sound, does not necessarily result in on-the-job application.

The Role of the Training Function Has Changed

Research conducted by the American Society for Training and Development (Bassi, Benson, & Cheney, 1998) shows that there is an increasing awareness that training functions need to change their role. A survey of training executives showed that they expected their department's role to shift from focusing predominantly on training to focusing increasingly on performance improvement. My experience suggests that although some training functions have made this transition, many have not.

Lesson learned: Some, but not all, training leaders recognize that the traditional training function needs to change.

Trainee Motivation Matters

A strong body of empirical research shows that trainee motivation plays an important role in the value of the training experience (Mathieu, Tannenbaum, & Salas, 1992; Baldwin, Magjuka, & Loher, 1991; Noe & Colquitt, Chapter Three, this volume; Tannenbaum, Mathieu, Salas, & Cannon-Bowers, 1991). Motivation can influence trainees' learning, confidence, and interest in applying what they have learned as well as their posttraining commitment. It is important that employees be motivated to attend training, to learn during training, and to apply what they have learned during training on the job (Mathieu & Martineau, 1997).

Lesson learned: Employees must perceive value in their learning experiences or they are much less likely to benefit from them.

Trained Skills Decay Over Time

Research has confirmed what practical experience suggests: the longer a person goes without using a new skill, the more that person will forget. A metanalytic review of skill decay shows that on average, trained skills demonstrate little or no decay one day after training but demonstrate a 92 percent decrement after one year (Arthur, Bennett, Stanuch, & McNelly, 1998). There can be little doubt that skill decay is a prevalent organizational problem, one that contributes to the low transfer rates described earlier.

Yet interestingly, relatively few companies offer refresher or remedial training. Most training courses are filled with first-time attendees. Two of the most prevalent times when training is offered are at the initial introduction of a new product or when there is a change in method or process (Bassi & Cheney, 1996).

Lesson learned: Unless we can find ways for people to apply what they learn immediately, or provide means for refreshing what they have learned, we can expect significant skill decay.

Poor Alignment Between Individual and Organizational Needs Hinders Transfer

A training needs analysis, in theory, ensures that training addresses individual and organizational needs (Goldstein, 1993). In fact, recent research has shown that the use of training needs analysis methods is positively related to training effectiveness (Bennett, 1995). But in practice, training needs analyses are often shortchanged, and the strategic or organizational analysis component of them is performed infrequently. Two studies examining best practices in industry concluded that a lack of alignment with strategic direction is a primary contributor to the low levels of transfer in organizational training efforts (Carnevale et al., 1990; Cassner-Lotto & Associates, 1988).

Lesson learned: Training and other learning experiences must address relevant needs and support organizational strategy.

Work Environment Matters

A large and convincing set of research studies shows that events that occur before and after training can play a significant role in the effectiveness of training (Tannenbaum & Yukl, 1992). In particular, supervisor and peer behaviors can greatly influence training effectiveness. Supervisor and peer support for learning, as demonstrated, for example, through communications and openness to new ideas or by covering for people when they attend training, sends powerful messages that ultimately affect transfer (Tracey, Tannenbaum, & Kavanagh, 1995; Rouillier & Goldstein, 1993).

Research has also shown that situational constraints such as lack of time or resources can significantly inhibit motivation to learn and subsequently transfer (Facteau, Dobbins, Russell, & Ladd, 1995; Mathieu, Martineau, & Tannenbaum, 1993). Moreover, organizations demonstrate significant differences in the extent to which their work environments support ongoing learning and application of trained skills (Tannenbaum, 1997; Eddy, Tannenbaum, & Flynn, 1999).

Lesson learned: Events that occur outside of training can be extremely important in determining training effectiveness.

Formal Training Is Not the Primary Source of Learning

Although training can play an important role in learning, research reveals that it is not the primary means by which people learn in organizational settings. In one study conducted in seven organizations, individuals consistently reported that they acquired less than 10 percent of their work competency from formal training courses (Tannenbaum, 1997). Furthermore, the Center for Workforce Development's study of one thousand employees in various organizations reported that up to 70 percent of workplace learning is informal (as cited in Pfeffer & Sutton, 2000). Yet others report that informal on-the-job instruction is three to six times more prevalent than formal training (Carnevale & Gainer, 1989; Rothwell & Kazanas, 1990).

Lesson learned: Formal training should not be the sole focus of an organization's strategy for learning and development.

Strategic Learning Imperatives

The business trends and research results described in the preceding sections reflect the current environment for organizations. They also offer insights into the types of strategic learning imperatives organizations should adopt. As mentioned earlier, learning imperatives can serve as a strategic road map to guide an organization's learning and training efforts. Strategic learning imperatives are the high-level actions that an organization must take to ensure its competitiveness.

Companies operate in different industries, have different goals, and possess different capabilities. Therefore, each one needs to establish what it considers to be its own strategic learning imperatives. An awareness of some of the most common imperatives can help stimulate analysis of company-specific imperatives. Consider which of the learning imperatives described here are most pertinent to your organization's success.

Diversify the Learning Portfolio

Research reveals that traditional training programs are not the primary source of learning for most employees (Tannenbaum, 1997). Moreover, we have seen that formal training programs often result in low levels of transfer (Baldwin & Ford, 1988). Yet classroom training continues to be the most common instructional method ("Industry report," 1997).

In most cases, organizations are dedicating a disproportionate amount of attention and resources to traditional training methods. Traditional training will continue to be important, but attention must also be paid to other means of building capabilities. To borrow a phrase from the investment arena, a strategic imperative for many organizations should be to diversify their portfolio of learning opportunities. They need to take a broader view of training.

It can be helpful to take an inventory of the learning options available to employees. How much of the training offered is in the form of traditional, classroom programs? How much is offered through media, such as Web-based or computer-based training? What other nontraining options are being used to enhance employee capabilities (for example, coaching, mentoring, performance support systems, 360-degree feedback, project assignments, access to Web sites, and knowledge management applications)? If there is a strong reliance on traditional training, where are there opportunities for other solutions?

Given the research trends discussed earlier, two areas in which organizations should consider focusing additional attention are informal learning and "N-of-1," or personalized learning.

Companies need to recognize the importance of informal learning opportunities and work on enhancing their value (Chao, 1997; Dixon, 1997). Informal learning occurs on the job as a result of interactions with others and through trial and error. Most learning occurs informally; some of it leads to positive behaviors, and some of it to bad habits. But although informal learning cannot be controlled in the same way as structured learning, it is worthy of additional attention because it is so prevalent. Organizations should consider how they can actively foster positive informal learning.

For example, opportunities may exist for encouraging positive role models to mentor colleagues informally (McDougall & Beattie, 1997). Employees could be taught metacognitive skills, such as self-regulation and self-correction, to enable them to extend what they have learned into new situations (Volet, 1991). Team leaders can be taught to conduct informal team debriefings during which teams discuss what is working for them and what they can do better (Tannenbaum, Smith-Jentsch, & Behson, 1998). Companies can also use work assignments to build experience-based expertise (McCall, Lombardo, & Morrison, 1988).

Another promising way to diversify the learning portfolio is to provide more N-of-1 or personalized learning opportunities. These learning methods provide greater control or customization for the person who needs to learn (Ford & Kraiger, 1995). Intelligent tutors, coaching, and 360-degree feedback are examples of such methods. Each provides the learner with customized feedback and has the potential to offer personalized developmental recommendations to address unique learning requirements. Other methods, such as self-paced training modules and performance support systems, may provide less customization but they allow individuals to acquire the knowledge they need when they feel they will be able to apply it on the job.

Two overarching questions are these: What capabilities must our employees possess for us to be successful? And what are the best means of building these capabilities? Formal training should clearly be one part of the mix. But given the low transfer rates of formal classroom training, other learning methods should be employed as well. Training functions should continue their transformation from the unit that develops and delivers training to the unit that identifies learning and performance needs, and helps ensure that creative solutions are in place to address those needs (Robinson & Robinson, 1995).

Expand the View of Whom to Train

Who should receive training? Any individual who must acquire specific capabilities to ensure an organization's success is a potential candidate for training. Historically, the pool of potential trainees would be made up of the company's core group of employees. But as noted earlier, organizational boundaries are blurring. The border between customers, suppliers, and even competitors is becoming fuzzier. For some organizations, a strategic learning imperative should be to expand their view of whom to train to include others outside the core group.

Collaboration across organizational boundaries can change the composition of the group that must be competent for the company to succeed. In some cases, a company's suppliers, customers, and collaborators become possible candidates for training. Naturally, a company cannot assume responsibility for addressing the training needs of all the groups it interacts with, but it should consider the value of supporting some of those groups in key areas.

If a company relies on its suppliers to ensure customer satisfaction and the supplier fails to fulfill its obligations, everyone suffers. For this reason, some organizations have begun training their key suppliers in quality management techniques. Similarly, if a company collaborates on a project with another organization, cross-dependencies may emerge. The members of such a project team often bring different skills and different assumptions about how to operate as a team. For this reason, some organizations provide project management or team training for joint project teams.

Customers are also candidates for training or other learning vehicles. A company that sells proprietary equipment to its industrial customers wants to ensure that they use the equipment properly. If they do not, the relationship with those customers is likely to deteriorate. Training increases the likelihood that the equipment will meet customer expectations and it can be a competitive advantage against other equipment manufacturers.

This logic can also extend to individual customers. Providing consumers with information about how to use products and services most effectively increases the chances that they will get the best value from the product and builds their trust and loyalty. For example, some financial institutions provide training for consumers on how to manage their finances. This increases the likelihood that the consumers will come to them for a loan or to invest their money, and it also decreases the likelihood that they will default on their loan.

The broader view of training discussed earlier may facilitate the extension of training beyond organizational borders. Web-based training and information sites provide easier access for consumers and suppliers. Internet technology has made it economically feasible to provide training to individuals outside an organization's core workforce.

Other nontraining options are possible too. Temporary assignments with suppliers or as part of a project team can serve dual purposes. They can provide opportunities to enhance an individual's capabilities but can also be a vehicle for building the capabilities of the supplier or project team. Some organizations have experimented with assigning people as temporary "coaches" at their suppliers' or customers' locations.

Clearly, there are some challenges in providing training across company boundaries. One is the additional expense of increasing the size of the trainee population. This cost must be weighed against the cost of poorly prepared suppliers and customers and the benefits of improved customer and partner relationships. A second challenge is managing proprietary information. When a company trains across boundaries, it sometimes has to juggle equipping partners and suppliers with the capabilities they need to support the company with not revealing any proprietary information that could hurt its future competitiveness. Despite these challenges, in many cases the benefits outweigh the risks.

Finally, when reviewing this strategic imperative, organizations should consider expanding or modifying the composition of their internal trainee pool as well. Some organizations offer most of their training to a relatively small group of employees. In many cases, managers and leaders get a disproportionately large share of training. This may be appropriate, and the ideal mix varies according to each organization's needs, but as part of this learning imperative, organizations should examine who—in their own company—currently receives training (and other learning opportunities) and determine if it is appropriate to reallocate or expand their resources to cover other groups better.

Accelerate the Pace of Employee Learning

Tom Kelly, vice president of Internet Learning Solutions at Cisco, faces the challenge of having to train three thousand people every sixty days on a new product, technology, or market (Muoio, 2000). This example reflects one of the business challenges described earlier: the pace of change is rapid and incessant. For many companies this means that a compelling strategic imperative must be to accelerate the pace of employee learning.

To do this, organizations need to understand two key time elements: How often and quickly do new learning needs emerge? And how long does it usually take to develop learning solutions? If the latter exceeds the former, then there is a problem. Because we cannot control the speed with which new learning needs emerge, we must reduce the time it takes to address those needs. Sometimes this means developing training solutions more rapidly; sometimes it calls for nontraining solutions. Exhibit 2.2 provides a framework for stimulating discussion about the pace of new learning requirements in key jobs.

When training is the right solution, what can organizations do to reduce the time it takes them to develop and produce it? Training developers are starting to gain access to a set of tools that can accelerate the training design process. A few technological developments are emerging that may help, including authoring tools, reusable learning objects, and learning libraries (for example, see American Society for Training and Development Research, 1998).

But reducing cycle time also requires a change in approach. For example, developing shorter training modules that people can access as they need them can accelerate learning. Similarly, rapid prototyping and developing quick 80 percent solutions can sometimes be more useful than 100 percent solutions that are implemented too late to address new learning requirements.

The key to shortening the training development cycle is balancing the need for speed with the need to ensure that the training hits the target. In other words, there is a need to perform fast, yet effective, training needs analyses (Lee & Owens, 2001). Currently, there is considerable room for improvement in that arena.

Accelerating the training development cycle is one way to increase the pace of employee learning. But unfortunately, the tra-

Exhibit 2.2. Pace of Learning Required Matrix.

Employee Groups	To perform effectively, employees in this group need to acquire 20 percent new knowledge and skills every . . .				
	1–4 Months	5–10 Months	11–18 Months	19–24 Months	25+ Months
Field sales					
Marketing					
Web programmers					
HR					
Accounting					
Customer service reps					

ditional instructional design process simply does not address quickly emerging learning needs. Organizational demands are such that employees are increasingly facing sudden learning needs. They often cannot wait for a formal classroom training experience to address the latest issue. In many cases, the solution must involve real-time learning and performance support.

In consequence, organizations will need to find ways to foster ongoing learning that is closely connected to the work at hand. For example, we can expect to see an increase in the use of electronic performance support systems (EPSS) that provide real-time, electronic access to information, advice, and guidance as employees need it. According to John Smith, general manager of Cadillac, "The days of a technician pulling up his toolbox to the car and using only the knowledge in his head to accomplish the task are over" (see American Society for Training and Development Research, 1998). Not surprisingly, GM is investing heavily in the development of EPSS. The company is not simply relying on training to put knowledge in employees' heads.

In general, to accelerate learning, organizations must provide people with access to information, tools, and learning resources on a real-time basis. Performance support systems can provide real-time access and just-in-time learning, as can some of the N-of-1 methods described earlier (for example, peer mentoring and knowledge management applications).

Prepare Employees to Deal with Customers Better

In many industries, the balance of power is shifting to the customer. Customers are better informed and better prepared than ever before. This creates greater challenges for the employees who interact with those customers. The ways in which sales professionals, billing clerks, account managers, and service providers deal with customers greatly influences a company's reputation and performance. For many companies, a strategic learning imperative in the current business environment must be to prepare these critical employees to address the customer challenge. They need preparation in at least three areas: knowledge, skills, and empowerment.

At a minimum, customer contact personnel cannot be at a "knowledge disadvantage" compared with customers. A knowledge disadvantage is when a customer has access to information that the employee does not, and that discrepancy makes it difficult for the employee to perform his job effectively. For example, when a customer has more recent information about the pricing and features of a competitor's product than does your sales representative, that discrepancy makes it difficult for the rep to position and sell the product appropriately.

When a customer knows the legal requirements about rental car insurance and your customer service representative (CSR) does not, that discrepancy puts the CSR at a disadvantage. If, as a result, the CSR provides incorrect information about insurance requirements, the customer may erroneously question your company's integrity, which would hurt its reputation and perhaps encourage the customer to use the competition.

Companies can even inadvertently create their own knowledge disadvantages. One of the most dreaded phrases an employee can hear during a customer interaction is, "That's not what it says on your Web site." All this suggests that organizations need to keep up with the information their customers have access to, and they must consider what that means about employee readiness. What do customers know about products, services, pricing, competitors, quality levels, regulations, order status, and so on? Organizations should identify any knowledge disadvantages that put employees in tenuous situations and then take action to remedy those discrepancies. Exhibit 2.3 provides a simple matrix that a group of subject matter experts can complete to identify potential knowledge disadvantages. Key knowledge areas are listed in the first column. For each knowledge area, the group identifies what customers and employees know about the area, and can begin to identify where potential knowledge disadvantages may occur. This matrix may be expanded to fit different customer groups and different employee groups who have contact with customers.

When building the capabilities of employees who deal with customers, it can be helpful to differentiate between information they must be able to recall from memory while with customers (need to know) and information they can look up either before, during, or after a customer interaction (able to access). The distinction is important because each type calls for a different solution. Information that employees need to know must be acquired and retained

Exhibit 2.3. Comparing Customer and Employee Knowledge.

Knowledge Domain: What Our Customers and Employees Know About . . .	Our Customers	Our Customer Service Reps	Potential Knowledge Disadvantage
Our products and services (features, quality)			
Competitors' products and services (features, quality)			
Price of our products and services			
Price of competitors' products and services			
Industry regulations and requirements			
Order status			
Etcetera			

prior to the interaction through training or coaching. In contrast, the second type of information can be accessible in a database, performance support tool, or tip sheet. Failing to distinguish between need-to-know information and able-to-access information can have several negative repercussions. Employees may not learn what they need to know, so they are unprepared for questions during customer interactions. Alternatively, if they assume that everything is need-to-know, it can overload them and inappropriately lengthen the time required for new employees to be considered ready. This is another example of the need for effective needs analysis.

Building the right knowledge base is essential. But employees must also have the right skills to interact with customers effectively. Customer expectations are extremely high, which puts employees in challenging situations. Knowledge is not sufficient to address such situations. Organizations must also ensure that employees have the skills they need to handle customer interactions.

The third part of employee preparation is empowerment. In this context, the term *empowerment* means that employees have a clear understanding of their decision-making authority. Can I discount the price? Can I accept a returned item? Can I make an exception to policy? Ideally, decision-making authority should be placed as close to the customer as possible. Yet regardless of where the decision-making authority lies, for employees to be equipped to deal effectively with customers, the organization must ensure that employee roles are communicated clearly and that managers take actions that are consistent with the established roles (for example, supporting employees' decisions). Without clear roles, the time spent developing knowledge and skills can go astray.

Make Sure Employees Believe They Have Opportunities to Learn and Grow

There is intense competition to attract and retain talent. Research has shown that organizations that provide better learning and growth opportunities have an advantage when competing for that talent (Buckingham & Coffman, 1999). These trends suggest that for many organizations, a strategic learning imperative should be to ensure that employees *believe* they have ample opportunities to learn and grow. Companies need to provide developmental opportunities, and be sure that current and prospective employees are aware of those opportunities, in order to attract, motivate, and retain employees.

In the current business environment, employee and corporate loyalty are generally low (Hall & Mirvis, 1995). Most employees no longer expect to spend their career with a single employer. Similarly, most employers reluctantly admit that they cannot expect their employees to work for them for thirty years. On a personal level, there is a growing recognition that to have a successful career, one needs to build competencies continually. To remain marketable, employees need to acquire new skills and knowledge, whether through training, new experiences and assignments, or interactions with others. Employees who do not feel they are growing in their current job are more likely to leave. This is particularly true for employees who possess the most valuable competencies, because they have a range of employment choices.

As a result, companies need to assess how their employees feel about the growth and learning opportunities they offer. Do employees feel they have sufficient opportunities to develop? Are they receiving the training they need? Are they receiving challenging, interesting assignments? Do they feel competent and capable? Are they ready and able to cope with change? Do they believe that someone cares about their personal growth? Has anyone talked with them about their career? This type of assessment is different from evaluating whether a particular training program is effective. To address this strategic imperative, employers must know how their employees perceive their personal development.

Employee perceptions about training play a part in this. Although employee reactions to training are often seen as less meaningful measures of training effectiveness, they can serve several important purposes. First, they provide an indication about whether a program is valued by employees. Although business needs may require the company to provide some important but unpopular courses, and to cancel a few popular but ineffective courses, there is merit in ensuring that employees view most training courses as meaningful. Second, research has shown that utility reactions, or trainees' perceptions of the value of a training program (rather than their simply liking the program), are related to subsequent job performance (Alliger, Tannenbaum, Bennett, Traver, & Shotland, 1997). Finally, programs that are perceived as meaningful gain positive reputations in the company. Based on that reputation, employees go into training with greater motivation, and motivated trainees gain more from training than less motivated trainees (Baldwin et al., 1991). So organizations should assess employee reactions to specific training programs and monitor their perceptions about whether the right types and amounts of training are being offered. Companies should use employee perceptions about training as one source of input when establishing their overall training plans.

But perceptions about personal growth and development go well beyond training programs. Some companies offer a great deal of training but are not perceived as positive learning environments. Others offer much less formal training but are perceived quite positively by employees (Tannenbaum, 1997). Factors that can influence employee perceptions about personal growth include the opportunities they have to interact with knowledgeable peers and the types of assignments they receive (and the way those assignments are communicated to them).

Any work assignment has two possible components: what needs to be accomplished for the organization (the task component), and what the employee can learn from the experience (the growth component). Some assignments are predominantly task-focused; for example, developing the same basic monthly report results in little or no growth. Others, such as attending training, are predominantly growth-focused. Yet many assignments include both task and growth elements. Consider an assignment to serve on a cross-functional task force. There is clearly a task component to this assignment—the employee is asked to serve on the task force to help it accomplish its goals. But there may be a good growth opportunity as well. Interacting with peers from other units can broaden an employee's knowledge base. Chairing the task force can be a chance to build team leadership skills.

Employees should have an appropriate mix of task and growth opportunities. A work assignment scorecard can offer insights into an employee's current mix (see Exhibit 2.4). The scorecard can reveal an imbalance between task and growth and can also serve as a springboard for discussing an employee's learning and development. If a manager asks an employee to serve on a task force but

Exhibit 2.4. Work Assignment Scorecard.

Assignment	Intended Task (%)	Intended Growth (%)	Intended Growth Goals	Actual Results
Work on new system implementation.	90	10	Chance to work with Joan; observe how she manages the project	
Chair cross-functional task force.	50	50	Learn about new business market; build team leadership skills, encouraging diverse team members to work together	
Teach the departmental reporting process to Jim.	85	15	Work on coaching skills	
Attend project management seminar.	100	0	Acquire project management skills	

never lets him know about the intended growth opportunities, that employee may simply see it as more work. In fact, research has shown that the way a learning experience is described can influence employee perceptions and subsequently employee learning (Martocchio, 1992). By learning the complete rationale for an assignment (for example, task: we need your technical expertise; growth: great chance to learn about our new business market) the employee can see that it is more than just additional work.

It is important to recognize that a work assignment does not have inherent task or growth weighting. The relative weighting is based in part on the skills and experiences of the employee who is completing the assignment. Take the example of chairing a task force. There will be a greater growth component in this assignment for an employee who has never done it before than for one who has chaired many task forces in the past. Providing an appropriate mix of work assignments and discussing the intended growth opportunities can help increase the likelihood that employees view the organization as supporting personal growth and learning.

Capture and Share Knowledge More Effectively

Intellectual capital has become as critical as financial capital for ensuring organizational success. As noted earlier, if products and services can be copied, then *knowing how* to innovate, refine processes, solve problems, and sustain critical relationships becomes an organization's primary advantage. Where does this critical knowledge reside? Usually in the heads of company employees. Because this knowledge is so important, a strategic learning imperative for some organizations should be to capture and share knowledge more effectively throughout the organization.

This imperative falls under the broad heading of *knowledge management*. Knowledge management means establishing the right mechanisms and culture to encourage the sharing and application of knowledge. It involves gathering, structuring, storing, and accessing information. Information and computer technology can be help an organization manage knowledge, but technology in and of itself is not knowledge management (Tannenbaum & Alliger, 2000).

If all employees possess knowledge, and some possess fairly unique knowledge, then organizations can be badly disrupted when employees leave. What happens when the only person who has detailed knowledge about the relationship with a key customer resigns? When the person who knows the most about repairing a troublesome piece of equipment leaves? When the person who is considered a top expert in developing packaging innovations retires? When the person who spearheaded the company's most successful new business ventures goes to work for another company? The answers to these questions can be very sobering. Therefore, organizations must attempt to capture and share knowledge in such a way that it lives beyond the tenure of any single employee.

The argument for knowledge management is compelling when we think about those cases where one person possesses unique knowledge. But the case can be equally compelling when the knowledge is distributed to different degrees throughout the organization. For example, consider a company that employs service personnel to diagnose and repair its products at customer locations around the world. Training has helped prepare them to address some of the most common problems. But at any point in time, some service personnel have acquired firsthand experience in debugging certain problems whereas others have not. In addition, service personnel try different ways to diagnose and resolve existing and new problems in the field—some more successfully than others. Would the service personnel perform better if they had access to the latest information about service problems and solutions that were emerging around the world? Would they perform better if they had some way of tapping into the collective expertise of their colleagues? Would their customers be better served? Would this be a competitive advantage? I would argue that the answer to all these questions is yes.

At the heart of knowledge management is capturing and sharing knowledge, through either formal or informal means. Organizations are trying a number of ways to accomplish this. Here are a few examples:

- Identifying internal experts, clarifying their areas of expertise, and publishing an electronic form of company yellow pages so employees know whom to contact when they need expert input on a particular topic

- Establishing shared databases so employees can access up-to-date information and monitor or mine trends about customers, accounts, common problems, inventory, and so on
- Capturing and documenting best practices and work processes so these can "live" beyond the tenure of any one individual and be proliferated throughout the organization as appropriate
- Using groupware, e-mail, Web sites, videoconferencing, and various intranet applications so a community of users can request input, share problems, and discuss ideas with colleagues at a distance
- Establishing a variety of forums that encourage knowledge sharing, including brown bag lunches, expert visits, and lessons-learned meetings

There are several elements to knowledge management. Three key ones are knowledge elicitation, knowledge organization, and knowledge dissemination (Tannenbaum & Alliger, 2000).

Knowledge elicitation refers to the process of capturing insights and information from knowledgeable people. An important first step is to have communication channels available so people can share their insights. For example, where can a retail clerk go to share what he has learned about a recurring problem with a product? Some companies have established technology-based channels such as a shared database to elicit employee insights. Other companies are trying informal mechanisms, such as lessons-learned meetings. Unfortunately, establishing open channels is only half the battle. Research has shown that experts are notoriously poor at articulating their expertise (Shiffrin & Schneider, 1977). Because they are not always able or ready to share their expertise, many knowledge management initiatives need to use systematic data-gathering methods to "elicit" or draw out expert and tacit knowledge. Interviews, focus groups, observation, and think-aloud protocols can be used to draw out expertise. For some companies, knowledge elicitation is a new competency they need to develop.

Knowledge organization refers to the translation and structuring of raw information into something that is meaningful and useful to others. Organizations possess more information than anyone can digest. Placing every policy, rule, and insight on the company intranet results in a collection of information that is overwhelming. It does not allow individuals to access the knowledge when they need it. Effective knowledge organization involves establishing logical frameworks, structures, schemas, or categories that serve as scaffolding for storing information. Categorizing information into a logical knowledge structure may also help individuals form mental models about key knowledge domains (Kraiger, Salas, & Cannon-Bowers, 1995). A logical knowledge structure can provide a starting point for deciding what information should be maintained in a database and where it should be stored. Some organizations are employing knowledge managers, people who oversee particular knowledge domains, screening and organizing content so that others can quickly and easily access what they need to address organizational issues.

Knowledge dissemination simply refers to the various means by which knowledge is dispersed in the organization. These can range from sophisticated knowledge management applications to informal get-togethers and resource guides. Effective dissemination relies on having the right mix of channels available and the right culture to encourage information sharing.

Although it is easy to concentrate on the technological elements of this imperative, it is actually the organizational culture that drives knowledge sharing. Many organizations have implemented sophisticated knowledge management applications only to discover that people do not use them (Alliger & Tannenbaum, 2000). Building employee motivation to share and to learn is primarily a function of key behaviors and organizational practices. It is more about the work environment than the technology. The impact of the work environment is discussed in a later section.

Ensure That Training and Learning Support the Strategic Direction

Research reveals that training does not always translate into effective behaviors and organizational results (Newstrom, 1986). One reason for this is a lack of alignment between the training and the company's strategic direction (Carnevale et al., 1990). Therefore, a strategic imperative for most companies is to ensure that the practices they employ to build readiness and capabilities are in fact aligned with their strategic direction. I will refer to this as *strategic capability alignment.*

One business trend that creates additional challenges for strategic capability alignment is the rapid pace of change. It has become increasingly difficult to project even a few years into the future, so the strategic planning horizon for most organizations has become shorter and shorter. The external environment is in a constant state of flux, so internal changes become more prevalent.

As a result, business units tend to change strategic direction more rapidly than before. New products, processes, structures, and initiatives are introduced with startling regularity. These changes can have important ramifications for the capabilities an organization needs to succeed. Consider the changes described in Exhibit 2.5 and the obvious implications about new capability requirements:

In practice, this imperative has several implications. First, organizations should perform a capability assessment for any important change or initiative. They need to ask which capabilities will be needed, how this compares to their current capabilities, and what they should do differently to bridge any capability gaps.

Second, leaders should periodically perform an overall strategic capability assessment for the company. What are the key strategic capabilities that are needed? What new capability requirements have emerged in the last year? What are we doing to build those capabilities (for example, training, hiring skilled employees, acquiring companies that possess those capabilities, using knowledge management applications)? Where should we dedicate resources to ensure that we have those capabilities going forward?

Third, training units should periodically audit their strategic alignment. They should review how they are dedicating resources to build capabilities against the key strategies of the organization. One way to do this is to compare current programs and services against the organization's strategic needs (see Exhibit 2.6). Training units can use this framework to discuss the following questions: Which current programs and services support which strategic needs? Which strategic needs could benefit from additional attention? Which of our offerings do not align with current strategic needs? Is that acceptable? Where should we focus resources going forward?

**Exhibit 2.5. Organizational Changes and
Their Impact on Capability Requirements.**

Organizational Change	Capability Implications
Deciding to become more aggressive in acquiring other companies	Company leaders will need better skills in screening acquisition targets; human resources and other groups will need to be able to assimilate the new acquisitions.
Restructuring the sales function from one that is organized by product (people sell one product in multiple regions) to one that is organized by region (people sell all products in a single region)	Sales professionals will need knowledge of a wider range of products and will need to understand how to sell a portfolio of products.
A push to become more innovative, not just in product development but throughout the organization	Individuals throughout the organization will need to learn skills and processes that foster innovation.
The implementation of a technology that streamlines transactions, freeing employees up to perform "higher value" work	Employees affected by the technology will need a complete new skill set related to the new work expectations.
The launching of a "quality" initiative	Employees will need to understand the importance of quality and acquire quality management skills.

Exhibit 2.6. Training Function Strategic Alignment Audit.

Current Programs or Services	Strategic Needs							
	Increase overall innovation	Reduce operating costs	Strengthen customer relations	Globalize business practices	Ensure supplier readiness	Manage change	Build leader depth	Break down silos
New product development program								
Best manufacturing practices program								
Creative thinking workshop								
Performance consulting services								
Team building support								
Succession planning facilitation								
Change transition for employees 101								
Product ideas database								
Customer service rep PSS								
Meet the leaders for lunch series								
Etcetera								

The results from this type of analysis can range from a simple confirmation of current efforts, to adding or dropping specific activities to align better with organizational needs, to reallocating future resources to address new strategic concerns, to changing the overall focus and mission of the training function to support the organization more appropriately.

Diagnose and Modify the Work Environment to Support Transfer and Learning

One of the most consistent and compelling findings from the training research literature is that the work environment is an important determinant of training effectiveness. Actions that take place before and after training greatly influence the extent to which training transfers to the job (Tannenbaum & Yukl, 1992). Similarly, as organizations undertake knowledge management efforts, a recurring lesson is that a company's work environment influences whether employees are willing to share their knowledge and expertise with others. For these reasons, most organizations should consider diagnosing and modifying their work environment to support transfer and learning as a strategic imperative.

Leader and peer behaviors, organizational policies, and work practices can all send signals to employees about the importance of learning and the relevance of specific learning experiences. For example, individuals who enter training knowing what to expect and who believe that some form of posttraining follow-up will occur are more motivated to apply what they have learned during training when they return to the job (Baldwin & Magjuka, 1991). Therefore, meeting with and preparing employees before training can yield positive dividends (Cohen, 1990).

As noted earlier, supervisors and peers can send strong messages about the value of training, learning, and knowledge sharing. Indeed, one negative comment by supervisors has been shown to wipe out the full effects of an assertiveness training program (Smith-Jentsch, Salas, & Baker, 1996). What types of behaviors send signals? Do employees help cover for colleagues who have gone to training, or are people informally "punished" for going to training "instead of" working? Do supervisors and peers encourage people to try what they learned in training, or do they send a different message ("That's not how we do it around here")? Is it acceptable for an employee to make a mistake when she is trying something new, or are mistakes intolerable? Are people promoted for being the only expert in an area (encouraging information hoarding), or is information sharing encouraged and rewarded? Are people assigned only to tasks they can do well, or are they given assignments that stretch them? Do leaders admit when they do not know something, or is it unacceptable to acknowledge a need to learn? Answers to questions like these reveal a great deal about the nature of the work environment and its conduciveness to continuous learning.

Situational constraints such as lack of time, resources, and equipment can also inhibit continuous learning. In an obvious example, consider employees who are trained on a new piece of equipment but have difficulty accessing the equipment on the job. They cannot transfer what they learned during training. Other constraints such as lack of time also limit opportunities to perform trained tasks, which accelerates skill decay. But even more insidiously, employees who experience many situational constraints over time enter training with lower motivation to learn (Mathieu et al., 1992). They realize they will not be able to apply new ideas to their job and so have little incentive to learn new ideas.

Greater business competition has increased the need for employees to innovate and think creatively. Many of the work environment attributes described earlier send signals about the relative need for and acceptability of new ideas. A final factor to consider when examining the work environment is the availability of physical space that is conducive to creative thinking. Many organizations are consciously examining how they structure and allocate space to foster teamwork, collaboration, and creativity. Dedicating space for that type of work also sends a signal about the importance of learning in the organization.

Organizations must periodically examine the work environment to identify what is facilitating and what is inhibiting ongoing learning and transfer of knowledge. A diagnosis of the readiness of the work environment should examine some of the factors listed in Exhibit 2.7. An example of one diagnostic tool can be found in Tannenbaum (1997).

**Exhibit 2.7. Work Environment Factors
That Affect Continuous Learning.**

- Toleration of mistakes during learning
- Use of assignments to develop people
- Openness to new ideas and change
- Training policies and practices
- Supervisor encouragement for learning and innovation
- Situational constraints to learning (time, resources)
- Coworker support
- Opportunities to try newly acquired skills on the job
- Encouragement to share knowledge
- Availability of space for collaboration
- Reward and recognition practices
- Channels of communication

Strategic Learning Imperatives and Strategic Alignment: A Summary

I have argued that leaders must take a strategic view of organizational training and learning to ensure ongoing competitiveness. In practice, what can companies do to ensure that their training and learning efforts support organizational success? In other words, how can companies assure strategic alignment?

To start, companies should establish their own set of strategic learning imperatives. The list should be short enough (approximately six to ten items) that it can provide a sense of focus and direction. The eight strategic learning imperatives described in this chapter can be a useful point of departure, but it is essential that each company identify and focus on imperatives that reflect its own business needs and goals. A question that should be asked about any proposed list of strategic learning imperatives is this: If we make considerable progress completing this list, will the probability of our company succeeding increase significantly? If the answer to this question is yes, then you have probably identified the right list of imperatives. If not, then the list should be revised.

As part of a strategic alignment, many organizations would benefit by conducting some form of strategic diagnosis. Strategic diagnoses can help establish the right learning imperatives and can guide actions to support those imperatives. It may be helpful to do the following:

- Examine the distribution of current training and learning offerings (by type and audience).
- Understand which jobs have the most rapidly changing knowledge requirements.
- Pinpoint where customer contact personnel may know less than the customers with whom they interact.
- Assess employee perceptions of growth and learning opportunities.
- Examine how organizational changes are affecting knowledge and skill requirements.
- Audit how well current offerings are aligned with strategic needs.
- Diagnose the readiness of the work environment to support continuous learning.

In addition to formal diagnosis, a key to ensuring continual alignment is consistently asking the right strategic questions. Asking the right questions can direct attention to the learning imperatives and can encourage actions that support organizational success. Who should ask these questions? Trainers, managers, business leaders, and anyone with a vested interest in ensuring that the company is taking the most appropriate actions to build organizational readiness should ask questions that help ensure that the company's strategic learning imperatives are met.

Exhibit 2.8 contains a set of sample questions based on the eight strategic learning imperatives described in this chapter. Note that one column pertains to a company's overall training or learning strategy, whereas the other contains questions that can be asked when planning a specific training program. In both cases, they are designed to foster a common strategic focus.

Exhibit 2.8. Sample Questions to Ensure Alignment of Strategic Learning Imperatives.

Strategic Learning Imperatives	Aligning Overall Training or Learning Strategy	Aligning a Specific Training Initiative
Diversify our learning portfolio	• What is the current distribution of our classroom training and other learning approaches? • How are our resources allocated? • Do we have an overreliance on classroom training?	• Is formal training the best solution in this case? • How else could people acquire the required knowledge or skill?
Expand our view of whom to train	• Who receives the training that we provide? • Is this the best mix? • Are there any strategic advantages to providing training to our suppliers, partners, or customers? • Should we redistribute training resources to support undertrained groups in our company?	• Could any other groups outside our organizational boundaries benefit from access to this training? • What might our suppliers, partners, or customers need to know about the content area under consideration? • How might we prepare our suppliers' or partners' trainers to provide this training?

Accelerate the pace of employee learning	• Which groups of employees need to acquire new knowledge most rapidly? • How long does it currently take us to develop training solutions for those groups? • Where are there needs or opportunities to offer faster solutions? • What tools and technologies could help us (for example, authoring systems)?	• When do people need to receive this training? • What is the trade-off between speed of development and quality of training in this case? • How could we accelerate the development process in this effort?
Prepare our employees to deal with customers better	• What information do our customers have access to? • What do our customers know that gives them an advantage when dealing with us? • How prepared are our employees who deal with customers? Where are the opportunities to better prepare our employees?	• What do our customers know about the topic covered in this training program? • How might this knowledge affect the way our employees interact with our customers? • What should we include in this training to ensure that our employees are not operating at a knowledge disadvantage with customers?

Exhibit 2.8. Sample Questions to Ensure Alignment of Strategic Learning Imperatives, Cont'd.

Strategic Learning Imperatives	Aligning Overall Training or Learning Strategy	Aligning a Specific Training Initiative
Make our employees believe they have opportunities to learn and grow	• How important is it that we be viewed as an employer of choice? • From a strategic perspective, where is it most critical to retain key employees? • What do our key employees value with regard to learning and developmental opportunities? • What actions can we take to ensure that employees believe they will grow more working for us than elsewhere?	• How will employees perceive this training opportunity (great opportunity, reward, punishment, distraction)? • How should we communicate this opportunity so that employees understand its value to them without overselling it?
Capture and share knowledge more effectively	• To what extent is knowledge sharing currently occurring in our company? • What mechanisms do we have for eliciting, organizing, and disseminating knowledge? • Which areas of our business (jobs, functions, tasks) would benefit most from better knowledge management? • What technological and cultural changes are needed to foster knowledge sharing?	• Who are the experts in this area and how can we best elicit knowledge from them? • What information do people need to know from memory and what information can they access? • How can we disseminate need-to-access information, posttraining? • Are there ways to foster ongoing knowledge sharing after the training program?

| Ensure that our learning and training efforts support our strategic direction | • How well do our current programs and services align with the strategic needs of the business?
• How are external and internal changes affecting the capabilities we need to be successful?
• How should we reallocate resources to ensure alignment?
• Do we need to change the focus and mission of our training function? | • Who should we interview during the needs analysis phase to ensure that we understand the needs of the business as we develop this program?
• How does this program align with the strategic needs of the business?
• Is this program a worthy use of organizational resources? |
| Diagnose and modify our work environment to support learning and transfer | • How does our work environment support or hinder continuous learning?
• Are our leaders and supervisors sending the right signals about the importance of learning (their use of work assignments, tolerance of mistakes while learning)?
• What changes can we make to policies, practices, physical space, and so on to create a more positive learning environment? | • What do we expect people to do differently as a result of this training program?
• What potential work environment obstacles might interfere with transfer (lack of equipment, supervisor support)?
• How can we use supervisors before and after the training to support transfer of training?
• What do we need from sponsors and other key stakeholders for this training to succeed? |

Conclusion

Billions of dollars are spent annually in attempts to train employees and build their knowledge and skills. To ensure a reasonable rate of return on that investment, organizations must take a strategic view of their training efforts. In this chapter I suggested that organizations could begin by establishing the right strategic learning imperatives, which should be based on an understanding of the business environment, an awareness of company aspirations, and insights into various training and learning options. Carefully conceived strategic learning imperatives can provide a sense of direction and serve as a high-level road map to guide learning and training efforts.

But learning imperatives are like vision statements—they are only valuable if they stimulate action. They can provide a sense of direction, but leaders and trainers must continually ask the right questions to ensure that their actions align with their company's learning imperatives.

Ultimately, strategic alignment is about taking the right actions. Companies that take actions to address their strategic learning imperatives successfully will be able to remain one step ahead of their competition; those that do not may suffer. So the final message of this chapter is this: think and act strategically about organizational training and learning.

References

Alliger, G. M., & Tannenbaum, S. I. (2000). You can build it, but will they come? *IHRIM Journal, 4,* 80–85.

Alliger, G. M., Tannenbaum, S. I., Bennett, W., Traver, H., & Shotland, A. (1997). A meta-analysis on the relations among training criteria. *Personnel Psychology, 50,* 341–358.

American Society for Training and Development Research (1998). *1998 learning technology research report.* [http://www.astd.org/virtual_community/research/1998_learning_technologies.html].

Arthur, W., Bennett, W., Stanuch, P. L., & McNelly, T. L. (1998). Factors that influence skill decay and retention: A quantitative review and analysis. *Human Performance, 11,* 57–101.

Baldwin, T. T., & Ford, J. K. (1988). Transfer of training: A review and directions for future research. *Personnel Psychology, 41,* 63–105.

Baldwin, T. T., & Magjuka, R. J. (1991). Organizational training and signals of importance: Linking pretraining perceptions to intentions to transfer. *Human Resource Development Quarterly, 2,* 25–36.

Baldwin, T. T., Magjuka, R. J., & Loher, B. T. (1991). The perils of participation: Effects of choice of training on trainee motivation and learning. *Personnel Psychology, 80,* 260–267.

Barley, S. R. (1994). *The turn to a horizontal division of labor: On the occupationalization of firms and the technization of work.* Paper prepared for the Office of Educational Research and Improvement. Washington, DC: Department of Education.

Bassi, L. J., Benson, G., & Cheney, S. (1998). *The top ten trends.* Alexandria, VA: American Society for Training and Development.

Bassi, L. J., & Cheney, S. (1996). *Results from the 1996 benchmarking forum.* Alexandria, VA: American Society for Training and Development

Bennett, W. (1995). *A meta-analytic review of factors that influence the effectiveness of training in organizations.* Unpublished doctoral dissertation, Texas A&M University, College Station.

Boulton, R.E.S., Libert, B. D., & Samek, S. M. (2000). *Cracking the value code: How successful businesses are creating wealth in the new economy.* New York: Harper Business.

Buckingham, M., & Coffman, C. (1999). *First break all the rules: What the world's greatest managers do.* New York: Simon & Schuster.

Carnevale, A. P., & Gainer, L. J. (1989). *The learning enterprise.* Washington, DC: American Society for Training and Development and Department of Labor.

Carnevale, A. P., Gainer, L. J., & Villet, J. (1990). *Training in America: The organization and strategic role of training.* San Francisco: Jossey-Bass.

Cassner-Lotto, J., & Associates (1988). *Successful training strategies.* San Francisco: Jossey-Bass.

Chao, G. T. (1997). Unstructured training and development: The role of organizational socialization. In K. Ford, S.W.J. Kozlowski, K. Kraiger, E. Salas, & M. S. Teachout (Eds.), *Improving training effectiveness in work organizations* (pp. 129–151). Hillsdale, NJ: Erlbaum.

Cohen, D. J. (1990). What motivates trainees? *Training & Development Journal, 36,* 91–93.

Connor, D. R. (1995). *Managing at the speed of change: How resilient managers succeed and prosper where others fail.* New York: Villard Books.

Dixon, N. M. (1997). The hallways of learning. *Organizational Dynamics, 25,* 23–34.

Eddy, E. R., Tannenbaum, S. I., & Flynn, D. (1999). *The impact of national culture on the continuous learning environment.* Paper presented at the 14th Annual Meeting of the Society of Industrial/Organizational Psychology, Atlanta.

Facteau, J. D., Dobbins, G. H., Russell, J.E.A., & Ladd, R. T. (1995). The influence of general perceptions of the training environment on pretraining motivation and perceived training transfer. *Journal of Management, 21*(1), 1–25.

Ford, J. K., & Kraiger, K. (1995). The application of cognitive constructs and principles to the instructional systems of model training: Implications for needs assessment, design, and transfer. In C. L. Cooper & I. T. Robertson (Eds.), *International review of industrial and organizational psychology* (Vol. 10, pp. 1–48). New York: Wiley.

Gagne, R. M., & Briggs, L. J. (1979). *Principles of instructional design.* Austin, TX: Holt, Rinehart and Winston.

Goldstein, I. L. (1993). *Training in organizations* (3rd ed.). Pacific Grove, CA: Brooks/Cole.

Hall, D. T., & Mirvis, P. H. (1995). Careers as lifelong learning. In A. Howard (Ed.), *The changing nature of work* (pp. 323–361). San Francisco: Jossey-Bass.

Harris, J., & Brannick, J. (1999). *Finding and keeping great employees.* New York: AMACOM.

Industry report 1997. (1997, October). *Training,* p. 56.

Jackson, S. E., & Schuler, R. S. (1990). Human resource planning: Challenges for industrial/organizational psychologists. *American Psychologist, 45,* 223–239.

Kraiger, K., Salas, E., & Cannon-Bowers, J. A. (1995). Measuring knowledge organization as a method for assessing learning during training. *Human Factors, 37,* 804–816.

Lee, W.W., & Owens, D. (2001). Rapid analysis model: Reducing analysis time without sacrificing quality. *Performance Improvement, 40,* 13–18.

Lipnack, J., & Stamps, J. (1993). *The teamnet factor: Bringing the power of boundary crossing into the heart of your business.* Essex Junction, VT: Oliver Wright.

Martocchio, J. J. (1992). Microcomputer usage as an opportunity: The influence of context in employee training. *Personnel Psychology, 45,* 529–552.

Mathieu, J. E., & Martineau, J. W. (1997). Individual and situational influences in training motivation. In K. Ford, S.W.J. Kozlowski, K. Kraiger, E. Salas, & M. S. Teachout (Eds.), *Improving training effectiveness in work organizations* (pp. 193–221). Hillsdale, NJ: Erlbaum.

Mathieu, J. E., Martineau, J. W., & Tannenbaum, S. I. (1993). Individual and situational influences on the development of self-efficacy: Implications for training effectiveness. *Personnel Psychology, 46,* 125–147.

Mathieu, J. E., Tannenbaum, S. I., & Salas, E. (1992). Influences of individual and situational characteristics on measures of training effectiveness. *Academy of Management Journal, 35,* 828–847.

McCall, M. W., Jr., Lombardo, M. M., & Morrison, A. M. (1988). *The lessons of experience*. San Francisco: New Lexington Press.

McDougall, M., & Beatttie, R. S. (1997). Peer mentoring at work: The nature and outcomes of non-hierarchical developmental relationships. *Management Learning, 28*(4), 423–437.

Muoio, A. (2000, October). Cisco's quick study. *Fast Company*, p. 286.

Newstrom, J. W. (1986). Leveraging management development through the management of transfer. *Journal of Management Development, 5*(5), 33–45.

Peters, T. (1992). *Liberation management: Necessary disorganization for the nanosecond nineties*. London: Pan Books.

Pfeffer, J., & Sutton, R. I. (2000). *The knowing-doing gap: How smart companies turn knowledge into action*. Boston: Harvard Business School Press.

Rapoport, C. (1994, November). Nestle's brand building machine. *Business Today, 7*, 156–161.

Robinson, D. G., & Robinson, J. C. (1995). *Performance consulting: Moving beyond training*. San Francisco: Berrett-Koehler.

Rothwell, W. J., & Kazanas, H. C. (1990). Planned OJT is productive OJT. *Training & Development Journal, 44*(10), 53–56.

Rouillier, J. Z., & Goldstein, I. L. (1993). The relationship between organizational transfer climate and positive transfer of training. *Human Resource Development Quarterly, 4*, 377–390.

Shiffrin, R. M., & Schneider, W. (1977). Controlled and automatic human information processing: Perceptual learning, automatic attending, and a general theory. *Psychological Review, 84*, 127–190.

Slywotzky, A. J., & Morrison, D. J., with Andelman, B. (1997). *The profit zone: How strategic business design will lead you to tomorrow's profits*. New York: Times Business.

Smith-Jentsch, K. A., Salas, E., & Baker, D. P. (1996). Training team performance-related assertiveness. *Personnel Psychology, 49*, 909–936.

Spitzer, Q., & Evans, R. (1997). *Heads, you win! How the best companies think*. New York: Simon & Schuster.

Stewart, T. A. (1997). *Intelligent capital: The new wealth of organizations*. New York: Doubleday/Currency.

Tannenbaum, S. I. (1997). Enhancing continuous learning: Diagnostic findings from multiple companies. *Human Resource Management, 36*, 437–452.

Tannenbaum, S. I., & Alliger, G. A. (2000). *Knowledge management: Clarifying the key issues*. Austin, TX: IHRIM Press.

Tannenbaum, S. I., Mathieu, J. E., Salas, E., & Cannon-Bowers, J. A. (1991). Meeting trainees' expectations: The influence of training fulfillment on the development of commitment, self-efficacy, and motivation. *Journal of Applied Psychology, 76*, 759–769.

Tannenbaum, S. I., Smith-Jentsch, K. A., & Behson, S. J. (1998). Training team leaders to facilitate team learning and performance. In J. A. Cannon-Bowers & E. Salas (Eds.), *Decision making under stress: Implications for training and simulation* (pp. 247–270). Washington, DC: APA Press.

Tannenbaum, S. I., & Yukl, G. (1992). Training and development in work organizations. *Annual Review of Psychology, 43,* 399–441.

Tracey, J. B., Tannenbaum, S. I., & Kavanagh, M. J. (1995). Applying trained skills on the job: The importance of the work environment. *Journal of Applied Psychology, 80,* 239–252.

Volet, S. E. (1991). Modeling and coaching of relevant metacognitive strategies for enhancing university students' learning. *Learning and Instruction, 1,* 319–336.

CHAPTER 3

Planning for Training Impact
Principles of Training Effectiveness

Raymond A. Noe, Jason A. Colquitt

Many organizations are reconsidering their investments in human resource practices such as training as they begin to recognize that the knowledge, skills, and competencies of their employees give them an advantage that is difficult for competitors to imitate. Organizations such as Motorola, Southwest Airlines, and Sun Microsystems have devoted considerable expense to training, whether provided by in-house personnel or out-of-house experts. They use training to facilitate learning but also to retain employees, improve their culture, and create incentives for good performance. Yet although there is no widespread systematic evaluation of the effectiveness of training, trainers are still responsible for making sure that managers affected by or in charge of training have a positive "gut feeling" that the training works and makes good use of their budget dollars and employee time.

The purpose of this chapter is to look at the factors that influence training effectiveness, with an emphasis on individual and organizational factors. We acknowledge that creating a learning environment plays a critical role in ensuring that learning and transfer of training occurs. However, despite the adoption and use of instructional design models based on education and psychology, learning and transfer are often inhibited or do not occur. Therefore, the primary focus of this chapter is on nondesign features that have often been considered under the broad umbrella of training motivation (for example, see Salas & Cannon-Bowers, 2001). We summarize more than twenty years of research on training motivation and provide guidelines based on this research for improving training effectiveness.

Before identifying the individual and organizational factors that influence training effectiveness, we will first discuss what training effectiveness means and how it is measured. Next, we will identify the features needed for effective training. Considering the features needed for effective training, as well as the outcomes used to measure training effectiveness, we will provide a model of individual and work environment characteristics that influence learning and transfer of training. The remainder of the chapter will be devoted to an in-depth discussion of each of the characteristics included in the model. Guidelines for practice are provided in each section; each also highlights how organizations and trainers can influence these characteristics to make training most effective.

Broadening the Model of Training Effectiveness

Training effectiveness refers to the processes that occur before, during, and after training to improve the likelihood that it will have an impact. Training evaluation is the measurement of the extent to which it is effective. Historically, most researchers and practitioners have evaluated the impact of training through outcomes proposed by Kirkpatrick (1976), including trainees' reactions to the program, learning, behavior change, and results. But the types of outcomes used to evaluate training programs have since been expanded to include cognitive, affective, and motivational outcomes (Kraiger, Ford, & Salas, 1993). Examples of affective and motivational outcomes include posttraining self-efficacy, customer service attitudes, tolerance for diversity, team commitment, and willingness to participate in future training programs. Examples of cognitive outcomes include technical vitality (anticipating learning to meet changing job demands) and contextual knowledge (recognizing contextual influences on performance).

The search for the "holy grail" in evaluation has occurred for two reasons. First, Kirkpatrick's outcomes are believed to be deficient and overly simplistic. Second, training is beginning to play a more strategic role in organizations, leading to demand for a more complete view of training outcomes. Training is becoming part of a continuous learning strategy that companies are striving to achieve. *Continuous learning* may be defined as a directed and long-term effort to learn, a desire to acquire knowledge and skills, participate in activities that facilitate learning, and apply what is learned for personal and organizational benefit (London & Smither, 1999). Indeed, the primary training focus on relevant knowledge, skills, abilities, and other factors (KSAOs) is changing, with the focus now on developing intellectual capital (Noe, 1999; Martocchio & Baldwin, 1997). Intellectual capital refers to cognitive knowledge (know what), advanced skills (know how), system understanding and creativity (know why), and self-motivated creativity (care why).

The real value of training may come not from individual learning but rather from having employees interact and share ideas that improve manufacturing, service, and interdepartmental processes. This is especially true for companies engaging in knowledge work (pharmaceutical, communications, and engineering organizations, for example), where so-called systems thinking and creativity are critical. Here training is viewed as part of a larger system in the company to create and share knowledge. That system includes technology for communications, delivering training, and sharing and storing knowledge, as well as traditional instructional design issues.

E-learning is a relatively new method that provides a good learning environment and facilitates knowledge sharing. E-learning uses the Web or company intranet to deliver instruction. From the trainees' perspective, e-learning can provide a rich learning environment, complete with learning objectives, feedback, opportunities to practice, and evaluation all built into the system. Trainees can learn at their own pace. E-learning also has the added advantage of allowing them to share learning, problems, and issues with one another. Learner-learner, instructor-learner, and learner-expert links can be easily established and used to facilitate learning and transfer of training. Despite calls for making training more strategic and for better determining the business benefits of training, the evidence continues to suggest that companies rely primarily on reaction criteria—so-called smile sheets—for measuring training effectiveness. These include self-report measures collected from trainees immediately after training that ask about their satisfaction with the content, instructor, and learning environment. Although few would argue that behavior and results outcomes are necessary to determine if transfer of training has taken place, a survey by the American Society of Training and Development suggests that these outcomes are used by less than 20 percent of companies (McMurren, Van Buren, & Woodwell, 2000). In contrast, over 75 percent of the organizations surveyed reported using reaction measures. Even more disturbing is that the use of behavior and results criteria did not vary significantly between those companies considered to make a large investment in training (the top 10 percent of companies surveyed in terms of total training hours, percent of eligible employees who received training, and use of new learning technologies) and those that did not.

What Is Needed for Effective Training?

For training to be considered effective, trainees must meet four criteria: they must be must be ready to learn, they must be motivated, they must learn the content of the training program, and they must transfer their training when back on the job.

Training readiness refers to abilities and skills (often termed *trainability*), personality factors, and attitudes that affect training motivation, actual learning, and transfer. One of the most common myths about training is that everyone is equally ready for training (Salas, Cannon-Bowers, Rhodenizer, & Bowers, 1999). When employees enter a training program they all bring different backgrounds, abilities, and experiences and—unless they are in an organization with a strong continuous learning culture—come from work environments that vary in their support for training.

According to studies in both educational and organizational settings, training motivation—or the desire on the part of the trainee to learn the content—influences both learning and transfer (Colquitt, LePine, & Noe, 2000). Motivation can affect whether an employee decides to attend training, how much effort he or she makes to learn, and whether he or she chooses to apply the skills on the job (Quiñones, 1997).

After completing the program, trainees must demonstrate increases in relevant cognitive, affective, and motivational outcomes. In exploring what factors to leverage to improve these outcomes, the focus is usually on the design of the instructional environment. Instructional designers and industrial/organizational psychologists have long recognized the features of the training or instructional environment that most enhance learning and transfer (for example, Gagne & Medsker, 1996; Cannon-Bowers, Rhodenizer, Salas, & Bowers, 1998). These features are shown in Exhibit 3.1.

Transfer of training includes effective and continual application of learned capabilities on the job, both generalization and maintenance (Baldwin & Ford, 1988). Generalization refers to the trainee's ability to apply learned capabilities to work situations that are similar but not identical to those emphasized in the instructional environment. Maintenance refers to the process of continuing to use new skills over time, even when opportunities to practice are limited and work constraints (such as time pressures, stress, or lack of manager support) exist.

Exhibit 3.1. Features of the Instructional Environment That Facilitate Learning and Transfer.

- Trainees understand the objectives of the training program—the purpose and outcomes expected.
- Training content is meaningful. Examples, exercises, assignments, concepts, and terms used in training are relevant.
- Trainees are given cues that help them learn and recall training content, such as diagrams, models, key behaviors, and advanced organizers.
- Trainees have the opportunities to practice.
- Trainees receive feedback on their learning from trainers, observers, video, or the task itself.
- Trainees have the opportunity to observe and interact with other trainees.
- The training program is properly coordinated and arranged.

Training effectiveness will be compromised if the individual does not meet the readiness, motivation, learning, and transfer requirements. Simply applying training design processes such as the instructional system design model will not guarantee success. As this discussion indicates, effective training requires a systems approach that focuses on both the instructional design and the characteristics of the trainees in the broader organizational context.

Guidelines for Practice: Effective Training

To improve the measurement of training impact, organizations must go beyond smile sheets and obtain a baseline measure of learning and transfer. How might this be done?

- *Analyze training program objectives to identify measurable outcomes.* Include both measures of learning and transfer. Measures of learning, including paper-and-pencil tests, performance in work samples, and role-plays, should be carried out at the end of training. Measures of transfer might include observation of behavior, manager or peer ratings, attitude surveys, or objective indicators of sales, quality, productivity, or internal or external customer satisfaction.
- *Do not give up evaluating effectiveness,* even if you cannot have a "rigorous" evaluation design (pretest, comparison group, random assignment). Keep in mind that the design that you use affects the confidence you have in the results and certainty of conclusion made. Any evaluation is better than no evaluation. Quasi-experimental designs (pretraining, posttraining with comparison group) are among the most rigorous tests of training, but other designs (posttest only) may be appropriate for some purposes (Sackett & Mullen, 1993; Tannenbaum & Woods, 1992). For example, determining how much change has occurred from pretraining levels requires a rigorous design, but determining whether trainees have reached a certain level of proficiency may not.
- *Consider using a cost-benefit analysis.* Organizations usually have accounting data that can be used to calculate direct costs (for example, costs associated with trainers, travel, materials, technology), indirect costs (clerical and administrative costs), and development costs (fees for program purchase, instructional design) for training. Benefits might be easily observable, such as reduction in errors or defects, accidents, or improved productivity. For "softer" outcomes, such as attitudes or interpersonal skills training, managers or human resource experts might be able to provide reasonable estimates of value (Phillips, 1996).

A Model of the Characteristics That Affect Training Motivation, Learning, and Transfer

Figure 3.1 presents a model of the factors that influence learning and transfer. This model is based on a larger model that was developed and empirically supported using metanalyses of over twenty years of research on training motivation (Colquitt et al., 2000). The model shows that individual characteristics (including trainability, personality, age, and attitudes) influence motivation, learning, transfer of training, and job performance. Work environment features (climate, opportunity to perform trained tasks, manager support, organizational justice, and an individual versus team context) also affect each stage of the training process. The model therefore illustrates that individual and work environment characteristics are critical factors before training (by affecting motivation), during training (by affecting learning), and after training (by influencing transfer and job performance).

It is important to note that although some of the individual characteristics may be more difficult for the organization to influence through policies and practices (for example, trainability and personality), job or career attitudes, pretraining self-efficacy, valence of training, and the work environment itself can be affected by the organization. In the following paragraphs we discuss each factor in the model and its implications for training, and provide guidelines for training practice.

Trainability

Trainability refers to the ability to learn the content of the training program. Individuals are trainable depending on their general cognitive ability (that is, intelligence) and their possession of basic skills such as reading, writing, and mathematics.

Cognitive Ability

Cognitive ability—the ability to process information actively—includes verbal comprehension, quantitative ability, and reasoning ability. Cognitive ability has been shown to be related to successful job performance and a critical resource for learning in novel

Figure 3.1. A Model of Individual and Work Environment

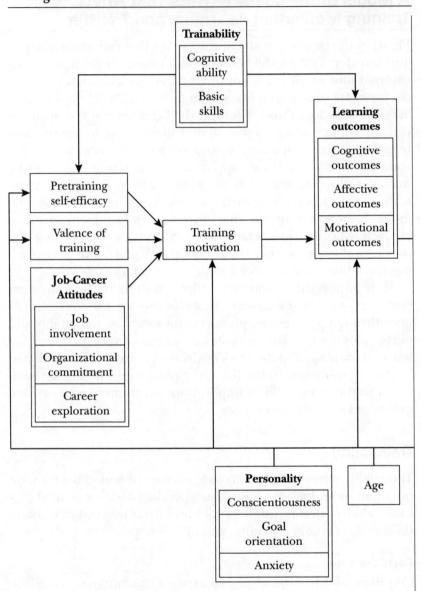

Characteristics Influencing Learning and Transfer of Training.

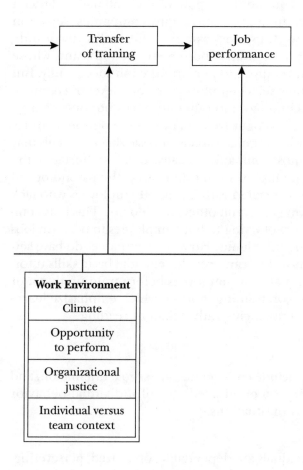

situations, such as in training (Hunter & Hunter, 1984; Gottsfredson, 1986). Some researchers have even characterized cognitive ability as the ability to learn (Hunter, 1986). It has been found to have a strong relationship with training success and proficiency across a wide variety of jobs (for example, Ree & Earles, 1991). Some academics believe that training success is accounted for solely by cognitive ability; however, research shows that although cognitive ability explains more variance in learning than motivational factors, the latter still account for significant variance (Colquitt et al., 2000).

Basic Skills

If trainees lack the requisite "horsepower," they will have a difficult time learning in training programs. Many companies' selection processes (interviews, tests, work samples) either directly or indirectly measure cognitive ability and screen out applicants whose ability is below that required to perform the job successfully. But what about when they select employees for one level of cognitive ability, but then technology and other advances not only change the job but increase its cognitive demands? One option is to "reselect" employees using cognitive ability or basic skill tests. This may be impractical for most companies because of labor shortages, the inability to reassign employees to other work, the psychological and financial costs associated with laying off employees who lack basic skills, and having to recruit others who do not. This puts companies in the dilemma of trying to train employees to perform jobs that stretch their cognitive limits. However, companies do have several realistic options. They can provide remedial basic skills tutoring in reading and math for employees before training them, or use video or on-the-job training, both of which emphasize learning by watching and practicing rather than by reading.

Personality

Personality factors include conscientiousness, goal orientation, and anxiety. Personality is a good predictor of individual behavior across a wide variety of situations.

Conscientiousness

Conscientious individuals are dependable, organized, persevering, thorough, and achievement oriented. Research has shown that conscientious individuals have more confidence in their ability to learn, value learning-related outcomes to a greater degree, have higher motivation levels, and are more committed to goals (Barrick, Mount, & Strauss, 1993; Colquitt & Simmering, 1998). Although this suggests that training outcomes may be best with conscientious trainees, research has also shown conscientiousness to be negatively related to some cognitive outcomes (for example, skill acquisition) (Colquitt et al., 2000; Martocchio & Judge, 1997). Conscientious individuals may have a tendency to be self-deceptive about learning progress. Such individuals also have a tendency to stay committed to courses of action that become improper because of situational changes (Barrick & Mount, 1993; LePine, Colquitt, & Erez, 2000; Hochwater, Witt, & Kacmar, 2000).

Goal Orientation

Goal orientation may be considered the individual's mental framework, which influences interpretation and behavior in learning activities. According to Dweck (Dweck, 1986; Dweck & Leggett, 1988), individuals have either a mastery goal orientation or a performance goal orientation. Individuals with a mastery orientation seek to gain competence through mastery of new skills or experiences. Those with a performance orientation seek to demonstrate competence by receiving positive evaluations from others. Persons with a mastery orientation will make a greater effort in the learning process, whereas persons with a performance orientation are likely to focus on testing well, regardless of whether they actually learn or not. A person with a mastery orientation is likely to be challenged by errors and negative feedback during learning; those with a performance orientation are likely to become frustrated by this. Research has shown that individuals with a mastery orientation were more motivated to learn, and learned more, than persons with a performance orientation (Colquitt & Simmering, 1998; Fisher & Ford, 1998; Phillips & Gully, 1997).

Anxiety

Anxiety is an acquired or learned fear that can result in physical arousal and a disruption in cognitive functioning and performance. Although anxiety is often cued by characteristics of the instructional environment, certain individuals have a predisposition to reacting anxiously in learning contexts. This can be damaging in a training environment because it can lead to off-task attention or cognitive disengagement. It can also exacerbate the effects of initial struggles, which are common when learning any new skill. Anxiety has therefore been shown to have a negative relationship with training motivation and learning (for example, Colquitt et al., 2000; Webster & Martocchio, 1993; Warr & Bunce, 1995).

Age

Older employees have been found to demonstrate less learning and participation in training programs than younger employees (Cleveland & Shore, 1992; Colquitt et al., 2000). In a study investigating age differences in the adoption and use of new technology, Morris and Venkatesh (2000) found that younger workers' decision to use technology was strongly influenced by their attitude toward using it. Older workers were more influenced by subjective norms and perceived behavioral control. This suggests that programs training employees to use new technologies should emphasize how the new technologies will help employees achieve more positive work outcomes (appeal to younger workers) as well as emphasize the ease of use of the new technology (appeal to older workers). This is relevant both when using technology to provide a product or service and when using it as a training delivery method (for example, Web-based training). Because of their work experiences and good knowledge of the institution, older employees may be dubious that training can be helpful to them (Sterns & Doverspike, 1989). They may also fear failing and looking "bad" in front of younger colleagues, whom they see as potentially replacing them.

Guidelines for Practice: Trainability, Personality, and Age

Know the audience members and modify the situation. Trainers need to be aware of their trainability, personality, and age. Although trainers may be unable to change their characteristics, they can modify situational and environmental factors to enhance the effects of positive characteristics and neutralize the effects of negative ones. If trainability is a concern:

* Incorporate basic skills training into training programs.
* Assess basic skills to identify deficits and send employees who are deficient to basic skills training.

- Perform a literacy audit of training materials to determine if the math and reading skills required for comprehension match those required for the job. For example, a readability assessment involves analysis of sentence length and word difficulty.
- Use video and work samples or on-the-job training if trainees can learn by watching and practicing rather than reading or calculating.

To motivate employees with high conscientiousness:

- Assign conscientious trainees specific goals for learning progress so that they have specific learning levels to strive for.
- Give frequent feedback, in the form of skill assessments, to prevent conscientious trainees from falling victim to self-deception on their progress.

If trainees have low levels of conscientiousness:

- Emphasize external incentives tied to training to make up for lower levels of internal motivation.
- Provide more structure during the training program so that trainees are not allowed to fall behind or fail to make an effort.

To reduce anxiety:

- Design pretraining activities to increase the trainees' familiarity with one another.
- Create an informal learning environment.
- Try to make trainees feel equal in status with respect to the training topic.
- Use anxiety-reduction techniques, such as positive imaging, and discourage negative self-talk.

To induce a mastery orientation:

- Set goals around learning and experimenting with new ways of performing trained tasks rather than trained task performance.
- Deemphasize competition with other trainees; instead, emphasize that trainees should help one another learn.
- Create a community of learning—encourage trainees to interact with each other, either face-to-face or using e-mail or chat rooms, to share insights about how they have applied training on the job.
- Allow trainees to make errors and experiment with new knowledge or skills during training. Create an expectation that they will be asked to take risks during training and they will not be evaluated on that.

To motivate older employees:

- Mix trainees of all ages in groups. Encourage employees from different cohorts to talk together and share experiences.
- Ask older workers to share their anecdotes and success stories.
- Use materials that are based on what the trainees already know.
- Emphasize that training is not a remedial activity but rather an important strategic activity for all employees.
- Get trainees involved through interaction and discussion.
- To counter resistance to change, emphasize the positive benefits of training.
- To help older trainees who have not been in a learning situation for several years feel comfortable, personally contact them before the session to introduce it and answer any questions.
- Allow trainees time to familiarize themselves with technology (for example, the Web) before using it for training

Motivational and Job or Career Attitudes

Self-efficacy, valence, job involvement, organizational commitment, and career exploration: these are important characteristics that trainees bring with them to training. All have been shown to be related to training motivation (Colquitt et al., 2000; Facteau, Dobbins, Russell, Ladd, & Kudisch, 1995; Noe, 1986; Noe & Schmitt, 1986; Tannenbaum, Mathieu, Salas, & Cannon-Bowers, 1991; Mathieu, Tannenbaum, & Salas, 1992).

Self-Efficacy

Self-efficacy describes an individual's belief that he or she can successfully organize and perform courses of action to attain certain outcomes. In a training situation, self-efficacy refers to a person's belief that he or she can successfully learn the content. Self-efficacy has been linked to positive outcomes in many types of training programs, including those focusing on interpersonal and computer software skills. One review found that self-efficacy had moderate to strong relationships with training motivation, declarative knowledge, skill acquisition, and job performance (Colquitt et al., 2000).

Valence of Training

Valence of training refers to the attractiveness of training outcomes. These outcomes are related to the individuals' current job, career, and personal life (Nordhaug, 1989) and include increased job performance, feelings of accomplishment, and greater potential for promotion. Trainees who value such outcomes show more training motivation (Mathieu, Tannenbaum, & Salas, 1992; Colquitt & Simmering, 1998; Colquitt et al., 2000).

Job Involvement

Job involvement, or the degree to which employees identify psychologically with their job and the importance of their work to their self-image, has been found to be related to training motivation (Noe & Schmitt, 1986). Those who are highly involved with their jobs are more likely to be motivated to learn because training can increase their personal capital (knowledge, skills, competencies), which will in turn improve their feelings of self-worth and contribute to enhanced job performance (for example, Mathieu, Tannenbaum, & Salas, 1993).

Organizational Commitment

Organizational commitment includes an affective component (belief in the organization's goals and values) and a behavioral component (willingness to make an effort for the organization). The greater the employees' organizational commitment, the more likely they are to view training as personally beneficial to themselves and the organization.

Career Exploration

Career exploration refers to a person's self-assessment of strengths, weaknesses, values, interests, goals, or plans, and search for information from peers, friends, managers, and family members (Stumpf, Colarelli, & Hartman, 1983). Employees who have explored careers have higher levels of training motivation because they can more clearly see how mastering training content can help them overcome their weaknesses and reinforce or complement their strengths.

Guidelines for Practice: Motivational and Job or Career Attitudes

Pay attention to the framing of the training program. The information that the organization provides about a training program can color trainees' perceptions of how to interpret it (Martocchio, 1992; Quiñones, 1997). To have a positive influence on trainee attitudes that affect learning, organizations should do the following:

- Provide information on the content of the training program, how it will benefit trainees' careers, current job performance, employability, promotability, and so on.
- Provide similar information on how the content of the training program can benefit the larger organization, help it meet the goals spelled out by its vision.
- If possible, allow trainees to bring problems and situations to use as practice exercises or examples in training.
- Use Web-based training or other methods that allow trainees to control the pace at which they proceed through the content and determine the amount of practice they need.

To increase self-efficacy:

- Communicate to employees that the purpose of training is to improve performance rather than identify skills in which they are deficient.
- Provide as much information as possible about the content and purpose of the training program before having employees attend training.
- Give employees examples of peers who have successfully completed training and explain how the content has been useful to them.

Characteristics of the Work Environment

The work environment can influence learning and transfer in several different ways. Behaviors and attitudes are influenced by the work employees do, relationships at work, and the overall psychological culture or climate of the organization. Interactions with the work environment influence motivation in two ways: going into training (which affects learning) and when back on the job (which affects transfer of training). Several work environment characteristics are important to consider during training, including the organization's climate, the opportunity to perform trained skills, managerial support for training, organizational justice, and the team demands of the work context.

Climate

Employees tend to behave according to their perceptions of the environment, known as the climate (Schneider & Reichers, 1983). In training, research suggests that a positive climate for learning and transfer can become very salient and affect behavior. Trainees who report working in a supportive climate are more likely to attend programs and exhibit high levels of motivation to learn (for example, Noe & Wilk, 1993; Maurer & Tarulli, 1994).

Climate for transfer refers to the trainees' perceptions of characteristics of the work environment that influence the use of what they have learned (Rouiller & Goldstein, 1993; Tracey, Tannenbaum, & Kavanaugh, 1995), such as manager and peer support, adequate resources, and positive consequences for using the training content. Research clearly demonstrates that the climate for transfer does influence motivation to learn as well as knowledge and skill acquisition and transfer of training (for example, Colquitt et al., 2000; Tracey et al., 1995).

Opportunity to Perform

Opportunity to perform includes three dimensions: breadth, activity level, and task type. Breadth refers to the number of trained tasks performed on the job. Activity level refers to the frequency with which trained tasks are performed. Task type refers to the difficulty or criticality of the trained tasks that are performed. Trainees who are given opportunities to perform are more likely to maintain learned capabilities than those given fewer opportunities (Ford, Quiñones, Sego, & Sorra, 1992). Opportunity to perform can be increased by formal job assignments or self-directed actions on the part of the trainee. Managers give trainees the opportunity by assigning job experiences (such as production or service problems, task forces) that require the use of training content. However, trainees also actively manage their learning by personally seeking out job experiences where they can use what they have learned.

Organizational Justice

Organizational justice refers to the perceived fairness of decision making in organizations. Employees perceive that there is organizational justice when they are given choices and allowed input into decisions; when they are treated consistently, politely, and without bias; and when they are provided with extensive explanations (Colquitt, Conlon, Wesson, Porter, & Ng, forthcoming; Folger & Cropanzano, 1998). Organizational justice is particularly relevant to the assignment of trainees to training situations. For example, research shows that trainees react more favorably when they choose to attend training, rather than being assigned to do so, and when they have some input into the training content (Baldwin, Magjuka, & Loher, 1991; Hicks & Klimoski, 1987). Justice is also particularly relevant when trainees are assigned to remedial or basic skills training. Quiñones (1995) showed that trainees who perceived that the remedial assignment decision had been made in a fair manner performed better during training.

Individual Versus Team Context

Often trainees learn skills in an individual learning environment but then return to work that is team-based. In team-based work, task performance depends on the contributions of other team members and requires teamwork skills in addition to job performance skills (McIntyre & Salas, 1995). Thus individuals may correctly transfer their individual KSAOs but fail to succeed nevertheless. Teams and training scholars agree that the training environment should be congruent with, and reinforce, the work environment. Therefore, if trainees work in teams then the task KSAOs emphasized by the training should be supplemented to include teamwork KSAOs (Cannon-Bowers, Tannenbaum, Salas, & Volpe, 1995; Stevens & Campion, 1994). Teamwork KSAOs may be relevant to almost any team task or may be task-specific (Cannon-Bowers et al., 1995). Stevens and Campion (1994) propose a list of generic teamwork KSAOs that include conflict resolution, collaboration, communication, performance management, and coordination. Similarly, Cannon-Bowers et al. (1995) note the importance of morale building, information exchange, consulting with others, and assertiveness. This notion of teamwork KSAOs is consistent with McIntyre and Salas's (1995) views on team training; they argued that team members must be trained not just for "taskwork" but also for teamwork.

Guidelines for Practice: Work Environment

Assess relevant features of the work environment. Many organizations conduct yearly attitude surveys in order to understand more clearly the factors that affect employee morale, retention, and performance. Although most surveys measure broader people issues, such as morale and satisfaction with various aspects of work, more focused surveys can be used to assess specific topics such as climate, support, opportunity, and organizational justice. Given the need for training departments to be accountable for results (that is, to show how their services contribute to the company's competitive advantage), yearly surveys of work environment features that influence training are essential. Information can be collected in two ways. One is to include items on the organization's attitude survey if it is part of the organization's human resource practices. Another is to measure work environment perceptions as part of training needs assessment surveys. Trainers usually use these surveys to identify the frequency and importance of competencies, skills, tasks, classes, and so on. Exhibit 3.2 presents sample items that can be used to assess the climate for transfer.

This kind of assessment helps trainers identify pockets of support and resistance for training activities and also the kinds of support strategies needed to enhance learning and transfer of training. Taking factors like climate, opportunity, and organizational justice into consideration can trainers help diagnose why seemingly

Exhibit 3.2. Sample Items to Measure Transfer Climate.

- My colleagues encourage me to use the skills I have learned.
- My manager sets goals that encourage me to use the skills I have learned in training.
- The resources I need to use what I learned in training will be available to me after training.
- Training is encouraged at my company.
- Maintaining the status quo is more important than learning new things at my company.
- My company provides paid release time for employee development purposes.
- Successful people at my company go to training.
- Before training I usually have a good idea of how it will help me perform my job better.
- Employees in this company receive rewards when they use newly learned skills on the job.
- Coworkers consistently suggest new approaches to solving problems based on their own experiences.
- Supervisors openly express their support of continuous learning.

Source: Based on Holton, Bates, & Ruona, forthcoming, Noe & Wilk, 1993, Rouiller & Goldstein, 1993, and Tracey, Tannenbaum, & Kavanaugh, 1995.

successful training is not resulting in proper transfer and job performance. For example, a task or skill has long been a key focus of training, yet former trainees report little opportunity to perform the task on the job. This may indicate the following:

- The task or skill is a candidate for a refresher course (designed to let trainees practice and review training content). This is especially important for tasks and skills that are determined to be critical for effective performance but are not needed frequently on the job.
- This specific aspect of the training content is not critical for performance of the job and therefore training time is being wasted.
- The work environment is interfering with the use of new skills. Managers may not be giving trainees the opportunity to use them, possibly because they are afraid initial job performance will decrease.

Besides offering an opportunity to perform, managers can create a supportive climate to encourage transfer of training. The levels of support (listed from high to low) include these:

- Permitting employees to attend training and acknowledging the importance of it (acceptance)
- Accommodating attendance at training by rearranging work schedules and endorsing employees' attending of training (encouragement)
- Attending training sessions themselves (participation)
- Discussing the progress that trainees are making in learning and using new skills, and asking how to support their use of training content (reinforcement)
- Allowing trainees opportunities to practice (practice skills)
- Becoming a trainer in the training program or designing instructional materials for the program (teaching)

When managers participate in train-the-trainer sessions they are prepared to offer the highest level of support. Those who are trainers themselves are more likely to provide many of the lower-level support functions (reinforcement, participation, and so on). They can create a supportive climate through action plans, which are documents that include the steps that both the manager and the trainee will take to ensure that training transfers to the job. Because goals can help energize, direct, and maintain behavior, action plans usually contain a goal that relates to a specific project or problem that the trainee will work on. The action plan also includes the resources that the manager agrees to provide, such as equipment, job experiences, financial resources, or a longer time period to complete a project. Finally, the action plan includes a specific set of dates and times when the manager and trainee

Exhibit 3.3. Ways to Gain Managerial Support for Training.

- Brief managers on the purpose of the program and its relationship to business objectives and strategy.

- Provide a schedule of training topics and a checklist of managers' responsibilities to ensure transfer of training.

- Encourage trainees to meet with their manager before training to identify projects and problems on the job. These can be brought to training and used as practice exercises.

- Communicate information on the benefits of the training program to managers.

- Hold managers accountable for ensuring that employees attend training by using a development dimension on their performance appraisal.

- Train managers in ways they can give employees opportunities to use learned skills through temporary assignments, task forces, job rotation, employee exchanges, or serving as an on-the-job trainer.

- Hold managers accountable for showing how their training budget is spent and how the training activities relate to individual, team, or division performance.

agree to meet to discuss progress toward attaining the established goals. Exhibit 3.3 shows several ways to enhance managerial support for training.

In addition to providing support, managers can improve the training climate by encouraging self-management. Given the influence of self-efficacy on learning and transfer, and the fact that most work environments are less than ideal for facilitating learning and transfer (that is, managerial support is low, time pressures and performance goals supercede efforts to apply training content to the job), it is necessary to teach trainees how to self-manage learning and transfer (Frayne & Geringer, 2000). Self-management includes having trainees do the following:

- Assess the degree of support they can expect for learning and transfer, and identify factors in the work environment that can inhibit transfer.
- Set goals for using training content on the job.
- Apply training content to the job.
- Monitor the degree of use of learned capabilities on the job.
- Reward themselves for using training content on the job.
- Write a contract with themselves that specifies expectations, plans, and contingencies for the behavior to be changed.

Self-management techniques are important because when trainees run into problems trying to apply new skills, they are likely to lapse back into previously learned, less effective techniques. Or, if trainees are using a new skill they may become frustrated and stop trying to use it. Lapses into old behaviors and skill patterns are common. Research suggests that trainees who are taught self-management techniques in the training program exhibit higher levels of transfer of behavior and skills than those who are not (for example, Frayne & Latham, 1987; Latham & Frayne, 1989; Gist, Bavetta, & Stevens, 1990). Unfortunately, most training programs overemphasize content but fail to prepare the trainee to understand how to cope with the reality of the work environment. Although devoting training to self-management may reduce the amount of training content, it will likely result in more effective training.

In addition to creating a positive climate through support, self-management, and the opportunity to perform, managers can promote training goals by fostering organizational justice. This can be accomplished by doing the following:

- Provide employees with input into the timing, sequence, and choice of training programs.
- Provide employees with input into the content of the training program.
- Offer programs that have several standardized modules as well as one or two modules that deal with specific issues raised by the trainees.
- Treat employees with dignity, sincerity, and respect when providing them feedback on their skill assessments or assigning them to remedial or basic skills training.
- Honestly and completely explain the reasons behind a training assignment (particularly if that assignment is remedial), and emphasize that the assignment was based on an unbiased view of the individual's current performance.

Finally, managers do well to consider the match between the training environment and the working environment by doing the following:

- Assess the degree of task interdependence among the trainees in their work environment. High levels of task interdependence require high levels of coordination and teamwork.
- Where interdependence is high, supplement task KSAOs with teamwork KSAOs, including conflict resolution, collaboration, communication, performance management, and planning and coordination (Cannon-Bowers et al., 1995; Stevens & Campion, 1994).
- Assess how long the teams have worked together. Teams that have been intact for several months may not require the teamwork KSAO module of the training program.
- Consider how long teams will remain stable in the future. Even teams that have existed for a while may be nearing the end of their project's tenure. If member-

ship is going to change rapidly, the nature of the KSAO training may be changed to focus more on generic team skills, less tailored to the specific team's tasks.

Conclusion

In this chapter, we have attempted to show how individual differences and work environment characteristics influence learning and transfer of training. Although solid training design is an essential prerequisite, it alone cannot guarantee learning and transfer of training. The trainability, personality, and attitudes that trainees brings with them have a great impact on their motivation and subsequent learning and transfer. Likewise, many facets of the work environment affect phases of the training experience. The research findings are unequivocal: individual and work environment characteristics influence learning and transfer. Organizations interested in making their training programs more effective would do well to assess these characteristics as part of the needs assessment process and design appropriate interventions to support training efforts.

References

Baldwin, T. T., & Ford, J. K. (1988). Transfer of training: A review and directions for the future. *Personnel Psychology, 41,* 63–105.

Baldwin, T. T., Magjuka, R. J., & Loher, B. T. (1991). The perils of participation: Effects of learner choice on motivation and learning. *Personnel Psychology, 44,* 51–66.

Barrick, M. R., & Mount, M. K. (1993). Autonomy as a moderator of the relationship between the Big Five personality dimensions and job performance. *Journal of Applied Psychology, 78,* 111–118.

Barrick, M. R., Mount, M. K., & Strauss, J. P. (1993). Conscientiousness and performance of sales representatives: Test of the mediation effects of goal setting. *Journal of Applied Psychology, 80,* 500–509.

Cannon-Bowers, J. A., Rhodenizer, L., Salas, E., & Bowers, C. A. (1998). A framework for understanding pre-practice conditions and their impact on learning. *Personnel Psychology, 51,* 291–320.

Cannon-Bowers, J. A., Tannenbaum, S. I., Salas, E., & Volpe, C. E. (1995). Defining competencies and establishing team training requirements. In R. A. Guzzo, E. Salas, & Associates (Eds.), *Team effectiveness and decision making in organizations* (pp. 9–45). San Francisco: Jossey-Bass.

Cleveland, J. N., & Shore, L. M. (1992). Self- and supervisory perceptions on age and work attitudes and performance. *Journal of Applied Psychology, 77,* 469–484.

Colquitt, J. A., Conlon, D. E., Wesson, M. J., Porter, C.O.L. H., & Ng, K. Y. (forthcoming). Justice at the millennium: A meta-analysis of 25 years of organizational justice research. *Journal of Applied Psychology.*

Colquitt, J. A., LePine, J. A., & Noe, R. A. (2000). Toward an integrative theory of training motivation: A meta-analytic path analysis of 20 years of research. *Journal of Applied Psychology, 85,* 678–707.

Colquitt, J. A., & Simmering, M. A. (1998). Conscientiousness, goal orientation, and motivation to learn during the learning process: A longitudinal study. *Journal of Applied Psychology, 83,* 654–665.

Dweck, C. S. (1986). Motivational processes affecting learning. *American Psychologist, 41,* 1040–1048.

Dweck, C. S., & Leggett, E. L. (1988). A social cognitive approach to motivation and personality. *Psychological Review, 95,* 256–273.

Facteau, J. D., Dobbins, G. H., Russell, J.E.A., Ladd, R. T., & Kudisch, J. D. (1995). The influence of general perceptions of the training environment on pretraining motivation and perceived training transfer. *Journal of Management, 21,* 1–25.

Fisher, S. L., & Ford, J. K. (1998). Differential effects of learner effort and goal orientation on two learner outcomes. *Personnel Psychology, 51,* 397–420.

Folger, R., & Cropanzano, R. (1998). *Organizational justice and human resource management.* Thousand Oaks, CA: Sage.

Ford, J. K., Quiñones, M. A., Sego, D. J., & Sorra, J. S. (1992). Factors affecting the opportunity to perform trained tasks on the job. *Personnel Psychology, 45,* 511–527.

Frayne, C. A., & Geringer, J. M. (2000). Self-management training for improving job performance: A field experiment involving salespeople. *Journal of Applied Psychology, 85,* 361–372.

Frayne, C.A., & Latham, G. P. (1987). The application of social learning theory to employee self-management. *Journal of Applied Psychology, 72,* 387–392.

Gagne, R. M., & Medsker, K. L. (1996). *The conditions of learning.* Orlando: Harcourt Brace.

Gist, M. E., Bavetta, A. G., & Stevens, C. K. (1990). Transfer training method: Its influence on skill generalization, skill repetition, and performance level. *Personnel Psychology, 43,* 501–523.

Gottfredson, L. (1996). The g factor in employment. *Journal of Vocational Behavior, 19,* 293–296.

Hicks, W. D., & Klimoski, R. (1987). The process of entering training programs and its effect on training outcomes. *Academy of Management Journal, 30,* 542–552.

Hochwater, W. A., Witt, L. A., Kacmar, K. M. (2000). Perceptions of organizational politics as a moderator of the relationship between conscientiousness and performance. *Journal of Applied Psychology, 85,* 472–478.

Hunter, J. E. (1986). Cognitive ability, cognitive aptitude, job knowledge, and job performance. *Journal of Vocational Behavior, 29,* 340–362.

Holton, E. F, Bates, R. A., & Ruona, W.E.A. (forthcoming). Development of a generalized learning transfer system inventory. *Human Resource Development Quarterly, 11,* 333–360.

Hunter, J. E., & Hunter, R. F. (1984). Validity and utility of alternative predictors of job performance. *Psychological Bulletin, 96,* 72–98.

Kirkpatrick, D. L. (1976). Evaluation of training. In R. L Craig (Ed.), *Training and development handbook: A guide to human resource development* (2nd ed., pp. 18.1–18.27). New York: McGraw-Hill.

Kraiger, K., Ford, J. K., & Salas, E. (1993). Application of cognitive, skill-based, and affective theories of learning outcomes to new methods of training evaluation. *Journal of Applied Psychology, 78,* 311–328.

Latham, G. P., & Frayne, C. A. (1989). Self-management training for increased job attendance: A follow-up and replication. *Journal of Applied Psychology, 74,* 411–416.

LePine, J. A., Colquitt, J. A., & Erez, A. (2000). Adaptability to changing task contexts: Effects of general cognitive ability, conscientiousness, and openness. *Personnel Psychology, 53,* 563–594.

London, M., & Smither, J. W. (1999). Career-related continuous learning: Defining the construct and mapping the process. In G. R. Ferris (Ed.), *Research in Personnel and Human Resource Management 17* (pp. 81–120). Greenwich, CT: JAI Press.

Martocchio, J. J. (1992). Microcomputer usage as an opportunity: The influence of context in employee training. *Personnel Psychology, 45,* 529–551.

Martocchio, J. J., & Baldwin, T. T. (1997). The evolution of strategic organizational training. In R. G. Ferris (ed.), *Research in personnel and human resource management* (Vol. 15, pp. 1–46). Greenwich, CT: JAI Press.

Martocchio, J. J., & Judge, T. A. (1997). Relationship between conscientiousness and learning in employee training: Mediating influence of self-deception and self-efficacy. *Journal of Applied Psychology, 82,* 764–773.

Mathieu, J. E., & Martineau, J. W. (1997). Individual and situational influences in training motivation. In J. K. Ford, S.W.J. Kozlowski, K. Kraiger, E. Salas, & M. S. Teachout (Eds.), *Improving training effectiveness in organizations* (pp. 193–222). Hillsdale, NJ: Erlbaum.

Mathieu, J. E., Tannenbaum, S. I., & Salas, E. (1992). Influences of individual and situational characteristics on measures of training effectiveness. *Academy of Management Journal, 35,* 828–847.

Maurer, T. J., & Tarulli, B. A. (1994). Investigation of perceived environment, perceived outcome, and person variables in relationship to voluntary development activity by employees. *Journal of Applied Psychology, 79,* 3–14.

McIntyre, R. M., & Salas, E. (1995). Measuring and managing for team performance: Lessons from complex environments. In R. A. Guzzo, E. Salas, & Associates (Eds.), *Team effectiveness and decision making in organizations* (pp. 9–45). San Francisco: Jossey-Bass.

McMurrer, D. P., Van Buren, M. E., & Woodwell, W. H. Jr. (2000). *The 2000 ASTD state of the industry report.* Alexandria, VA: American Society for Training and Development.

Morris, M. G., & Venkatesh, V. (2000). Age differences in technology adoption decisions: Implications for a changing workforce. *Personnel Psychology, 53,* 375–403.

Noe, R. A. (1986). Trainee attributes: Neglected influences on training effectiveness. *Academy of Management Review, 11,* 736–749.

Noe, R. A. (1999). *Employee training and development.* Burr Ridge, IL: Irwin.

Noe, R. A., & Schmitt, N. (1986). The influence of trainee attitudes on training effectiveness: Test of a model. *Personnel Psychology, 39,* 497–523.

Noe, R. A., & Wilk, S. L. (1993). Investigation of the factors that influence employees' participation in development activities. *Journal of Applied Psychology, 78,* 291–302.

Nordhaug, O. (1989). Reward functions of personnel training. *Human Relations, 42,* 373–388.

Phillips, J. J. (1996, February). ROI: The search for best practices. *Training and Development,* pp. 42–47.

Phillips, J. M., & Gully, S. M. (1997). Role of goal orientation, ability, need for achievement, and locus of control in the self-efficacy and goal-setting process. *Journal of Applied Psychology, 82,* 792–802.

Quiñones, M. A. (1995). Pretraining context effects: Training assignments as feedback. *Journal of Applied Psychology, 80,* 226–238.

Quiñones, M. A. (1997). Contextual influences on training effectiveness. In M. A. Quiñones & A. Ehrenstein (Eds.), *Training for a rapidly changing workplace* (pp. 177–200). Washington, DC: American Psychological Association.

Ree, M. J., & Earles, J. A. (1991). Predicting training success: Not more than g. *Personnel Psychology, 44,* 321–332.

Rouiller, J. Z., & Goldstein, I. L. (1993). The relationship between organizational transfer climate and positive transfer of training. *Human Resource Development Quarterly, 4,* 377–390.

Sackett, P. R., & Mullen, E. J. (1993). Beyond formal experimental design: Toward an expanded view of the training evaluation process. *Personnel Psychology, 46,* 613–627.

Salas, E., & Cannon-Bowers, J. A. (2001). The science of training: A decade of Progress. In S. Fiske, D. Schacter, & C. Zahn-Waxler (Eds.), *Annual Review of Psychology.* Palo Alto, CA: Annual Reviews Inc.

Salas, E., Cannon-Bowers, J. A., Rhodenizer, L., & Bowers, C. A. (1999). Training in organizations: Myths, misconceptions, and mistaken assumptions. In G. R. Ferris (Ed.), *Research in personnel and human resource management* (pp. 123–162). Greenwich, CT: JAI Press.

Schneider, B., & Reichers, A. E. (1983). On the etiology of climates. *Personnel Psychology, 36,* 19–39.

Sterns, H. L., & Doverspike, D. (1989). Aging and the training and learning process. In I. Goldstein (Ed.), *Training and development in organizations* (pp. 299–332). San Francisco: Jossey-Bass.

Stevens, M. J., & Campion, M. A. (1994). The knowledge, skill, and ability requirements for teamwork: Implications for human resource management. *Journal of Management, 20,* 503–530.

Stumpf, S. A., Collarelli, S. M., & Hartman, K. (1983). Development of the career exploration survey (CES). *Journal of Vocational Behavior, 22,* 191–226.

Tannenbaum, S. I., Mathieu, J. E., Salas, E., & Cannon-Bowers, J. (1991). Meeting trainees' expectations: The influence of training fulfillment on the development of commitment, self-efficacy, and motivation. *Journal of Applied Psychology, 76,* 759–769.

Tannenbaum, S. I., & Woods, S. B. (1992). Determining a strategy for evaluating training: Operating within organizational constraints. *Human Resource Planning, 15,* 63–81.

Tracey J. B., Tannenbaum, S. I., & Kavanaugh, M. J. (1995). Applying trained skills on the job: The importance of the work environment. *Journal of Applied Psychology, 80,* 239–252.

Warr, P., & Bunce, D. (1995). Trainee characteristics and the outcomes of open learning. *Personnel Psychology, 48,* 347–375.

Webster, J., & Martocchio, J. J. (1993). Turning work into play: Implications for microcomputer software training. *Journal of Management, 19,* 127–146.

CHAPTER 4

Leveraging Hidden Expertise

Why, When, and How to Use Cognitive Task Analysis

David A. DuBois

In the conventional view, the conceptual foundations and basic procedures of a field (that is, declarative and procedural knowledge of it) are learned in the classroom, whereas expertise is acquired from long experience on the job. Consider what knowledge is missing in the following performance vignettes gathered from cognitive task analyses of three different military jobs:

A navy computer technician is changing the computer tapes when he notices several indications of a computer malfunction. Before he can begin troubleshooting the problem, several officers converge in the computer room to help resolve the problem, which has interrupted the performance of an important mission. As a result, the computer technician is now at an impasse and unsure how to proceed.

A marine infantryman has lost his way navigating from one point to another in thick woods. He knows several procedures for recovering to the planned route when lost but is unsure of which one to use in this situation.

A navy pilot is taking off on runway 29 at the San Diego Naval Air Station. At one hundred knots the number 1 hydraulic pressure light illuminates on the master caution panel. The wind is at twelve knots with a cloud ceiling of fifteen hundred feet. He is uncertain whether to proceed with the takeoff.

These examples of real situations illustrate a need for the kind of knowledge that is not taught in a classroom. In the first case, the computer technician was well trained in each of the topic areas he faced—electronic troubleshooting, computer operations, and communications with officers—but was not prepared to address a situation that involved all three simultaneously. The interactive effects of these tasks produced a novel situation that required unique knowledge, much more than minor modifications of instructed knowledge. Similarly, the marine had been instructed in several procedures for recovery when lost, but he had not been trained in how to decide which procedure to use in specific situations. The navy pilot was well informed about handling a variety of emergencies but did not recognize which situation he was in. Each of these situations required knowledge, essential to effective performance, that was not learned in classrooms. Because of its importance to performance in dynamic contexts, these knowledge requirements are referred to as *adaptive knowledge* or *adaptive expertise* (see Chapter Nine). Together with declarative and procedural knowledge, they form a complete set of content for job knowledge requirements.

When we consider the determinants of high levels of performance, it is clear that knowledge is indeed power. In quantitative summaries of decades of scientific studies (that is, using metanalyses), job knowledge emerges as the dominant determinant of performance effectiveness (for example, Schmidt & Hunter, 1998). Most of this expertise comes from experience on the job. The kind of knowledge gained on the job can differ markedly from the kind that is learned formally through education, training, technical references, job descriptions, and other job materials and aids. Whereas formal training focuses on the facts, concepts, and procedures of a job, expertise gained through experience usually involves knowledge that helps people make effective decisions, understand the big picture while also noticing essential details, and adapt procedures to new situations (see Exhibit 4.1).

Often, this expertise is achieved through observing or modeling others, performing tasks repeatedly, seeing consequences of

Exhibit 4.1. The Nature of Job Expertise.

- Proficient in fundamental skills
- Adapts procedures and standards to situation
- Makes good decisions quickly
- Sees the big picture
- Notices details

- Understands system effects
- Maintains situation awareness
- Perceives trends through time
- Learns efficiently

actions and changes in contexts, and so forth. In fact, this tacit knowledge becomes second-nature to expert performers, so that they report difficulty in describing clearly what they know that others do not know (compare Ericsson & Simon, 1993). For this reason, special methods, called *cognitive task analyses,* must be used to elicit this store of expertise.

My goal in this chapter is to describe why, when, and how cognitive task analysis (CTA) can be used to improve individual and organizational effectiveness. The need for CTA results from recognizing that critical mental skills and knowledge requirements are frequently missing in human resource applications such as job descriptions, despite their criticality to job performance. A central thesis of this chapter is that we gain much by making these cognitive tasks and knowledge explicit through cognitive task analysis.

In this chapter I identify the need for CTA, the organizational factors or reasons for its use, and indicators that suggest when it may be useful. I go on to describe the CTA process. Cognitive task analysis methods tend to be as complex as the skills and knowledge they attempt to describe. Similar to these complex skills, CTA methods work best when adapted to the specific goals and context. Consequently, I attempt to identify and describe the critical decisions that are made in CTA, so that the methods you choose can be adapted effectively to your needs. Finally, I present guidelines and tips intended to serve as an aid to implementation and to provide some ideas on how CTA can be incorporated into standard organizational practice.

Cognitive Task Analysis (CTA)

Cognitive task analyses are methods for decomposing job and task performances into discrete, measurable units, with special emphasis on eliciting mental processes and knowledge content. A variety of methods are available for two central stages of this process, which are knowledge elicitation and knowledge representation. The selection of optimum methods will depend on your purpose for doing CTA, your available resources, constraints (number of subject matter experts, time available, project time line, and so on), as well as on your working model or theory of cognition. These details will be discussed in the following section on implementation.

Cognitive task analyses differ from conventional task analyses because they provide explicit methods for identifying the mental aspects of job performance. Where conventional task analyses focus on observable behaviors such as procedural skills (typing, driving), cognitive task analyses describe activities such as decision making, problem solving, pattern recognition, and situation assessment, which are not directly observable. Where conventional task analyses tend to emphasize what gets done, cognitive task analyses focus on the details of how it gets done (cues, decisions, strategies, goals, standards, and so on). In many cases, cognitive task analysis can be used to supplement traditional methods to identify cognitive tasks and knowledge requirements that are difficult to describe using standard procedures. In some cases, conventional methods can simply be modified to address these knowledge requirements.

As a rule, cognitive task analysis is especially useful in jobs that are complex, dynamic, and have high-stakes outcomes. These jobs tend to involve great judgment, knowledge, and experience. Given a predominance of cognitive tasks in these jobs, cognitive task analysis procedures may be especially suited to identify the essential requirements. However, even jobs that are considered essentially physical in nature (for example, digging ditches) often contain important cognitive elements that can be identified through cognitive task analysis (for example, Shalin, Geddes, Bertrim, Szczepkowski, & DuBois, 1999).

Exhibit 4.2. Cognitive Versus Conventional Task Analyses.

Cognitive	Conventional
• Mental	• Physical
• Unobservable	• Observable
• How tasks are done	• What tasks are done

Purpose of CTA

The purpose of any type of task analysis is to describe the nature of job performance. Task analyses are used to specify the components of job performance, to describe the essential tasks that get performed on the job. They provide essential information for the entire range of human resource activities and outcomes, including job descriptions, training needs, performance appraisal forms, job evaluation, training content, and job and organization design.

In addition, task analyses are sometimes performed to define user requirements for software design and for developing the user interface. They are used to develop selection measures, such as biodata or personality inventories, and criteria for the validation of selection measures. Task analyses are also used to develop career paths, evaluate affirmative action and equal employment opportunity programs, and identify reasonable accommodations for persons with disabilities. Quite simply, a clear description of the activities of a job is helpful virtually all the time, and can be used in virtually any application of CTA data.

Cognitive task analysis is especially suited to training and development activities because it directly addresses the job's knowledge requirements. In addition to identifying the facts, concepts, and procedures that support task performance, cognitive task analysis can identify the decisions, cues, judgments, and perceptions that contribute to effective performance. By making this expertise explicit through CTA, the time required to become highly proficient may be sharply reduced through appropriate training and development activities.

Unique Contribution of CTA

Achieving high levels of performance often requires ten years or more on the job. Even performance on relatively simple, routine tasks continues to improve after several years of experience (Schmidt, Hunter & Outerbridge, 1986). For jobs that are complex, technical, dynamic, or with high-stakes outcomes, the amount of expertise acquired through experience can be extremely large. Cognitive task analysis allows us to describe explicitly what these experts implicitly learned from experience.

Unlike the descriptions of facts, concepts, and procedures contained in textbooks and technical references, the expertise of high performers also includes knowledge that helps in decision making, problem solving, pattern recognition, and situation assessment. This cognitive knowledge and these skills are often the most critical influences on individual and organizational effectiveness. Yet because this expertise is usually acquired informally and implicitly, experts themselves find it difficult to describe what it is that they know that others do not. Therefore, the unique contribution of cognitive task analysis is uncovering the nature of this expertise.

Applications

Uncovering hidden expertise greatly expands the opportunities for improving performance. Once expertise has been made explicit, it can be leveraged in many ways to improve individual and organizational effectiveness.

Training

Most directly, job expertise can be incorporated into formal training, described in technical references, and incorporated into performance aids (for example, integrated into an electronic performance support system [EPSS]). If they are given training in essential yet previously missing areas, trainees are more likely to transfer this knowledge into performance in the work setting and less likely to face performance impasses because of lack of knowledge. Importantly, if they are provided with more complete knowledge, it should reduce substantially the time they require to attain high levels of performance.

For example, in an application to aviator training (DuBois & Gillan, 2000), we assisted a navy training school by using cognitive task analyses to identify important decisions that affected flight skills and crew performance. These performance vignettes were then used to create a decisions-skills training program and scenario-based testing in which brief scenarios, developed from actual incidents, were presented to trainees to let them gain expertise in decision making. This cognitive approach to training was integrated into a curriculum that previously gave instruction only in individual skills and systems. We wrote similar scenarios for assessments of training and flight simulator exercises. Our intention was to provide many opportunities for trainees to practice these essential decision-making skills. The expectation was that performance in this task would improve steadily with practice. In the future, we plan to implement additional training programs for other essential cognitive flight skills, such as error management, situation awareness, and managing transitions.

Development

Once the complete set of knowledge requirements of high performance levels is defined, it can lead to further performance improvements. An explicit set of knowledge requirements can be used to diagnose performance deficiencies and prescribe useful strategies for overcoming impasses. Mentors and coaches can use this information to set clear, specific learning goals for on-the-job training and self-directed learning. For example, coaches may explain that decisions about goal priorities and choice of methods in specific situations are important knowledge requirements that need to be learned from experience. By making this learning goal explicit, individuals have the opportunity to discuss options, monitor their own performance, and improve their effectiveness.

Performance Reviews

These knowledge requirements can also be incorporated into performance assessment and appraisal tools to provide feedback for skills improvement. It seems obvious, yet critical cognitive skills such as planning and decision making are omitted frequently from performance assessments and reviews. Yet these skills are essential to performance effectiveness and career progress.

Let us take decision skills as an example. Two main types of decisions are made at work: decisions about goals and decisions about the methods used to achieve the goals. A typical stumbling block for novices is to conflate methods and goals. They sometimes develop "method fixation," becoming unproductively attached to a particular way of getting the work done. Among research scientists like myself, for example, a common example of method fixation is to use a particular analytic technique (usually because the investigator is familiar with it) regardless of how inappropriate it may be for the situation at hand.

If a supervisor understands this knowledge requirement, she can work with her subordinate. In the review process, she can clarify the goal, separate the goal from alternative methods for accomplishing it, and then coach her subordinate on effective decision strategies for selecting the optimum method for the current context. Inevitably, this involves understanding how the advantages and disadvantages of each method match the salient contextual factors, conditions, and constraints.

Recognizing the Need for CTA

When should cognitive task analysis be used? Many indicators, or cues, suggest when it may be helpful. Once a need is recognized, then the potential for performance improvement, cost or time reduction, and so forth can be evaluated. Highly favorable ratios of benefits to costs can then drive the commitment to the project.

Indicators

One need not wait until a serious accident or costly error occurs to recognize the need to identify the critical cognitive skills underlying effective performance. Accidents are usually the result of a cascading series of errors and preexisting conditions (Reason, 1999). It is helpful to examine the patterns of existing performance problems, typical errors, and training transfer difficulties. If these deficiencies occur during the performance of a task, then there is probably a problem with training, equipment, or the procedures themselves. However, if problems occur in recognizing what to do, when to do it, when the context requires adaptation of standard procedures, or when making a transition between tasks or phases of tasks, then the problem more likely involves cognitive skills, and there is a need for cognitive task analysis.

Other indicators can be found by examining the content of training programs, performance reviews, and technical references of an organization. Do they explicitly include knowledge requirements that support decisions (knowing how goal priorities shift across changes in the situation, or knowing which methods are best in each context)? Do training materials include realistic scenarios of how the knowledge gained will be applied in the work setting? If not, and if you are confident that decision skills, pattern recognition, and other cognitive content are important for the target job, then cognitive task analyses will be useful. If essential cognitive content is missing from training, it may also show itself in difficulties in transferring skills from the classroom to the work setting.

Drivers

There are two main reasons why CTA may be needed: performance deficiencies and improvement goals for human resource applications. Common performance deficiencies are costly errors or serious accidents.

For example, the driver for CTA in a navy aviation group came from a review of serious aviation mishaps throughout the navy. The review determined that over 60 percent of them involved human factors. Further analyses revealed the nature of the human factors: poor judgment, faulty decisions, misperceptions, and ineffective communication. These performance elements were not explicitly addressed in the training programs at the time. The results of these deficiencies were very costly in both human lives and high-performance aircraft. Further, the errors were cognitive—missing from existing training and from the task analyses that produced the training. Consequently, cognitive task analyses were selected to address these deficiencies.

More proactively, cognitive task analysis can also be employed to make substantial improvements in applications such as testing, performance diagnoses, training, and software design. For example, another motivation for the military services to use cognitive task analysis is to shorten the learning curve required to achieve

Exhibit 4.3. Recognizing the Need for CTA.

Indicators of a Need for CTA

- There are persistent performance problems.
- There are costly errors or accidents.
- Training transfer is deficient.
- Learning curves to achieve high performance are long.
- Training, performance reviews omit cognitive skills.

Drivers of CTA

- Reduce errors and accidents.
- Reduce training costs.
- Improve assessment validity.
- Improve performance diagnoses.
- Reduce time to performance effectiveness.

high levels of performance. By identifying previously hidden expertise, this knowledge can be explicitly incorporated into training, testing, and practice (DuBois & Gillan, 2000) to speed the knowledge acquisition process.

The CTA Process

There are four steps in conducting a cognitive task analysis: planning, knowledge elicitation, knowledge representation, and application development. Each of these is described in the following paragraphs.

Planning the CTA

As with any project, successful outcomes depend on effective planning. For cognitive task analysis, the core of this planning involves a series of key decisions, shown in Exhibit 4.4.

Purpose

The first decision is choosing the application that will be addressed by the CTA results. The nature of the application determines the focus of the CTA (whether special attention will be given to goals,

Exhibit 4.4. CTA Planning Decisions.

- Purposes
- Methods
- Sampling
- Project personnel

---

decisions, cues, strategies, conditions, constraints, perceptions, patterns, standards, and so on) and affects the choice of method, the level of detail required, and so on.

An important advantage of CTA is that the results can be used across a very wide range of applications. This is an important consideration because CTA is usually more costly than conventional task analyses. These extra costs may be recouped through cost sharing. For example, you may have a need for CTA to improve training quality. After some examination, you may determine that the results would also contribute to process reengineering efforts, Web site design, and EPSS design. In fact, CTA results are especially useful for software and systems design because they can reveal information that is often implicit, such as operant goals that guide problem solving or task performance.

The decision about the appropriate purposes for CTA is usually straightforward. Still, it is important to specify these uses up front because of their impact on how the process will be carried out. Suppose the primary motivation is to redesign an internal Web site, but additional uses of CTA results are identified for technician training and certification. In the former application, the focus would be on goal structure and task processes; the latter would probably require an emphasis on situation assessment and decision making. Knowing the purposes of data collection, along with the implications of these purposes for the CTA methods, will produce a much stronger return on the effort.

Methods

When planning a CTA project, a decision about the method to use must also be made: Will it will be knowledge elicitation or knowledge representation? *Knowledge elicitation* is the process of specify-

**Exhibit 4.5. Factors in Choosing
a Knowledge Elicitation Method.**

Factor	Range of Possible Values	
Costs, job-organizational outcomes	Low stakes	High stakes
Time, duration of cognitive task	Days, hours	Minutes, seconds
Contextual dependencies	Low	High
Problem or task focus	Process	Content
Preferred method	Interview	Protocol analysis

ing the knowledge requirements for effective performance. *Knowledge representation* is the process of analyzing, reducing, and organizing the data gathered in the knowledge elicitation phase. Because of its centrality to CTA effectiveness, the decision criteria for selecting methods of knowledge elicitation are discussed in some detail here. Brief descriptions of methods of knowledge elicitation and representation are given in the following paragraphs.

A wide range of methods for knowledge elicitation are available. These methods differ in scope, detail, accuracy, and cost. For example, interviews with subject matter experts are reasonably quick and straightforward but not as accurate or detailed as protocol analyses. The goal of the knowledge elicitation phase is to identify completely the important knowledge requirements for performance. The optimum method to meet this goal depends on several factors, including the nature of the expertise involved in the targeted task or job (for example, decision making versus perception), the applications that will be developed, the resources available, and the constraints (time, subject matter experts). Exhibit 4.5 summarizes several key factors to consider when matching CTA methods to application needs.

The nature of the problem being addressed determines how much latitude you will have with accuracy and completeness. For example, if the problem is to improve training for computer programmers, accountants, or architects, some inaccuracies and omissions are probably acceptable in order to reduce the cost of data collection. You can conduct reasonably brief interviews with SMEs, using directed probes targeted to essential cognitive content and skills of the job, to help them recall relevant information. In contrast, if the problem involves high-stakes outcomes, such as with airline pilots, firefighters, and physicians, then more resource-intensive procedures, such as protocol analyses, should be employed. The return on investment is higher because of the superior accuracy and completeness of protocol analyses compared with retrospective interviews.

A second factor to consider is the amount of contextual dependencies in the target job. For example, compare the three high stakes jobs mentioned in the previous paragraph to the three low stakes jobs. The expertise of the former is contextually sensitive. Effective performance depends on noticing and responding to subtle changes in the environment. Consequently, it is important to conduct protocol analysis with SMEs in their natural performance context, so that the relevant cues, strategies, and important contextual characteristics can be readily identified.

A third factor to consider is the duration of the critical cognitive activities of the job. For example, senior executives may take weeks or months to gather information and decide whether to build or lease a new building for their business. In contrast, a fire crew chief may make a series of quick decisions when responding to an advancing fire in a building. The ability to recall and describe accurately and completely the decision process, critical cues, strategies, and alternatives is much greater in the former situation than in the latter. Interviews may produce equivalent results in the former situation, but they are less likely to do so in the latter.

The fourth factor is the type of information required for effective performance. The distinction between content and processes is a useful one to guide decisions about choice of methods. Training, testing, and performance measurement tend to require a stronger focus on the content of cognition. Process reengineering, software design, and systems design tend to emphasize identification of processes. Thus for some situations and applications, the focus will be on processes—the steps required to get the job done. For other situations and applications, it may be necessary to pay special attention to the content of knowledge to accomplish a task. For example, in these situations knowledge requirements such as cue and pattern recognition, situation assessment, and the adaptation of goals, methods, and standards need more attention in the CTA. Most situations involve both, but it is a question of emphasis.

Although the content-process distinction is a useful one, it is certainly not absolute when it comes to classifying methods of cognitive task analyses; all methods will reveal useful information about both the content and processes of cognition. Thus, it should be employed as a flexible heuristic in determining the best match for the need. There are other considerations as well: availability of persons with cognitive task analysis experience, availability of subject matter experts, and theoretical positions about the nature of the task and the nature of cognition.

Taken together, these considerations are complex, subtle, and without conclusive empirical evidence to guide choices. The choice among methods rests on two main criteria: matching the method to the situation, and evaluating trade-offs between costs and benefits.

Trade-offs between costs and benefits play an important role in selecting an appropriate method of knowledge elicitation. Interviews are the least expensive method. As noted, they are especially productive when stakes are low, knowledge requirements are not context dependent, the time span of critical cognitive events is reasonably long, and the focus is on describing processes with long duration. But when the knowledge requirements are comparatively implicit and hard to describe, more expensive methods such as protocol analyses will provide the best return on investment. Advice from people with experience in cognitive task analysis can be especially useful when you are selecting an appropriate method for knowledge elicitation.

Fortunately, the decision about which knowledge representation method to use is simpler and has less of an impact on CTA quality. The goal here is to analyze, reduce, and organize the data gathered from the knowledge elicitation phase into a form suitable for the targeted applications. The content-process distinction is especially helpful for decisions about methods of knowledge representation. For example, text and tabular methods of knowledge representation work best in content-oriented applications, such as training, testing, and performance measurement. Graphical representation methods, such as decision trees and flowcharts, are especially suited for process reengineering, and software and systems design applications. The main consideration for this decision is to select a format that is easy to work with. Because both task analysts and application developers will need to work with these data, the best method will suit both groups. Sometimes, that may mean using two methods of knowledge representation.

Sampling

Once decisions about knowledge elicitation and knowledge representation methods have been made, it is important to develop a sampling plan to ensure that the representation of knowledge developed from the cognitive task analysis is reliable, valid, and useful. It need not be complex, but it is important to judge how much the CTA results may vary across three factors: people, tasks, contexts. A sampling plan for each of these three factors will ensure that results are sound, useful, and address the questions that need answering.

Depending on the application, it may be important to sample subject matter experts from different organizational locations and departments, with different levels of experience, equipment configurations, and so forth. For example, in a testing application for the Marine Corps, I found big differences in the nature of experts' land navigation knowledge for infantry located in mountainous areas versus flat, forested areas, although both sets of experts were highly proficient. Sometimes it is also useful to understand better what novices, journeymen, and decayed experts know (and do not know). (So-called decayed experts are people who were highly proficient in the past but have not performed the tasks for some time.) Interviewing subject matter experts with different levels of expertise, beginning with the experts and moving successively to less experienced personnel, provides a developmental view of knowledge requirements for a job (Ford & Kraiger, 1995). It can be especially helpful for training and development applications to know the progression, so appropriate assistance can be provided along the way.

Sampling across tasks is especially important when the application is broad and resources do not permit careful consideration of each task. This might occur for projects that cover an entire job, such as job performance measurement, or for projects that cut across jobs, such as reengineering customer service.

Contextual characteristics, such as time pressure, resource availability, and environmental or mission changes, also affect the nature of expertise. For example, in a training application with navy computer technicians, I found substantial differences in knowledge requirements for performing the same tasks in different contexts. Troubleshooting computer problems involved very different procedures when in port or when at sea or when engaged in combat. Differences were also noted for different equipment configurations, availability of parts, and changes in weather (rough rather than calm seas).

Consequently, by incorporating these three factors into the plan for eliciting knowledge from experts, you greatly increase the usefulness of the results you obtain. Importantly, you also reduce the risks that the application developed from the CTA will need to be substantially revised.

Project Personnel

Selecting appropriate people as cognitive task analysts and subject matter experts (SMEs) will increase project efficiency and effectiveness. As with any project, experienced personnel is invaluable. The current challenge for the practice of cognitive task analysis is that well-developed procedures are not readily available. Consequently, a key decision for a CTA project is to define the best mix of external consultants and in-house personnel. As with methods, trade-offs between costs and benefits will have a strong impact on this decision. The first step is to come to a preliminary decision about which CTA methods are most appropriate for the project. This will tell you who to approach for advice and help in conducting it. However, most cognitive task analysts have method-specific expertise: they do CTA their way. Their methods may, *or may not,* be most appropriate for your situation. Getting second and third opinions at the beginning of the project will likely save many headaches toward the end of the project, when application developers use the CTA data to design or revise the application.

From the perspective of reducing costs, some strategies to decrease the workload of in-house personnel include the following: use consultants to provide training and guidance in conducting the task analysis, have consultants develop organization- and application-specific examples of CTA methods and results, use well-developed sampling methods to reduce the amount of data that need to be gathered, and institutionalize the CTA process in the organization so that it is a continuous process rather than an occasional—and major—project.

To increase project effectiveness, a time-honored practice is to assemble a technical review panel of experts and stakeholders to provide assistance and guidance as the project proceeds.

When selecting subject matter experts, there are two main considerations. First, make sure that an appropriate sampling strategy is used. It is important that the SMEs chosen have the relevant expertise. For example, if the application involves software design, it is important that SMEs from the various user groups (by location or by function) be involved to ensure that all important factors and knowledge requirements are identified. Second, SMEs who are verbally fluent (as well as experienced in their work) and committed to the project provide the best information.

Eliciting Knowledge

The main challenge when it comes to knowledge elicitation is that experts themselves often cannot report with accuracy the knowledge they use during performance (Ericsson & Simon, 1993). Nor are they always able to describe what knowledge they possess and others, who are less skilled, do not. As we have already seen, the reason for this is that much of what the experts know was acquired implicitly from long experience. Substantial differences may be found between the knowledge experts say they use and the knowledge they actually use. The challenge of the cognitive task analyst is to identify and articulate this tacit knowledge.

The main source of this information, of course, is the experts themselves. Hence, their verbal reports lie at the heart of most (but not all) methods of cognitive task analysis. But given the omissions and inaccuracies in their descriptions, the goal of cognitive task analysis is to provide the tools and methods to help them provide accurate and complete information.

There are numerous methods for identifying the knowledge requirements and cognitive processes used in job performance. Variants of two general methods—interviews and protocol analyses—are usually used (see Exhibit 4.6). This section provides brief descrip-

Exhibit 4.6. Methods of Knowledge Elicitation.

Method	References
Interviews:	
Critical decision method	Klein, Calderwood, & MacGregor, 1989
PARI	Hall, Gott, & Pokorney, 1995
Protocol analyses:	
Cognitively oriented task analysis	DuBois & Shalin, 2000
Team communications analysis	Orasanu & Fischer, 1992

tions of a few methods of knowledge elicitation to familiarize those of you who have not already been exposed to cognitive task analysis. If you require more details on the goals, assumptions, strategies, and implementation of these methods, I encourage you to read the references cited. In addition, detailed discussions about these and other knowledge elicitation methods are available from a number of useful sources (for example, Cooke, 1994; Ford & Kraiger, 1995; Ford & Wood, 1992; Schraagen, Chipman, & Shalin, 2000).

Critical Decision Method

The critical decision method (CDM; Klein, Calderwood, & Mac-Gregor, 1989), adapted from the critical incident method of Flanagan (1954), focuses on key decisions and events that occur on a job. The task analyst uses a structured approach in interviewing SMEs, asking them to recall specific incidents when they made important decisions. A structured series of follow-up questions elicits information about the cues that affected the decision, the strategies and options that were considered, and why this decision could be difficult for novices. In a variation on this procedure, structured questions are used to identify important knowledge requirements for the job. These knowledge requirements are based on characteristics of experts' knowledge, including knowledge of

- *Past and future:* seeing where situations are headed and where they came from
- *Big picture:* understanding how elements fit together as a whole
- *Noticing:* detecting important details and seeing meaningful patterns
- *Job smarts:* adapting standard procedures to be more efficient for the situation
- *Self-monitoring:* checking how well one is doing and adapting to get the job done

Here are some questions for eliciting information about the big picture: Can you give me an example of what is important about the big picture for this task? What are the major elements you have to know and keep track of?

Structured interviews can be effective even when SMEs have only a short amount of time (less than thirty minutes) to meet with task analysts. Furthermore, because they require descriptions of actual situations, the results are usually rich in context and detail, serving as excellent examples and case studies for training. Another advantage of this method is that it can be adapted to other aspects of cognitive performance, including goal adaptation, teamwork, and systems knowledge.

A limitation is that it takes some training and experience for task analysts to be consistently effective in conducting interviews. Fortunately, Klein Associates, the originators of the method, have developed some job aids and training tools to support the development of interviewing skills using the CDM approach. A second limitation of this method is a tendency by users to overgeneralize the results from individual SMEs or to overlook some essential tasks and knowledge. These concerns can be addressed by developing an appropriate sampling plan.

PARI

The PARI approach to knowledge elicitation also uses structured interview techniques (Hall, Gott, & Pokorney, 1995). Developed initially for electronics troubleshooting tasks, the task analyst presents a SME with a work scenario to solve (for example, a challenging troubleshooting task, developed with the assistance of another SME). After the SME has had some time to study the scenario, the task analyst probes systematically for information on the following four aspects of the task:

- *P*recursors, indicators or cues, that suggest the nature of the situation
- *A*ctions that the SME would take
- *R*esults that the SME expects to occur from the actions taken
- *I*nterpretation of what the results mean

Appropriate scenarios are important for effective use of this method. The scenarios should address the range of essential tasks and contexts for the job or project that is the target of the CTA. With the assistance of other job experts, the scenarios should also be sufficiently challenging in order to reveal the knowledge and strategies used on the job. The interview can be conducted with the assistance of a collaborating expert (the person who developed the scenario) so that he or she can provide answers to queries by the SME about the effects of specific actions.

Similar to the CDM method, this approach can readily be adapted to tasks other than electronics troubleshooting. A limitation is that important aspects of the context can easily be missed, especially if the interview is conducted away from the normal work environment. The seriousness of this limitation depends on the extent to which expertise for the target task is contextually dependent.

Cognitively Oriented Task Analysis (CoTA)

Cognitively oriented task analysis (DuBois, Shalin, Levi, & Borman, 1997) incorporates several methods—interviews, video protocol analyses, and critical incidents. Brief preliminary interviews with SMEs are conducted to identify the important tasks, knowledge, and contexts of the job, project, or task. Ratings are also obtained to assess the relative importance of the tasks, knowledge, and contexts. This information is used to develop detailed sampling plans for tasks, knowledge, and contexts and to formulate appropriate scenarios for the protocol analysis phase.

Protocol analyses are usually conducted in the normal task environment, using four-person teams (two SMEs and two task analysts, one to probe for information and one to do the videotaping). For each protocol session, one SME is presented with a written scenario, along with instructions for conducting the protocol analysis session. These instructions simply request the SME to conduct his work as normal, only to "think aloud" while doing so. Thinking aloud is explained and demonstrated as verbalizing the contents of one's thoughts—not explaining or interpreting behavior for the task analyst. That is, the task analyst wants to know what information SMEs use when they are actually performing their work, not how they explain their work to others. As discussed previously, the difference between the two can be substantial.

After planning their strategy, the two-person team of SMEs begins their work of accomplishing the requested task while the task analysts consistently prompt them to verbalize their thoughts but not suggest interpretations. The performance is videotaped, providing a record of team communications as well as capturing important features of the context (equipment used, cues, constraints, resources, lighting, layout, and so on). Additional queries are sometimes made to illuminate key features of expertise, including probes about goals, cues, decision options and criteria, performance standards, and so forth. The protocols are then reviewed, and the knowledge content is represented in both tabular and graphical form (plan-goal graphs, which will be described in the section on knowledge representation).

A big advantage of this approach is that the protocols clearly reveal the knowledge requirements of the job. Unlike other methods, this approach elucidates in rich detail the influence of the work context on knowledge content and processes. It also affords the task analyst ample opportunities to observe task performance directly, in the natural environment. The primary disadvantage of this approach is the amount of time and task analyst expertise required to perform it.

Analysis of Team Communications

In another variation of protocol analysis, ordinary communications within a team provide a verbal record of cognition that can be recorded and examined (Orasanu & Fischer, 1992). In addition to revealing information that is shared among team members, this method reveals information about technical terms, equipment used, and so forth. Goals and cues can be inferred from the behaviors and verbalizations observed. Of course, a limitation of this approach is that it is less informative about teammates' shared knowledge because there is a tendency not to discuss aspects of task performance that are well understood by all.

A strategy for increasing the task analyst's understanding is to have team members retrospectively provide commentary while watching the videotaped protocol session. Especially if this is done relatively soon after the performance was recorded, the participants may be able to recall accurately their goals, strategies, cues, and other essential information. A benefit of this approach is that data collection can be directed to selected portions of the videotape that are most informative, thus saving time. This strategy of having SMEs comment on performance videos is also useful if it is not feasible to gather protocols during performance. This may happen, for example, when several tasks are being performed or when thinking aloud disrupts performance. (For example, air traffic controllers must simultaneously talk with aircrews while deciding how to assign planes to routes; thinking aloud would disrupt communications.) This approach can be less resource intensive than standard protocol analysis methods and potentially less intrusive.

Representing Knowledge

The knowledge representation provides an efficient summary of knowledge elicitation results organized in a format that is appropriate for the application development phase. For example, in a cognitive task analysis of land navigation (DuBois et al., 1997), over sixteen hours of videotaped protocols, representing hundreds of pages of data, were collected. The data were analyzed, reduced, and organized into a table of results with three levels of analysis: a half-page matrix of tasks by knowledge categories, a two-page list of tasks, and a three-page list of methods of performing the tasks.

Hence, one important purpose of the knowledge representation phase is to abstract only those portions of the data that are important to the purpose. Estimations of the reliability and validity of the data are also usually conducted at this stage of the project to ensure that the representation is reasonably accurate and complete.

There are three general ways to organize and represent the data gathered in the knowledge elicitation phase: text, lists, and tables; graphics (flowcharts); and models (computer simulations).

The method chosen will depend on the purpose of the application. The purpose in turn determines the optimal structure, amount of detail, and the importance of completeness for the representation of knowledge.

Texts, Lists, and Tables

For most training purposes, organizing the knowledge elicitation data into paragraphs, lists, or tables will probably be the most efficient and easiest approach to take. For example, the data can be organized into a matrix of tasks and knowledge requirements, as shown in Exhibit 4.7, which is an excerpt of a knowledge representation of land navigation for the U.S. Marines infantry.

Note that three tasks are listed in the table, each defined by a goal. The cognitive task analysis results (DuBois et al., 1997) identified some unique cognitive requirements for land navigation previously unspecified in training objectives or in technical reference materials. In some cases, the cognitive knowledge requirements represented unique tasks. In other cases, unique knowledge requirements were identified for existing tasks. In both cases, the tasks and knowledge were not described explicitly in existing documentation or training, although they were routine.

The first task shown in the exhibit is an example of a decision task. Although essential to performance, this task was omitted from training probably because it is primarily cognitive in nature and

Exhibit 4.7. Tasks by Knowledge Requirements.

Tasks	Knowledge			
	Procedures	Decisions	Cues	Standards
Select an optimal method for situation.		X		
Determine location by resection.	X		X	X
Determine location by terrain association.	X		X	X

thus not directly observable. The next two tasks represent alternative methods for determining one's location. Existing training instructed the steps for performing these tasks in detail. However, additional cognitive knowledge requirements for effective performance were identified: recognizing cues that initiate and guide performance, and knowing how standards of performance vary with the context (that is, mission, environment, and presence of a threat).

Hence, in some cases CTA will identify unique tasks and in others it will identify unique knowledge requirements. In the representation provided in Exhibit 4.7, the knowledge requirements were represented by an *X*, as this was an efficient strategy for denoting more detailed descriptions given elsewhere.

Graphics

The same information can also be represented graphically, in a flowchart for example. Figure 4.1 provides a generic illustration, using an adaptation of the plan-goal graph method of Sewell and Geddes (1990).

The plan-goal graph illustrates how performance is decomposed. It is decomposed into goals (circles) and plans or methods (rectangles) for achieving the goals. Additional knowledge requirements include decisions (triangles). Cues, procedures, and standards are shown as well (rounded rectangles).

This graphical approach to representing knowledge displays at a glance the structure of a task. Although it is especially useful for applications such as software design, job design, or process engineering, it is also a very useful CTA exercise for training. The discipline of constructing the graphs helps ensure that knowledge requirements are completely represented. The flowchart structure clearly displays any omissions of goals, methods, or supporting knowledge requirements (that is, cues, procedures, standards, conditions, constraints).

In particular, this approach requires stating a goal for each task. Doing this is often much less straightforward than may be imagined, and very informative in itself. Once a goal is clearly formulated, new and sometimes more efficient or effective methods suggest themselves.

Figure 4.1. An Excerpt of a Plan-Goal Graph.

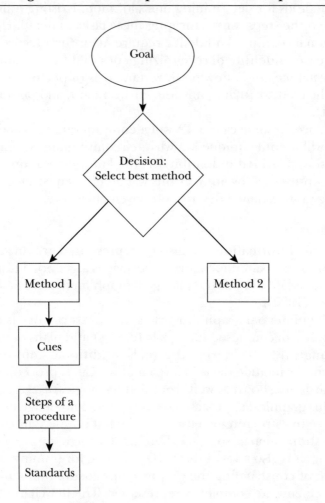

Source: Adapted from Sewell & Geddes, 1990.

There are many ways to represent knowledge graphically, including hierarchical task analyses and decision trees. The approaches differ in style, in definitions of what content should be depicted (for example, supporting knowledge requirements, how plans and goals are defined, and so on), or in constraints put on the decomposition process (for example, limiting procedural steps to the seven items of short-term memory capacity). However, the basic principle of a hierarchical analysis of tasks is common to all the methods.

Models

Another useful way to represent CTA results is to embed the data into a computer simulation, or model, of performance (compare Williams, 2000; Zachary, Ryder, & Hicinbothom, 2000). This is often done when the CTA purpose involves modeling human-computer interactions (HCI) or seeks to model human performance in intervals of seconds or less. For example, computer simulations are useful for modeling the responses of air traffic controllers, emergency dispatchers, and telephone operators to screen information. The simulation usually contains an information-processing model of human cognition (for example, attention, short-term memory, and long-term memory) along with the specific information obtained from the CTA. An advantage of this approach is that the validity of the data can be checked by comparing performance times between a running version of the simulation and actual human performance. One way this information can be useful is to compare alternative screen designs to determine which is more efficient.

Applying the Results

The final step in the CTA process is to transform the knowledge representation results into the application. Sometimes this involves the additional step of adapting the application for use with cognitive content. For example, in the testing application for the marines that looked at experts' land navigation knowledge, both test design principles and the test development process had to be changed in order to incorporate cognitive content. The test design principles were modified by formally incorporating knowledge requirements into the test plan. That is, the test plan specified both the task and the knowledge requirement (for example, decisions, cues, procedures, and standards) that each test question should address.

Some examples of test development procedures had to be developed because existing tests assessed only knowledge of facts, concepts, and procedures. There were no examples of test questions that assessed decisions, conditions, cues, or standards to aid instructors in preparing questions that assessed this content. Exhibit 4.8 compares two land navigation questions on the same topic: determining direction. The conventional question requests a fact—the name of a standard location determination procedure. In contrast, the second question requires a decision. Hence, the second question assesses one unique element of knowledge (in compari-

Exhibit 4.8. Land Navigation Test Questions.

1. To measure an azimuth, you look through a rear sight notch and align the sights by centering the front sight hairline in the rear sight notch. What is the name of this direction finding technique?

   A. Compass to cheek

   B. Recon technique

   C. Compass-point technique

   D. Centerhold technique

2. PVT Rojas is following an azimuth of 166° to a checkpoint 1200 meters from his start point. He has moved 600 meters through a forest and believes he may have drifted off-course while weaving through the trees. From his map, he sees that the last 400 meters of the route goes through a clearing with a road across his path at 1000 meters. He scans the immediate area but can't see far because of the trees. What should he do to get back on course?

   A. Return to the start point and begin again.

   B. Recon the area and plan a new route.

   C. Continue on his azimuth until the road, then adjust.

   D. Perform resection to determine his current position.

son to other land navigation tests, training and reference manuals, and so on) discovered using the CTA procedures.

In addition to being used as content for test questions, the CTA results were used to design a test development process that specifically incorporated cognitive content. This process focuses on three components of test questions: scenarios, question content, and errors, with the CTA process providing the content for each. Scenarios were developed based on ratings obtained in the initial interviews about important contextual features for marine infantry—the missions, environments, and threats relevant to effective performance. Second, the CTA results provided both the content and a specific blueprint for the number of each type of question that should be included in the test—decisions, procedures, pattern recognition, standards, conditions, and constraints. Third, the CTA process provided a list of errors that commonly occur for each land navigation procedure along with a description of the relative frequency of errors. This information was used to specify the content of response alternatives (that is, the incorrect options). In summary, the CTA process not only provided the necessary content for testing but also suggested a specific strategy for test development and test design.

CTA results can similarly be used to adapt training content and strategies. They suggest several practical ways to improve training. First, cognitive content can be used to provide more complete and effective training. For example, if specific skills are being taught, CTA results suggest that in addition to instructing the steps of the procedure, information should be provided on how the procedure and standards may differ in different contexts, and how cues initiate and guide its implementation. Second, CTA results may suggest entirely new topics and skills for training. In work with the aviation community, training in decision making, situation assessment, and teamwork were added to the curriculum (DuBois & Gillan, 2000). The CTA results were used to provide performance vignettes for discussion in class, along with a process for making tactical decisions. These episodes were used to augment their experiential learning on the job (that is, flying in the aircraft) by providing realistic scenarios to practice their decision and team skills.

Guidelines for Practice

Conducting an effective cognitive task analysis project is both a science and an art. If knowledge elicitation represents the scientific core, then getting the project started, managing the inevitable challenges, and keeping up the momentum represents the art of good practice. Drawing on experience, this section describes some lessons learned in implementing cognitive task analysis projects. These guidelines are organized as follows: getting started, managing challenges, and maintaining momentum (see Exhibit 4.9).

Getting Started

The amount of expertise gained through job experience is enormous. Tapping into this expertise for inclusion in formal organizational programs can provide enormous benefits to individual and organizational effectiveness. This hidden expertise can be incorporated into a host of programs, including training; supervising, coaching, and mentoring; technical resources and job aids; and software and systems design.

Knowledge Audit

One approach to beginning is to conduct a knowledge audit of the organization. The information provided in Exhibit 4.3 on the indicators and drivers of CTA will

Exhibit 4.9. Guidelines for Implementation.

Getting started:

- Conduct a knowledge audit.
- Achieve goals, adapt methods.
- Build project momentum early.

Managing the challenges:

- Achieve high quality results.
- Distinguish between resource-critical and resource-flexible CTA activities.
- Set and manage expectations.
- Avoid pitfalls.
- Know when you are "there."

Maintaining momentum:

- Leverage the results.
- Institutionalize the process.

help you evaluate the usefulness of conducting this kind of analysis. For example, examine the content of training materials, tests, and technical reference materials to determine if they explicitly provide the knowledge required for effective performance. Determine whether knowledge and support are provided for decisions, judgments, situation assessments, and team communications. Keep in mind the many uses for CTA results.

Goals and Methods

It is axiomatic to recommend that project goals be stated clearly and precisely. A reason for caution here is the complex nature of job expertise. Much expertise involves knowledge of how to handle the interactive effects of multiple tasks and dynamic contexts. This chapter began with a vignette about a computer technician. His challenge was to complete multiple tasks with changing contexts and priorities. The critical knowledge requirements would have been missed if the cognitive task analysis had focused narrowly on technical problem solving or effective communications in isolation from other tasks and the overall context. Once useful project goals have been set, they can provide clear guidance for the many decisions required throughout the project.

In contrast to a firm, precise set of goals, project methods should be adaptable to serve the goals. Adapting the methods used to the particulars of the situation makes good sense. Given the goals, resources, and constraints, some modifications to standard procedures (in the amount of detail gathered, probes used, mix of methods employed) can improve the efficiency and effectiveness. It is important to avoid obsessive concern about implementing methods in a rigid manner. Maintaining the quality of the goal you want to achieve is paramount.

Project Momentum

One way to build project momentum is to conduct a couple of small trials before committing serious resources to the project. Try out the task analysis procedures and iron out any bugs. Even if an experienced consultant is not hired to conduct the process, it may be a good idea to hire one just to conduct the initial trials and train the staff. It is most important to develop a prototype of the application that will be developed. This will provide a clear idea of where you are headed and what information you need—and will reveal what information is not needed. In fact, conducting the cognitive task analysis using several iterations of the process is an effective strategy for enhancing quality and fine-tuning procedures. Once you know the process and products, you have the information you need to set and communicate realistic expectations for the project.

Telling the story of why and how CTA will benefit your organization is a key element in achieving success with the project. All the major stakeholders need to hear and understand this story. They will also need to have positive yet realistic expectations about both the benefits of CTA and the effort required to achieve them.

Stakeholders may need repeated explanations before they can grasp the opportunities presented by use of CTA.

Managing the Challenges

Inevitably, the CTA project will meet many challenges before its successful completion. Most of the challenges involve trade-offs between the complexity and details of the process and the organizational constraints on resources. Achieving the optimal balance between costs and benefits involves understanding the trade-offs and communicating effectively with the primary stakeholders.

Critical and Flexible CTA Activities

Three CTA activities are essential to the project's effectiveness: planning the project, especially the knowledge elicitation methods and the sampling method; conducting the knowledge elicitation; and developing examples of the application using the CTA results.

Devoting sufficient resources (including time) to these activities produces ample rewards in project quality and outcomes, especially in the early stages of the project. Conversely, trimming resources here because of constraints can place the project's success at risk. For example, a poor match of the knowledge elicitation method to the target task or job can cause difficulties in developing the desired application. Getting these three activities wrong usually means beginning the project over, with substantial restart costs and diminished credibility and morale. Instead of trimming these activities if schedules or resources become tight, it is better to reduce the scope of the project. Then, when resources permit a continuation of the project, little momentum is lost. For example, when limited resources required that a test development project I was involved with be shortened, we completed the knowledge elicitation phase but only developed example test questions for each type of knowledge requirement (decisions, situation assessment, and so on) for all of the thirty-two training topics. Using the examples for guidance, tests for each of the topics could be developed later without a need for additional CTA.

Quality Control

Because of the relative newness and potential complexity of CTA, it is useful to employ several controls to maintain the quality of the process and outcomes. For example, it is helpful to have two or three SMEs review CTA results at each stage of the project—knowledge elicitation, knowledge representation, and development of application examples. It is especially helpful to do this early in the project, when everyone is learning about standards for quality. Similarly, it is useful to have an external review committee help evaluate technical decisions and outcomes. This is especially useful when selecting and adapting knowledge elicitation methods, and during the initial design and development of an application.

Avoiding Pitfalls

To ensure success, it is also important to anticipate potential pitfalls. One pitfall is "failing to see the forest for the trees." The results of CTA are necessarily detailed. With the practical constraints that normally accompany any project, it is important to focus on essential details only. In fact, useful adaptations of the CTA methods are likely to occur in the iterative process of comparing the scope and depth of detail with the overall goals as the project unfolds. It is worth repeating that the development of an initial prototype of the application early on will contribute to a clear sense of which details are essential and which are distractions. As will be discussed next, understanding how much CTA is enough is important for effectiveness and efficiency.

A second trap is to become obsessively concerned about methodological precision but pay too little attention to project goals. An experienced cognitive task analyst can help by providing a range of possible techniques to adapt to a situation.

Finally, it is important to communicate with all stakeholders throughout the project. Maintaining their support, answering questions, and addressing any obstacles that arise are all essential to effective CTA projects.

Knowing When You Have Reached the Goal

An important and useful lesson gained from experience is understanding the characteristics of effective CTA—knowing when your project goal has been satisfied. High-quality cognitive task analysis has three characteristics. First, collect an appropriate amount of detail for the application you intend to develop. For computer modeling, this usually involves a lot of detail so that performance can be modeled down to the second, or even finer. In contrast, if the goal is a good job description, far less detail is required. Training and testing applications usually require a moderate amount of detail. Gathering detail one step past what is needed is a good rule of thumb.

Another sign of a well-done cognitive task analysis is that the content obtained is sensible and suited to the application. For training applications, this probably entails information about decisions, situation assessment, adaptation of standards to contexts, management of transitions, and teamwork. Often, job incumbents and instructors will say, "I knew that," because the content identified is a necessary and important part of their job. Yet this content was not in training, technical objectives, or other job documents. In this sense, an important contribution of cognitive task analysis is to provide descriptive expressions for workers' mental experience. They tacitly and regularly employ cognitive strategies, mental models, cue recognition, decision making, and the like, but without CTA they do not have an effective means of communicating or discussing these phenomena.

The last sign of a job well done is that the results make important differences in the application—substantial improvements in performance quality, quantity, speed, and cost.

Maintaining Momentum

There are several ways to increase the productivity of CTA efforts. Most directly, CTA results may be leveraged for other organizational uses. CTA can also readily be incorporated into standard organizational processes.

Additional Uses of CTA Information

Although cognitive task analysis can be resource-intensive, the details of cognitive contents and processes essential to job performance are useful in a variety of ways. For example, the decision-making vignettes gathered for test development for the marines were later used by instructors as cases in the classroom, scenarios for flight simulator practice, and content in performance measures. The rich contextual detail based on actual job performance provided trainees with many opportunities to consider how the conceptual and procedural knowledge acquired in the classroom would transfer to their performance on the job.

Institutionalizing the Process

Incorporating these methods into organizational procedures can further extend the benefits of CTA. For example, an ongoing database of performance examples of critical decisions can be used as training vignettes. Instructors and supervisors can contribute to the database when they observe interesting examples. Benchmark examples of exceptional performances ("gold standards") can be used to demonstrate model performance. Similarly, examples of poor performance ("lead standards," with anonymity given to the participants) can be used to help trainees learn how to diagnose their own performance.

For navy aircrew training, these examples are gathered electronically during simulator exercises, using both video and flight instruments to capture the detail. These performance vignettes serve a wide variety of purposes. Using only the key events from each performance, they can be replayed during crew debriefs to assist the team in reviewing their own performance. After faces and voices are electronically altered to avoid being identified, the key events are included in the performance database, indexed by performance dimension and scenario (type of mission, environment, threat, and so on). Trainees may review vignettes when planning future missions or use them for study. Instructors use the vignettes as examples of main points and for discussion in class. Examples are also selected to anchor rating scales in measures of performance and to standardize rater training. Instructional designers can review the examples to determine training needs and analyze performance trends. Most importantly, this information serves as a rich source of evaluation data. Performance trends can be actively monitored. Because the cognitive performance vignettes are so detailed and critical to effectiveness, the outcomes are usually very positive. Communicating these results throughout the organization is one of the most effective ways to ensure ongoing success.

Using CTA results for a variety of purposes also has the added benefit of leveraging the investment in the CTA process. By using these results in many functions— such as classroom training, testing, simulations, performance measurement, debriefing and coaching, planning, training evaluation and design, performance support, and others—the database of experiences that will contribute to the development and maintenance of expertise in an organization will be built.

References

Cooke, N. J. (1994). Varieties of knowledge elicitation techniques. *International Journal of Human-Computer Studies, 41*, 801–849.

DuBois, D. A., & Gillan, C. A. (2000, November). *Cognitive training initiatives: A case study of aircrew training.* Interservice/Industry Training, Simulation, and Education Conference, Orlando.

DuBois, D. A., & Shalin, V. L. (2000). Describing job expertise using cognitively oriented task analyses (CoTA). In J. M. Schraagen, S. F. Chipman, & V. L. Shalin (Eds.), *Cognitive task analysis.* Hillsdale, NJ: Erlbaum.

DuBois, D. A., Shalin, V. L., Levi, K., & Borman, W. C. (1997). A cognitively oriented approach to task analysis. *Training Research Journal, 3,* 103–142.

Ericsson, K. A., & Simon, H. A. (1993). *Protocol analysis: Verbal reports as data.* Cambridge, MA: MIT Press.

Flanagan, J. (1954). The critical incident technique. *Psychological Bulletin, 51,* 327–358.

Ford, J. K., & Kraiger, K. (1995). The application of cognitive constructs and principles to the instructional systems model of training: Implications for needs assessment, design, and transfer. In C. L. Cooper & I. T. Robertson (Eds.), *International review of industrial and organizational psychology, 10,* 1–48.

Ford, J. M., & Wood, L. E. (1992). Structuring and documenting interactions with subject matter experts. *Performance Instruction Quarterly, 5*(1), 2–24.

Hall, E. P., Gott, S. P., & Pokorney, R. A. (1995). *A procedural guide to cognitive task analysis: The PARI methodology* (TR 1995–0108). San Antonio, TX: AFMC, Brooks Air Force Base.

Klein, G. A., Calderwood, R., & MacGregor, D. (1989). Critical decision method for eliciting knowledge. *IEEE Transactions on Systems, Man, and Cybernetics, 19,* 462–472.

Orasanu, J., & Fischer, U. (1992). Team cognition in the cockpit: Linguistic control of shared problem solving. In J. K. Kruschke (Chair), *Proceedings of the 14th Annual Meeting of the Cognitive Science Society* (pp. 189–194). Hillsdale, NJ: Erlbaum.

Reason, J. (1999). *Human error.* Cambridge, UK: Cambridge University Press.

Schmidt, F. L., & Hunter, J. E. (1998). The validity and utility of selection methods in personnel psychology: Practical and theoretical implications of 85 years of research findings. *Psychological Bulletin, 124,* 2, 262–274.

Schmidt, F. L., Hunter, J. E., & Outerbridge, A. N. (1986). Impact of job experience and ability on job knowledge, work sample performance, and supervisory ratings of job performance. *Journal of Applied Psychology, 71,* 432–439.

Schraagen, J. M., Chipman, S. F., & Shalin, V. L. (2000). *Cognitive task analysis.* Hillsdale, NJ: Erlbaum.

Sewell, D. R., & Geddes, N. (1990). A plan and goal-based method for computer-human system design. In *Human Computer Interaction, INTERACT 90,* proceedings of the IFIP TC 13 Third International Conference (pp. 283–288). Amsterdam: North-Holland.

Shalin, V. L., Geddes, N. D., Bertram, D. L., Sczepkowski, M., & DuBois, D. (1997). Expertise in dynamic physical task domains. In P. Feltovich, K. Ford, & R. Hoffmann (Eds.), *Expertise in context: Human and machine.* Cambridge, MA: MIT Press.

Williams, K. E. (2000). An automated aid for modeling human-computer interaction. In J. M. Schraagen, S. F. Chipman, & V. L. Shalin (Eds.), *Cognitive task analysis.* Hillsdale, NJ: Erlbaum.

Zachary, W. W., Ryder, J. M., & Hicinbothom, J. H. (2000). Building cognitive task analyses and models of a decision-making team in a complex real-time environment. In J. M. Schraagen, S. F. Chipman, & V. L. Shalin (Eds.), *Cognitive task analysis.* Hillsdale, NJ: Erlbaum.

PART 2

Innovations in Training and Development Methods

CHAPTER 5

Training for a Diverse Workplace

Donna Chrobot-Mason,
Miguel A. Quiñones

Beginning in the late 1980s organizations were inundated with projections of significant changes in workforce demographics. The message was clear: the future labor pool would be significantly less white and less male (Johnston & Packer, 1987). For the most part, these predictions are coming true. From 1980 to 1995, the percentage of women in the workforce increased by 3.4 percent, blacks by 1 percent, and Hispanics by 3.6 percent (Tsui & Gutek, 1999). It is projected that by 2008, white non-Hispanic persons will make up a decreasing share of the labor force, dropping from 73.9 to 70.7 percent (U.S. Department of Labor, 2000). By 2050, the Bureau of the Census predicts that nearly half of the population will be Hispanic, black, American Indian, or Asian (Fine, 1995). These demographic shifts, as well as predictions of an increasingly diverse labor pool and customer base, have forced U.S. companies to take a hard look at how to prepare for a much more heterogeneous workforce.

One of the ways organizations have attempted to prepare for a diverse workforce has been through diversity training. There has been a dramatic rise in the number of such programs in the last decade. The consulting firm Towers Perrin released a report indicating that nearly 75 percent of companies have, or plan to begin, diversity training programs (Towers Perrin, 1992). When asked about the primary motivation to implement diversity training in their organizations, 85 percent of respondents in a Conference Board study cited as primary motivators business need and the perception that it is a competitive business issue (Wheeler, 1994).

Although the number of diversity training programs implemented in U.S. companies continues to rise, recent evidence suggests such efforts may be ineffective at best and harmful at worst. Some researchers report positive outcomes associated with diversity initiatives, such as increased productivity, competitiveness, workplace harmony (Morrison, 1992), increased creativity, and better-quality decisions (Jackson, 1992a; Lobel, 1999). Others, however, argue that poorly implemented or mandatory diversity training programs can lead to even more negative attitudes toward diversity (Joplin & Daus, 1997), raise expectations of minority group members, only to be followed by disappointment (Hemphill & Haines, 1997), or make group distinctions even more salient, resulting in lower cohesiveness (Jackson, 1992b).

If organizations are to realize the benefits of diversity as a competitive business strategy, they must pay more attention to the development and evaluation of effective diversity training initiatives. Although many have criticized current diversity training practices (for example, Davidson, 1999; Hemphill & Haines, 1997; Noe, 1999) and called for significant changes such as incorporating a thorough needs assessment (Wheeler, 1994) and training evaluation (Ivancevich & Gilbert, 2000), few specifics are provided to guide the practicing diversity program manager. However, research on training development and evaluation has much to offer for developing more effective diversity training practices. Thus, it is our intent in this chapter to integrate research findings in the training literature with diversity training in practice. Our goal is to provide detailed suggestions for improving diversity training practices based on sound, empirical, academic research findings in the training literature.

Problems with Current Diversity Training Initiatives

Despite organizational efforts to increase employee awareness and sensitivity to diversity issues through training, reports of negative incidents continue to rise. From 1990 to 1994, there was a 34 percent increase in the number of claims of sex, race, and age discrimination, and sexual harassment (Hemphill & Haines, 1997). High-profile lawsuits suggest organizations have not been particularly successful in eliminating or even reducing claims of harassment and bias. For example, in 1994 Texaco paid $140 million to resolve a lawsuit filed by black employees after the transcripts of a meeting with top officials were released to the public (Eichenwald, 1996; Fisher, 1998). The transcripts contained strongly offensive racial remarks about black employees. Another high-profile case involved a $54.4 million settlement from Denny's to resolve two discrimination lawsuits in 1994 brought by black customers who claimed some restaurants refused to seat or serve them (Faircloth, 1998).

Cases such as these, which make headlines and tarnish an organization's image, beg the question, "Why have diversity training efforts failed to help companies realize the competitive advantage of a diverse workforce?" Perhaps the biggest problem with current diversity training programs is that organizations often implement them in a knee-jerk response to a lawsuit or employee pressure, or to follow the lead of other companies. We suggest several reasons for this failure: unclear objectives, the backlash effect of diversity programs, a short-term focus, and lack of evaluation and feedback. Each of these areas of concern are discussed in some detail in the following paragraphs.

Unclear Objectives

Despite expert advice to clarify training objectives and goals, very few organizations seem to take the time to engage in this important step (Hollister, Day, & Jesaitis, 1993). Moreover, when asked, respondents at most organizations suggest that the main objective of their diversity training is to improve employee awareness of diversity issues (Wheeler, 1994). However, choosing attitude awareness and change as the primary outcome for diversity training has been strongly criticized (Noe, 1999) in part because the focus is on changing attitudes rather than behavior. Hemphill and Haines (1997) argue that focusing on changes in personal value systems, beliefs, and biases is a mistake. Such long-held beliefs may be extremely difficult to change, particularly when employees are not motivated to do so. Instead, organizations should focus efforts on changing tangible behaviors in the workplace and providing examples of expected behaviors rather than communicating only what *not* to do.

The Backlash Effect

Another criticism of diversity training is that many programs focus only on increasing awareness of group differences, which often results in making prejudices and stereotypes more salient and work group cohesiveness seem even more difficult, because differences are emphasized (Bond & Pyle, 1998; Thomas, 1998). White males may feel particularly threatened or resentful if they perceive they will be squeezed out of the organization (Ellis & Sonnenfeld, 1994; Heilman, McCullough, & Gilbert, 1996) or are being included in diversity training simply as targets for blame (Hemphill & Haines, 1997; Lynch, 1997). In addition, diversity training aimed specifically at whites may have an oversensitizing effect, so that participants may actually avoid interactions with minority group members because of anxiety about offending them (Lindsley, 1998). Meanwhile, white women and people of color may feel burdened with expectations to serve as spokespersons for their group (Ellis & Sonnenfeld, 1994) or may develop increased expectations of change, only to be disappointed. Inexperienced trainers who are ill-prepared to handle emotional discussions or the inevitable resistant participants who can sabotage training efforts may lose credibility quickly, resulting in participant cynicism and distrust (Arredondo, 1996).

Short-Term Focus

Perhaps one of the harshest criticisms of most diversity training programs is the lack of follow-through. Despite good intentions, many participants confess that in the long run, very little changes in the way diversity is managed in the organization (Davidson, 1999). Most diversity training involves a one-shot, one-size-fits-all approach (Cox, 1994) that is probably very ineffective in changing long-lasting attitudes, values, and beliefs about diversity. In a study involving 785 Society for Human Resource Management members, Rynes and Rosen (1995) found that most training programs last only a day or less (72 percent) and consume less than 10 percent of the total training budget. In addition, only 33 percent of respondents believed that their training programs were successful over the longer term. Diversity training is usually not part of a long-term comprehensive change initiative (Thomas, 1991) but rather a stand-alone program that lacks integration with other organizational practices and policies. Thus, diversity training becomes an annual event that gets checked off a to-do list.

Lack of Evaluation and Feedback

Finally, almost no rigorous evaluation of diversity training effectiveness can be found in the literature (Ivancevich & Gilbert, 2000). Without a thorough evaluation of diversity training programs, organizations cannot even begin to understand how to modify their programs to achieve the greatest effectiveness (see Chapter Three, this volume, by Noe & Colquitt). Without evaluation, organizations are practicing *single-loop learning* rather than *double-loop learning* (Wooten & Hayes James, 2000). In single-loop learning, the organization responds to diversity issues by fixing the problem at hand but fails to understand the root causes. Double-loop learning occurs only when the organization takes a comprehensive look at why the problem surfaced and how to fix the underlying issues. In addition, a lack of training evaluation and feedback results in a lack of accountability on the part of employees and managers to engage in behavioral change. Long-term follow-up evaluations of training and explicit managerial rewards for increasing diversity were both found to be important factors contributing to successful diversity training programs (Rynes & Rosen, 1995) but are often overlooked in current diversity training programs.

A Systematic Approach to Diversity Training

The literature suggests that diversity training programs fail to eliminate prejudice and discrimination in the workplace because of a whole variety of reasons. However, we believe that the situation is not hopeless and that we have a great deal to learn from previous mistakes. Throughout this chapter, we will address each of these criticisms by suggesting alternative approaches based on what we know from research on training development, delivery, and evaluation. We propose a more systematic approach (see Figure 5.1) that involves preparing for diversity training through needs assessment and development of clear objectives, developing training content based on a three-phase approach to learning, planning for success by gaining management buy-in and stimulating motivation to learn, and evaluating and maintaining the intervention.

Our recommendations are based on models of training effectiveness, according to which training must be systematic to succeed. It must be systematic in its interface with the larger organization (Kozlowski & Salas, 1997) and in the design and delivery of the training program (Goldstein, 1993). For example, Goldstein (1993) presents what is sometimes referred to as the instructional design (ISD) model. The ISD model forces the training developer to consider why training is needed, what should be covered in training, and how training outcomes will be measured. A simplified version of the ISD model is presented in Figure 5.2. Specific steps outlined in the model and how they can be applied to diversity training are discussed in the following sections of this chapter.

Preparing for Diversity Training

Diversity training is more effective if it is only one aspect of a larger organizational development intervention. Consider an organization that espouses the virtues of diversity in a training program but at the same time relies on referrals from its primarily white male workforce to fill job openings. Similarly, an inhospitable workplace where racial joke telling is the norm is unlikely to change as a result of diversity training if there are no repercussions for individuals who continue this tradition. Diversity initiatives should be more than just diversity training. Recruitment, selection, compensation, promotions, and other practices must be reevaluated. In addition, corporate climate and work group norms can facilitate or hinder the goals of a well-designed diversity training program.

Therefore, we recommend that the first step in preparing for diversity training is to conduct an organizational needs assessment to determine the nature and severity of diversity problems or issues in the organization. Only then can a comprehensive, long-term diversity strategy be created, of which training is but one piece (others

Figure 5.1. A Systematic Approach to Diversity Training.

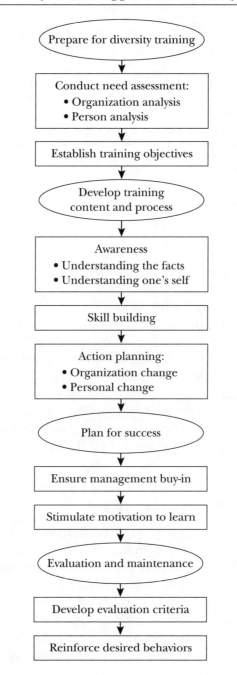

Figure 5.2. Instructional System Design Model.

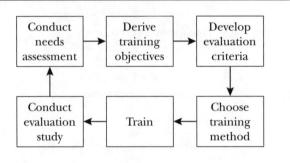

Source: Adapted from Goldstein, 1993.

may include changing reward structures and selection and re-cruitment practices, establishing a mentoring program, and so on). In addition, a thorough needs assessment is absolutely critical to determine the appropriate content and delivery mechanism for training. Skipping the needs assessment will undoubtedly result in the development of a training program that fails to address the most important diversity issues facing the organization or to initiate any lasting change in employees—thus wasting valuable training resources. Before a training program is designed and delivered, an organization must first figure out what it hopes to accomplish. As Gagne (1962) put it, one must first figure out, "What is to be learned?"

Conducting a Needs Assessment

To determine how training can be properly implemented, a needs assessment must be conducted first. A needs assessment consists of organizational, task, and person analysis (for example, Goldstein, 1993). The process can be used to ensure that the content and im-plementation of training is consistent with the organization's broader goals and that the content is appropriate for the organiza-tion's unique circumstances. In discussing diversity training pro-grams, we will focus on organizational and person analysis. Although task analysis is generally an important part of a needs assessment, it is not relevant to our discussion of diversity training because we are assuming that all jobs, regardless of the tasks performed, may benefit from the training initiative.

No single method for conducting a needs assessment is best. In fact, ideally a combination of methods will be used to increase the richness of the data collected (Noe, 1999). For example, focus groups with a small number of employees can be used to develop the content of a survey that can then be sent out to the entire organization. Focus groups can help identify common themes and issues that would otherwise be missed by a generic organizational survey. A lot can also be learned about a job by observing job incumbents perform their everyday activities. However, it is critical that the observer be well-trained in how to remain unobtrusive. In addition, technical manuals and organization records can be a rich source of information. Finally, one-on-one interviews with job incumbents, managers, customers, and other relevant parties can also reveal issues and critical incidents that can form the content of a diversity training program.

Organizational Analysis

An organizational analysis determines an organization's goals (both short- and long-term), challenges, work environment, and resources, as well as internal and external constraints that may support or hinder the effectiveness of a training program (Goldstein, 1993; Kozlowski & Salas, 1997). Organizations are not always clear about what their goals are. In addition, the goals that are specified may not be directly relevant to diversity initiatives. The organizational analysis process forces organizations to think about how a diversity initiative can help them achieve their broader goals. For example, does having a diverse workforce allow an organization to increase its market share in a particular community or demographic group? Does a diversity initiative allow an organization to attract and retain a more qualified workforce? Does diversity training help decrease overall operational costs by reducing lawsuits? A clear specification of the goals is needed before diversity training's role in achieving those goals can be specified.

There is, in fact, a growing literature demonstrating the need to link organizational HR strategies with strategic goals. For example,

Wright and McMahan (1992) argued that an organization's human resources could be a source of continued competitive advantage. However, this is only true if the strategy is complementary to the knowledge, skills, and abilities possessed by the workforce. Schuler and Jackson (1987) argued that competitive strategies such as growth, innovation, or cost saving require very different types of employees. In a series of recent studies, Huselid and colleagues have found links between an organization's human resource strategy and organizational outcomes such as productivity and turnover (Huselid, Jackson, & Schuler, 1997; Huselid, 1995). Clearly, a diverse workforce can help organizations achieve their competitive strategies. However, this link must be made explicit in order to design an intervention that makes use of the unique advantages provided by a diverse workforce.

Organizational analyses can also be used to determine if the conditions are right for introducing a training course. Conditions such as management support can make or break a training program (for example, Kozlowski & Doherty, 1989; Quiñones, 1997). For example, if a diversity training program stresses the importance of zero tolerance for racist and sexist jokes but managers continue to make such jokes and fail to punish those who do, it is very unlikely that the goals of that diversity training program will be met. Other conditions that need to be considered are resources such as space to conduct the training program, money for trainers and materials, and time off for employees to attend. Finally, an organizational analysis can help focus attention on other organizational practices such as recruitment, socialization, mentoring, and reward structure. It is critical that all of these practices be compatible with the new diversity initiative.

Although there are few valid and reliable measures to assess an organization's climate for diversity, Cox (1991) provides a list of six dimensions on which to evaluate a multicultural organization that values and manages diversity effectively. Cox's six dimensions provide a useful framework to guide data collection efforts during the needs assessment phase of diversity training. To gain a better understanding of employee perceptions of the extent to which the organization is a supportive multicultural workplace, survey items or focus group questions may be developed for all six dimensions. (See Exhibit 5.1.)

Exhibit 5.1. Six Dimensions of a
Multicultural Organization.

Dimension	Definition
Pluralism	Socialization is a two-way process in which minority employees have influence on organizational norms and values.
Full structural integration	All groups are represented at all levels of the organization and job status.
Integration in informal networks	All organizational members have access.
Cultural bias	Discrimination and prejudice in the workplace are eliminated.
Organizational identification	All employees can be committed to and identify with the company.
Intergroup	Interpersonal conflict resulting from diverse group conflict membership is minimized.

Source: Adapted from Cox, 1991.

It may also be important to examine the historical context of the company's approach to dealing with diversity issues and its operating paradigm for managing diversity (Chrobot-Mason & Thomas, 2000). For example, many companies have traditionally focused on representation of minorities (EEO policies, affirmative action), whereas others have attempted to take a more proactive approach to managing diversity at all stages of the employee's career (Thomas, 1991). Some organizations have adopted what Thomas and Ely (1996) refer to as an access and legitimacy paradigm, which motivates them to celebrate and embrace differences because doing so makes business sense. However, the authors argue that it is only when an organization adopts a learning and effectiveness paradigm, where employees can capitalize on their differences in day-to-day activities, that diversity becomes a competitive advantage.

Person Analysis

A person analysis is usually conducted to determine who needs training (Goldstein, 1993). However, diversity training is most likely to include all employees or all employees at a certain level of the organization, rather than singling out individuals or groups (for example, white males). Therefore, person analysis in this context can be used to decide how the training should be conducted and promoted. It is important to assess how comfortable employees or certain groups are with diversity issues, how much experience they have had interacting and working with people who are different, and how receptive they are to learning about different cultures. In essence, we recommend evaluating employee readiness for diversity training (see Noe, 1986).

Employees are likely to vary in their comfort level with discussing sometimes emotional and sensitive topics such as race relations, sexual orientation, gender roles, and so on. In fact, research has shown that personality style may contribute to how well an individual can adapt to working with dissimilar others. For example, research on sojourners (employees assigned to overseas assignments) suggests that in addition to technical competence, employees who succeed in another culture have personality characteristics such as empathy, interest in the local culture, flexibility, and tolerance (Kealey, 1989). Other personality traits such as locus of control and extroversion (Ward & Kennedy, 1993) have been identified as important characteristics that may help explain why some individuals are more receptive to interacting with new people and respecting differences in others.

Although personality may help explain employee differences in diversity training readiness, variability in diversity skills may also be important to evaluate. Researchers argue that as the United States becomes more diverse, organizational leaders who succeed in the future will be competent in a multicultural or diverse environment (Chemers & Murphy, 1995; Chrobot-Mason, 2000a; Cox & Beale, 1997; Morrison, 1992). That is, some employees have developed skills to help them respond to the challenges and opportunities posed by diversity (Cox & Beale, 1997). Garcia (1995) defines such competence as the ability to demonstrate respect and understanding, to communicate effectively, and to work collaboratively with people from different cultural backgrounds. Others speak of the need for future workers to develop emotional intelligence (Goleman, 1998)—the ability to understand their own emotions and how they affect work relationships. Enhancing interpersonal skills to cope effectively with a more heterogeneous workforce will be a critical leadership skill in the future (Joplin & Daus, 1997).

Life experience may also play an important role in determining receptivity to diversity training. Douthitt, Eby, and Simon (1999) developed a scale to measure diversity of life experiences and found that individuals who reported traveling, living in many places, and having an interest in a variety of cultures, and whose families encouraged openness or whose friends were racially diverse, were more likely to show receptiveness to dissimilar others. Likewise, current experiences with diversity may influence employee readiness for diversity training. Employees of companies located in a more demographically diverse location (for example, an urban setting) may be more sensitive to diversity issues than employees who work in a more rural setting, where the population is largely homogeneous.

Finally, research suggests that individuals vary in their own racial and ethnic identity development (Helms, 1990; Phinney, 1992) and this may also affect receptiveness to diversity training. Some have spent more time understanding their own ethnic identity (including a white identity), reflecting on racial issues and how their ethnic group membership affects interactions with others (Phinney, Lochner, & Murphy, 1990). There is considerable evidence that individuals progress through developmental stages in racial identification (Cross, 1978; Helms, 1990). Racial identity development usually begins with a naive stage, at which an individual accepts racial stereotypes. As the individual interacts more frequently with dissimilar others and experiences greater conflict or dissonance, he or she begins to question previously accepted stereotypes. Finally, the individual develops a healthier racial identity while realizing the positive attributes of people and cultures outside of his or her own reference group (Rowe, Bennett, & Atkinson, 1994). It is argued that this process of self-exploration may help individuals compare options and make conscious decisions about how to deal with racial issues and conflicts when confronted with them (Chrobot-Mason, 2000b; Phinney et al., 1990; Thomas, 1998).

One strategy for conducting a person analysis as part of the needs assessment is to gather data (questionnaires, focus groups) before developing training content. These data may then be analyzed to determine level of comfort and experience with diversity at the work group level or broader, and thus guide development of training content. So, for example, results of the person analysis may provide information that suggests various levels of diversity training are needed in the organization (awareness versus skill building) or that certain training groups collectively are more advanced in their understanding of diversity issues than others. Kirkland and Regan (1997) recommend administering a survey to assess employee perceptions of corporate policies and practices, racial attitudes, interaction patterns with others, racial identity development, and coping strategies.

A second strategy for conducting a person analysis may be to administer self-assessments (personality questionnaires) to help trainees understand their own level of receptiveness to diversity. This information can be useful to both trainees and trainers before the start of training because it provides baseline data. Trainees are made aware of the gap between their current level of awareness or skills and where the company wants them to be. Trainers may also find such information useful in helping to select certain exercises, set the pace of training, and prepare for future obstacles or barriers to learning.

Guidelines for Practice

- Conduct an organizational needs assessment to evaluate the current climate for diversity and establish specific training goals. Remember to evaluate current diversity practices and policies as well as other HR practices to assess compatibility with diversity training goals.
- Develop a long-term and comprehensive diversity strategy. Keep in mind that implementing a diversity training program alone, without supporting structures and policies, will not be sufficient to create lasting change.
- Conduct a person analysis to determine employee readiness for diversity training. A successful training effort requires gathering data to determine the best approach to training and how it should be promoted. A one-size-fits-all approach simply will not work.

Establishing Clear Training Objectives

As mentioned previously, one of the biggest mistakes made in diversity training efforts is to proceed without clear objectives. If the goal of diversity training is not identified, content may be weak or ineffective and the company will have no way of knowing how to evaluate its effectiveness. Most training efforts are intended to increase employee awareness of diversity and cultural issues (Wheeler, 1994). However, diversity experts argue that awareness is simply the first step and that the benefits of a diverse workforce can only be realized when the organization's diversity strategy encompasses a long-term, comprehensive culture change (Thomas, 1991; Burkart, 1999; Ferdman & Brody, 1996). Cox (1994) suggests that advanced training should include building specific skills and helping individuals to understand their role in implementing the organization change process. He also stresses the importance of diversity training as an ongoing program rather than a onetime event.

Generally, diversity training in the workplace is intended to accomplish three broad goals: improve the work environment for all employees, improve work relationships, and improve the quality and efficiency of work being done. These broad goals, however, must be clarified and specified. Successful diversity training efforts must detail *how* training can accomplish these goals.

In general, learning objectives should be specific enough that it may be determined if they have been achieved. Learning objectives should specify the situation in which the action is performed, the learned capabilities required to perform the action, the object of the action, and any special constraints that can influence the performance of the action (Gagne, Briggs, & Wager, 1992). For example, stating that trainees should be more sensitive after the completion of the training program may be a difficult learning objective to evaluate. What specific observable actions indicate increased sensitivity? The key is to focus on those specific actions that are directly measurable and observable when developing learning objectives.

Kraiger, Ford, and Salas (1993) identify three categories of learning outcomes—cognitive, skill-based, and affective—that may be useful to this discussion. Cognitive or knowledge outcomes generally precede higher-order development. For example, trainees usually must learn information about a subject (for example, traffic laws and symbols) before they are able to develop procedural knowledge (how to drive a car). The first step in learning thus involves transition from knowledge that is declarative to knowledge that is procedural. Skill-based outcomes are achieved when the learner has practiced to the point that newly acquired behaviors become automatic or routine. Finally, affective outcomes may involve inner growth, self-awareness, and motivational changes.

In the case of diversity training, initial goals are likely to focus on cognitive or knowledge outcomes such as increased awareness of diversity issues, discrimination, and bias in the workplace. Objectives at this stage of development may also include knowledge of the business case for diversity and an introduction to expected behaviors in the workplace. In the second stage of learning, trainees may begin practicing new ways of communicating with dissimilar others and strategies for dealing with diversity conflict. The goal at this stage is to give trainees an opportunity to practice these skills so that they begin to feel more natural and comfortable. In the third stage of development, affective outcomes are usually the goal of diversity training, such as inner growth and awareness of how each employee can contribute to a more positive work environment for all. At this stage, one of the primary objectives may be for the individual to recognize the value of new behaviors and attitudes and personally buy into the value of diversity for the organization. Another term for this stage may be *action planning*—facilitating employee development of and commitment to plans to act on the knowledge and skills acquired during training.

Based on the Kraiger, Ford, and Salas (1993) model, we propose a list of examples of diversity training objectives at three levels of development: awareness (cognitive outcomes), skill building (skill-based outcomes), and action planning (affective outcomes). (See Exhibit 5.2.)

The list shown in the exhibit is not intended to be exhaustive but rather a guide for generating your own training objectives. We recommend that objectives be based on this three-stage development model and tailored to meet the needs of specific employee groups. For example, diversity training as part of a new employee orientation process should focus on awareness and

Exhibit 5.2. Examples of Diversity
Training Objectives at Three Levels.

Goal 1: Improve the work environment for all employees.

Awareness objectives	Acknowledge bias and discrimination that occurs in the workplace.
	Recognize racist and sexist comments in the workplace.
	Have knowledge of all relevant laws (EEO, ADA, and so on).
Skill building objectives	Define and discuss appropriate and inappropriate behavior at work.
	Enforce zero tolerance policy for racist or sexist language in the workplace.
Action planning objectives	Examine current organizational practices and policies for bias and take steps to create a work environment that supports and values diversity:

  • Recruitment

  • Selection

  • Reward and recognition

  • Mentoring

  • Employee development or training

  • Performance appraisal

Goal 2: Improve work relationships.

Awareness objectives	Acknowledge one's own biases, prejudices, and assumptions.
	Understand general differences between cultural groups.
	Facilitate self-exploration toward the development of higher levels of racial awareness.
Skill building objectives	Discuss coping strategies for dealing with discrimination and stereotypes.
	Listen and empathize with those who experience bias or discrimination.
	Practice conflict management skills to facilitate collaboration among dissimilar others.

Exhibit 5.2. Examples of Diversity
Training Objectives at Three Levels, Cont'd.

Action planning objectives	Make personal commitment to diversity and continuous growth.
	Value and encourage differences in interacting with others.

Goal 3: Improve the quality and efficiency of the work being conducted.

Awareness objectives	Understand how differences can be an asset to the organization.
	Understand how differences can become a barrier to productivity.
Skill building objectives	Value and encourage differences of opinion and styles of work.
	Practice communication skills to understand diversity issues and problem solve.
Action planning objectives	Assist the organization in identifying issues and concerns about the way employees perceive and cope with racial diversity issues.
	Work collaboratively with others toward common goals.

skill building (or behavioral change). Training for more tenured employees should include action planning sessions to discuss changing organizational practices and policies to better foster diversity.

Guideline for Practice

- Develop specific and measurable goals for the three levels of development. For each goal, remember to generate specific observable behaviors that are expected from employees.

Developing Training Content and Process

Once the needs assessment is complete—diversity training is seen to be a viable piece of the overall diversity strategy and objectives have been clarified—then development of training content and process can begin. Again, we recommend an ongoing approach to diversity training that involves all three levels of change (awareness, skill building, and action planning). Others agree that reducing prejudice is not an all-or-nothing event (Devine & Vasquez, 1998) but rather a gradual process akin to breaking a bad habit that begins with motivation to change and proceeds to developing the skills necessary to change behavior. Cross-cultural training experts recommend that programs begin by helping participants become aware of differences and then acquire knowledge necessary for adjustment, explore the emotional challenges of change, and finally develop skills and practice behavioral change (Brislin & Yoshida, 1994).

In the following section, we provide suggestions for training content and delivery at all three stages based on the writings and research in the diversity literature as well as in cross-cultural training, social psychology, and multicultural counseling. Our intent is not to provide off-the-shelf lectures or exercises, because there are already many valuable resources available (for example, Cox & Beale, 1997; Gardenswartz & Rowe, 1993; Thomas, 1999), but rather to provide arguments based on research findings that will help guide you in making sound decisions when selecting a training consultant, developing an in-house training program, or adopting existing materials for use in a particular organization.

Awareness

Increasing one's awareness of diversity issues involves an understanding of both the factual issues and the personal feelings and attitudes surrounding diversity.

Understanding the Facts

Many diversity training programs begin with a presentation of facts and figures (for example, projected demographic changes in the workforce) intended to increase awareness of the importance of diversity issues to the organization's bottom line. One of the goals may be to educate employees on the organizational policies regarding diversity and the legal issues and implications of harassment and bias in the workplace. The training literature refers to this as a set induction—an instructional event at the beginning of training designed to increase trainee motivation, interest, or attention (Ausubel, 1968). In diversity training, a set induction may include recent research evidence that diversity can have a positive impact on the bottom line through stock valuation (Wright, Ferris, Hiller, & Kroll, 1995), increased creativity and innovation (Jackson, 1992a), and firm performance when the company has adopted a growth business strategy (Richard, 2000). The interest of trainees may be captured by beginning diversity training with an example of a specific case of discrimination from the perspective of the victim.

Generally, this information is presented in a lecture format, so there is very little active processing on the part of trainees. Although presentation of this information may be a valuable piece of the overall diversity training program, it should be a very small part of it. Numerous studies have shown that learning is more likely to improve when trainees take a more active role in the learning process (Baldwin, 1992; Decker & Nathan, 1985; Noe, 1999). We recommend beginning diversity training at the awareness level with a group discussion of the definition of diversity and differences. The trainer may then wish to present the organizational definition of diversity, emphasizing a broad definition that includes differences in work styles, values, experiences, and so on that seeks to include all employees and not alienate certain group members (particularly white males).

Although it may be important to present information about group differences such as cultural norms and values or historical differences in power and status between majority and minority groups (Linnehan & Konrad, 1999), we recommend this type of awareness training be conducted only by an experienced trainer as part of a long-term training program in which both group differences *and* similarities are discussed (Bond & Pyle, 1998). Otherwise, the organization runs the risk of reinforcing stereotypes, emphasizing group differences, and creating a threatening environment for some who feel blamed by and alienated from coworkers. Although intergroup inequality must be addressed as part of an effective diversity initiative, and confronting emotionally charged issues is an inevitable part of change (Linnehan & Konrad, 1999), inexperienced trainers who emphasize group differences but do not help employees learn the skills to bridge the differences and work together effectively may create a backlash effect and cause more harm than good.

Understanding One's Self

Many have argued that knowledge of self is a critical first step in understanding how one's own attitudes, beliefs, coping strategies, work style, and so on affect interactions with dissimilar others (Thomas, 1996; Ely, 1995; Jacques, 1997). As human beings we naturally categorize people into groups (like us or not like us) to make sense of our world. This tendency to categorize may unintentionally lead us to act based on stereotypes. Considerable evidence suggests that many people are unaware of their unconscious biases and prejudices and the subsequent impact on interpersonal interactions. For example, McConahay (1986) has shown that unlike the blatant racist attitudes and remarks people made in decades past, racism in the United States today is much more subtle, involving a general belief that racism is a thing of the past and minorities are pushing for undeserved gains. There is also research to suggest that racial bias on the part of whites is not really the result of a belief in black inferiority but rather a belief in white superiority (Dovidio & Gaernter, 1991). Many of us may be successful at consciously suppressing negative feelings about others who are different, but we tend not to notice the natural positive bias we hold for people who are like us. Self-knowledge of both positive and negative biases is an important first step in overcoming the stereotypes we all hold of one another.

Although it is sometimes difficult to look inside ourselves and recognize the stereotypes and biases we hold, research has found that awareness of prejudice and guilt associated with such attitudes can be a strong motivational force for learning how to avoid prejudice in the future and reduce the effects of prejudice on judgments (Devine & Monteith, 1993). Thus, being made aware of our own biases and prejudices through diversity training can help us begin to monitor and change our reactions toward others. This may be a very important step in the process of reducing prejudice. We recommend that trainers employ a variety of interactive techniques to facilitate increased self-awareness, including self-report questionnaires, interviews with dissimilar others, small group discussions, and a presentation of racial or ethnic identity stages of development (see Cox & Beale, 1997, for examples), and so on.

Skill Building

It is important not only to educate and inform trainees about inappropriate behaviors in the workplace and the negative consequences of bias and discrimination but also to foster the development of skills necessary to break bad habits and change often unconscious and unintended prejudice. Research on various methods of intercultural training has shown that both an informational type of training and a more interactive–skill development type of training have significant benefits in preparing managers for intercultural work assignments (Earley, 1987). Instructing participants in positive behaviors may also improve their confidence that they can interact with members of different demographic groups in an unprejudiced way.

Skill Building Theories and Methods

A number of theories have been presented in the literature as possible explanations for how and why training may facilitate positive changes in behavior toward people who are different. For example, Black and Mendenhall (1990) argued that the effectiveness of cross-cultural training may be explained by the general principles of social learning theory (SLT). Social learning theory proposes that learning is affected by both observation and experience. Research has shown that learning can be facilitated through modeling, which occurs when participants observe appropriate behaviors in others, mentally rehearse them, and then actively practice the modeled behavior (see Bandura, 1977). In applying SLT to cross-cultural training, Black and Mendenhall (1990) suggest that training may be effective when trainees' confidence in themselves and their ability to act appropriately in cross-cultural settings is increased by practicing appropriate behaviors and receiving positive reinforcement.

Other researchers suggest training may be effective if it helps people to manage the anxiety and uncertainty associated with intercultural interactions (Gudykunst, 1998). Another explanation of why training may be effective in creating behavior change comes from impression management theory (Giacalone & Beard, 1994; Mendenhall & Wiley, 1994), or the self-regulation process (Tsui & Ashford, 1994). The idea is that training can provide opportunities for employees to practice diverse interactions and deal with diversity issues in a relatively safe context, where they can receive feedback and monitor their behavior accordingly. Previous research involving managers has shown that seeking negative feedback conveys a sense of sincerity and eagerness to be responsive to the needs and expectations of others (Ashford & Tsui, 1991). Therefore, if people learn to seek feedback and adapt their behavior, it may help reduce their anxiety about making a mistake when dealing with dissimilar others and increase their confidence.

Based on previous research, we recommend that the skill-building phase of diversity training include many opportunities for participants to observe both appropriate and inappropriate behavior, practice dealing with diversity issues and conflicts, and receive feedback to make adjustments to future behavior. For example, videos or role-plays are often very effective methods for having trainees observe workplace situations in which diversity conflicts arise or bias and discrimination exist. Many videos show a scene where a diversity issue is handled poorly. The tape is stopped so the group can discuss the situation, and the scene is then replayed to show how behavior can be changed to support diversity and foster positive diverse interactions at work.

Another method that has been proven effective in cross-cultural training is the use of critical incidents (Flanagan, 1954), also referred to as culture assimilators in intercultural training (Bhawuk & Brislin, 2000). This training tool consists of a number of real-life scenarios involving cross-cultural interactions that lead to misunderstandings because of cultural differences between two people. Trainees are then given several alternative behavioral choices and explanations or feedback about why an alternative is preferred or not (Bhawuk & Brislin, 2000). This type of training method has also been shown to be effective in reducing stereotyping of blacks by whites in an American sample (Triandis, 1977). An experienced trainer may wish to seek anonymous input from training participants about actual diversity conflicts that have come up in that particular organization. These actual workplace examples can then become the critical incidents that the group can analyze and then offer alternative responses and discuss appropriate responses.

Diversity Training Success in Practice: Case Study 1

We highlight the Diversity Alive program here as an example of an interactive and multidimensional approach to diversity training (Smagala, personal communication with the authors, July 2000). In Rochester, New York, a theater-based training group (Learn It Live) has been working with companies since 1992 to deliver live demonstrations. Professional actors portray characters in a short scene involving a diversity issue in the workplace. Afterwards, the actors remain in character and trainees have an opportunity to ask questions of each of them—about their motives, what they were thinking and feeling, and how they would have liked the situation to be different. Next, trainees practice communication skills in small groups, where they take turns performing dialogues with one of the actors, who plays a supporting role. The actor improvises responses to each trainee based on how well that person is using effective communication skills. Finally, the actor steps out of character to provide coaching feedback to improve the trainees' skill level.

This highly interactive and entertaining approach to diversity training presents a nonthreatening way for participants to see themselves and their coworkers, through the characters portrayed by the actors. Diversity Alive is multidimensional because it involves raising awareness of diversity issues in the workplace, seeks to educate employees about appropriate behaviors in the workplace, and provides an opportunity to practice and refine new skills and strategies for dealing with diversity issues.

Action Planning

To create a more affirming work environment for diversity, commitment to both organizational and personal change is necessary.

Organizational Change

If diversity training efforts are to lead to real changes in the organization, a long-term approach that integrates diversity with other business processes and objectives is needed. It is important not to treat diversity training as a onetime event that remains disconnected from the "real" business of the organization. This means critically examining organizational processes, policies, and practices to understand where bias and discrimination may be occurring. It also means taking steps to correct those problems and constant monitoring of the work environment for diversity. Managing diversity is a long-term, comprehensive effort requiring cultural change for full implementation (Thomas, 1991).

We believe that trainees are unlikely to be able to make the connection between what they have learned about diversity and about themselves to make significant changes in their own work environment unless they are given some guidance and practice in creating plans for change. Thus, we recommend that the third phase of diversity training include a facilitated process of seeking input from trainees on changes that need to be made to organizational practices (for example, recruitment, selection, reward, and recognition). After identifying problems, trainees should develop an action plan for change that includes roles and responsibilities, a time line, and evaluation measures (increase minority applicants by 5 percent in six months, for example). This phase of training will be most effective with intact work teams or functional groups. Creating action plans helps ensure that each participant takes responsibility and ownership for improving the racial climate in the organization (Kirkland & Regan, 1997).

In addition to working together to identify and resolve specific diversity issues, this phase of diversity training may also include problem-solving activities related to more general workplace dilemmas in which organizational identity supercedes other group identities as group members work interdependently (Tsui & Gutek, 1999). Research has shown that group identities (such as racial or gender groups) can become less salient when a superordinate goal or a larger group identity becomes more salient. For example, the literature has consistently shown that when group boundaries are made salient, in-group–out-group or we-versus-they categorizations increase intergroup bias (Gaertner & Dovidio, 1986). In organizations, a superordinate social identity such as identification with the organization or functional group may begin to break down we-versus-they group differentiation and increase work group effectiveness (Brewer, 1995). Thus, this phase of training may be referred to as something other than diversity training (such as a task force) in which two goals are met: problem solving intended to resolve an organizational issue or improve a process, and strengthening an organizational or functional group identity to increase perceptions of similarity and eliminate in-group bias along racial or gender lines.

Personal Change

In addition to facilitating change in organizational practices and work group interactions, one of the goals of diversity training may be to foster individual change in attitudes toward diversity and workplace interactions with dissimilar others. Although personal growth may begin with awareness followed by the acquisition and practice of communication and interpersonal skills, long-term change is unlikely unless participants make a personal commitment to continued growth and development and practice their new skills in real-word situations. Therefore, this phase of diversity training should also include time for individuals to develop a personal action plan for change that includes specific activities or experiences to practice interacting with dissimilar others and reduce anxiety, as well as anticipated dates for completion of the plan. For example, research on the development of multicultural competence in counselors has shown a relationship between white racial identity development, comfort with people of other races, and multifaceted training programs that include awareness, skill development, and multicultural action planning (Brown, Parham, & Yonker, 1996; Parker, Moore, & Neimeyer, 1998). Researchers recommend that a number of experiences be included in a personal action plan, such as working with multicultural populations, becoming involved with diverse community groups or activities, or generating two or three personal goals for approaching interracial encounters with sensitivity and competence. Other examples in a work context may include attending a diversity conference, learning about a coworker's cultural background, and reading about historical issues for minorities. The most important thing to be learned during this part of diversity training is that personal growth and development must go beyond the diversity training program and often beyond work boundaries.

Diversity Training Success in Practice: Case Study 2

Laurence (Larry) Payne, president of the Educational Excellence Resource Group, has been doing diversity work with organizations for twenty-one years. Larry emphasizes the importance of framing diversity as more than just training or affirmative action. In fact, he only works with companies that are willing to develop a long-term consulting relationship intended to improve the work environment and workplace interactions for all employees. For example, Larry has worked with one client for five years. The relationship began with a promise from senior leaders to take a hard look at the organization's diversity issues. Larry first conducted small focus groups with employees at *all* levels of the organization. Although every organization has written policies and rules, the purpose of the focus groups is to understand not how things *should* happen but how they actually happen—the unwritten rules. "Often the biggest disparity found in an organization lies between what we say we are in print, and how things really operate. There is often a disconnect between word and deed, preached and practiced. The challenge then becomes aligning organizational members' thoughts, feelings, and actions" (Laurence Payne, personal communication, July 19, 2000).

From these conversations, Larry was able to identify common themes among employees and pinpoint where he thought the organization could make both short-term and long-term improvements. In planning a diversity strategy, he immediately integrated diversity with business objectives, rather than viewing it as a standalone initiative. In fact, Larry did not even mention the word diversity. Instead, the change strategy he created revolved around creating a work environment that fosters cooperation. "Creating a multicultural society involves transitioning from an 'I' or 'me' thinking of the issues to a 'we' or 'us' view of diversity" (Laurence Payne, personal communication, July 19, 2000). As part of the change strategy, 350 company managers attended awareness workshops focusing on changing behavior, developing effective listening skills, and creating personal and corporate action plans for diversity.

The program works as follows. The first phase of training, self-awareness through individual reflection, involves the use of role-plays, interview questions, exercises, and homework assignments (for example, participants examine their own ethnic background with respect to struggles, perspectives, and experiences with other groups). The second phase, at the group level of development, focuses on developing the skills necessary to function professionally in a multicultural environment. There are a series of group discussions about difference, films, lectures, and so on. "The goal is to have people listen and learn, not to agree with each other. We want people to come to understand that different is different, amen, period. Not better than, more than, or less than; just different" (Laurence Payne, personal communication, July 19, 2000). Finally, the third phase involves communal or organizational level of development, focusing on the creation and reinforcement of expected norms of behavior for diversity in the workplace. All employees are then held accountable for their behaviors, and provided incentives in their paychecks, bonuses, stock options, and so on.

Guidelines for Practice

- Develop a customized diversity training program that involves three levels of development: awareness, skill building, and action planning.
- Keep in mind that although lectures may be a part of the training program, employees will get more out of the training if they are actively involved.
- Hire a qualified and experienced trainer to deliver the training; otherwise, you run the risk of creating a threatening environment where learning fails to occur.
- Ensure that trainees have multiple opportunities to practice the skills they have learned.
- Consider the use of both individual and work group or organizational action plans for change.

Planning for Success

To create a successful initiative, ensure management buy-in and stimulate participants' motivation to learn.

Taking Steps to Ensure Management Buy-In

A key predictor of successful diversity programs is top management support (Davidson, 1999; Ferdman & Brody, 1996; Rynes & Rosen, 1995). Unless senior leaders are committed to diversity, employees will not take training seriously or feel responsible for initiating personal or organizational change. In addition, minority employees may feel betrayed when organizational leaders make promises about diversity issues that remain unfulfilled (Chrobot-Mason & Zeman, 2000). Therefore, it is critical that an organization planning to begin diversity training communicate a strong message to employees (in both words and actions) that the issue is a high priority relative to other business issues (Rynes & Rosen, 1995).

There are several ways to gain management buy-in, beginning with the initial planning stages of diversity training. It is important to make sure key stakeholders are involved in the interviews and surveys conducted as part of the needs assessment. The perspective of organizational leaders—what they feel the key diversity issues are in the company—should be heard. It may also be important to determine the level of racial identity development of the very top leaders in the company to understand the extent to which they have reflected on diversity issues and their coping strategies for dealing with such conflicts in the organization (Kirkland & Regan, 1997). Understanding the motivation and perspective of organizational leaders can bring to light barriers or obstacles to success of the diversity training initiative. Once data have been gathered and analyzed as part of the needs assessment, it will be critical again to schedule time with senior leaders to go over the data and collaboratively develop an overall diversity strategy. The strategy should include both long-term and short-term goals and everyone should agree on it.

It is important that organizational leaders understand the role they play in supporting diversity efforts. When top managers actively mentor, coach, develop, and place people of color and women in their own ranks, they send a powerful message to employees about the organization's commitment to diversity (Fernandez, 1999). Based on their study of best practices in diversity training programs, Ellis and Sonnenfeld (1994) recommend that the chief executive address sessions in person or on videotape to explain why the company genuinely cares about workforce diversity. Others believe a diversity champion (a visible advocate for diversity who will push all obstacles aside) is critical to training success (Sessa, 1992). Another critical success factor is when organizational leaders create a corporatewide philosophy that governs and enforces diversity policies (Gilbert & Ivancevich, 2000). This may include incorporating statements of valuing diversity to gain a competitive business advantage in company vision or mission statements and strategic objectives.

Stimulating Motivation to Learn

To encourage trainees to participate and to help them learn more, trainers will want to take steps to create a safe learning environment that is relatively free of blame and guilt. Ideally, training groups should include approximately equal numbers of racial and ethnic group members and men and women (Ellis & Sonnenfeld, 1994; Kirkland & Regan, 1997) to minimize the likelihood that individuals feel obligated to assume the role of unwilling representative for their group. It may be beneficial in the early phases of diversity training to have management and employee groups trained separately to avoid discomfort in situations that require a great deal of self-disclosure, and with that, a lot of personal risk taking (Kirkland & Regan, 1997).

Although certain feelings of guilt may be an inevitable part of the change process for majority members (Helms, 1990; Linnehan & Konrad, 1999; Regan & Huber, 1997), it is important that the training include sufficient debriefings to ensure that a group can still function after tense exchanges and that individual dignity is protected (Ellis & Sonnenfeld, 1994). A critical component of success then becomes selecting qualified and competent trainers who can effectively manage the emotions that often ensue following discussions about diversity, power, and privilege. Ferdman and Brody (1996) recommend careful consideration of diversity trainers based on the role they will perform in the overall intervention. They should be able to address issues of ethnicity, race, gender, lifestyle, and so on without reinforcing previously held stereotypes or inventing new ones (Ellis & Sonnenfeld, 1994). They should be able to demonstrate both diversity education competence (for example, familiarity with the business reasons for diversity) and technical competence (for example, designing and evaluating a training program), and have experience both in training and working in multicultural settings (Arredondo, 1996). One suggestion is to have trainers involve participants in establishing group norms and ground rules to provide a sense of safety and comfort for all participants.

Research findings also suggest ways to increase motivation to learn (Colquitt, LePine, & Noe, 2000; Quiñones, 1997). First, trainees will be motivated if they believe their assignment to training was fair (Quiñones, 1995; see also Folger & Cropanzano, 1998). It is likely that if individuals are singled out for training they will feel the assignment was unfair. This is another reason for training everyone in the organization. Second, trainees will be motivated if the content of the course matches their expectations (Tannenbaum, Mathieu, Salas, & Cannon-Bowers, 1991). Therefore, it is critical that all communications with employees portray the content and purpose of the program accurately. Finally, how the training is framed can influence motivation, anxiety, and subsequent learning and transfer (Martocchio, 1992; Quiñones, 1995).

One strategy for framing diversity training for managers is to emphasize that managing a diverse workforce is only part of a broader skill set required to be a successful manager. Diversity training may be thought of as a way for managers to increase their overall skills or prepare for future jobs in which they may be required to manage a diverse team or work with an international customer. Again, communication about the purpose of diversity training is needed. If employees think they are being given diversity training as a punishment for past behavior their motivation is likely to be low. But if diversity training is framed as an opportunity to increase the productivity and well-being of the organization, then motivation will be enhanced.

Guidelines for Practice

- Be sure to include key stakeholders in the needs-assessment and objective-setting phases of planning. Their involvement in these early phases will help solidify their support for the project.
- Encourage organizational leaders to champion the diversity training effort by openly showing support for it.
- Take steps to create a psychologically safe training environment for all. Create racial, gender, and ethnic balance in training groups whenever possible. Make sure there is sufficient time to debrief when tensions run high.
- Motivate trainees to learn by setting realistic expectations and framing training as an opportunity to enhance work performance.

Evaluating Training and Maintaining the Intervention

Finally, the initiative must be evaluated and maintained.

Developing Measurable Evaluation Criteria

As mentioned previously, diversity training initiatives are very rarely evaluated, yet it is critical to monitor progress toward intended goals, maintain an ongoing diversity strategy that changes over time, and link such efforts to organizational savings and productivity. Two issues must be considered when determining a strategy for evaluation: What are the objectives to be evaluated? How should the evaluation be conducted?

Earlier in the chapter we outlined three broad goals for diversity training: to improve the work environment for all, to improve work relationships, and to improve the quality and efficiency of the work being done. Linked to each of these broad goals are training objectives for the three levels of diversity training: awareness, skill building, and action planning. Each objective should be evaluated in some measurable way after training.

Besides evaluating specific objectives, progress toward the overall diversity strategy (of which training is but one part) should also be measured over time. Successful multicultural organizations tend to monitor their progress on multiple criteria rather than a single index (Gilbert & Ivancevich, 2000). For example, although it is important to evaluate minority and female representation at all levels of the organization, other measures of success should also be examined, including retention rates, employee satisfaction, support of diversity efforts both internally and externally, response time for resolving problems and concerns, and so on. Cox (1994) emphasizes the importance of measuring both diversity-related goals and the impact of managing diversity on other organizational performance indicators. He suggests evaluating affective outcomes, including attitude change, individual achievement measures such as intergroup differences in promotion rates, and organizational performance indicators such as turnover and market share (see also Kirkpatrick, 1967; Kraiger et al., 1993).

In determining how to conduct the evaluation, a variety of methods and measurement criteria should be considered. Several self-report measures taken at the conclusion of diversity training can help evaluate the extent to which participants feel that they are more comfortable interacting with dissimilar others, have benefited from training, and believe they will use what they learned when they return to the workplace. Knowledge of diversity laws and organizational policies may also be assessed as part of the evaluation. Tracking completion rates of both personal and organizational action plan activities may indicate some measure of success. In addition, some type of 360-degree feedback instrument involving diversity behaviors may be used; employees are rated by their supervisor, subordinates, peers, and themselves. This type of feedback instrument can provide not only a measure of training success but also valuable developmental feedback to survey respondents when a gap exists between self and other ratings.

The quality of the evaluation efforts will also depend on the type of evaluation design used. The key question to be answered is the extent to which any observable changes can be attributed to the training program. Ideally, an evaluation design should include a trained and an untrained group for which criterion data are collected before and after training (Arvey & Cole, 1989). If criterion scores change more for the trained than the untrained group, one can be confident that the observed changes are due to attending the training program. A critical aspect of this design is that assignment to trained and untrained groups be done randomly.

Clearly, the ideal evaluation design is difficult to implement in real-world situations. For example, if everyone in the organization is trained, it is difficult to come up with a control group. A solution here might be to stagger the implementation of the training program so that individuals who will attend training at a later point can serve as a control group for those who attend early on. One concern is that early attendees might communicate with the others and influence their pretraining responses. This would make it difficult to find changes that result from training.

An alternative is to include posttest-only designs, nonequivalent group designs (where no random assignment takes place), and time-series designs (see Goldstein, 1993). These can be used to get a general idea of the effectiveness of training but are difficult to interpret. Although one may be tempted to assume that a poorly designed evaluation is better than no evaluation at all, this is not always true. A poorly designed evaluation can lead an organization to drop a perfectly fine diversity training program or continue an inferior program. Good decisions always require good data.

Guideline for Practice

- Monitor ongoing progress toward intended goals by collecting a variety of measures, including self-reports, knowledge assessment, demographic changes, and so on.

Reinforcing Desired Behaviors

Both positive reinforcement and efforts to ensure accountability have been identified as critical factors in a long-term diversity culture change effort. Gilbert and Ivancevich (2000) report that one organization linked 25 percent of each employee's pay to positive interactions with diverse individuals. Other organizations report holding managers accountable for diversity behaviors by developing quantitative measures that include a culture group profile of employees mentored and persons moved for development purposes, or presenting recognition awards to managers for excellence in managing diversity (Cox, 1994). Other companies such as Xerox included the extent to which managers and executives met balanced workforce goals as part of their performance appraisal (Sessa, 1992).

Changes resulting from training are also reinforced by a supportive organizational climate (Rouiller & Goldstein, 1993). If supervisors are supportive of employees trying out new skills, provide opportunities to practice (Ford, Quiñones, Sego, & Sorra, 1992), and give time off to attend refresher courses or other relevant courses, transfer of training is enhanced. In addition, posttraining interventions such as goal setting and self-management skills have been found to increase the likelihood that trainees will transfer their new skills and knowledge back to the workplace (for example, Marx, 1982). This latter approach teaches trainees to be aware of situations in which they may slip back into old behaviors and provides them with coping skills for dealing with potential relapses.

Guideline for Practice

- Reinforce individuals and work groups when they demonstrate positive behaviors and make progress toward action plan goals. Consider modifying the organizational performance appraisal system to reward achievement of diversity goals.

Conclusion

As the workplace continues to diversify, organizations will have to make a choice: either ignore this trend and continue business as usual or take steps to prepare for diversity. Ignoring demographic changes may cause such problems as an inability to attract and retain minority employees or a hostile work environment that increases the risk of litigation. In contrast, organizations that work to change or create organizational practices and policies that support a diverse workforce may not only minimize exposure to discrimination lawsuits but also realize the benefits of the creativity and problem-solving capabilities that a diverse workforce can provide.

In this chapter, we have outlined a systematic approach to diversity training, based on both the training literature and current best practices in diversity training. It is our belief that many of the failings of diversity training initiatives may be avoided if organizations take the time to develop a comprehensive plan for diversity. The plan should be organization-specific and developed after a thorough needs assessment. If training becomes a part of the overall diversity strategy, then specific objectives should be developed to guide content and process, as well as the evaluation strategy. An effective diversity training initiative will not only increase awareness of the issues but enable employees to interact more effectively with people who are different, and motivate them to search for ways to see differences as an asset rather than a liability to the organization.

References

Arredondo, P. (1996). *Successful diversity management initiatives.* Thousand Oaks, CA: Sage.

Arvey, R. D., & Cole, D. A. (1989). Evaluating change due to training. In I. L. Goldstein & Associates (Eds.), *Training and development in organizations* (pp. 89–117). San Francisco: Jossey-Bass.

Ashford, S. J., & Tsui, A. S. (1991). Self-regulation for managerial effectiveness: The role of active feedback-seeking. *Academy of Management Journal, 34*(2), 251–280.

Ausubel, D. P. (1968). *Educational psychology: A cognitive view.* Austin, TX: Holt, Rinehart and Winston.

Baldwin, T. T. (1992). Effects of alternative modeling strategies on outcomes of interpersonal-skills training. *Journal of Applied Psychology, 77,* 147–154.

Bandura, A. (1977). *Social learning theory.* Englewood Cliffs, NJ: Prentice-Hall.

Bhawuk, D.P.S., & Brislin, R. W. (2000). Cross-cultural training: A review. *Applied Psychology: An International Review, 49,* 162–191.

Black, J. S., & Mendenhall, M. (1990). Cross-cultural training effectiveness: A review and a theoretical framework for future research. *Academy of Management Review, 15,* 113–136.

Bond, M. A., & Pyle, J. L. (1998). Diversity dilemmas at work. *Journal of Management Inquiry, 7,* 252–269.

Brewer, M. B. (1995). Managing diversity: The role of social identities. In S. E. Jackson & M. N. Ruderman (Eds.), *Diversity in work teams* (pp. 47–68). Washington, DC: American Psychological Association.

Brislin, R. W., & Yoshida, T. (1994). The content of cross-cultural training: An introduction. In R. W. Brislin & T. Yoshida (Eds.), *Improving intercultural interactions. Modules for cross-cultural training programs* (pp. 1–14). Thousand Oaks, CA: Sage.

Brown, S. P., Parham, T. A., & Yonker, R. (1996). Influence of a cross-cultural training course on racial identity attitudes of white women and men: Preliminary perspectives. *Journal of Counseling & Development, 74,* 510–516.

Burkart, M. (1999). The role of training in advancing a diversity initiative. *Diversity Factor, 8,* 2–5.

Chemers, M. M., & Murphy, S. E. (1995). Leadership and diversity in groups and organizations. In M. M. Chemers, S. Oskamp, & M. A. Costanzo (Eds.), *Diversity in organizations: New perspectives for a changing workplace* (pp. 157–188). Thousand Oaks, CA: Sage.

Chrobot-Mason, D. (2000a). *Multicultural competence for managers: Same old leadership skills or something new.* Paper presented at the Conference on Psychological and Organizational Perspectives on Discrimination in the Workplace, Rice University, Houston.

Chrobot-Mason, D. (2000b). *An examination of intra-group differences in majority managers' ethnic identity and its effect on minority employee perceptions of managerial support.* Paper presented at the annual meeting of the Society for Industrial/Organizational Psychology, New Orleans.

Chrobot-Mason, D., & Thomas, K. (2000). *The intersection of individual and organizational multicultural identity development.* Paper presented at the annual meeting of the Society for Industrial/Organizational Psychology, New Orleans.

Chrobot-Mason, D., & Zeman, R. (2000). *Keeping the promise: Violations of the psychological contract for minority employees.* Paper presented at the Academy of Management Conference—Gender and Diversity in Organizations Division, Toronto, Canada.

Colquitt, J. A., LePine, J. A., & Noe, R. A. (2000). Toward an integrative theory of training motivation: A meta-analytic path analysis of 20 years of research. *Journal of Applied Psychology, 5,* 678–707.

Cox, T., Jr. (1991). The multicultural organization. *Academy of Management Executive, 5,* 34–47.

Cox, T., Jr. (1994). *Cultural diversity in organizations.* San Francisco: Berrett-Koehler.

Cox, T., Jr., & Beale, R. L. (1997). *Developing competency to manage diversity.* San Francisco: Berrett-Koehler.

Cross, W. E., Jr. (1978). Models of psychological nigrescence: A literature review. *Journal of Black Psychology, 5,* 13–31.

Davidson, M. N. (1999). The value of being included: An examination of diversity change initiatives in organizations. *Performance Improvement Quarterly, 12,* 164–180.

Decker, P. J., & Nathan, B. R. (1985). *Behavioral modeling training: Principles and applications.* New York: Praeger.

Devine, P. G., & Monteith, M. J. (1993). The role of discrepancy-associated affect in prejudice reduction. In D. M. Mackie & D. L. Hamilton (Eds.), *Affect, cognition, and stereotyping: Interactive processes in group perception* (pp. 317–344). San Diego: Academic Press.

Devine, P. G., & Vasquez, K. A. (1998). The rocky road to positive intergroup relations. In J. L. Eberhardt & S. T. Fiske (Eds.), *Confronting racism: The problem and the response* (pp. 234–262). Thousand Oaks, CA: Sage.

Douthitt, S. S., Eby, L. T., & Simon, S. A. (1999). Diversity of life experiences: The development and validation of a biographical measure of receptiveness to dissimilar others. *International Journal of Selection and Assessment, 7,* 112–125.

Dovidio, J. F., & Gaertner, S. L. (1991). Changes in the nature and expression of racial prejudice. In H. Knopke, J. Norrell, & R. Rogers (Eds.), *Opening doors: An appraisal of race relations in contemporary America* (pp. 201–241). Tuscaloosa: University of Alabama Press.

Dovidio, J. F., & Gaertner, S. L. (1998). On the nature of contemporary prejudice. In J. L. Eberhardt & S. T. Fiske (Eds.), *Confronting racism: The problem and the response* (pp. 3–32). Thousand Oaks, CA: Sage.

Earley, P. C. (1987). Intercultural training for managers: A comparison of documentary and interpersonal methods. *Academy of Management Journal, 30*(4), 685–698.

Eichenwald, K. (1996, November 16). Texaco to make reward payout in bias lawsuit. *The New York Times,* pp. 1, 23.

Ellis, C., & Sonnenfeld, J. A. (1994). Diverse approaches to managing diversity. *Human Resource Management, 33,* 79–109.

Ely, R. J. (1995). *The role of dominant identity and experience in organizational work on diversity.* In S. E. Jackson & M. N. Ruderman (Eds.), *Diversity in work teams: Research paradigms for a changing workplace* (pp. 161–186). Washington, DC: American Psychological Association.

Faircloth, A. (1998, August 3). Guess who's coming to Denny's. *Fortune,* pp. 108–110.

Ferdman, B. M., & Brody, S. E. (1996). Models of diversity training. In D. Landis & R. S. Bhagat (Eds.), *Handbook of intercultural training* (pp. 282–303). Thousand Oaks, CA: Sage.

Fernandez, J. P. (1999). *Race, gender, and rhetoric.* New York: McGraw-Hill.

Fine, M. G. (1995). *Building successful multicultural organizations.* Westport, CT: Quorum Books.

Fisher, A. (1998, May 11). Texaco: A series of racial horror stories. *Fortune, 137*(9), 186.

Flanagan, J. (1954). The critical incident technique. *Psychological Bulletin, 51,* 327–358.

Folger, R., & Cropanzano, R. (1998). *Organizational justice and human resource management.* Thousand Oaks, CA: Sage.

Ford, J. K., Quiñones, M. A., Sego, D., & Sorra, J. (1992). Factors affecting the opportunity to perform trained tasks on the job. *Personnel Psychology, 45,* 511–527.

Gaertner, S. L., & Dovidio, J. F. (1986). Prejudice, discrimination, and racism: Problems, progress, and promise. In J. F. Dovidio & S. L. Gaertner (Eds.), *Prejudice, discrimination, and racism* (pp. 315–332). Orlando: Academic Press.

Gagne, R. M. (1962). Military training and principles of learning. *American Psychologist, 17,* 83–91.

Martocchio, J. J. (1992). Microcomputer usage as an opportunity: The influence of context in employee training. *Personnel Psychology, 45,* 529–552.

Marx, R. D. (1982). Relapse prevention for managerial training: A model for maintenance of behavior change. *Academy of Management Review, 7,* 433–441.

Mendenhall, M. E., & Wiley, C. (1994). Strangers in a strange land. The relationship between expatriate adjustment and impression management. *American Behavioral Scientist, 37*(5), 605–620.

McConahay, J. B. (1986). Modern racism, ambivalence, and the modern racism scale. In J. F. Dovidio & S. L. Gaertner (Eds.), *Prejudice, discrimination, and racism.* Orlando: Academic Press.

Morrison, A. M. (1992). *The new leaders: Leadership diversity in America.* San Francisco: Jossey-Bass.

Noe, R. A. (1986). Trainees' attributes and attitudes: Neglected influences on training effectiveness. *Academy of Management Review, 11,* 736–749.

Noe, R. A. (1999). *Employee training and development.* Burr Ridge, IL: Irwin.

Parker, W. M., Moore, M. A., & Neimeyer, G. J. (1998). Altering white racial identity and interracial comfort through multicultural training. *Journal of Counseling & Development, 76,* 302–310.

Phinney, J. S. (1992). The multigroup ethnic identity measure. *Journal of Adolescent Research, 7,* 156–176.

Phinney, J. S., Lochner, B. T., & Murphy, R. (1990). Ethnic identity development and psychological adjustment in adolescence. In A. R. Stiffman & L. E. Davis (Eds.), *Ethnic issues in adolescent mental health* (pp. 53–73). Thousand Oaks, CA: Sage.

Quiñones, M. A. (1995). Pretraining context effects: Training assignment as feedback. *Journal of Applied Psychology, 80,* 226–238.

Quiñones, M. A. (1997). Contextual influences on training effectiveness. In M. A. Quiñones & A. Ehrenstein (Eds.), *Training for a rapidly changing workplace: Applications of psychological research.* Washington, DC: American Psychological Association.

Regan, A. M., & Huber, J. S. (1997). Facilitating white identity development: A therapeutic group intervention. In C. E. Thompson & R. T. Carter (Eds.), *Racial identity theory: Applications to individual, group, and organizational interventions* (pp. 113–126). Hillsdale, NJ: Erlbaum.

Richard, O. (2000). Racial diversity, business strategy, and firm performance: A resource-based view. *Academy of Management Journal, 43*(2), 164–177.

Rouiller, J. Z., & Goldstein, I. L. (1993). The relationship between organizational transfer climate and positive transfer of training. *Human Resource Development Quarterly, 4,* 377–390.

Rowe, W., Bennett, S. K., & Atkinson, D. R. (1994). White racial identity models: A critique and alternative proposal. *Counseling Psychologist, 22,* 129–146.

Rynes, S., & Rosen, B. (1995). A field survey of factors affecting the adoption and perceived success of diversity training. *Personnel Psychology, 48*(2), 247–270.

Schuler, R. S., & Jackson, S. E. (1987). Linking competitive strategies with human resource management practices. *Academy of Management Executive, 1,* 207–219.

Sessa, V. I. (1992). Managing diversity at the Xerox Corporation: Balanced workforce goals and caucus groups. In S. E. Jackson & Associates (Eds.), *Diversity in the workplace: Human resource initiatives* (pp. 37–64). New York: Guilford Press.

Tannenbaum, S. I., Mathieu, J. E., Salas, E., & Cannon-Bowers, J. A. (1991). Meeting trainees' expectations: The influence of training fulfillment on the development of commitment, self-efficacy, and motivation. *Journal of Applied Psychology, 76,* 759–769.

Thomas, D. A., & Ely, R. J. (1996). Making differences matter: A new paradigm for managing diversity. *Harvard Business Review,* 79–90.

Thomas, K. M. (1996). Psychological privilege and ethnocentrism as barriers to cross-cultural adjustment and effective intercultural interactions. *Leadership Quarterly, 7*(2), 215–228.

Thomas, K. M. (1998). Psychological readiness for multicultural leadership. *Management Development Forum, 1,* 99–112.

Thomas, R. R. (1991). *Beyond race and gender.* New York: AMACOM.

Thomas, R. R. (1999). *Building a house for diversity.* New York: AMACOM.

Towers Perrin. (1992). *Workforce 2000 today: A bottom-line concern—Revising corporate views on workforce change.* New York: Author.

Triandis, H. C. (1977). Theoretical framework for evaluation of cross-cultural training effectiveness. *International Journal of Intercultural relations, 1,* 19–45.

Tsui, A. S., & Ashford, S. J. (1994). Adaptive self-regulation: A process view of managerial effectiveness. *Journal of Management, 20,* 93–121.

Tsui, A. S., & Gutek, B. A. (1999). *Demographic differences in organizations.* San Francisco: New Lexington Press.

U.S. Department of Labor. (2000). *Occupational outlook handbook 2000–2001.* Washington, DC: U.S. Department of Labor.

Ward, C., & Kennedy, A. (1993). Where's the "culture" in cross-cultural transition? *Journal of Cross-Cultural Psychology, 24,* 221–249.

Wheeler, M. L. (1994). *Diversity training: A research report* (Report No. 1083–94-RR). New York: The Conference Board.

Wooten, L., & Hayes James, E. (May, 2000). *Workplace discrimination: Why do firms continue to make the same mistakes?* Paper presented at the Conference on Psychological and Organizational Perspectives on Unfair Discrimination in the Workplace, Houston.

Wright, P., Ferris, S. P., Hiller, J. S., & Kroll, M. (1995). *Academy of Management Journal, 38,* 272–287.

Wright, P. M., & McMahan, G. C. (1992). Theoretical perspectives for strategic human resource management. *Journal of Management, 18,* 295–320.

CHAPTER 6

Management Development
Coaching and Mentoring Programs

David B. Peterson

Coaching has achieved such popularity that many organizations now refer to their managers as coaches. In fact, consultants in fields as diverse as financial investing and health and beauty are calling themselves coaches in order to cash in on the term's cachet. Coaching and mentoring—potentially powerful tools for management development—now face the risk of devolving into faddish buzz words and trendy but marginally effective programs. To reduce that risk, and to help you and your organization capture the full potential of coaching and mentoring, this chapter presents a practical framework for accelerating learning and development through coaching, examines best practices in coaching, highlights common pitfalls and what you can do to avoid them, and outlines specific recommendations for designing effective programs in three areas: an individual coaching program, an organizational program for coaching groups of individuals, and a companywide mentoring program.

Note: I am extremely grateful to Mary Dee Hicks, Seymour Uranowitz, and Donna M. Genett for their helpful comments and suggestions on this chapter.

The primary focus of this chapter is on coaching because it has broader applicability and a more generalizable skill set than mentoring.[1] Consider the following comment from an insightful senior manager at a Fortune 50 high-tech company: "There is a huge difference between coaching and mentoring. Coaching is part of your job as a manager and you have to do it. Mentoring is about chemistry; if you don't have the chemistry between two people you can't force it. A mentor needs the time, the bandwidth, and the propensity to do it. A mentor needs to be someone you look up to, someone you respect, and they have to be interested in, and actually like, the person they are mentoring" (Mike Rose, personal communication with the author, January 8, 1996). That fits with the distinction drawn by Peterson and Hicks (1996), "Mentors typically share insights and lessons from their personal storehouse of experiences and opportunities. Coaches paint development with a broader brush; they understand the process of learning and help create the conditions for it to occur" (p. 16).

A Paradigm Shift

Before 1990, a suggestion that a manager needed a coach was invariably perceived as a personal indictment of the individual's skills or performance. Most people referred to coaching were, in fact, viewed as talented but flawed. Similarly, coaches tended to emphasize the negative and remedial aspects of working with people, from overcoming resistance (Jellison, 1993) to preventing derailment (Kaplan, 1991; Lombardo & Eichinger, 1989).

By the late 1990s, coaching had taken on a positive, proactive tone (for example, Executive Coaching Forum of Boston, 2000; Whitworth, Kimsey-House, & Sandahl, 1998; see also Hicks & Peterson, 1997; Seligman & Csikszentmihalyi, 2000). A suggestion that a manager needs coaching today is likely to be met with "Well, of course I do. Everything around here is changing so fast that I need new skills just to keep pace," rather than with denial or defensiveness. Yet even though the paradigm of coaching has shifted, many of the techniques of and assumptions about coaching still rest on either negative or irrelevant vestiges of the past, such as those presented in the left column of Exhibit 6.1.

Exhibit 6.1. Old and New Assumptions About Coaching.

Assumptions in Remedial Approaches to Coaching	Assumptions for Positive, Proactive Coaching
People resist change and the coach's task is to motivate them to develop.	People are motivated to learn and grow; the coach's task is to tap into that motivation to develop.
Coaching needs to start with a thorough assessment or needs analysis so people have an accurate picture of themselves and their development needs.	Insight is a never-ending discovery process that is nurtured throughout the entire coaching process; all that is necessary to begin is a good starting point.
Coaches need to provide feedback to the people they coach.	Although feedback from the coach may be helpful, the coach's primary role is to help people improve their ability to nurture deeper insights by gathering their own feedback.
Coaches have a more objective understanding than the participant.	Both coaches and participants have important insights and information. By working together, they can put together a more useful picture of what is happening.
Coaches need to be experts in a given topic in order to teach it to people.	Coaches need to be experts in how people learn so they can help people actually change behaviors and become more effective. One of the most valuable things a coach can do is help people learn how to learn for themselves.
Coaching takes a lot of time and effort.	Coaching is about finding leverage so that people focus on the one or two things that will have the greatest payoff.
Coaching is about fixing problem behaviors (an assumption that often leads to a focus on the past).	Coaching is about improving future performance; it works best when the focus is on understanding what works for the person, what does not work for her, and what she will do the next time she is in that situation.

Even though many of the stated approaches to coaching reflect partnership and positive development, the actual approaches reveal implicit assumptions that people resist change and that the coach has the right ideas and motivations while the learner does not. Such assumptions perpetuate a top-down approach to development, which diminishes motivation and inhibits learners from taking responsibility for their own learning (Hicks & Peterson, 1997). Coaching will have the greatest impact when the techniques are aligned around positive values for learning and partnering with people. Think about it yourself. What kind of coach would you want to work with? One who assumes you will resist change or one who partners with you? As you read this chapter, keep these ideas in mind and examine yourself to get a better understanding of your own implicit assumptions.

What Makes a Great Coach?

Back in 1997, I started asking two questions of participants at my workshops and seminars (Peterson, 2001). First I asked them to discuss and then list the characteristics of a good coach. By far the two most common responses were being a good listener and displaying genuine interest in the person being coached. These were followed by several other themes: good coaches are seen as trustworthy, honest, with high integrity; direct, able to confront and challenge appropriately; and flexible and willing to adapt to the person they are coaching.

The second question is similar, but with enough of a difference that it produces a distinctly different set of answers: What are the characteristics of a *great* coach, and how do great coaches differ from good ones? Most groups respond to this question with several moments of silence. In over half the groups, someone will then declare, "Great coaches get results." This moment of insight is what I am looking for, when people realize that a list of qualities or behaviors is not what makes a great coach. Great coaches focus on achieving the desired outcome, through a variety of techniques and tools. The discussion at this point often turns to deeper insights, such as these:

- Great coaches are goal-oriented. They use listening, empathy, and honesty to help people achieve a desired outcome.
- Great coaches know when to listen and when to interrupt or challenge (rather than just be a good listener). As one person observed, "A great coach takes the whole set of tools we listed, and like a true artist, knows how to do the right thing at the right time."
- Great coaches are rarely wedded to specific methods or techniques because they search for what each individual needs in order to learn. They focus on what the person needs rather than on the coaching itself.
- Great coaches are good learners themselves.

What has continually amazed me in all of these discussions is that not one person has mentioned expertise in learning or in human behavior as an important quality for a coach to have. There has been no mention that good coaches understand what motivates people, how people learn, and how people act and interact with others. Even more puzzling is why most professional books, articles, and discussions of coaching barely mention these topics (see Peterson & Hicks, 1999). Yet this issue rests at the heart of how we define coaching. If the purpose of coaching is to help people gain insight, learn new things, change their behavior, and improve their effectiveness and satisfaction in life's activities, then expertise in those areas—cultivating insight, facilitating new learning, guiding the application and transfer of new insights and skills—is essential to being a great coach.

Necessary Conditions for Learning

Along with a shifting view in the field of coaching, the early 1990s saw several attempts to consolidate decades of research on how best to facilitate individual learning (Curtis & Stricker, 1991; Druckman & Bjork, 1991; Hellervik, Hazucha, & Schneider, 1992; Mahoney, 1991; Prochaska, DiClemente, & Norcross, 1992; Prochaska, Norcross, & DiClemente, 1994). My colleague Mary Dee Hicks and I sought to translate this psychology of individual learning into tools and techniques that are accessible to a wide range of people in organizations (Hicks & Peterson, 1997, 1999a, 1999b; Peterson

Figure 6.1. The Development Pipeline.

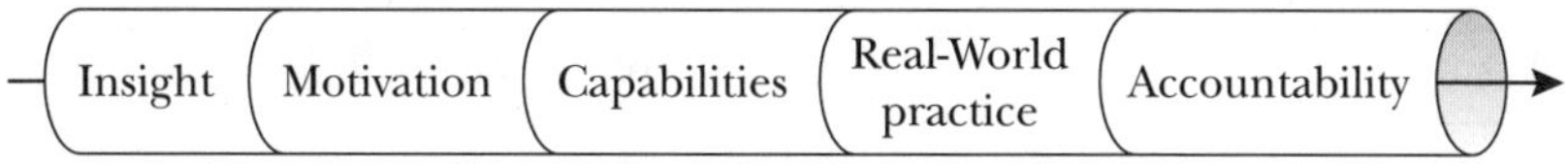

& Hicks, 1995, 1996, 2000). The foundation of our approach is the development pipeline (Hicks & Peterson, 1999a; see Figure 6.1), which outlines the necessary and sufficient conditions for systematic learning.

Coaching, like any management development approach, needs to consider how to address the essential ingredients of development, as summarized in Exhibit 6.2.

The pipeline metaphor is useful in diagnosing where development interventions such as coaching have the greatest value. By analogy, the amount of water that will flow through a pipe is determined by the size of the pipe at its narrowest point. Similarly, we look for the constraints in the development pipeline to determine the most productive point to begin coaching. Two common examples reveal the value of this framework:

- A decentralized organization is trying to improve cross-group collaboration and speed of operation in order to keep up with new competitors. After months of dialogue and skills training, most managers understand what is expected of them (insight), recognize the need to change (motivation), and have the basic skills (capabilities) and opportunities to use them, but their primary accountability is still for the performance of their separate divisions, not for the organization as a whole. Until the organization starts measuring and rewarding collaboration, few people will change their behavior. In this situation, feedback and skills training techniques will have little effect until the real issue—accountability—is addressed.

- An R&D manager is told, "We'd like you to attend a class on active listening, because the people in marketing feel that you don't listen to them or take their views seriously." This assumes that a lack of capability is the problem. However, this same manager demonstrates effective listening skills with his team and his superiors. On further exploration, it is discovered that he does not fully

Exhibit 6.2. The Development Pipeline:
Necessary and Sufficient Conditions for Development.

Necessary Conditions	What Coaches Can Do
Insight: Do people know what to develop?	• Help people clarify their personal goals, values, and motivators. • Help people understand what others expect of them and what it takes to be successful in their environment. • Teach people to get feedback from others. • Identify where skill enhancement or development of new capabilities will have the greatest payoff.*
Motivation: Are people willing to invest the time and energy it takes to develop themselves?	• Identify both personal and organizational reasons for change. • Identify personal and organizational-environmental barriers that will make change difficult. • Seriously examine the trade-offs and make a realistic decision to proceed. • Discuss specific steps for addressing barriers and challenges.
Capabilities: Do people have the skills and knowledge they need?	• Share new ideas and best practices. • Help people find appropriate resources and opportunities. • Explore alternative ways to handle difficult situations. • Practice new skills and behaviors in realistic situations.
Real-world practice: Do people have opportunities to try their new skills at work?	• Identify specific situations where change is appropriate. • Help people determine how they will put small changes into practice every day. • Work with people to create personal strategies for assessing what is working well and what they need to do differently.
Accountability: Do people internalize their new capabilities to improve performance and results?	• Encourage people to make specific commitments for action. • Follow up on learning assignments and personal commitments for action. • Encourage people to enlist others to give them feedback and discuss progress.

*See Peterson and Hicks (1995, 1996) for a discussion of GAPS (goals and values, abilities, perceptions, and success factors), a summary of the various types of information necessary for full insight.

understand the growing importance of marketing for designing products that can compete in the marketplace (insight) and therefore is little motivated to spend time discussing such topics with the marketing team. In this case, directly addressing insight would alleviate the most significant constraint and allow change to happen.

When coaches follow the same game plan with everyone they work with, they squander one of the greatest advantages of coaching: customization. It is common to hear coaches describe a rote process: "First we'll do a 360-degree feedback survey, then we'll have a two-hour feedback session, then we'll write our coaching plan, then we'll work on active listening skills . . ." Such an approach wastes the participant's time if she already has a clear sense of her development priorities. A better approach is to determine first if insight is constrained, and then to determine whether 360-degree feedback is an appropriate tool for this person. This targets the real need and enables the coach to focus time and energy where it will have the greatest payoff. The development pipeline as a framework for the necessary conditions for change aids the coach in searching for the most significant constraints and then in designing an approach customized to that person's needs. This focused approach produces the most rapid and efficient learning.

Peterson and Hicks (1996; see also Peterson, 1996; Hicks & Peterson, 1999b) outline five strategies that coaches can use to work through the necessary conditions for learning outlined in the development pipeline.

Forge a Partnership

The coach's first big challenge is to build sufficient trust and understanding so that people want to work with him. Unless this is established, coaches are unlikely to have the opportunity they need to effectively address the development pipeline conditions.

Inspire Commitment

The next stage is to build insight and motivation—the first two components of the pipeline—so people focus their energy on goals that matter. Coaching participants need an objective picture of their abilities and how they are perceived by others. In addition, coaches can tap into a powerful motivation for development by ensuring a good understanding of what really matters to the person and those around him or her. This complete picture of insight facilitates identifying development priorities that will have a high payoff for both the person and the organization.

Build Skills

At this point, the coach can help the person build the new capabilities he needs to do what is required. Coaches may directly teach new skills or guide the person to draw on a wide range of other learning opportunities for acquiring new knowledge and skills.

Promote Persistence

One of the most neglected aspects of coaching and developing others is helping them maintain the discipline to break old habits and establish new ones through actually practicing their new skills in real-world settings. Two opposite challenges arise at this point. First, it often feels risky for people to replace tried-and-true behaviors with new approaches they are not comfortable with. Second, once they have begun the process, rapid gains in improvement are usually followed by plateaus; it is a slow, tedious process consciously to work on a behavior until it becomes natural. It is easy for people to give up at this point, unless they have continued monitoring and support from their coach.

Shape the Environment

Too often coaches focus only on the one-on-one nature of the coaching relationship and neglect to orchestrate the environment to reward learning and remove barriers that the person will run into. At a minimum, coaches can work with their clients' organizational sponsors so that they provide regular feedback and encouragement to the person.

Research Findings: Evaluating the Impact of Coaching

Apart from one recent study by Manchester Consulting (Fisher, 2001; Manchester Consulting, 2000) and studies conducted primarily by researchers from Personnel Decisions International

(Birkeland, Davis, Goff, Campbell, & Duke, 1997; Davis & Petchenik, 1998; Peterson, 1993a, 1993b; Thompson, 1986), very little empirical work has been conducted on coaching outcomes (Kilburg, 1996, 2000).[2]

Researchers at Manchester Consulting (2000; see also Fisher, 2001) found that one hundred executives who participated in coaching reported improvements in the following areas: working relationships with direct reports (reported by 77 percent of executives), working relationships with immediate supervisors (71 percent), teamwork (67 percent), working relationships with peers (63 percent), job satisfaction (61 percent), conflict reduction (52 percent), organizational commitment (44 percent), and working relationships with clients (37 percent).

They also report significant benefits to the organization, noting improvements in the following areas: productivity (reported by 53 percent of executives), quality (48 percent), organizational strength (48 percent), customer service (39 percent), reducing customer complaints (34 percent), retaining executives who received coaching (32 percent), cost reductions (23 percent), and bottom-line profitability (22 percent).

Thompson (1986) conducted a follow-up study of over two hundred individuals who had participated in coaching during the early 1980s. According to self-reports and ratings by superiors, these coaching participants had made substantial improvements in their skills as a result of coaching and had sustained them over time. Peterson (1993a, 1993b) examined pre-, post-, and follow-up ratings (including ratings on a set of control items) from participants, their superior, and their coach. Considering just the superiors' ratings, the average participant ($N = 370$) showed 1.54 SDs of change on their learning objectives. This represents over three times the amount of change achieved in the average well-designed management training and development program examined by Burke and Day (1986). In addition to dramatic improvement in specific skills, participants also showed a significant improvement in overall performance, based on ratings by superiors (Peterson, 1993b).

Another study (Birkeland et al., 1997; Davis & Petchenik, 1998) evaluated the impact of coaching on over seventy participants at Amoco, which was at the time a Fortune 50 organization in the petrochemical industry. Based on ratings from participants and their superiors, those who participated in coaching demonstrated the following, in comparison to a representative group of managers who did not participate in coaching: improved performance, usually from below average performance in a particular skill to above average performance; increased rate of advancement; higher average salary increases.

Although it is obviously difficult to control for all the variables affecting these outcomes, those who participated in the coaching study reported that their coaching was the single most significant factor in their improvements in these areas (Birkeland et al., 1997).

Coaching was one of the variables examined by Sloan (2001) in her research on executive education. She found that participants in executive education programs offered by leading universities and business schools who worked with a coach or mentor before or after their program, or both, reported substantially greater benefits in the following areas compared with participants who did not work with a coach or mentor: better self-confidence and improved skills in developing others, strategic thinking, operational management, and other areas.

In summary, although systematic research on coaching is not widespread, the available evidence strongly indicates that it is a powerful method for helping people learn new capabilities that can have a direct impact on important organizational outcomes.

When Coaching and Mentoring Are Most Beneficial

Compared with training courses, university programs, Web-based education, and most other management development options, coaching and mentoring are high-cost, high-impact, and high-value investments. However, because both are so popular, they may sometimes be used when better alternatives are available. To gain the greatest benefits from coaching, consider using it when the following characteristics are important (Peterson & Hicks, 1999):

Customization Is Needed

Because of its one-on-one nature, coaching can be automatically customized to the unique needs of the person being coached. Both the content (what is learned) and the process (when, where, and how it is learned) can be customized. Thus, unique needs can be met in one process. For example, coaching could support a senior financial person who needs to learn greater assertiveness, political savvy, strategic thinking, and how to build better external relationships. This principle was demonstrated recently when top executives in a leading computer organization realized that their general managers had received very little leadership development. Because their audience had very different development needs, the organization implemented a large-scale coaching program to bring the general managers up to speed quickly.

Another consideration in choosing coaching is how well a customized learning approach fits with the organizational culture. A leading mutual fund organization determined that coaching was the development method of choice because of its distinctive fit with the organizational norms. Lawrence (1998) observed that our culture doesn't support group-oriented, systematic development efforts. She then described a culture characterized by a strong action orientation, self-sufficiency and independence, and an appreciation for novelty and idiosyncrasy, all of which are favorable to the personal and individual nature of coaching.

Learning Must Be Just-in-Time

When the development need is urgent, coaching can almost always be arranged more quickly than other learning modes such as classroom training, university courses, or action learning. For example, a sales organization in a multinational medical supply company was suffering from a high failure rate in newly promoted sales managers. The group began to offer just-in-time coaching whenever anyone was promoted into that position. Another rapidly growing high-tech company had a poor track record of bringing in external managers until it started assigning a coach to each person on his or her first day on the job.

Little Time Is Available

Coaching is often recommended when a person's time is more valuable than the cost, such as with senior executives, financial gurus, and other key individuals. Coaching tends to provide the maximum learning for the time invested because the curriculum is continuously tailored exactly to the topics and the level of the person. Group learning modes necessarily aim for a common denominator that introduces inefficiency in time commitments for any given individual. For example, a leading consulting firm offers coaching as the primary development tool for its 110 highest-performing senior partners.

Significant Results Are Necessary

Well-designed coaching incorporates virtually all of the best principles of learning, more than any other method. It also provides a supportive relationship, which is often cited as one of the most powerful factors in significant personal change (Mahoney, 1991; Orlinsky & Howard, 1986). The multiple-session design provides for spaced practice, fine-tuning of skills, personal accountability, and continued strategizing around on-the-job application of skills. A financial services firm that was facing dramatic changes in its industry responded with an initiative to change its culture to move faster, make decisions quicker, and operate more strategically at a global level. Hoping to ensure positive role models and effective leadership to make this dramatic change quickly, it provided coaching for the fifteen people identified as most critical to the successful implementation of this new leadership style. In another case, a large-scale process was instituted by a traditional manufacturing organization attempting a significant strategic shift. The company provided three different coaching programs, each tailored to a specific audience of its twelve top executives, the next fifty senior leaders, and the remainder of its top three hundred managers. Both of these organizations chose coaching because they were facing significant challenges and had to achieve dramatic changes quickly.

Confidentiality Is Needed

Coaching generally takes place in the context of a close, trusting relationship, where it is safe to discuss sensitive personal and business issues. For senior leaders in particular it provides a confidential and objective sounding board for issues that they are reluctant or unable to discuss with other members of their team.

Other Considerations

Two other considerations are important in deciding when to use coaching:

Topics Best Suited to Coaching and Mentoring

Peterson (1993b) found that a well-designed coaching program was effective in enhancing skills and improving performance in a wide range of areas:

- Interpersonal skills, including relationship building, tact and sensitivity, assertiveness, conflict management, working across cultures, and influencing without authority
- Communication, including listening skills, presentations, and speaking with impact
- Leadership skills, including delegating, coaching and mentoring, and motivating others
- Certain cognitive skills, such as prioritizing, decision making, and strategic thinking
- Self-management skills, including time management, emotion and anger management, and work-life balance

What these topics have in common is a lack of universal rules or fact-based principles to follow. Each person's actions are based on his or her values, skills, and appraisal of the situation. A coach can help clarify values, build skills, and improve the person's ability to appraise the situation accurately. In contrast, formal instruction and other training methods are often more effective for factual topics with clear rules or legal guidelines (such as history, finance, technology, science). Nonetheless, for virtually all topics, it is often helpful to differentiate acquisition of skills and knowledge from real-world application. It is often best to learn the principles and methods of a topic, whether finance, marketing, or leadership, through books, lectures, and case discussion. But coaching is a powerful tool for helping people apply in the real world what they have learned in the classroom. As a caveat, it is important to point out that coaching is rarely appropriate for therapeutic issues such as depression, substance abuse, or marital problems. Such topics are better handled through a company's employee assistance program (EAP) or other counseling providers.

Mentoring is particularly well-suited to transferring personal insights and wisdom about how to be successful in an organization and any areas requiring experience and seasoned judgment, such as ethics, integrity, organizational politics, and courageous leadership. Mentoring is particularly recommended for organizations seeking to do the following:

- Accelerate the career progress of underrepresented groups, whether based on ethnicity, gender, background, or even functional area.
- Transmit the culture and values to newer managers. Mentoring can even be used to help change the culture, if it selectively emphasizes a few of the most critical values.
- Pass on the accumulated wisdom of seasoned leaders, especially in areas where personal insight and sound judgment are essential.

People Most Likely to Benefit

Birkeland et al. (1997) found that the payoff from coaching was significantly greater for leaders who had been designated as having high potential than those deemed to be solid performers or at risk for derailment. Specifically, the high potentials received higher ratings on the amount of skill improvement from coaching and in their subsequent performance appraisals. Although there are many good reasons, as listed earlier, for offering coaching to a wide range of employees, organizations are advised to focus their efforts on high potential performers and highly valued employees in order to get the greatest return on their investments in coaching. Top priority candidates for coaching might be found among new promotions into critical roles; high potentials, especially from underrepresented populations; talented incumbents in roles with high failure rates; leaders responsible for major turnaround or change initiatives; highly valued employees where retention is an issue; and leaders facing difficult and unpredictable business challenges, such as managing mergers and acquisitions.

Designing an Individual Coaching Program

There are four major considerations in designing a coaching program for an individual: identifying the participant, selecting and orienting the coach, following a well-designed coaching process, and providing appropriate supports for learning.

Identifying the Participant

In addition to the general factors discussed in the preceding section, organizations are encouraged to develop specific criteria for determining who will receive coaching. One organization outlined a set of questions, including the following, that must be addressed before an individual can participate in coaching (Lawrence, 1998):

- Is there a genuine development need?
- Is that development need linked to business performance?
- Is the issue something the individual has control over, or is it symptomatic of a larger organizational problem that needs to be addressed on a broader scale?
- Is the person open to learning and feedback?
- Is the person motivated to change?
- Is coaching the most appropriate development option?

Selecting and Orienting the Coach

It is not unusual to hear requests such as "We want a coach who's been a manufacturing executive in the automobile industry, because that's the type of person he'll be coaching." This is a common pitfall: trying to match participants with coaches on the basis of similar backgrounds and experiences rather than on the coach's ability to help such a person. Instead of matching coaches and leaders according to surface similarities, two qualities are essential in the right coach.

Can the Coach Work Well with the Person?

It is important to make sure that the coach can relate to the person and the world that person lives in. Find out how well the coach has worked with others in similar situations by asking the following questions: (1) What kinds of people have you worked with? What results did you achieve? (2) Where do you do your best work? With what kinds of people and topics do you work best? (3) Who would you turn down and why? (The last question helps make sure the coach recognizes her own limits.)

How Effectively Can the Coach Help the Person Develop?

A coach should be able to walk a person through all the important steps of learning, as shown in the development pipeline. The following questions are useful in assessing a coach's approach to the learning process.

How will you determine what the person needs to work on? Evaluate how thoughtful and strategic the coach is in zeroing in on important issues. Pay attention to how coaches partner with others to plan the development priorities and process.

How will you help the person learn new ways to do things? The best coaches translate insights and good ideas into practical steps that build new capabilities and stronger performance in the real world.

How will you ensure they get results? Determine up front how coaches will help break old habits and put change into action. Find out what they will do to ensure what is learned is translated into real, sustainable change.

Once you have selected a coach, make sure that person understands the broader context, such as organizational culture and values, business environment, and strategic priorities. This background information will help ensure their coaching is more closely aligned with the organizational objectives. Discuss relevant ground rules and expectations with the coach as well, including confidentiality, communication, and involvement of other members of the team.

It is also worth examining the role of *internal* and *external* coaches. In the last few years, several organizations have hired professional coaches to serve full time. More often, internal coaches are human resource and organizational development professionals, or even managers who have some training or experience in coaching. External coaches are most appropriate in a few specific cases:

- When you need rapid learning and behavior change. Few organizations have internal coaches with the depth of skill and experience that is readily available among external coaches.
- For dealing with people who are resistant to change or who are cynical toward the coaching process. There is less risk if an external person fails as a coach.
- For relatively confidential or sensitive issues where the person does not want an internal person involved.

- When internal coaches are unavailable or in different locations.
- When internal coaches do not have the particular expertise that is desired.
- When an objective, independent viewpoint is critical.

In contrast, internal coaches are most appropriate in these cases:

- As part of regular, ongoing development activities, such as supporting a specific development program
- When deep knowledge of the personalities or relationships among a given cast of characters is important
- When knowledge of organizational politics or how things really get done inside the organization is critical

Following a Well-Designed Coaching Process

There are dozens of approaches to the coaching engagement itself, reflecting preferences for different assessment techniques, meeting formats (length of the coaching session and whether conducted in person, over the phone, or on-line), and philosophy of development. However, any well-designed coaching process should address the following issues.

Contracting

There are several aspects of contracting. The first focuses on the content, outlining the purpose of the coaching, establishing specific learning goals, and setting clear expectations for how and when performance will improve. The second is procedural, defining various stakeholders and their roles, as well as clarifying guidelines for confidentiality and communications.[3] Finally, contracting involves financial arrangements, such as fees, expenses, and billing schedules.

The contracting process often begins by identifying the key stakeholders, usually the coach, the person being coached, that person's superior boss or designated organizational sponsor, and the human resource contact. The coach should discuss expectations, roles, and responsibilities with each of them. For additional useful detail on the contracting process, consider *The Executive Coaching Handbook* (Executive Coaching Forum of Boston, 2000).

Coaching Sessions

So that everyone gets the most value for the time actually spent in coaching sessions, coaches should have a strategy for identifying what parts of the development pipeline are constrained and what actions will have the greatest impact. As a result, it is difficult to provide a standard outline of what the coaching sessions should look like. There are typically three parts:

The Opening. In the very first meeting the opening is a chance to clarify expectations, solidify the working agenda, and get to know each other. This may be the first time the coach and the participant meet face to face, although they have usually been in communication with each other in arranging the coaching process. The coach needs to pay particular attention to building trust and rapport by understanding what the person hopes to accomplish through coaching. In subsequent meetings, the first part of each session allows time to reestablish that rapport, catch up on what has happened since the last session, and prioritize the agenda for the day. The development pipeline issue of accountability is brought into play when the coach asks for a report on what the individual has done on her action plan from the preceding session.

Practice. The middle segment is the heart of the coaching engagement. Here, through hands-on practice of real-world situations, instruction, modeling, feedback, and discussion, the coach facilitates the kind of learning that participants can carry back with them.

Action Planning. This is often the most neglected aspect of learning. It is relatively easy for participants to leave each session with new insights and skills and a genuine motivation to put them into action. Without a specific plan, however, they are often sidetracked. We encourage participants to visualize exactly what will happen when they try to put a new behavior into action. When do they plan to do it? How will they remember to do it? What will get in their way? What will they do to stay on track? How will they evaluate the outcome of their new action? How will they get feedback from others? When will they try it again? How will they modify or build on what they tried the next time they use it?

Real-world practice and accountability, the fourth and fifth parts of the development pipeline, are also addressed by the two following activities.

On-the-Job Activities Between Sessions

Between coaching sessions, participants are expected to apply what they have learned. Attention to this is essential for breaking old habits and establishing new ones. Participants need to be encouraged to push their comfort zone on a daily basis. Similar to an exercise program, regular activity is necessary to ensure fitness. For development, meaningful progress can be made in most areas with just five minutes a day of practice (Peterson & Hicks, 1995).

Evaluation of Progress

It is often assumed that a multirater feedback instrument is a useful way to measure progress in coaching. But such instruments rarely provide the level of specificity needed to capture the true impact of coaching. If a formal process for evaluating progress is desired, then consider using a completely customized rating form based on the agreed-upon learning objectives for the person. Such a form should be used immediately at the outset of coaching to provide a behavioral baseline. Subsequently, the survey could be used at three-month intervals or as desired. This approach has the advantages of brevity and of zeroing in on the exact behaviors of interest. It can be filled out by the person, the coach, the person's manager, and any other key stakeholders. Such a method is described in detail by Peterson (1993a, 1993b).

A less formal process of evaluating progress is to discuss progress periodically with each of the stakeholders. We recommend that participants regularly seek feedback, encouragement, and support from their organizational sponsors and share their own perspective on what they have learned and what progress they are making. In addition to helping participants gauge their progress, this ensures that others are aware of their progress in areas they may not be able to observe directly.

Providing Supports for Learning

Coaching works best when it does not stand alone but rather is part of a broader, orchestrated process of learning. There are multiple accountabilities in ensuring the continuous growth of a leader. In some cases, assigning a coach can inadvertently lead to an abdication or easing of those responsibilities. Some managers may feel they are let off the hook; the coach is now responsible. Therefore it is important to outline clearly support roles to ensure that optimal learning takes place. The following recommendations to the person's manager, HR person, and any other organizational sponsors, will help enhance the impact of coaching.

- *Have clear expectations.* Even when expectations are clear at the outset, they frequently evolve over the coaching engagement. It is important to continue to communicate them.
- *Provide ongoing feedback.* It is important not to bombard the person with feedback at every opportunity, but periodic feedback is essential to work on how he is coming across. One of the best things sponsors can do is simply ask the person when and how he would like to discuss his progress and get feedback.
- *Encourage and support.* Learning new skills is often hard for managers, who are used to being competent and successful at most things they do. So it helps to provide encouragement and reinforcement simply for the effort they are putting into learning.
- *Give room to experiment, try new things, and make mistakes.* Anyone who works on significant new skills will use them awkwardly and inefficiently at first. Sometimes using new skills even leads to a temporary decrement in performance. It is important to give people the space they need to practice their new skills in real situations.

Designing an Organizational Coaching Program

In a survey of Global 1,000 organizations, fewer than 5 percent had any kind of systematic or coordinated approach to coaching (Peterson & Hicks, 1999). In fact, the use of coaching was so diffuse and decentralized that not one of those surveyed was willing even to estimate how much money his or her organization spent on coaching. Recently, however, organizations have realized the powerful role that coaching can play when channeled into supporting their strategic priorities. We are seeing a growing number of leading-edge corporations take steps to design a consistent process, target specific audiences and high-priority needs, and establish criteria for choosing an appropriate pool of coaches. Often, they see coaching as a focal point for introducing a new performance management process, accelerating organizational changes, or dealing with emerging priorities such as improving retention of key talent. This

to work with the coaches (including confidentiality, communications, and roles). The organization also holds periodic update meetings. Although these meetings are an additional cost, the group claims that the benefits, such as greater alignment between the coaches and organizational priorities, are well worth it.

Asking Coaches for Feedback

Either formally or informally, it is important to seek periodic feedback and input from coaches working inside your organization. For example, find out what they see as most effective techniques for working with your leaders, what they are learning about the organization and its talent, where they see gaps, and what else they might recommend.

Evaluating the Coaches' Performance

Based on the purpose of the coaching, identify who can most appropriately evaluate progress against the desired outcomes. For example, if the purpose is to enhance insight and personal effectiveness, the participant may be the ideal source. If the purpose is to improve performance, the participant and his or her superior might be interviewed. If the purpose is a broader strategic agenda, key stakeholders might rate the group's progress as a whole. Keep in mind that evaluation does not have to occur only at the end of the project. Regular monitoring can help you make midstream corrections that will ultimately lead to a better outcome.

Design the Process

The basic steps in the coaching process are outlined earlier and can be adapted relatively easily to a companywide program. One additional factor arises from the scope of such an endeavor: simply managing and administering the project. Like any other program, it is necessary to keep track of eligible candidates, actual participants, the pool of coaches, financial arrangements, and other details. If specific instruments or tools, such as multirater feedback, are used, they need to be coordinated smoothly. Several years ago, a coaching program being rolled out by a fast-paced Internet company failed miserably simply because its 360-degree survey process was so poorly implemented that participants gave up in frustration. In terms of other administrative tasks, you may want to track everyone's learning objectives, progress, and accomplishments. A further level of record-keeping entails tracking participants' progress in the organization for several years after their programs in order to determine the long-term impact of coaching.

A primary pitfall of large-scale coaching programs is building in too much standardization as a way to manage the process. Customization, one of the chief values of coaching, can be overshadowed by an organization's need for structure and consistency. For example, it is common for organizations to mandate multirater feedback. In one organization we worked with, several managers were required to complete a similar 360-degree feedback survey three times—once as part of a divisionwide development process, once as members of a high potential program, and yet again if they were interested in individual coaching. This kind of overkill ignores the principle that the coaching process should be customized to each person. Even when the organization wants to ensure minimum standards for consistency, the focus should be on general process and desired outcomes, not on a lockstep procedure. For example, it is important that people identify clear goals for their coaching, so the organization might require submitting a set of goals and a careful rationale. Such goals can be determined, however, by reflection and self-examination, personal interest, 360-degree feedback, management recommendations, organizational need, or by filling out a self-rating checklist against a relevant competency model. It is also important to realize that one's goals may change as a result of the coaching, and to allow for such an evolution.

The opposite end of the customization spectrum is reflected in the menu of coaching options put together by a leading telecommunications company for its general managers and vice presidents. As a result of an increasingly competitive landscape, senior executives were encouraging all members of this group to be more proactive about upgrading their skills. Their coaching menu includes such items as a multirater feedback and development planning session; a high impact program, where the coach works intensively with the person for several sessions over a six-week period; a skills coaching package, similar to a one-on-one training program, with a clearly defined learning objective; a leadership improvement package, which includes a broad-based leadership assessment and a long-term coaching relationship; an observation process, where the coach shadows the person as he engages in a number of important activities and then offer feedback, observations, and advice; and a "build-your-own" program where the manager sits down with a coach and designs a personalized coaching process from scratch.

A second potential pitfall for organizations is overengineering the beginning of the coaching program (matching coaches and participants, assessing needs, contracting) and then essentially neglecting the actual learning and change process that occurs during and between coaching sessions. This seems to happen because it is relatively easy to define key steps for gathering feedback and for writing objectives but far more difficult to quantify the steps in learning and applying a new skill. In order to provide better balance and drive the learning process to completion, organizations should strive to address each component of the necessary conditions for change as outlined in the development pipeline (Hicks & Peterson, 1999a). Druckman and Bjork (1991) raise a similar concern when they point out that most development programs tend to emphasize skill acquisition over skill application, even though skill application is the ultimate goal.[4]

In one example, Coleman (2000) falls prey to this pitfall. His presentation outlines a nine-step coaching process in which "regular meetings with the coachee" (p. 3) is just one step. The other eight steps clearly address the insight, motivation, and accountability sections of the development pipeline. In addition, he deals at length with how to manage the coaching relationship with the client. However, there is very little mention of how to help people sharpen their skills or acquire new capabilities, and nothing at all on how to transfer those skills to real-world practice. Unfortunately, Coleman is not alone in this regard.

Evaluate Outcomes

Finally, organizations should evaluate the impact of the coaching. We were surprised by our finding (Peterson & Hicks, 1999) that few organizations were measuring coaching outcomes. Those surveyed often described their belief that coaching was known to be effective, and that was sufficient. However, coaching can be used for a wide variety of objectives, and we encourage organizations to measure how effectively it is achieving their specific goals. For example, an important East Coast financial services firm was spending over a million dollars a year on coaching for its senior executives. When a new head of HR was appointed, she surveyed those who had participated in the process. Their response was unanimously positive. But when she surveyed the managers of those participants, they were rarely able to point to any observable outcomes. Our perspective is that if the coaching was intended as a retention strategy, it was effective. Participants found personal value and were pleased that the company was investing in them. But if the purpose of coaching was to improve performance, then it was less than successful. That was the conclusion of the new HR head, too, who promptly set up a new procedure for determining who would receive coaching and how it would be evaluated. One unintended but intriguing consequence was that several of the executives then negotiated for personal coaches as part of their executive compensation package.

Designing an Organizational Mentoring Program

Many of the considerations for implementing a mentoring program are similar to those for a coaching program, such as having a clear purpose, planning ahead for the tremendous administrative tasks involved in managing a project with many different players, and providing for ongoing evaluation of the process and its outcomes. However, there are several critical differences that warrant separate treatment.

First, most mentoring programs are staffed internally, usually by senior managers.[5] This necessitates different selection criteria for the mentors than for coaches. Primary considerations include these: having something important and useful to share with others, credibility inside the organization, willingness to spend time sharing their knowledge, and basic interpersonal and communications skills. Once selected, most mentors will benefit from training in active listening and other fundamental coaching skills.

Second, mentors usually benefit from having a clear road map to follow. Miller and Costantino (1999) emphasize that successful mentoring programs provide clear roles and expectations and follow well-established practices regarding how often to meet, what types of topics to discuss, and how to manage mentoring conversations.

Third, the reality in mentoring is that the protégé is more likely to be driving the process than the mentor or the two of them together. Participants need to understand their role in ensuring that the relationship continues in a productive fashion. Because mentors are essentially volunteers, they are more likely to continue their involvement if they get something out of the process and feel their time is well spent. It is essential to provide participants with guidelines on how to work the process—and make sure that the benefits are mutual—if organizations wish to see the program succeed. In fact, explicitly designing reciprocal mentoring programs is a growing trend.

In essence, these last two points suggest that mentoring programs should begin with separate workshops for training mentors to be effective coaches and for training participants to be effective self-guided learners and partners in the mentoring process. Further, providing them with ongoing support is critical. Grewe and Lassiter (2000) used regular communications, including follow-up phone calls and monthly e-mail newsletters, to answer questions that would arise. Regular meetings between participants and between mentors provide a vehicle for maintaining focus and allowing people to share what they are learning with others.

Finally, one-on-one conversations, so integral to the coaching engagement, are rarely the primary way that people benefit from mentoring. It is common for organizations to design mentoring programs that recommend a two-hour meeting each month. One of the most common reasons that mentoring programs fail is that mentors find it too difficult to keep these regular time commitments. In personal conversations with participants in mentor programs, they often cite exposure to senior management activities as one of the primary benefits of working with a mentor several levels above them in the organization. Being able to shadow a mentor through significant events in their work lives, and then discuss them afterwards, has a dramatic impact on learning. For example, one marketing manager was given the opportunity to attend a worldwide meeting of her company's top executives. She was impressed with their intense focus on financial metrics and what she described as mundane operational issues. She walked away with much greater insight into how she could focus her own activities to add more value to the company. Certainly, mentoring participants can benefit from many types of activities, but our suggestion is to focus the mentoring on broader exposure and the ensuing dialogue about real-time issues.

Conclusion

Until science allows us to download new capabilities directly into people—as depicted in the movie *The Matrix*—coaching and mentoring are arguably the best methods we have for helping people learn. In fact, coaching and mentoring are ideally suited to today's times. In a world where many leaders are hungry for learning, overwhelmed with their workload, and confronted by new challenges every day, coaching provides

- Highly efficient, just-in-time learning for managers who never have enough time
- Practical, real-world solutions for people confronted by new challenges every day
- A safe, supportive environment where it is acceptable to take risks and try new things
- A caring, supportive relationship that allows people to explore difficult issues and ask tough questions about what is really important

Although coaching and mentoring often require significant investment in time, money, and energy, the substantial returns (Birkeland et al., 1997; Manchester Consulting, 2000; Peterson, 1993) clearly warrant the expenditure whenever better performance is critical to organizational success. And because talent has become the most critical variable for many organizations, those that excel at coaching and mentoring are most likely to thrive.

Notes
1. No widely accepted definition of coaching and mentoring has yet emerged (Peterson & Hicks, 1999). I often advise clients not to worry about the terminology and simply use the language that makes the most sense in their organization. Then, regardless of the label, focus on helping people gain insight, enhance their capabilities, and improve their performance.
2. See Peterson (1996) for a case study of the coaching process and the resulting benefits for one individual, featuring commentary from her performance appraisals immediately before and after her coaching experience.

3. My personal recommendation regarding confidentiality is for the coaching process to be as open as possible, similar to how we might view a person attending a workshop or a university program. Of course, legal and professional standards must be followed, such as those involving psychological instrumentation and assessment results. In addition, it is critical to respect the client's desire for confidentiality on specific topics. Beyond those areas, I encourage people to talk openly about their coaching objectives and their own progress. This demonstrates a genuine commitment and facilitates additional feedback that is essential to effective learning.

4. Chapter Three in their book (Druckman & Bjork, 1991) is highly recommended for its excellent distillation of research on the techniques that actually facilitate transfer and generalization of new skills.

5. With the rise of the Internet, questions about how to manage Generation X, and concerns about retaining and advancing individuals who are members of minority groups, several organizations have reported an increasing use of younger mentors to coach older managers. Nostrand (2000) uses the term *reverse mentoring* to describe Procter & Gamble's program, which provides female mentors to more seasoned male managers.

References

Birkeland, S., Davis, B., Goff, M., Campbell, J., & Duke, C. (1997). *AMOCO individual coaching study.* Unpublished research report, Personnel Decisions International, Minneapolis.

Burke, M. J., & Day, R. R. (1986). A cumulative study of the effectiveness of managerial training. *Journal of Applied Psychology, 71,* 232–246.

Coleman, D. (2000, May). *Principles and guidelines for practitioners: A coach's lessons learned.* Paper presented at the Linkage Coaching and Mentoring Conference, Chicago.

Curtis, R. C., & Stricker, G. (Eds.). (1991). *How people change: Inside and outside therapy.* New York: Plenum Press.

Davis, B. L., & Petchenik, L. (1998). *Measuring the value of coaching at Amoco.* Paper presented at the Linkage Coaching and Mentoring Conference, Washington, DC.

Druckman, D., & Bjork, R. A. (Eds.). (1991). *In the mind's eye: Enhancing human performance.* Washington, DC: National Academy Press.

Executive Coaching Forum of Boston. (2000). *The executive coaching handbook: Principles and guidelines for a successful coaching partnership.* Boston: Executive Coaching Forum of Boston.

Fisher, A. (2001, February 19). Executive coaching: With returns a CFO could love. *Fortune,* p. 250.

Grewe, B., & Lassiter, G. B. (2000, May). *The Seagate Technologies executive mentor program.* Paper presented at the Linkage Coaching and Mentoring Conference, Chicago.

Hellervik, L. W., Hazucha, J. F., & Schneider, R. J. (1992). Behavior change: Models, methods, and a review of the evidence. In M. D. Dunnette & L. M. Hough (Eds.), *Handbook of industrial and organizational psychology* (2nd ed., Vol. 3). Palo Alto, CA: Consulting Psychologists Press.

Hicks, M. D., & Peterson, D. B. (1997). Just enough to be dangerous: The rest of what you need to know about development. *Consulting Psychology Journal, 49*(3), 171–193.

Hicks, M. D., & Peterson, D. B. (1999a). The development pipeline: How people really learn. *Knowledge Management Review, 9,* 30–33.

Hicks, M. D., & Peterson, D. B. (1999b). Leaders coaching across borders. In W. H. Mobley, M. J. Gessner, & V. J. Arnold (Eds.), *Advances in global leadership* (Vol. 1, pp. 295–314). Greenwich, CT: JAI Press.

Jellison, J. M. (1993). *Overcoming resistance.* New York: Simon & Schuster.

Kaplan, R. E. (1991). *Beyond ambition.* San Francisco: Jossey-Bass.

Kilburg, R. R. (1996). Toward a conceptual understanding and definition of executive coaching. *Consulting Psychology Journal, 48*(2), pp. 134–144.

Kilburg, R. R. (2000). *Executive coaching: Developing managerial wisdom in a world of chaos.* Washington, DC: American Psychological Association.

Lawrence, C. (1998). Using executive coaching to accelerate just-in-time learning at Fidelity Investments. Paper presented at *Fast Development for Fast Companies,* Personnel Decisions International, San Francisco.

Lombardo, M., & Eichinger, R. (1989). *Preventing derailment: What to do before it's too late.* (Technical Report No. 138). Greensboro, NC: Center for Creative Leadership.

Mahoney, M. J. (1991). *Human change processes: The scientific foundations of psychotherapy.* New York: Basic Books.

Manchester Consulting. (2000). *Return on investment for executive coaching process.* Unpublished research report.

Miller, P., & Costantino, R. (1999, April). *A grassroots approach to corporate mentoring: Developing and implementing a formal mentoring system.* Paper presented at Linkage Coaching and Mentoring Conference, Boston.

Nostrand, K. (2000, May). *Retaining women through Procter & Gamble's "mentoring up" program.* Paper presented at the Linkage Coaching and Mentoring Conference, Chicago.

Orlinsky, D. E., & Howard, K. I. (1986). Process and outcome in psychotherapy. In S. L. Garfield & A. E. Bergin (Eds.). *Handbook of psychotherapy and behavior change* (3rd ed.). New York: HarperCollins.

Peterson, D. B. (1993a). *Measuring change: A psychometric approach to evaluating individual coaching outcomes.* Paper presented at the annual conference of the Society for Industrial and Organizational Psychology, San Francisco.

Peterson, D. B. (1993b). *Skill learning and behavior change in an individually tailored management coaching and training program.* Unpublished doctoral dissertation, University of Minnesota, Minneapolis.

Peterson, D. B. (1996). Executive coaching at work: The art of one-on-one change. *Consulting Psychology Journal, 48*(2), 78–86.

Peterson, D. B. (2001, April). *Psychological science and executive coaching: Are we neglecting our secret weapon?* Paper presented at the annual conference of the Society for Industrial and Organizational Psychology, San Diego.

Peterson, D. B., & Hicks, M. D. (1995). *Development FIRST: Strategies for self-development.* Minneapolis: Personnel Decisions International.

Peterson, D. B., & Hicks, M. D. (1996). *Leader as coach: Strategies for coaching and developing others.* Minneapolis: Personnel Decisions International.

Peterson, D. B., & Hicks, M. D. (1999, February). *The art and practice of executive coaching.* Paper presented at the annual conference of the Division of Consulting Psychology, Phoenix.

Peterson, D. B., & Hicks, M. D. (2000). Unleashing talent. *Executive Excellence, 17*(6), 7–8.

Prochaska, J. O., DiClemente, C. C., & Norcross, J. C. (1992). In search of how people change: Applications to addictive behaviors. *American Psychologist, 47,* 1102–1114.

Prochaska, J. O., Norcross, J. C., & DiClemente, C. C. (1994). *Changing for good.* New York: William Morrow.

Seligman, M.E.P., & Csikszentmihalyi, M. (Eds.) (2000). Positive psychology [special issue]. *American Psychologist, 55*(1).

Sloan, E. B. (2001). *The contribution of university-based executive education to corporate executive talent management results.* Joint research project conducted by the International University Consortium for Executive Education (UNICON) and Personnel Decisions International. Minneapolis: Personnel Decisions International.

Thompson, A. D., Jr. (1986). *A formative evaluation of an individualized coaching program for business managers and professionals.* Unpublished doctoral dissertation, University of Minnesota, Minneapolis.

Whitworth, L., Kimsey-House, H., & Sandahl, P. (1998). *Co-active coaching: New skills for coaching people toward success in work and life.* Palo Alto, CA: Davies-Black.

CHAPTER 7

Using Computer Technology in Training
Building an Infrastructure for Active Learning
Kenneth G. Brown, J. Kevin Ford

"How technological capabilities are utilized is more critical than the capabilities themselves. Simply put, more is not necessarily better. Designers must be aware of the cognitive demands their systems place on learners and thoughtfully apply techniques that support, not interfere with, learner effort. . . . It is far easier to create something with great cosmetic appeal than an integrated learning system that is consistent with available research and theory" (Hannafin, Hannafin, Hooper, Rieber, & Kini, 1996, p. 391).

Recent evidence suggests there has been a dramatic shift away from instructor-led, classroom training toward learner-centered, technology-mediated training. Based on benchmark data from the American Society of Training and Development, Bassi and Van Buren (1999) predict that companies will have reduced classroom training nearly 20 percent between 1997 and 2000, with much of that time converted to training delivered via CD-ROMs, intranets, or the Internet. Although each learning technology has some unique features, they all use computers to deliver training. Thus, computer-based training, in its many forms, is the future of training—and the future has arrived.

The appeal to managers of delivering training by computer is that it has considerable potential to streamline the learning process. Trainees do not have to coordinate their schedules with a trainer and other learners; they can learn when they want to. They do not have to take courses whenever they are offered but rather can learn "just in time." And finally, they do not have to leave work to gain knowledge but can receive the instruction they need on-site. The presumed result is individualization of learning that increases efficiency and reduces costs.

Although there is some evidence that computer-based training can reduce long-term training costs for certain courses (for example, Hall, 1997) and reduce training time for learners (Kulik & Kulik, 1991), lingering questions about how to implement it effectively in organizations remain. Most of the literature on computer-based learning has focused on the technology (interface, navigation, and screen design) without making in-depth investigations of learning processes and outcomes (Montazemi & Wang, 1995; Yang & Moore, 1995). In addition, most of the research on computer-based learning has been conducted with elementary, secondary, or college students (Bates, Holton, & Syler, 1996). Therefore, the question remains how computer-based training can live up to the promise of individualized learning in the workplace.

Clearly, the effectiveness of this type of training will depend in large part on the way it is used. Most authors agree that the most powerful influence on learning from instructional technologies like computers is not the nature of the technology itself but what is delivered with it (Binder, 1989; Clark, 1994; Lanza, 1991). In other words, poorly designed training will not stimulate and support learning no matter how appealing or expensive the technology used. As a result, it is imperative that the growth in computer-based training be matched by a greater understanding of how to use technology in order to support learning.

The individualized nature of computer-based training calls for the development of design and delivery principles that expand on the ones derived from traditional classroom instruction (see Brown, Ford, & Milner, 1998). Although active rather than passive learning is clearly important for effective instruction in both classroom settings and computer-based training, there is an important distinction. In computer-based instruction, the designer must consider the choices learners might value and find engaging so they will become active participants in their own learning experience. Everything that can be done to motivate them to be active learners has to be determined and programmed in ahead of time. In classroom instruction, the instructor can customize the design to better meet learner needs at the time learning is taking place, based on feedback from them. Thus in classroom instruction the instructor and the trainees share the responsibility for making sure the training is worthwhile and engaging. In contrast, once the computer program is set up, the burden for active learning switches to the learner.

Attention to important learner characteristics must be built into the technology so that both designer and learner efforts to individualize training facilitate, rather than hinder, learning. In particular, with learners involved in making important decisions about what to learn, principles must address how to encourage them to make choices that enhance rather than detract from their learning experience. In computer-based instruction, learners need to be led (or perhaps coaxed) into taking an active role in their own development. The purpose of this chapter is to distill knowledge about how to design computer-based instruction so that it facilitates active learning among trainees. We examine the existing conceptual and empirical literature on how to stimulate active learning in computer-based instruction and, in the process, increase the desired training outcomes.

This chapter defines computer-based training as text, graphics, and/or animation presented via computer for the express purpose of teaching job-relevant knowledge and skills. This definition includes training that previously has been given many different labels, including computer-based instruction, computer-aided instruction, multimedia learning environments, Internet-based instruction, Web-based instruction, and more recently, e-learning (for example, Kiser, 1999). Many of the technical distinctions that underlie these terms are transparent to the learner, such as where the bulk of the program and data reside and how easily they can be updated. In other words, from a learning perspective, the differences between these technologies are often negligible. The key instructional feature they share, and the focal point of our review and guidelines, is individualization of the learning experience. The intent of this chapter is to present empirically derived guidelines for how to use this feature of computers to design effective learning experiences.

Bassi and Van Buren (1999) clearly indicate that the greatest growth in instructional technology has occurred in Web-delivered and CD-ROM formats. Therefore, we restricted our focus to these two technologies. Our review did not include other computer-mediated technologies such as full-scale simulations (Salas, Bowers, & Rhodenizer, 1998), virtual reality training (for example, Steele-Johnson & Hyde, 1997), or intelligent tutoring systems (for example, Burns & Parlett, 1991).

The chapter includes three broad sections. First, we present and describe the components of an input-process-output model of learning that depicts how computer technology learning principles influence learner states and learning outcomes. Second, we present guidelines for effective design and delivery of computer-based instruction organized around four themes. Third, we move past design issues to consider practical issues that affect the appropriateness of computer-based training, how to select a vendor, and what to emphasize during formative evaluation of a computer-based instruction program.

A Model of Learning

Training research and practice have been criticized for being atheoretical (Campbell, 1988) and failing to attend to relevant knowledge regarding learning and instruction (Campbell, 1989). Despite some progress on these fronts (see Ford, 1997), many training approaches continue to treat learning as a "black box" between the implementation of a training program and the measures used to evaluate it. For example, studies about training design often compare alternative interventions for their influence on a range of outcome variables without assessing what learners actually think, do, or feel as they progress through the training (Bretz & Thompsett, 1992; Simon & Werner, 1996). To remedy this limitation and ensure that training design has a foundation in learning theory, we present a model of learning that depicts the process by which design influences learning.

This model, presented as Figure 7.1, is organized as an input-process-output model of learning. The inputs to this model are the computer-based instruction technologies of the Internet and CD-ROM or multimedia. For these training technologies to be effective, they must stimulate learners to participate actively in their own learning. The three active learning states listed in the model represent the key psychological processes that must be affected through the design of the computer-based instruction. When Internet and CD-ROM programs are designed to elicit mastery-oriented, mindful, and motivated learning, the result will be positive changes in learner outcomes. The components of the model, starting from the goal of enhancing learning and moving backward to the learning states, are described in the following paragraphs.

Learning Outcomes

Kraiger, Ford, and Salas (1993) proposed a three-part model of learning outcomes: cognitive, skill-based, and affective. Each is a distinct and important element of learning.

Cognitive Outcomes

Cognitive outcomes refer to variables capturing the quantity and type of knowledge as well as the relationships among knowledge elements. Three types of knowledge are included in this category: verbal information, knowledge organization, and cognitive strategies.

The first type of knowledge, verbal information, is also called declarative knowledge. Declarative knowledge is information about

Figure 7.1. An Input-Process-Output Model of Learning.

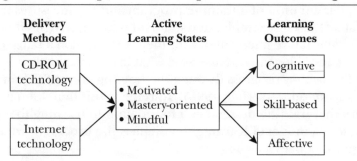

topics and ideas that is stored in the memory, available for retrieval in the form of spoken or written communication. For example, customer service representatives in the banking industry must know the features of the products offered by their bank. Being able to recite these features would demonstrate their verbal knowledge. The second type of knowledge, knowledge organization, refers to the mental connections or links that learners hold with regard to their declarative knowledge. Rouse and Morris (1986) use the term *mental models* to describe knowledge organization, and they suggest that these models describe functions of tasks, explain integration of tasks, and anticipate future task requirements. Returning to the example, a customer service representative who could explain how products are related would be displaying evidence of knowledge organization. The third type of knowledge is cognitive strategies, which refers to methods trainees use to control their own cognition. Recent research has emphasized the importance of metacognition as a general cognitive strategy. Metacognition is knowledge of and control over one's cognition (Flavell, 1979). When a customer poses a problem to a customer service representative, that representative would display metacognition by recognizing the limits of her own knowledge and seeking outside help to solve the customer's problem. As discussed by Kraiger, Ford, and Salas (1993), each of these cognitive outcomes is an important element of effective task performance. Compared to a novice or a poor performer, an expert customer service representative would possess a greater store of verbal information about products and customers, more well-organized knowledge, and the capacity to recognize his or her own strengths and weaknesses with regard to that knowledge.

Skill-Based Outcomes

Skill-based outcomes concern the development of technical or motor skills (Gagne, Briggs, & Wager, 1992). Theories of skill development posit that trainees move from initial skill acquisition, where knowledge is largely declarative, toward skill automaticity, where knowledge becomes proceduralized (Anderson, 1982; Fitts & Posner, 1967).

Procedural knowledge entails integrating discrete steps into a single act, freeing up the individual's attention to perform other tasks. Procedural knowledge enables faster, less error-prone performance than declarative knowledge. Individuals with proceduralized knowledge are more likely to detect the appropriate situations for using a skill and to individualize skill acts to situational demands. As anyone who has taught a teenager to drive would agree, the best drivers have moved beyond declarative knowledge (that is, possessing knowledge about the rules of the road) to procedural knowledge (that is, possessing skills necessary to obey those rules).

Affective Outcomes

Affective outcomes are values, attitudes, or beliefs that may develop or change as a result of training. Kraiger, Ford, and Salas (1993) suggest that organizational commitment (that is, identification with an organization and desire to maintain membership) or norm-related beliefs (understanding what is appropriate and inappropriate behavior) may be important outcomes for particular programs. Similarly, some training programs may seek to change personal values, so that success would be defined when learners develop deeply held convictions about the training topic. For example, the express purpose of a safety training program would be to increase the value trainees place on personal responsibility at work.

Kraiger, Ford, and Salas (1993) include motivational outcomes such as self-efficacy in this category of outcomes. Self-efficacy is technically defined as a judgment of capability to organize and execute courses of action to attain particular types of performance. More concisely, it is confidence that a task can be performed effectively. Research supports the importance of self-efficacy as an attitudinal outcome because of its predictive power for subsequent behavior (see Bandura, 1997). Specifically in the training context, posttraining self-efficacy has been found to predict skill generalization (Ford, Smith, Weissbein, Gully, & Salas, 1998; Kozlowski et al., 2001) and attempts at transfer (Ford, Quiñones, Sego, & Sorra, 1992). Thus, for example, learners who leave sales training confident that they can use techniques learned will be most likely actually to attempt those behaviors during a sales encounter.

Active Learning States

In computer-based training the learner is a critical intermediary between training features and training outcomes. In other words, the activities and choices of the learner are the most powerful and immediate determinants of cognitive, skill-based, and affective learning outcomes. The learner must be an active participant in training or none of the desired outcomes will be achieved. Thus, the concept of active learning is central to understanding whether learning will occur. We suggest that active learning involves the presence of three related psychological states in the learner: motivation, mastery orientation, and mindfulness. Each of these states is explained as follows.

Motivation

The level of an individual's motivation during training is predictive of a number of outcomes, such as the declarative and procedural knowledge gained from training (Colquitt, LePine, & Noe, 2000; Noe & Colquitt, Chapter Three, this volume). The issue of trainee motivation becomes more complex when the medium over which material is transmitted is the computer. Nevertheless, we have a rich source of data on factors affecting trainee motivation that is relevant to improving the effectiveness of computer-based instruction.

In general, motivated learners have been found to hold two beliefs: if they make an effort during training it will result in learning, and the material they learn will be useful for achieving valued outcomes back on the job. The first belief, that effort will result in learning, is not as clearly emphasized in ISD models but has extensive support in both theoretical and empirical literature. Expectancy theory emphasizes that in addition to utility perceptions, confidence that effort will result in desired performance is an important determinant of motivational force. Empirically, this idea has been studied as pretraining self-efficacy or learning self-efficacy. For example, Warr and Bunce (1995) demonstrated that people with higher learning self-efficacy gained more knowledge from a training program than people with lower self-efficacy. Similarly, Phillips and Gully (1997) demonstrated that higher self-efficacy improves learning even when general cognitive ability and relevant personality characteristics are controlled. Thus, to date, research strongly supports the contention that learners who believe that their efforts will pay off in learning, and that their learning will pay off back on the job, will gain more knowledge and skill than learners who do not hold these beliefs.

Many models of instructional design indicate the importance of the second belief when they indicate that interest in and attention to training material is essential for learning (for example, Dick & Carey, 1996; Gagne, Briggs, & Wager, 1992). There is extensive theoretical and empirical support for the importance of this belief. For example, expectancy theory suggests that the motivating force for particular choices derives in large part from perceptions of the utility of that choice. Individuals are more likely to pursue choices and make an effort when they believe valued outcomes will result (Vroom, 1964). Empirical support for the importance of utility perceptions can be found in research demonstrating that beliefs in the value of training are highly correlated with specific motivation to do well in that training (Alliger, Tannenbaum, Bennett, Traver, & Shotland, 1997; Warr & Bunce, 1995).

Mastery Orientation

Believing in one's ability to learn and the importance of learning is not sufficient for active learning; the orientation that learners take to the learning situation is also critical. Research has identified different approaches that learners may take. A mastery-oriented approach coincides with a belief that ability can be improved and mistakes are attributable to effort. Learners with this belief are persistent during learning, persevering through challenges. In contrast, a performance-oriented approach involves a belief that ability is fixed and mistakes are attributable to ability. These learners are sensitive to feedback, which may lead them to stop making an effort after a challenge (Dweck, 1986; Farr, Hofmann, & Ringenbach, 1993). Although some research suggests that there is a dispositional component to the orientation adopted by a learner (Meece, Blumenfeld, & Hoyle, 1988), there is sufficient evidence to suggest that situational features, such as the design features of instruction, influence the orientation adopted (Kozlowski et al., 2001; Stevens & Gist, 1997).

Research has shown that learners with high mastery orientation make a greater effort in learning and develop higher self-efficacy than learners with low mastery orientation. For example, Fisher and Ford (1998) found that those with greater mastery orientation focused their attention more and exerted more effort in the training task. Kozlowski et al. (2001), Ford, Smith, Weissbein, Gully, and Salas (1998), and Phillips and Gully (1997) demonstrated that higher mastery orientation resulted in higher self-efficacy. Similarly, Brett and VandeWalle (1999) demonstrated that learners seeking to improve their skill performed better at the end of training than those seeking to prove their ability or avoid appearing incompetent. Kozlowski et al. (2001) provided evidence that learners who were oriented toward learning key task concepts (as opposed to performing well) showed evidence of better knowledge organization. Consequently, learners who adopt a mastery-oriented approach to training are much more likely to strive consistently throughout training to master the material, and as a result will have better cognitive, skill-based, and affective training outcomes.

Mindfulness

Mindfulness is a concept borrowed from the information processing literature. It refers to the deliberate and systematic process of making a cognitive effort to evaluate information and integrate it with previous knowledge (for example, Beach & Mitchell, 1978). Processing characteristics opposite to mindfulness have been described as automatic, shallow, mindless, schema-driven, and peripheral (for example, Petty & Cacioppo, 1986). In automatic processing, simple decision rules are used rather than thorough analysis of information. An example would be a learner reading material for a case and going through the motions of choosing an action without giving it much thought. The learner may proceed until the "correct answer" is obtained in order to finish quickly. Mindful processing, in contrast, suggests that the learner makes an effort to engage the material during the learning process. In this case, the learner would read the case material carefully and thoughtfully and spend considerable time and effort gaining an understanding of the content. This learner would deliberate before selecting answers to case-related questions. This capacity for the self-regulation of learning means that a learner devotes effort to planning, monitoring, and evaluating his own progress (Ford & Schmitt, 2000). In planning, the learner analyzes a learning situation such as computer-based instruction and determines what strategy is likely to lead to successful acquisition of trained knowledge and skills. In monitoring, learners make active attempts to track their allocation of attention as well as gauge how well they are comprehending material. In evaluating, the learners actively assess their success in knowledge and skill acquisition and their likelihood of successfully transferring the learned skills to the job. Greater planning, monitoring, and self-evaluation has been demonstrated empirically to increase knowledge (Fisher & Ford, 1998) and skill (Kanfer & Ackerman, 1989) acquisition.

Interrelationships Among Action Learning States

These psychological states are not independent of each other. Research has indicated that mastery-oriented learners are more likely to engage in mindful processing of information (Fisher & Ford, 1998; Meece, Blumenfeld, & Hoyle, 1988). Similarly, it seems likely that learners who see utility in the training content will be more likely to adopt a mastery-oriented approach. In all likelihood, these are reciprocal states that reinforce each other over time. In total, when all three states are present, learners are engaged and willing to make a considerable effort to improve their knowledge. This is the essence of active learning, and stimulating it is the most critical issue in building effective computer-based training. The following section presents key design and delivery learning principles and guidelines specifically targeted to increase active learning.

Emerging Design Factors for New Training Technologies

Based on considerable research on factors affecting learning, principles and guidelines for effective design and delivery have been developed (for example, Dick & Carey, 1996; Gagne, Briggs, & Wager, 1992). A principle is an underlying truth about a phenomenon, in this case about learning and instruction. Guidelines are specific steps that can be taken to improve instruction that are consistent with the learning principles (see Salas, Cannon-Bowers, & Blickensderfer, 1997).

The commonly accepted design principles of today are largely predicated on traditional classroom delivery, which uses a structured and sequenced learning environment for helping learners master training content. For example, training design research stresses that instructional events should be sequenced to mirror the developmental process—that trainers should take trainees through successive approximations of mastery by presenting learnable knowledge increments that always build on their prior level of understanding (Annett, 1991). Feedback research suggests that correct behavior should be reinforced and that feedback should be frequent and specific (Gopher, Weil, & Siegal, 1989). Thus, two design principles from traditional research are to provide developmentally appropriate material that builds on prior understanding and to provide frequent and specific feedback following training activities. Current delivery principles have focused on the role of the instructor in the traditional classroom. For example, classroom management principles focus on the role of the instructor in managing training time so that most of it is spent in learning. Thus training can be made more efficient by preparing, establishing rules at the beginning of training, and pacing lessons and making transitions smoothly (Brophy & Good, 1986). The instructor also informs trainees of the lesson objectives, describes the behaviors that will be tested or required, and provides timely feedback to questions so that trainees can understand the material and successfully complete the course (Borich, 1989).

These principles of effective design and delivery are relevant to computer-based training. For example, designers of computer-delivered instruction must consider issues of sequencing and feedback. But there are also important differences between classroom and computer-based instruction that have implications for the relevance of particular principles. The first difference is that classroom instruction is inherently group-focused and normative. Because of the instructor's central role and limited availability, classroom training is usually targeted to average learners in a projected distribution of participants. Instruction is designed based on an understanding of how to move most individuals in a group toward desired training outcomes. In contrast, with emerging training technologies, training can be customized to meet individual needs. This means that training must be designed with a greater emphasis on understanding the knowledge and skill needs of particular learners. In addition, learners can be given options relevant to the type of feedback that is available to ensure that learning is occurring. In this way, individuals can choose the type of feedback desired at various points in the learning process.

The second difference is that, rather than a structured experience led by an instructor, computer-based instruction puts control of the training in the hands of the learners. Learners structure and guide their own learning. In such environments, learners, in partnership with computer programs, become their own trainers through the choices they make on the content they focus on, the sequence of their learning, and the learning strategies they invoke.

The features of customization and learner control are in some sense opposite sides of the same coin. The key instructional feature of computer-based training is that it offers the potential to individualize learning experiences based on the desires, abilities, experiences, and ongoing activities of learners. Customization, as it has been discussed here, represents *designers'* efforts to build programs that modify elements of instruction based on important learner characteristics. Learner control, in contrast, represents efforts by *learners* to modify the training for their own purposes. Thus, fundamentally, computer-based training is designed to be adaptive to individual learners.

To identify emerging design principles particularly relevant to computer-based instruction, we reviewed empirical, theoretical, and practice literatures on the design and delivery of computer-based instruction and training. Searches of PsycInfo and ERIC databases and reference sections from selected articles were used to identify potential articles. More than one hundred articles and books were screened for consideration in the creation of design and delivery principles. Preference was given to straightforward conclusions from empirical studies. Articles that simply echoed other authors' suggestions were eliminated. In the end, sixty-six articles and book chapters were included in our analysis.

Summaries of each paper were written and key design and delivery principles distilled. For empirical articles, normative prescriptions implied by the study findings were noted. For conceptual and practical papers, the advice suggested by the researchers was summarized. The principles were identified and categorized as a way of translating empirical and conceptual research into practical guidance about training design and delivery (see Salas, Cannon-Bowers, & Blickensderfer, 1997, for a similar approach). The principles and guidelines discussed in this chapter focus on training design characteristics with the potential for direct and powerful influence on learning outcomes.

From these sixty-six studies we generated four themes for effective technology-mediated training design and delivery. These are specific to computer-based platforms and are offered in addition to principles and guidelines for traditional instructional settings. The four key thematic areas are information structure and presentation, learner control and guidance, learning activities and feedback, and metacognitive monitoring and control. Each principle encourages active learning on the part of the trainee. For each principle a number of design and delivery guidelines were identified.

Information Structure and Presentation

Computer-based training offers considerable freedom in how training material is structured and presented. This freedom can be used effectively by training designers to motivate learners and stimulate mindful engagement, or it can be misused to overwhelm and confuse. This section examines research to develop guidelines that ensure training structures and presents information in a way that supports rather than interferes with active learning. This section focuses on three relatively independent design elements for structure and presentation: structure of the materials, user interface, and form of presentation.

Structure of the Materials
The first issue to consider in developing a supportive learning architecture is how to structure the material. For the purposes of this discussion, structure refers to both how the material is organized into chunks of information and how that information is connected together. Much has been written on the topic of organizing material for delivery by computer systems. Most authors agree that material should be organized in small, meaningful chunks of related information or "nodes" (Binder, 1989; Kearsley, 1988; Kommers, Grabinger, & Dunlap, 1996; Yang & Moore, 1995). This type of structure requires modularizing the material into self-contained sections that deal with a single meaningful idea or concept (Lanza, 1991; MacLachlan, 1986; Park & Hannafin, 1993). Decisions about how to modularize material should be driven by the objectives of the training and the nature of the content. For example, a system designed to teach a problem-solving process might have nodes represent major steps (or substeps) in this process, whereas a system

designed to teach a concept might have nodes organized around important elements and examples of the concept. Failing to organize materials into manageable nodes can result in material that is overwhelming and confusing to the learner.

Nodes must be connected or "linked" in a manner that facilitates active learning. Generally speaking, nodes should be connected according to the objectives of training and the nature of the content. For example, if the intent of training is to develop cognitive strategies such as troubleshooting or problem solving, then providing less structure to the connections among nodes may slow learner progress initially but ultimately facilitate development of these skills (Gall & Hannafin, 1994). For training designed to facilitate verbal knowledge and knowledge organization, hierarchical structures with default paths may be most useful. Hierarchical structures place nodes into sequences that clearly indicate the relationship and relative importance of nodes to each other. Default paths are suggested sequences of nodes for learners to follow. Hierarchical structures convey meaningful information about the task domain and may help to improve knowledge organization. In addition, learners can skip over material linked to a node that they are familiar with but go into more depth on nodes where the linked information is new. Thus, linking hierarchically can help to accommodate differences in prior knowledge (Park & Hannafin, 1993) while maintaining motivation and enhancing mindful engagement.

A potentially powerful feature of Web-based and Internet-based training is the capability to provide links to material that elaborates on the training material. Elaborative links can be very useful but they can also dilute the trainees' efforts because they may focus on material that is not central to the training objectives. In addition, these links can disorient trainees if they have difficulty returning to the point where they initiated the elaborative effort. Therefore, elaborative links should be used only for the material that is important in training (Binder, 1989; Cates, 1992; Gall & Hannafin, 1994), and learners should be able quickly and easily to return to their original position in the training materials.

Research has demonstrated learning benefits for providing outlines of the structure to learners prior to learning. For example, Kiewra, Kauffman, Robinson, Dubois, and Staley (1999) demonstrated that providing either an outline or another form of organizational information improved relational learning when compared to text-only presentations. Research on advance organizers, or structuring information presented prior to training, supports the positive effects of providing structural information to learners (for example, Kraiger, Salas, & Cannon-Bowers, 1995). Presumably, such structure provides valuable information about the nature of the connections in the material to be learned.

User Interface

The second issue to consider about information presentation is the user interface. A concept that is central to this area is working memory. Working memory is short-term memory that contains readily accessible information. An important feature of working memory is that it is limited, a fact that has been understood for more than a century (Miller, 1956). An analogy often used to understand the functioning of working memory is that of a fixed pool of "attention resources" that can be divided among mental activities that an individual is performing (Howell & Cooke, 1989; Kahneman, 1973; Kanfer & Ackerman, 1989; Wickens, 1984). Mayer (1997) emphasizes that learning usually occurs when individuals retain and organize information in working memory storage. When working memory is taken up with mental activities unrelated to the material being learned, such as when learners think about off-task topics or ruminate over how to get the computer to show particular types of information, learning is hindered (for example, Kanfer & Ackerman, 1989). It is in this light that the Hannafin et al. (1996) quote at the start of this chapter was offered, "Designers must be aware of the cognitive demands their systems place on learners." Learning architectures that support learning ensure that working memory is reserved for training material. In other words, designers seek to build training so that using the interface demands as little attention as possible.

Extremely complex, ambiguous, and inconsistent user interfaces demand attention and limit mindful engagement with the training material by using working memory capacity. For example, complex interfaces do not provide clear information to learners about where they are and how they can perform basic functions required to progress through the learning experience. This kind of ambiguity makes learners focus on the system in order to figure out how to navigate the experience. And as suggested by attention allocation models, this will reduce the resources available to focus on the training content itself (Park & Hannafin, 1993). For experienced computer users, following established software conventions is sufficient for avoiding ambiguity (Wilson & Jonassen, 1989). But for novice computer users, it may be necessary to use common metaphors that provide meaningful clues to system functions. Perhaps the most common example of metaphor use is to provide arrow icons to represent forward and backward functions along a default path (Kearsley, 1988; Milheim, 1996). The metaphor selected should be clear and efficient. In addition, an "undo" feature can be very useful for eliminating problems with incorrect use of the interface and as a result can reduce user anxiety (Gall & Hannafin, 1994; Wilson & Jonassen, 1989).

Regardless of the specific interface characteristics, inconsistent application of them will demand the attention of the learner. Consistent mapping of action to outcomes, such as with a particular button moving the user along a default path, is easily learned and performed without paying attention. Inconsistent mapping of action to outcomes, however, such as when the same button changes its function depending on what material is displayed on the screen, is much more difficult to learn and will draw attention away from the training task.

Another issue to consider during the user interface design is whether the interface demands that users perform thoughtful tasks that do not contribute to learning. Interfaces should be designed so that basic functional tasks are performed by the computer and not left to the learner. For example, a common task that should be performed during learning is tracking, or keeping records of what sections have been read and what activities have been completed. Keeping specific track of activities and sections completed is generally unnecessary for learning, so asking learners to do it steals working memory capacity from more valuable activities. Similarly, if learners have to take a few minutes to figure out where they are in a particular learning sequence, that time may be wasted. These issues highlight the importance of formative evaluation and pilot testing (which are discussed in the final section of this chapter) before rolling out Web-based or CD-ROM or multimedia programs.

Finally, despite all attempts to design an easy-to-use interface, some users are likely to experience difficulty. As a result, encountering new material in a complex computer program almost always requires guidance on using the system until trainees are comfortable and familiar with it (Park & Hannafin, 1993; Gay, Trumbull, & Mazur, 1991). In addition, the system should provide context-sensitive, on-demand help to resolve questions such as, Where am I? What do I need to do in order to go to a particular part of the program? How can I repeat a section? If this information is readily available, it can help avoid early frustration and build a belief that making an effort will produce learning.

Information Presentation

The concept of working memory is also relevant for selection of the different types of information presentation that should be used. The selection of presentations, such as text, graphics, and audio, should be driven by concerns about whether they facilitate active learning. Research suggests that presentations that compete for working memory include those that use similar input modalities. Mayer and Moreno (1998) demonstrated that individuals have difficulty learning from text and pictures presented simultaneously because both seem to compete for similar working memory store. Visual images and auditory information, however, do not seem to compete. Therefore, it is a good idea to present narration (rather than text) with graphics and animation.

There are a number of broader issues relating to presentation. Most authors agree that a variety of presentations are useful for accommodating individual differences (Park & Hannafin, 1993; Wilson & Jonassen, 1989; Yang & Moore, 1995). In fact, research suggests that presenting a variety of different examples can be useful for improving long-term retention of training materials (Schmidt & Bjork, 1992). When training materials are varied it prevents learners from using mindless or heuristic processing of the material, so their mindful engagement is increased and retention improved. Therefore, presenting material in abstract as well as concrete form, such as with examples, can be very useful. In addition, the most important information should be recast in different formats so that it is repeated and clearly emphasized (Park & Hannafin, 1993).

Learner Control and Guidance

Computer-based training often allows learners to take control of their learning. Decisions about providing learner control over various aspects of the learning process should be made cautiously. Not all learners make good decisions when they are put in control of their own learning. Tennyson (1980) demonstrated that many of them stop practicing too early, before they are proficient with the training task (see also Nelson & Leonesio, 1988; Sasscer & Moore, 1984).

These less than perfect choices result in part from an inability to assess knowledge and skill levels accurately. The less learners knows about a subject, the less likely they will be to recognize their own limitations (Kruger & Dunning, 1999). Consequently, learners with the least knowledge are the ones most likely to overestimate their knowledge. By extension, these same learners are most likely to make bad choices about their learning experience. As noted by Kruger and Dunning (1999), those with the least knowledge suffer a dual burden: "Not only do they reach erroneous conclusions and make unfortunate choices, but their incompetence robs them of the ability to realize it." Imagine employees who know very little about legal issues in human resource management making decisions about which areas of law are most (and least) relevant to a discrimination case and using those judgments to guide their learning and subsequent handling of an internal complaint. Because they lack a basic knowledge of law, these employees may elect to learn irrelevant things and make choices that increase the company's liability, all the while believing they are making excellent decisions. Clearly, the question of how to ensure that control is given appropriately by designers, and used wisely by learners, is central to building effective computer-based training.

There are two perspectives on how to address the dilemma of poor choices by learners. The first is to have the program retain control over the critical elements of instruction, and the second is to provide learners with guidance so they make informed decisions. Although these positions may be seen as adversarial, we believe they are complementary; each has merit in particular circumstances.

The first solution is for the program to retain control. This idea is captured in the extreme in early efforts as programmed learning, such as Skinner's description of a teaching machine (Skinner, 1961). Teaching machines reinforce correct responses in order to shape the learner's behaviors. This form of teaching is often called programmed instruction. Although the terms *teaching machine* and *programmed instruction* have fallen into disfavor because of the shift toward more cognitive explanations for human learning (for example, Ford, 1997), many of the concepts discussed in this area of research are relevant today (Bostow, Krich, & Tompkins, 1995). In addition, this work has much in common with emerging "intelligent tutoring systems" (Burns & Parlett, 1991). Thus, we believe there is a role for training designs that allow the program to retain control over what the learner does during training.

Programmed instruction demands clear learning objectives involving basic knowledge or skill. The computer must be able to judge the learner's behaviors as consistent or inconsistent with the desired outcomes. In order to make this judgment, the knowledge or skill must be straightforward enough to be analyzed for its appropriateness by a computer program (for example, options selected on the computer screen). Research has demonstrated that programmed instruction is effective for teaching elementary probability (Roe, 1962) and logic (Coulson, Estavan, Melaragno, & Silberman, 1962). Teaching more complex skills, such as problem solving, would be much more difficult to do using programmed instruction. In addition, allowing learner control may be useful for facilitating the development of higher-order thinking skills. Therefore, program control should be used for training simple knowledge and skills. Fortunately, this is also the level of skill development at which learners will need the most help.

Programmed instruction does have disadvantages, however, not the least of which is the potential to reduce learner motivation (Milheim & Martin, 1991). Learners may be frustrated by the fact that the computer is making decisions about what they do during training. They may begin to believe that they do not need to make an effort to learn. Moreover, their frustration may reduce both mindful engagement with the material and learning. It seems likely that learners who come to training with prior knowledge and experience would be most apt to become frustrated with program control. They would try to skip material they already know and feel limited by a program that does not allow them to do so. Evidence suggests that those with prior knowledge learn more from learner-controlled than programmed-controlled training (Lee & Lee, 1991) but that those without prior knowledge have considerable difficulty learning from learner-controlled training (Gay, 1986). Therefore, learners should be tested for prior knowledge, and those with higher prior knowledge should be allowed to opt out of program control.

If program control is deemed appropriate, the computer should be designed to examine learning and make decisions for the learner. More specifically, the program should examine learner errors and provide continued practice for weak areas. In addition, the program should attempt to stop any potential motivation problems by emphasizing that the learners' success is largely determined by their effort. This ensures motivation and helps to facilitate mastery orientation.

The second solution to the problem of learner control is to provide guidance on the learner's knowledge and progress. An excellent example is provided by Tennyson's Minnesota Adaptive Instructional System (MAIS) (see Tennyson, Christensen, & Park, 1984). This system uses on-task information to advise students about their progress toward mastery. In research summarized by these authors, learners learned more when they controlled training than when they were provided with continuous information about their performance relative to a mastery standard.

With learner control, specific types of support should be provided to help learners make good decisions. Guidance should include an introduction to the choices that they are allowed to make, so they understand their role during training (Wilson & Jonassen, 1989). It should also include suggestions about what material to focus on and how to learn the material effectively as well as help on how to use the instructional medium in these efforts (Hannafin, 1984). Providing prompts and hints about appropriate learning strategy is one way to help learners use their control effectively. This information is particularly important for people with low general intelligence or low confidence because they are more likely to become confused or frustrated in a learner-controlled environment (Chung & Reiguluth, 1992). Extra assistance in the form of a guided tour and suggested activities could be provided to learners who demonstrate these characteristics.

Learning Activities and Feedback

Researchers from Thorndike (1913) to the present day have emphasized that the dominant influence on skill acquisition is practice. Thus, it is critical that learners practice using the knowledge and skill that is the focus of the training objectives. In addition, they must be given feedback about how effectively they are using their newly acquired knowledge and skill. Thus, practice and feedback are essential to learning. Research suggests that particular types of practice (cognitively complex and collaboration) and feedback (varied by level of expertise and explanatory) should be provided in computer-based learning environments.

Learning Activities

Research suggests the importance of complex and collaborative activities for learning. First, the computer should provide cognitively complex activities for the learners (Aberson, Berger, Emerson, & Romero, 1997; Gall & Hannafin, 1994; Reeves & Reeves, 1997). Cognitively complex activities require more than simple recognition and recall of main points. Instead, learners should be asked to organize data, judge information, represent data in new ways, and predict outcomes. For example, learners could be provided partial information (such as three steps to a four-step process) and then be asked to suggest the final step (MacLachlan, 1986). Or they could be provided initial and final conditions (in a system) and then be asked to test whether a theory fits the data (Park & Hannafin, 1993). Each of these activities demands involvement with the material, and as a consequence is likely to generate a deeper and longer-lasting understanding of it. Moreover, asking learners to engage in complex activities is likely to motivate them because it offers them an interesting and engaging challenge.

Computer-based instruction should also include collaborative opportunities. Computer-based learning has the potential to isolate learners. Yet research has demonstrated the value of cooperative learning (Lindauer & Petrie, 1997; Slavin, 1990). Cooperative learning involves small groups of individuals helping each other to learn the material. There appear to be two potential benefits of cooperative activity: informational and motivational.

The first benefit is informational in that learners receive greater exposure to relevant information when peers reflect, discuss, and question each other about it. Similarly, learners gain information by watching others make mistakes and perform. For example, Arthur and colleagues demonstrated that two individuals using a particular dyadic learning protocol can learn as much in a shorter period of time as individuals working alone (Arthur, Day, Bennett, McNelly, & Jordan, 1997). Similarly, Dossett and Hulvershorn (1983) presented research suggesting that peer groups taking computer instruction were able to complete the instruction more efficiently than individuals, with no loss in knowledge gain. Hiltz and colleagues (Hiltz, Coppola, Rotter, Turoff, & Benbunan-Fich, 2000) present evidence that on-line academic courses using collaborative group projects are much more effective than those using individual activities.

The second benefit of collaborative learning is that it builds a learning atmosphere emphasizing a mastery-oriented approach. Research suggests that classroom environments vary in the degree to which they encourage learners to adopt a mastery orientation (Elliott & Dweck, 1988). Emphasizing collaboration among learners is one way to push learners to adopt learning goals. Johnson, Johnson, and Stanne (1985) demonstrated that individuals working in cooperative groups performed better on various knowledge tests than individuals working competitively or on their own. Thus, positive benefits of working together do not come simply from having individuals work on the same material but from asking them to collaborate during their work.

There are, however, limitations to group activities as well. Consistent with the idea that anxiety generates thoughts that load working memory, learners who are anxious about those activities may not learn from them. Supporting this hypothesis, Arthur, Young, Jordan, and Shebilske (1996) demonstrated that anxiety about interpersonal interaction can reverse the benefits of a dyadic training protocol over individual training. Thus, individuals should be allowed to pass on collaborative activities if they are prone to experience anxiety as a result.

Feedback

Feedback on the success of one's learning efforts is also an important element of successful training. A metanalysis by Azevedo and Bernard (1995) demonstrates the importance of feedback in computer-based training. Combining data from twenty-two research studies, these authors revealed that students given feedback learn more than others who are not given feedback. Moreover, their analyses suggest that immediate feedback is more effective than delayed feedback. Thus, feedback is a critical design element in computer-based training (see also Brown, Milner, & Ford, forthcoming).

It is important to note that immediate feedback may not be appropriate for all learners. Withholding feedback from more experienced learners can help them think more critically about their own performance and as a result improve retention and generalization of training materials (Schmidt & Bjork, 1992). Consistent with this hypothesis, the positive effects of immediate feedback are reduced when the measures used to assess learning are different from the activities during training that yielded feedback (Clariana, Ross, & Morrison, 1991). Thus, to build knowledge and skill that will be retained over time and can be generalized to new situations, training should shift—providing immediate feedback to novices and providing less frequent feedback to more experienced learners.

In addition to the timing of feedback, its content is critical. Feedback should help learners diagnosis problems with their learning. Gilman (1969) demonstrated that learners provided with correct-incorrect feedback plus information about why it was correct or incorrect learned more and had better retention than learners provided only with correct-incorrect feedback. Gall and Hannafin (1994) suggest that the computer should go a step further by giving learners advice on approaches that may help remedy the knowledge deficiency that caused the mistake.

Negative feedback can stimulate task withdrawal, particularly among learners who are focused on performing well relative to others (Dweck, 1986). Consequently, feedback should not emphasize relative performance but personal performance relative to a mastery standard. Moreover, mistakes should be emphasized as learning opportunities (Aberson, Berger, Emerson, & Romero, 1997; Ivancic & Hesketh, 1995–96). For this to occur, learners must be given an opportunity to correct inadequacies in their thinking by reviewing material or answering a question again (Aberson, Berger, Emerson, & Romero, 1997). Feedback should be designed to build motivation by encouraging rather than simply critiquing the learner (Milheim, 1996).

Metacognitive Monitoring and Control

There has been considerable research on how different learning strategies—or approaches to learning—influence learning outcomes. Generally speaking, research suggests that more in-depth strategies lead to better learning (for example, Warr & Bunce, 1995). However, the critical issue for learning is whether learners adopt the most appropriate strategy for them. Appropriate use of learning strategies based on existing knowledge and goals is related to the notion of metacognition, which is the awareness and control of cognition (Flavell, 1979). Halpern (1998) writes that "metacognition is the executive or 'boss' function that guides how adults use different learning strategies and make decisions about the allocation of limited cognitive resources" (p. 454). Individuals with high metacognitive skills actively monitor their progress on a task, identify issues or problems with learning the task, and adjust learning strategies to meet their goals better.

Facilitating metacognition provides a powerful way to get learners to be mindful of their own cognition and control it in service of learning. Metacognition has been demonstrated to provide learning benefit in a number of studies (see Georghiades, 2000). For example, Ford, Smith, Weissbein, Gully, and Salas (1998) found that learners who engaged in more metacognitive reflection gained more declarative knowledge from a training episode than those who did less of it. They also demonstrated that mastery orientation is an important determinant of metacognition. Mastery-oriented learners engaged in more metacognition than other learners. Volet (1991) developed student metacognitive skills in an introductory computer course by focusing on the use of planning, monitoring, and evaluation strategies. The study found that a significantly greater number of the students trained in metacognitive skills passed a follow-up computer course.

One successful metacognitive intervention is teaching learners question-generation strategies to allow them to self-monitor their understanding of course material. For example, King (1992) found that open-ended or fill-in-the-blank questions provided to learners during a course (for example, How does x affect y?) resulted in greater comprehension and retention of instructional material than a control group. A recent metanalysis by Rosenshine, Meister, and

Chapman (1996) found that generic question stems that forced learners to test their own knowledge at various points throughout an instructional sequence led to great increases in comprehension. These questions were specifically designed to stimulate mindful engagement with the material, but in the process they also stimulated reflection about the current state of knowledge. Thus, the effectiveness of these questions suggests the benefit of raising learners' awareness about the current state of their knowledge. Students who determine that they have not learned the material sufficiently will put further effort into learning. Other research has found that prompting or questioning should not occur immediately after presentation of the material but should be delayed for a short time so that individuals have some time to assess their current level of knowledge (Keleman & Weaver, 1997).

To help learners assess their learning, the objectives for the lesson must be clear (Cates, 1992; Park & Hannafin, 1993). Indicating at the beginning of major sections what learners should be trying to gain provides a clear indication of the training outcomes to monitor. Asking content-related questions about material can also be used to ensure that there is monitoring. The computer can also provide strategic tips and advice when requested (Reeves & Reeves, 1997). For example, when a learner asks for assistance the computer could suggest a particular learning strategy. In a training program with an objective to memorize verbal knowledge about a product, the computer could suggest a mnemonics technique. Or, if the objective involves understanding the relationship between products, the computer could suggest depicting the relationship among important product characteristics in a series of diagrams. Research has also found that simply prompting individuals to self-reflect can have an impact on knowledge acquisition (Ridley, Schultz, Glanz, & Weinstein, 1992).

Guidelines for Practice

Based on an extensive literature review, we offer four design principles to help ensure active learning, and in each category we offer research-based conclusions. Exhibit 7.1 presents these conclusions in the form of design and delivery guidelines. For example, information structure and presentation guidelines include making sure that the material is organized into manageable chucks, that the user interface is

Exhibit 7.1. Guidelines for Effective Computer-Based Instruction.

Information Structure and Presentation

- Is the material organized into manageable chunks-nodes and linked to the desired learning outcomes and characteristics of the training material?

- Are links for deeper investigation available for important (but not peripheral) definitions or topics and can the learner return to her original position quickly and easily after following a link for deeper investigation?

- Is an orientation to the system provided to avoid early confusion and is there an outline or similar orientation to the content's structure available to the learner at all times?

- Does the system have an intuitive interface that is consistent throughout the program and does not demand attention to perform basic navigational tasks?

- Does the system store information for the learner and retrieve it when requested, including tracking information about what tasks and activities the learner has completed?

- Is information provided in multiple forms, including explanations and examples, and does the system amplify, repeat, and recast important terms, concepts, and principles?

- Does the system use graphics and animation to depict important relationships and processes?

- Does the system use auditory (rather than text) explanation of graphics when the two are presented simultaneously?

Learner Control and Guidance

- Are the training objectives clear and focused enough so learners can monitor their own progress against these objectives?

- Do learners have enough prior knowledge to allow for informed choices in a computer-based course?

- Can the program analyze learner errors and provide appropriate material and practice?

- Does the program emphasize that learner effort is critical to success?

- Does the system prepare learners for the choices they can make during training by providing an orientation to the operation of its features?

- Is guidance provided as requested in the form of strategy prompts and hints?

- Does the system provide extra assistance to low-ability and to low-confidence trainees in the form of guided tours and suggested activities?

Exhibit 7.1. Guidelines for Effective Computer-Based Instruction, Cont'd.

Learning Activities and Feedback

- Does each lesson include practice and feedback consistent with the desired learning outcomes?
- Does the system *stimulate* cognitively complex activity by learners, such as recognizing and judging information, predicting outcomes, organizing data, and representing data in new ways?
- Are data and resources that allow the learner to create and test theories in action readily available?
- Can learners who want to interact with other learners in relevant discussions and activity do so?
- Does the system provide immediate feedback, particularly to novice learners?
- Does the system provide feedback that guides the learner to correct responses, rather than simply providing the answers or forcing the learner to discover them?
- Is feedback provided so that the learner can understand why a mistake was made how to address the possible underlying causes of the error?
- Does the system emphasize mistakes as learning opportunities?

Metacognitive Monitoring and Control

- Are learning objectives of each lesson clearly identified?
- Does the system highlight the importance of planning, monitoring, and revising learning strategies?
- Are learners prompted from time to time to self-reflect on whether their learning strategy is appropriate or should be revised to meet training objectives?
- Does the system provide open-ended or fill-in-the-blank questions at various times during the instruction following the most important material so learners can monitor their own progress?
- Does the system provide assistance with planning and evaluating learning strategies?
- Are strategic tips and advice available when requested about different learning strategies?
- Does the system prompt the learner to diagram or depict relationships among the important characteristics being studied?

consistent throughout the entire program, and that the information is provided in different forms including explanations and examples. For learner control and guidance, some guidelines include making sure that the system prepares the learners for the choices they can make during training, provides data and resources that allow the learner to create and test theories in action, and provides immediate feedback, especially for novices. With stimulating metacognitive monitoring and control, designers can engage the learner by having them recognize and judge information, predict outcomes, organize data, and represent data in new ways, provide strategic tips and advice when requested, and prompt trainees throughout the program to consider whether their current learning strategy is effective.

The principles and guidelines emphasize the importance of considering the desired outcomes and the task content when determining training design. Moreover, the guidelines can help organizational decision makers build training that actively engages learners so that the desired learning outcomes are likely to occur. Once the design is completed, the principles and guidelines can be used to evaluate the quality of the computer-based instruction from a psychological perspective—that is, the extent to which the training is likely to lead to motivated, mastery-oriented, mindful learning.

Following these guidelines does not ensure efficient training, nor does it ensure success of a particular computer-based training intervention. However, it will ensure that increasingly common training technologies are used to the best of the current knowledge on the learning process. Moreover, continued testing and refinement of these principles will help ensure that our knowledge of *how* to use computer technology keeps apace with developments in the technology itself.

Other Issues

This final section of the chapter focuses on practical considerations when building the infrastructure for learning in work organizations. Three key issues have important implications for the quality of computer-based instruction: (1) What material is most suitable for computer-based instruction? (2) How can we select a vendor that will make good design decisions? (3) What type of formative evaluation should be conducted prior to the rollout of a program?

Suitable Material

Although many authors have speculated about what material is suitable for computer-based presentation versus instructor presentation (for example, Driscoll, 1998), the research is equivocal. In fact, after hundreds of studies comparing instructor-led courses with computer-based courses, no clear pattern has emerged. Some authors suggest that computer-based training is slightly more effective than instructor-led training (for example, Kulik & Kulik, 1991), but others say that this effect occurs because of confounds between media and instructional techniques (that is, changing media means adopting different instructional techniques) and between media and novelty (computer media's novelty motivates learners; Clark, 1994).

Further muddying the conclusions that can be drawn from existing research, studies have been limited to a small range of learning outcomes. Most of the research on computer-based training has focused on cognitive outcomes, such as verbal knowledge tests, and simple skill-based outcomes. There is little research comparing media effectiveness for more complex skill or affective outcomes. Thus, it seems worthwhile to caution readers against using computer-based training to build complex skills or to change attitudes. Current limitations of computer technology make detailed observation and feedback (helpful for complex skill development, particularly those skills having a heavy psychomotor component) and interpersonal interaction and discussion (helpful for changing attitudes) difficult to implement.

Most important of all, we would like to encourage readers to view technology not as an all-or-nothing decision but rather as one choice in the design process. Moreover, we believe that it is important to recognize this choice as occurring across all desired outcomes, so that different technology may be adopted for different outcomes in a single training effort. Imagine how we would ridicule a college professor who asked whether he should use lectures or textbooks, classroom discussion, or overheads! Effective teachers use a combination of media to reach the desired learning outcomes. Thus, the issue for the adoption of technology in training should not be whether it is used to replace human interaction but how it is used to add value to learning activities. Thus a course could use computer-based instruction to help learners gain verbal knowledge, build mental models, and learn simple skills but use an instructor and classroom to help learners change their attitudes on the use of their new knowledge and skill. Using the computer in this way would free up instructor time for working on outcomes that may be less easily achieved with the computer. Thus, the question of using computers as training tools is not "if" and it is not "all or nothing." The appropriate questions are when and how.

Vendor Selection

As training becomes more technology-focused and complex, many companies are outsourcing training development. There are a number of potential benefits to outsourcing elements of the training function, perhaps the most important of which is the ability to partner with companies that have core competencies with the technology to be used. There are also many potential disadvantages with outsourcing. The checklists provided in Exhibit 7.1 offer one means to evaluate vendors. A vendor's product could be examined to determine if it has the potential to stimulate active learning. However, the checklists do not necessarily offer guidance on how to make the broader decision about which vendors to select as partners. Three characteristics of excellent vendors are noted in the following paragraphs: they are need-focused, learner-focused, and process-oriented. It is our contention that companies that meet these characteristics are most likely consistently to produce tools that stimulate active learning.

Need-Focused Vendors

The training media and instructional strategies selected should depend on the need identified and the desired training objectives. Picking a vendor with expertise in a single subject matter or with a single technology virtually guarantees that the solution will involve that area of expertise. Therefore it is imperative either to select a company that has breadth in focus and is willing to match training content and technology to the need or to consider carefully the need prior to selecting a vendor. Following traditional guidelines for needs assessment can be very helpful in ensuring that the solution adopted is appropriate to the organization's strategy, need, or problem.

Learner-Focused Vendors

The technology used should depend on the people who will undergo training. The temptation is often to incorporate bells and whistles—the latest capabilities. But as we made clear earlier in our discussion of working memory, some of these characteristics can actually interfere with learning. Animation, for example, may stimulate interest but end up taking attention away from key learning points. Animation should be used, but only if it serves a learning objective. In addition, there may be systematic differences in learners in different organizations. For example, individuals in one company may be particularly competitive, so additional efforts to instill mastery orientation during training may be needed. A vendor that is willing to modify training based on the particular learners in an organization will be more likely to stimulate active learning in that population.

Process-Oriented Vendors

Many companies use off-the-shelf products as training tools in order to get the greatest profit. Although these products may work, they are less likely to work in a specific company than a tool that was developed or at least modified based on characteristics of the organization and its employees. Vendors that recognize this sell not only a product but also a design and implementation process, which systematically examines the organization's and the learners' needs. Moreover, they will often do some testing of the product to ensure that it is working as intended.

Few training vendors would ever admit to having a focus solely on technology and a strategy that relies heavily on prepackaged products. Therefore, examining their past work and comparing it to the checklists in Exhibit 7.1 is an effective way to determine whether their espoused model of design and development is congruent with their actual model. Although such an examination lengthens the time it takes to select vendors, there should be a resulting gain in learning outcomes.

Formative Evaluation

Formative evaluation is the formal process of evaluating the program as it is being developed and designed for implementation (Tessmer, 1993). The purpose is to improve the quality of the program being developed so it is likely to achieve its stated objectives. Although formative evaluation is important for any training program, it is particularly crucial when designing computer-based instruction. For example, changing a few pages in a training manual is relatively easy to do compared with reissuing hundreds of CD-ROMs. In addition, although Web-based instruction is touted as being able to make content or process changes immediately because of its just-in-time round-the-clock availability, many individuals may have completed the program before the errors are noticed. Perhaps more importantly, places where a computer-based program freezes up or does not allow a user to move to another link can lead to much frustration in the learner that may affect how well the material is acquired and retained.

A case example follows. We were asked to conduct both a formative and summative evaluation of a Web-based training program for a large manufacturing company. The program was very well developed, and in fact, won an award as one of the top Web-based courses of 1998. Despite the large amount of effort already invested in the development of the course, we wanted to provide an intensive formative evaluation to catch any problems or issues that were not readily apparent in looking at the large amount of Web-based text for the training program. As part of the formative evaluation, we pilot-tested the program with nearly eighty engineers. Facilitators kept a log of all questions asked and problems encountered. Afterward, each trainee was asked open-ended questions about what she or he liked best and least, and how things could be improved. Trainees raised over 150 issues or problems while going through the training program and made more than forty suggestions for improvements in these posttraining interviews. Most of the problems and suggestions were relatively minor, yet they were annoying or got in the way of learning. Some items from the problem log included the following:

- It was not clear to me from the earlier screen that you were going to show the worksheet as you work through the example. Perhaps make that clear at the top of this screen. Will they be able to print it out?
- What is an escape point? I do not remember reading about this at all. Is it in Module 4? If it is not explained thoroughly before this point, it should be defined here. Even so, we may want to add a one-sentence reminder.
- Make sure we have some transition even if it's a header difference into Section 2 after a long journey through Section 1.
- Are the quizzes going to be linked directly off the software page? In some modules I think it is like that—in this module it

is on a separate page. Let's pick one and be consistent—to lower the number of screens, we could just link off the bottom of the software page

- Provide another example of a problem and symptom, one that is more production oriented (for example, slow production times for a certain line is symptom, problem is one machine keeps breaking down).

Based on the comments, the designers made final revisions by adding error-catching routines so that trainees could not make mistakes in the program, such as exiting the program; fixing navigational links so the right material would pop up when requested; correcting spelling, wording, or grammar; adding links on pages to aid trainees in navigating the program quickly; providing a FAQ page that trainees could access that addresses many concerns about what to do next; improving explanation and providing additional optional practice exercises in certain modules; providing more options for trainees to print out material such as case summaries to aid performance when exploring the case; and simplifying certain screens so they would not be as distracting. Responses to the open-ended questions after training focused on issues such as providing hard copy reference materials, improving access to information necessary to complete cases, reducing the amount of time in front of the computer on a given day, adding some human interaction and discussion, and providing more feedback to quizzes and case studies.

The richness of the information obtained from the formative evaluation resulted in an improved program for final delivery. Thus, even with a well-designed computer-based program, there are often glitches that need to be resolved. In addition, it is critical to make sure that active learning states (motivation, mastery orientation, and mindfulness) are stimulated by the training program through case studies, quizzes, feedback, self-reflection prompts, and practice exercises.

Conclusion

The move to computer-based instruction presents an opportunity for designers to develop engaging and creative training programs. The threat that accompanies this opportunity is that the organizational focus may shift to reducing training costs. The empirical evidence of cost reductions as a result of a move to CD-ROM and Web-based training technologies is scant. More importantly, an emphasis on cost reductions ignores critical issues of learning, retention, and transfer. As noted in the quotation that opens this chapter, how technological capabilities are used is more critical than the capabilities themselves (Hannafin et al., 1996). Reductions in costs, if realized, must not come at the expense of lower trainee motivation, mindfulness, or mastery orientation.

We have attempted in this chapter to provide a review of the current thinking and empirical findings on developing active learners in technology-mediated, self-paced learning contexts. Active learners are motivated, mastery-oriented, and mindful throughout the learning process. We have identified four emerging design themes that can affect active learning states: information structure and presentation, learner control and guidance, learning activities and feedback, and metacognitive monitoring and control. For each design factor, a checklist of issues to consider to create engaging and creative training programs has been identified. We hope that the model presented in Figure 7.1 guides future research on factors that affect learning and retention from computer-delivered instruction. In addition, we hope that the checklists presented in Exhibit 7.1 guide practice in the creation of effective individualized learning programs.

References

Aberson, C. L., Berger, D. E., Emerson, E. P., & Romero, V. L. (1997). WISE: Web-interface for statistics education. *Behavior Research Methods, Instruments, & Computers, 29,* 217–221.

Alliger, G. M., Tannenbaum, S. I., Bennett, W., Traver, H., & Shotland, A. (1997). A meta-analysis of the relations among training criteria. *Personnel Psychology, 50,* 341–358.

Anderson, J. R. (1982). Acquisition of cognitive skill. *Psychological Review, 89,* 369–406.

Annett, J. (1991). Skill acquisition. In J. E. Morrison (Ed.), *Training for performance: Principles of applied human learning.* New York: Wiley.

Arthur, W., Jr., Day, E. A., Bennett, W., Jr., McNelly, T. L., & Jordan, J. A. (1997). Dyadic versus individual training protocols: Loss and reacquisition of a complex skill. *Journal of Applied Psychology, 82,* 783–791.

Arthur, W., Jr., Young, B., Jordan, J. A., Shebilske, W. L. (1996). Effectiveness of individual and dyadic training protocols: The influence of trainee interaction anxiety. *Human Factors, 38,* 79–86.

Azevedo, R., & Bernard, R. M. (1995). A meta-analysis of the effects of feedback in computer-based instruction. *Journal of Educational Computing Research, 13,* 111–127.

Bandura, A. (1997). *Self-efficacy: The exercise of control.* New York: W. H. Freeman.

Bassi, L. J., & Van Buren, M. E. (1999). Sharpening the leading edge. *Training and Development Magazine.* [http://www.astd.org/virtual_community/research/].

Bates, R. A., Holton, E. F., & Syler, D. L. (1996). Principles of CBI design and the adult learner: The need for further research. *Performance Improvement Quarterly, 9,* 3–24.

Beach, L., & Mitchell, T. R. (1978). A contingency model for the selection of decision strategies. *Academy of Management Review, 3,* 439–449.

Binder, C. (1989). Hypertext design issues. *Performance Improvement Quarterly, 2,* 16–33.

Borich, G. D. (1989). Air Force instructor evaluation enhancement: Effective teaching behaviors and assessment procedures (AFHRL-TP-88–55). Brooks AFB, TX: Training Systems Division.

Bostow, D. E., Krich, K. M., & Tompkins, B. F. (1995). Computers and pedagogy: Replacing telling with interactive computer-programmed instruction. *Behavior Research Methods, Instruments, and Computers, 27,* 297–300.

Brett J., & VandeWalle D. (1999). Goal orientation and goal content as predictors of performance in a training program. *Journal of Applied Psychology, 84,* 863–873.

Bretz, R. D., & Thompsett, R. E. (1992). Comparing traditional and integrative learning methods in organizational training programs. *Journal of Applied Psychology, 77,* 941–951.

Brophy, J., & Good, T. L. (1986). Teaching behavior and student achievement. In M.C. Wittrock (Ed.), *Handbook of research on teaching* (3rd ed., pp. 328–374). New York: MacMillan.

Brown, K. G., Ford, J. K., & Milner, K. R. (1998). *The design and evaluation of interactive distance learning courses.* Ann Arbor, MI: National Center for Manufacturing Sciences.

Brown, K. G., Milner, K. R., & Ford, J. K. (forthcoming). Repurposing instructor-led training into web-based training: A case study and lesson learned. In B. Khan (Ed.), *Web-based training.* Englewood Cliffs, NJ: Educational Technology Publications.

Burns, H., & Parlett, J. W. (1991). *Intelligent tutoring systems: Evolutions in design.* Hillsdale, NJ: Erlbaum.

Campbell, J. P. (1988). Training design for performance improvement. In J. P. Campbell, R. J. Campbell, & Associates (Eds.), *Productivity in organizations* (pp. 177–215). San Francisco: Jossey-Bass.

Campbell, J. P. (1989). The agenda for theory and research. In I. Goldstein & Associates (Eds.), *Training and development in organizations* (pp. 469–486). San Francisco: Jossey-Bass.

Cates, W. M. (1992). Fifteen principles for designing more effective instructional hypermedia/multimedia products. *Educational Technology, 32,* 5–11.

Chung, J., & Reiguluth, C. M. (1992). Instructional prescriptions for learner control. *Educational Technology, 32,* 14–20.

Clariana, R. B., Ross, S. M., & Morrison, G. R. (1991). The effects of different feedback strategies using computer-administered multiple-choice questions as instruction. *Educational Technology Research and Development, 39,* 5–17.

Clark, R. E. (1994). Media will never influence learning. *Educational Technology Research and Development, 42,* 21–29.

Colquitt, J. A., LePine, J. A., Noe, R. A. (2000). Toward an integrative theory of training motivation: A meta-analytic path analysis of 20 years of research. *Journal of Applied Psychology, 85,* 678–707.

Coulson, J. E., Estavan, D. P., Melaragno, R. J., & Silberman, H. F. (1962). Effects of branching in a computer controlled autoinstructional device. *Journal of Applied Psychology, 46,* 389–392.

Dick, W., & Carey, L. (1996). *The systematic design of instruction* (4th ed.). White Plains, NY: Longman.

Dossett, D. L., & Hulvershorn, P. (1983). Increasing technical training efficiency: Peer training via computer-assisted instruction. *Journal of Applied Psychology, 68,* 552–558.

Driscoll, M. (1998). *Web-based training: Using technology to design adult learning experiences.* San Francisco: Jossey-Bass.

Dweck, C. S. (1986). Motivational processes affecting learning. *American Psychologist, 41,* 1040–1048.

Elliott, E. S., & Dweck, C. S. (1988). Goals: An approach to motivation and achievement. *Journal of Personality and Social Psychology, 54,* 5–12.

Farr J. L., Hofmann, D. A., & Ringenbach, K.L. (1993). Goal orientation and action control theory: Implications for industrial and organizational psychology. In C. L. Cooper & I. T. Robertson (Eds.), *International Review of Industrial and Organizational Psychology* (pp. 193–232). New York: Wiley.

Fitts, P., & Posner, M. I. (1967). *Human performance.* Pacific Grove, CA: Brooks/Cole.

Fisher S. L., & Ford, J. K. (1998). Differential effects of learner effort and goal orientation on two learning outcomes. *Personnel Psychology, 51,* 397–420.

Flavell, J. H. (1979). Metacognition and cognitive monitoring: A new area of cognitive-developmental inquiry. *American Psychologist, 34,* 906–911.

Ford, J. K. (1997). Advances in training research and practice: A historical perspective. In J. K. Ford & Associates (Eds.), *Improving training effectiveness in work organizations* (pp. 1–16). Hillsdale, NJ: Erlbaum.

Ford, J. K., Quiñones, M. A., Sego, D. J., & Sorra, J. S. (1992). Factors affecting the opportunity to perform trained tasks on the job. *Personnel Psychology, 45,* 511–527.

Ford, J. K., & Schmitt, A. (2000). Emergency response training: Strategies for enhancing real-world performance. *Journal of Hazardous Materials, 75,* 195–215.

Ford, J. K., Smith, E. M., Weissbein, D. A., Gully, S. M., & Salas, E. (1998). Relationships of goal orientation, metacognitive activity, and practice strategies with learning outcomes and transfer. *Journal of Applied Psychology, 83,* 218–233.

Gagne, R. M., Briggs, L. J., & Wager, W. W. (1992). *The principles of instructional design* (4th ed.). Orlando: Harcourt Brace Jovanovich.

Gagne, R. M., & Medsker, K. L. (1996). *The conditions of learning: Training applications.* Orlando: Harcourt Brace Jovanovich.

Gall, J. E., & Hannafin, M. J. (1994). A framework for the study of hypertext. *Instructional Science, 22,* 207–232.

Gay, G. (1986). Interaction of learner control and prior understanding in computer-assisted video instruction. *Journal of Educational Psychology, 78,* 225–227.

Gay, G., Trumbull, D., Mazur, J. (1991). Designing and testing navigational strategies and guidance tools for a hypermedia program. *Journal of Educational Computing Research, 7,* 189–202.

Georghiades, P. (2000). Beyond conceptual change learning in science education: Focusing on transfer, durability and metacognition. *Educational Research, 42,* 119–139.

Gilman, D. A. (1969). Comparison of several feedback methods for correcting errors by computer-assisted instruction. *Journal of Educational Psychology, 60,* 503–508.

Gopher, D., Weil, M., & Siegal, D. (1989). Practice under changing priorities: An approach to the training of complex skills. *Acta Psychologica, 71,* 147–177.

Hall, B. (1997). *Web-based training cookbook.* New York: Wiley.

Halpern, D. F. (1998). Teaching critical thinking for transfer across domains: Dispositions, skills, structure training, and metacognitive monitoring. *American Psychologist, 53,* 449–455.

Hannafin, M. J. (1984). Guidelines for using locus of instructional control in the design of computer-assisted instruction. *Journal of Instructional Development, 7,* 6–10.

Hannafin, M. J., Hannafin, K. M., Hooper, S. R., Rieber, L. P., & Kini, A. S. (1996). Research on and research with emerging technologies. In

D. H. Jonassen (Ed.), *Handbook of research for educational communications and technology* (pp. 378–402). New York: Macmillan.

Hiltz, S. R., Coppola, N., Rotter, N., Turoff, M., & Benbunan-Fich, R. (2000). Measuring the importance of collaborative learning for the effectiveness of ALN: A multi-measure, multi-method approach. *Journal of Ansynchronous Learning Networks, 4*(2) [http://www.aln.org/alnweb/journal/jaln-vol4issue2.htm].

Howell, W. C., & Cooke, N. J. (1989). Training the human information processor: A review of cognitive models. In I. L. Goldstein (Ed.), *Training and development in organizations* (pp. 121–182). San Francisco: Jossey-Bass.

Ivancic, K., & Hesketh, B. (1995–96). Making the best of errors during training. *Training Research Journal, 1,* 103–125.

Johnson, R. T., Johnson, D. W., & Stanne, M. B. (1985). Effects of cooperative, competitive, and individualistic goal structures on computer-assisted instruction. *Journal of Educational Psychology, 77,* 668–677.

Kahneman, D. (1973). *Attention and effort.* Englewood Cliffs, NJ: Prentice Hall.

Kanfer, R., & Ackerman, P. L. (1989). Motivation and cognitive abilities: An integrative aptitude-treatment interaction approach to skill acquisition [Monograph]. *Journal of Applied Psychology, 74,* 657–690.

Kearsley, G. (1988). Authoring considerations for hypertext. *Educational Technology, 28,* 21–24.

Keleman, W. L., & Weaver, C. A. (1997). Enhanced memory at delays: Why do judgments of learning improve over time? *Journal of Experimental Psychology: Learning, Memory, and Cognition, 23,* 1394–1409.

Kiewra, K. A., Kauffman, D. F., Robinson, D. H., Dubois, N. F., & Staley, R. K. (1999). Supplementing floundering text with adjunct displays. *Instructional Science, 27,* 373–401.

King, A. (1992). Facilitating elaborative learning through guided student-generated questioning. *Educational Psychologist, 27,* 111–126.

Kiser, K. (1999). E-learning takes off at United Airlines. *Training, 36*(12), 66–72.

Kommers, P.A.M., Grabinger, S., & Dunlap J. C. (Eds.). (1996). *Hypermedia learning environments: Instructional design and integration.* Hillsdale, NJ: Erlbaum.

Kozlowski, S.W.J., Gully, S. M., Brown, K. G., Salas, E., Smith, E. M., & Nason, E. R. (2001). Effects of training goals and goal orientation traits on multi-dimensional training outcomes and performance adaptability. *Organizational Behavior and Human Decision Processes, 85,* 1–31.

Kraiger, K., Ford, J. K., & Salas, E. (1993). Application of cognitive, skill-based, and affective theories of learning outcomes to new methods of training evaluation. *Journal of Applied Psychology, 78,* 311–328.

Kraiger, K., Salas, E., & Cannon-Bowers, J. A. (1995). Measuring knowledge organization as a method for assessing learning during training. *Human Factors, 37,* 804–816.

Kruger, J., & Dunning, D. (1999). Unskilled and unaware of it: How difficulties in recognizing one's own incompetence lead to inflated self-assessments. *Journal of Personality and Social Psychology, 77,* 1121–1134.

Kulik, C. C., & Kulik, J. A. (1991). Effectiveness of computer-based instruction: An updated analysis. *Computers in Human Behavior, 7,* 75–94.

Lanza, A. (1991). Some guidelines for the design of effective hypercourses. *Educational Technology, 31,* 18–22.

Lee, S., & Lee, Y.H.K. (1991). Effects of learner-control versus program-control strategies on computer-aided learning of chemistry problems: For acquisition or review? *Journal of Educational Psychology, 83,* 491–498.

Lindauer, P., & Petrie, G. (1997). A review of cooperative learning: An alternative to everyday instructional strategies. *Journal of Instructional Psychology, 24,* 183–187.

MacLachlan, J. (1986). Psychologically based techniques for improving learning with computerized tutorials. *Journal of Computer-Based Instruction, 13,* 65–70.

Mayer, R. E. (1997). Multimedia learning: Are we asking the right questions? *Educational Psychologist, 32,* 1–19.

Mayer, R. E., & Moreno, R. (1998). A split-attention effect in multimedia learning: Evidence for dual processing systems in working memory. *Journal of Educational Psychology, 90,* 312–320.

Meece, J. L., Blumenfeld, P. C., & Hoyle, R. H. (1988). Students' goal orientations and cognitive engagement in classroom activities. *Journal of Educational Psychology, 80,* 514–523.

Milheim, W. D. (1995). Learner interaction in a computer-based instructional lesson. *Journal of Computing Research, 13,* 163–172.

Milheim, W. D., & Martin, B. L. (1991). Theoretical bases for the use of learner control: Three different perspectives. *Journal of Computer-Based Instruction, 18,* 99–105.

Miller, G. A. (1956). The magical number seven, plus or minus two: Some limits on our capacity for processing information. *Psychological Review, 63,* 81–97.

Montazemi, A. R., & Wang, F. (1995). An empirical investigation of CBI in support of mastery learning. *Journal of Educational Computing Research, 13,* 185–205.

Nelson, T. O., & Leonesio, R. (1988). Allocation of self-paced study time and the "labor-in-vain effect." *Journal of Experimental Psychology: Learning, Memory, & Cognition, 14,* 676–686.

Park, I., & Hannafin, M. J. (1993). Empirically-based guidelines for the design of interactive media. *Educational Technology Research & Development, 41,* 63–85.

Petty, R. E., & Cacioppo, J. T. (1986). The Elaboration Likelihood Model of persuasion. In L. Berkowitz (Ed.), *Advances in experimental social psychology* (Vol. 19, pp. 123–205). San Diego, CA: Academic Press.

Phillips, J.M., & Gully, S.M. (1997). Role of goal orientation, ability, need for achievement, and locus of control in the self-efficacy and goal-setting process. *Journal of Applied Psychology, 82,* 792–802.

Reeves, T. C., & Reeves, P. M. (1997). Effective dimensions of interactive learning on the Word Wide Web. In B. H. Khan (Ed.), *Web-based instruction* (pp. 59–66). Englewood Cliffs, NJ: Educational Technology Publications.

Ridley, D. S., Schutz, P. A., Glanz, R. S., & Weinstein, C. E. (1992). Self-regulated learning: The interactive influence of metacognitive awareness and goal setting. *Journal of Experimental Education, 60,* 293–306.

Roe, A. (1962). Automated teaching methods using linear programs. *Journal of Applied Psychology, 46,* 198–201.

Rosenshine, B., Meister, C., & Chapman, S. (1996). Teaching students to generate questions: A review of the intervention studies. *Review of Educational Research, 66,* 181–221.

Rouse, W. B., & Morris, N. M. (1986). On looking into the black box: Prospects and limits in the search for mental models. *Psychological Bulletin, 100,* 349–363.

Salas, E., Bowers, C. A., & Rhodenizer, L. (1998). It is not how much you have but how you use it: Toward a rational use of simulation to support aviation training. *International Journal of Aviation Psychology, 8,* 197–208.

Salas, E., Cannon-Bowers, J. A., & Blickensderfer, E. L. (1997). Enhancing reciprocity between training theory and training practice: Principles, guidelines, and specifications. In J. K. Ford (Ed.), *Improving training effectiveness in work organizations* (pp. 291–322). Mahwah, NJ: Lawrence Erlbaum Associates.

Sasscer, M. F., & Moore, D. M. (1984). A study of the relationship between learner-control patterns and course completion in computer-assisted instruction. *Programmed Learning and Educational Technology, 21,* 28–33.

Schmidt, R., & Bjork, R.A. (1992). New conceptualizations of practice: Common principles in three paradigms suggest new concepts for training. *Psychological Science, 3,* 207–217.

Simon, S. J., & Werner, J. M. (1996). Computer training through behavior modeling, self-paced, and instructional approaches: A field experiment. *Journal of Applied Psychology, 81,* 648–659.

Skinner, B. F. (1961). Teaching machines. *Scientific American, 205,* 9–107.

Slavin, R. E. (1990). *Cooperative learning: Theory, research, and practice.* Englewood Cliffs, NJ: Prentice-Hall.

Steele-Johnson, D., & Hyde, B. G. (1997). Advanced technologies in training: Intelligent tutoring systems and virtual reality. In M. A. Quiñones & A. Ehrenstein (Eds.), *Training for a rapidly changing workplace: Applications of psychological research* (pp. 225–248). Washington, DC: American Psychological Association.

Stevens, C. K, & Gist, M. E. (1997). Effects of self-efficacy and goal-orientation training on negotiation skill maintenance: What are the mechanisms? *Personnel Psychology, 50,* 955–978.

Tennyson, R. D. (1980). Instructional control strategies and content structure as design variables in concept acquisition using computer-based instruction. *Journal of Educational Psychology, 72,* 525–532.

Tennyson, R. D., Christensen, D. L., & Park, S. I. (1984). The Minnesota adaptive instructional system: An intelligent CBI system. *Journal of Computer-Based Instruction, 11,* 2–13.

Tessmer, M. (1993). *Planning and conducting formative evaluations.* Bristol, PA: Taylor & Francis.

Thorndike, E. L. (1913). *Educational psychology: Vol. 2. The psychology of learning.* New York: Teachers College Press.

Volet, S. E. (1991). Modeling and coaching of relevant metacognitive strategies for enhancing university students' learning. *Learning and Instruction, 1,* 219–336.

Vroom, V. (1964). *Work and motivation.* New York: Wiley.

Warr, P., & Bunce, D. (1995). Trainee characteristics and the outcomes of open learning. *Personnel Psychology, 48,* 347–375.

Wickens, C. D. (1984). Processing resources in attention. In R. Parasuraman & R. Davies (Eds.), *Varieties of attention* (pp. 63–101). New York: Academic Press.

Wilson, B. G., & Jonassen, D. H. (1989). Hypertext and instructional design: Some preliminary guidelines. *Performance Improvement Quarterly, 2,* 34–49.

Yang, C., & Moore, D. M. (1995). Designing hypermedia systems for instruction. *Journal of Educational Technology Systems, 24,* 3–30.

CHAPTER 8

What We Know About Designing and Delivering Team Training
Tips and Guidelines

Eduardo Salas, C. Shawn Burke,
Janis A. Cannon-Bowers

In December 1978, United Airlines Flight 232 crashed near Portland, Oregon, when it ran out of fuel while the crew attempted to deal with a landing gear malfunction. The National Transportation Safety Board (1979) found a breakdown in teamwork to be the primary cause of the accident (as cited in Driskell, Salas, & Johnston, 1999). Specifically, the captain was preoccupied with an individual task, the first officer's main responsibility was to monitor the captain—this was not done—and the flight engineer's responsibility was to monitor the captain's and first officer's actions—this was not done either.

A research and development team in a large southeastern organization was asked to write a proposal to obtain more funding from the federal government in order to continue its current line of research. Because the proposal was large and needed expertise in various disciplines, a multidisciplinary team was put together to work on it. Early on, tasks were divided up, and in areas where there was overlap it was planned that individual team members would get together to determine who would do what in order not to duplicate efforts and to keep one another informed. As the deadline approached, individual team members forwarded their sections of the proposal to the team leader, whose job it was to integrate them into a coherent whole. But as the team leader began to read the sections he found that two members of the five-person team had tackled exactly the same topic, and in addition, had presented conflicting views on it! With only one week left, the team leader was faced with a big hole in the proposal caused by a breakdown in communication between members.

A fire-and-rescue team responded to a call from dispatch reporting a man complaining of chest pains. On arriving at the scene, the first unit observed a man down in the front yard of his house; behind him the house was engulfed in flames. The unit informed dispatch of the situation and more units were sent. Meanwhile, the teams on the scene began dividing up responsibilities, with the firefighters beginning to tackle the house and the team of rescue workers working on the downed man. Rescue teams revived the man and began transport to the hospital. On arriving at the hospital, a member of the rescue team realized that in the confusion no one had determined the man's current regime of medication. This breakdown in teamwork resulted in time being lost and could have been life-threatening.

Although these examples come from different domains the core problem is the same: a breakdown in teamwork. The dramatic increase in the use of teams as an organizational strategy (see Guzzo & Dickson, 1996), combined with the fact that they are not always or automatically successful, makes team training a cornerstone of effective organizations.

What We Know About Teams

As teams have become increasingly popular in work organizations, the amount of research conducted on promoting, training, and measuring effective teams and teamwork has increased (Cannon-Bowers & Salas, 1998; Brannick, Salas, & Prince, 1997; Guzzo & Salas, 1995; Sundstrom, McIntyre, Halfhill, & Richards, 2000). As a result, several tips and guidelines can be extracted that can be used to help practitioners understand the requirements for effective teamwork. The remainder of this chapter delineates tips and guidelines drawn from the team performance and teamwork literatures. See Exhibit 8.1 for a complete list of them.

Exhibit 8.1. Tips and Guidelines on Team Training.

Tips	Guidelines
1. It takes more than technical skill to make an effective team—it's about teamwork.	• Training should foster both individual and team skills. • Team members' knowledge should reach a threshold level before they can go on to acquire teamwork skills. • During team training, individuals should be made aware of the relationship between (1) individual development and team performance and (2) team performance and individual preparation and accomplishment.
2. A complex set of interrelated behaviors, cognitions, and attitudes underlie effective teamwork.	• Team members should learn teamwork skills, such as situation awareness, communication, team leadership, adaptability, and compensatory behavior. • Team members should learn each other's roles and develop realistic expectations of task performance. • Team members should be made aware of the importance of clear concise communication, including requesting clarification if information is ambiguous. • During team training, members should be urged to make verbal gestures of support to one another. • Team members need motivational guidance; factors that may hinder motivation should be highlighted.
3. All teams are not created equal and therefore instructional strategies may vary.	• Training for transportable competencies must be done at the individual level. • To learn team-contingent or context-driven competencies, teams must receive feedback that facilitates formation of shared expectations of task performance. • To learn task-contingent or context-driven competencies, teams need to be trained as close to the actual environment as possible. • To train task-contingent competencies, simulations of the task environment will be useful, as will cross-training and passive demonstration.

Exhibit 8.1. Tips and Guidelines on Team Training, Cont'd.

4. The power of team-based task analysis (behavioral, cognitive) should not be underestimated.	• Begin with a traditional task analysis. • Use subject matter experts and source documents to identify the tasks that need to be coordinated. • Rate tasks that have been deemed to require coordination or interaction. • Begin to articulate the conditions, events, or situations in which coordinated tasks occur. • Identify the competencies needed for coordinated tasks.
5. Training should be designed to facilitate information presentation, demonstration of learned behaviors, guided practice, and constructive feedback.	• A climate of learning may be fostered if participation is encouraged in an uncritical environment. • Where feasible, hands-on guided practice should be provided. • During training, difficult, but achievable goals should be set. • Models and demonstrations of desired behaviors should be provided. • Feedback should be timely, focused on the task (not the person), and constructive. • Advance organizers should be used when possible. • Prepractice briefs help promote shared expectations about training. • Training should include varied practice situations and events to increase transfer and team adaptability.
6. Opportunities for guided, hands-on practice should be built into training.	• Scenarios of different difficulty levels should be used throughout the training program; problems should not have easy solutions or only one answer. • Scenarios should allow members to take different courses of action. • Scenarios should allow participants to exhibit desired behaviors at several times. • Scenarios should be developed with goals for the specific knowledge, behaviors, and attitudes to be exhibited; they should provide opportunities to practice important teamwork competencies. • Events should elicit expected actions to measure the desired skill.

Exhibit 8.1. Tips and Guidelines on Team Training, Cont'd.

	• When developing scenarios, small details should be included, such as tools and documentation that would be used in real operations and constraints that would occur in actual operational settings. • Role-plays should provide practice and feedback of specific behaviors; they should be semistructured. • Each participant should have a role in the role-play. • Guidelines for running the role-play should be provided.
7. The prepractice environment has an effect on trainees.	• Advance organizers may be used before training to help participants develop a basic structure for the information they will learn in the practice environment. • Preparatory information may be given before training to set participants' expectations about the events to occur and their consequences. • The trainer may use prepractice briefs to clarify team performance expectations and set team member roles and responsibilities. This serves to develop shared knowledge and increase coordination. • Participants tend to have higher motivation to learn when mastery goals, rather than performance goals, are set.
8. Training can be delivered through various proven strategies.	• Team coordination training should be used to help team members learn to employ the resources of the entire team effectively, especially in stressful situations. • Team coordination training can be delivered through task simulation, principles, guidelines, information, and demonstration of effective and ineffective behaviors. All methods should be accompanied by feedback. • Cross-training should be used when exposure to and practice with other teammates' tasks, roles, and responsibilities is needed. • Cross-training can be delivered through lectures, role-plays, or multimedia.

Exhibit 8.1. Tips and Guidelines on Team Training, Cont'd.

	• Team self-correction training uses lectures, demonstration, practice, and feedback to teach teams how to debrief. • Event-based training uses trigger events embedded into scenarios to structure team training in complex environments where decision making and coordination skills need to be practiced. The events are based on training objectives.
9. Timely feedback is critical, to allow team members to adjust their knowledge before incorrect behaviors become deeply ingrained.	• Both process and outcome feedback should be delivered. • Feedback should be clear, concise, and constructive (focusing on the task, not the person). • Checklists and benchmarks aid in providing feedback. • Feedback must be given on all important aspects of team functioning. • Feedback should be based on training objectives. • Before practicing, the relationship between teamwork processes and the outcomes that will be used as a basis for feedback should be clarified. • Team self-correction techniques can be used as a tool for providing feedback to the team; peer involvement is important.
10. Team performance measurement is a critical part of a successful team training system.	• Measurement tools should provide trainers with information about the achievement of training objectives. • Observation of team members is inevitable. • Performance should be measured at several points as the team matures. • Measurement should be tied back to team training objectives and debriefings. • Measurement should be done at the team and individual levels. • Shared knowledge should be measured. • Measurement must be diagnostic; both process and outcome measures should be collected. • Team process measures determine how team achieve its objectives; outcome measures determine the effectiveness of the team as a whole in meeting its objectives.

Source: Adapted from Salas & Canon-Bowers, 2000.

Tip 1: It Takes More Than Technical Skill to Make an Effective Team—It's About Teamwork

Organizational team members must have two general types of skills (Morgan, Glickman, Woodard, Blaiwes, & Salas, 1986). *Taskwork skills* refer to those skills needed by team members to master the actual task (operational skills). Because team members must co-ordinate their actions and work interdependently, they must also possess *teamwork skills,* which are the behavioral, cognitive, and attitudinal skills needed to communicate, interact, and coordinate tasks effectively with other team members (including adaptability, performance monitoring and feedback, and leadership–team management). Although taskwork skills are the foundation for the operational side of performance, teamwork skills are the foundation for the necessary synchronization, integration, and social interactions that must occur between members for the team to complete the assigned goal. For example, although all the members of a product design team may have the technical skills to design their individual parts of a new product, if there is no communication between them there may be redundant efforts or a lack of integration, resulting in a failed product.

Both taskwork and teamwork skills need to be designed into a team training system. That is, individual proficiency is a necessary, but not sufficient, condition for effective teamwork. The following guidelines suggest how a team training system can be designed to take the aforementioned requirements into account:

Guidelines for Practice: Types of Skills to Foster

- Training should be designed to foster both individual and team skills.
- Training should develop team members' knowledge to a threshold level before focusing on acquiring teamwork skills; individual skills should be taught before teamwork skills.
- Training should make individuals aware of the relationship between their own development and team performance, as well as the relationship between team performance and their own preparation.

Tip 2: A Complex Set of Behaviors, Cognitions, and Attitudes Underlie Effective Teamwork

The recent literature has clearly concluded that teamwork is characterized by a set of behaviors, knowledges, and attitudes that allows members to function effectively in a coordinated fashion (see Salas & Cannon-Bowers, 2000b). For example, knowledge of the team's mission, goals, objectives, and available resources gives members needed direction. This is a simple requirement that organizations often overlook. Yet when team members have this knowledge it yields significant improvement in the team's capability (see Cannon-Bowers & Salas, 1998). In addition, because team members must work interdependently, they need to know about the team norms (typical behavior patterns) as well as their own specific roles and responsibilities. Interdependence also means that team members must have a shared understanding of teammates' characteristics, such as their task knowledge, skills, abilities, and preferences. This shared knowledge allows members to coordinate their actions by guiding expectations. Finally, team members must understand cue-strategy associations. Specifically, they must understand the relationship between environmental cues and particular teamwork strategies (which cues should elicit which strategy).

Although knowledge provides the foundation for effective teamwork, members must also have the skills to apply the behaviors. For example, they must be able to monitor their own actions as well as the actions of teammates in order to provide feedback in a timely manner, catch mistakes, and know when another member needs support. A hallmark of effective teams is flexibility—they monitor one another's performance and when they see a member in trouble (overloaded, overwhelmed), they step in and provide assistance. Effective teams are also flexible in that they are able to adjust to the moment-to-moment demands of the task as well as to other team members; they can thus coordinate their actions and adapt strategies as needed. (For a more detailed listing of relevant teamwork behaviors see Cannon-Bowers, Tannenbaum, Salas, & Volpe, 1995.)

The last quality important for effective teamwork is that members must have *attitudes that promote the use of teamwork*. For example, effective teams have members who believe in the team's capability, want to be part of the team, possess a common vision for the team's mission, trust one another, believe that teamwork is important, and work well with others (have good interpersonal relations). See Exhibit 8.1 for guidelines.

Tip 3: All Teams Are Not Created Equal and Therefore Instructional Strategies May Vary

Although a core set of team competencies exists, the importance of each one may vary according to the specific type of team (see Cannon-Bowers et al., 1995; Sundstrom, 1999). This is why time spent up front conducting a systematic team training needs analysis is so important (we will discuss this in more depth later). For example, in a typical organization it is easy to identify several different types of work teams—production, service, management, project, and action—each with a different purpose. Given the various types of work teams and their varying purposes, team competencies can be divided into four general categories (see Cannon-Bowers et al., 1995), depending on whether they are applicable across teams or tasks or are specific to the current team or task.

For example, teams with fairly stable membership that perform a relatively small range of tasks and face situations where the task is highly demanding, requiring members to adapt their strategies quickly, need members with competencies that are *context driven.* Basically, these competencies are important to the current team and task; they do not generalize across tasks or to other combinations of team members. It is important that members of these teams, such as firefighting teams, have accurate knowledge about one another because this knowledge forms the basis of actions and expectations about what everyone is likely to do in a given situation. This is extremely important in stressful, time-demanding situations. On the opposite extreme are teams that work on a variety of tasks with a variety of members (the membership is not stable). Teams that fall into this category usually require more general competencies that are *transportable,* or applicable, across teams and tasks. Otherwise, these members would be in a constant state of retraining.

In the middle range between these two extremes are two other types of teams. The first type performs a small range of tasks but has variable membership. These team members usually need to have competencies that are task-specific but transportable—that is, *task-contingent* competencies. The second type works on a wide range of tasks but has a fairly stable membership. These teams need *team-contingent* competencies, or competencies that are generalizable across a multitude of tasks but help to promote coordination in the specific team the members find themselves in. (For more information on how specific teamwork competencies break down into each of the previously mentioned categories, see Cannon-Bowers et al., 1995, and Salas & Cannon-Bowers, 2000b.)

Guidelines for Practice: Types of Competencies

To promote the needed team competencies in a team training system, we offer the following guidelines:

- Training for transportable competencies must be done at the individual level.
- Training for team-contingent or context-driven competencies must include feedback that facilitates formation of shared expectations about task performance.
- Training for task-contingent or context-driven competencies should be carried out as close to the actual task environment as possible.
- Simulations of the task environment, as well as cross-training and passive demonstrations, are useful in training task-contingent competencies.

What We Know About Team Training

Many of the tools used in the design and delivery of a team training system are similar to those used in individual skills training. Recently, Salas and Cannon-Bowers (2000a) provided a framework through which we can understand what is needed to design and deliver an effective team training system (see Figures 8.1 and 8.2). Figure 8.1 lays out a framework for understanding the components involved. Specifically, a skill inventory is taken to identify the tasks of the job in question as well as the team competencies (knowledge, skills, and attitudes) associated with particular tasks. This aids development of training objectives. The training objectives then drive the development of exercises and events. Furthermore, measurement criteria flow from the training objectives and are tied to the team competencies taught in the training exercises. Finally, based on the information obtained from the measurement system, feedback is delivered to both the team as a whole and individual team members.

Where Figure 8.1 depicts the process of designing a team training system, Figure 8.2 presents the overall structure—the anatomy—of team training. Team training strategies are at the heart of this model. These strategies come to be as a result of tools and methods (the delivery medium), combined with training objectives, as defined by the required competencies. Together, these tools, methods, and content form an instructional strategy.

Tip 4: The Power of Team-Based Task Analysis (Behavioral, Cognitive) Should Not Be Underestimated

Unless there is a systematic analysis of training needs, the training is guaranteed to fail. It may take time and resources to complete a training needs analysis, but it is the foundation for training because

Figure 8.1. Designing Team Training.

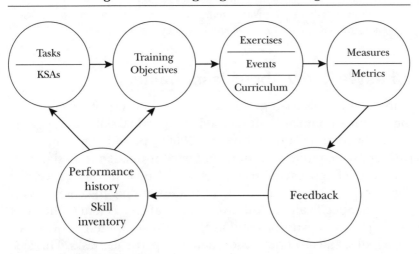

Source: Cannon-Bowers, Burns, Salas, & Pruitt, 1998. Copyright © 1998 by the American Psychological Association. Reprinted with permission.

it provides answers to the question of who, where, and what needs to be trained. In many ways the front-end analysis required for the design of a team training program is similar to that required for a typical individual training program. For example, as when developing individual training, a task analysis must determine the behavioral and cognitive skills required. In addition, also similar to the training needs analysis for individual training, an organizational analysis and a person analysis should be conducted. Because

Figure 8.2. Structure of Team Training.

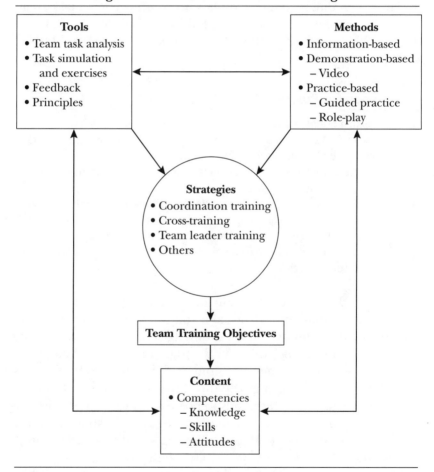

Source: Salas & Cannon-Bowers, 2000b. Reprinted by permission of The Gale Group.

these last two analyses are identical to the procedures that would be used in developing an individual training program they will not be reviewed here; for more information see Goldstein (1993) and Chrobot-Mason and Quiñones (Chapter Five, this volume).

The main difference in conducting a needs analysis for team training is the focus on determining where the interdependencies lie and what skills are necessary to master the coordination requirements present within team tasks. Specifically, the objective in conducting a team task analysis is to identify the team competencies (knowledge, skills, and attitudes) needed for the task at hand because they will help create training objectives. Although there has not been much guidance on how to conduct a team task analysis, some general guidelines are listed here. (See Bowers, Baker, & Salas, 1994, and Levine, Penner, Brannick, Coovert, & Llobert, 1988, for more details.)

Guidelines for Practice: Team Task Analysis

- Begin with a traditional task analysis.
- With the help of subject matter experts and source documents, identify the tasks that require coordination (cooperation among members).
- Rate (in frequency and importance) the tasks that have been deemed to require coordination or interdependent action.
- With the help of subject matter experts, begin to articulate the conditions, events, or situations in which the coordinated tasks occur.
- Identify the competencies required for these coordinated tasks.
- Create training objectives and measurement schemes that tie training objectives to needed competencies.

A second difference in conducting a training needs analysis for a team rather than an individual is that there is a heavy focus on identifying the cognitive skills (knowledge) needed for interacting as a team. This is accomplished through a team-based cognitive task analysis (see Schraagen, Chipman, & Shalin, 2000). To properly design team training, the developer must understand the knowledge each member needs to possess in order to perform effectively, as well as what information needs to be shared among team members. In general, the following should be investigated: knowledge of task-specific goals; knowledge of task procedures, strategies, and timing; knowledge of team members' roles and responsibilities; interpositional knowledge; and knowledge of teamwork. To investigate these types of knowledge, the developer may conduct individual and group interviews, review existing documents, observe performance, use questionnaires, and probe for recall of past important events. (For more information on these tools, see Blickensderfer, Cannon-Bowers, Salas, & Baker, 2000.)

Tip 5: Training Should Be Designed to Facilitate Information Presentation, Demonstration of Learned Behaviors, Guided Practice, and Constructive Feedback

Organizations spend prodigious amounts of money to train their workers, and with advances in technology, delivery mechanisms sometimes overshadow the need to base team training on sound principles of human learning. Although principles of human learning may not seem as exciting, they are the second part of the foundation that ensures that a training system will be effective—the first being a well-designed team-based cognitive and task analysis. Team training does not happen in isolation, and many other factors will affect its success, including organizational variables, task characteristics, team characteristics, and individual characteristics. Therefore, it is vital to make every effort to make it easy for team members to learn—to remove the barriers.

Guidelines for Practice: Creating the Right Environment

Perhaps the first step in removing barriers to learning is to create a training climate that will promote learning. The following are a few guidelines for achieving this environment:

- The organization should provide a comfortable training facility so that team members will focus on the material and not on the environment.
- Participation should be encouraged.
- The training environment should be perceived as uncritical and nonthreatening.
- Team members as well as instructors should be encouraged to provide constructive feedback.

Although many of these guidelines apply to individual training, they become even more important in a team context. For example, a hallmark of effective teams, already mentioned, is the teammates' ability to monitor each other's actions and provide feedback or step in to offer support when needed. When participation during team training is encouraged, and constructive feedback is given, norms (behavioral patterns) begin to take hold. In addition, when a non-threatening training environment is promoted, participation will be more likely. In turn, this participation may begin to foster the social interactions needed among effective team members.

Once a learning climate has been created, team training should then allow for demonstration of learned behaviors as well as feedback on the demonstration of team competencies (knowledge, behaviors, attitudes). At least two relevant guidelines have been offered for facilitating the demonstration of learned behaviors. First, it has been suggested that members receive training on technical skills prior to receiving instruction on teamwork skills. The argument here is that if individual skills are not fully developed, the team may not be able to perform the actual task no matter how good their teamwork skills are (see Salas, Cannon-Bowers, & Blickensderfer, 1993). Second, systematic opportunities for guided practice must be created during training. Guided practice sessions not only help ensure that trainees are practicing the relevant competencies but also offer opportunities for timely feedback. To promote learning and self-efficacy this feedback should be constructive (not attack the person) and focus on the task, with suggestions for resolving problems. (See also Salas & Cannon-Bowers, 2000b, and Swezey & Salas, 1992b.)

Tip 6: Opportunities for Guided, Hands-On Practice Should Be Built into Training

By guiding practice and ensuring that participants practice the relevant cognitive skills, behaviors, and attitudes, the trainer is setting the stage to make the best use of practice time. This is important in organizations where training time is at a premium. While several tools can be used to guide practice, what follows is a brief review of two of the most popular: scenarios and role-plays. (For more information on tools for structuring guided practice, see Salas & Cannon-Bowers, 2001.)

Scenarios

Because most would agree that practice should not be a random event, many team training developers have begun to use a priori developed scenarios to structure and guide practice during training (Prince, Oser, Salas, & Woodruff, 1993; Oser, Cannon-Bowers, Salas, & Dwyer, 1999). More specifically, with the help of subject matter experts, scenarios are developed that contain embedded cues or triggers. These cues, based on the training objectives, represent structured opportunities for team members to practice the behaviors, knowledge, and attitudes targeted by training. Use of such scenarios ensures that opportunities to practice targeted team competencies will occur. It also makes collecting feedback (to deliver to team members) easier because observers know when the targeted behaviors should occur in the scenario. Another benefit of using scenarios to guide practice is that team members feel some freedom, because from their standpoint the scenarios seem free-flowing.

Guidelines for Practice: Scenarios

The following are some guidelines for developing scenarios (for more details, see Hall, Dwyer, Cannon-Bowers, Salas, & Volpe, 1993):

- Design scenarios with different difficulty levels to use throughout the training program. Include problems that do not have easy solutions or only one answer.
- Develop scenarios that allow team members to take different courses of action.
- Develop scenarios that allow participants to exhibit desired behaviors several times.
- Develop scenarios that have behavioral objectives that contain the specific knowledge, behaviors, and attitudes that should be exhibited. Provide opportunities to practice important teamwork competencies.
- Create events that elicit expected actions to measure the desired skill.
- Consider the addition of small details in scenarios; include tools and documentation that would be used in real operations as well as constraints that would occur in actual operational settings.

Role-Plays

Role-plays are a low-cost tool that use scenarios, targeted practice, and feedback to involve trainees in hands-on practice. Although role-plays vary in the degree to which they are scripted or structured, the general flow of events is as follows. First, participants are given a description of a scenario and their role in it. In most cases they are told to assume they are in the scripted situation and should respond to both the situation itself and the actions of the other players. At the conclusion of the role-play, guided discussion allows team members to receive performance feedback, as well as feedback on any other targeted areas.

Guidelines for Practice: Role-Plays

The following are a few guidelines on role-plays; for more information see Beard, Salas, and Prince (1995).

- If providing practice and feedback of specific behaviors, role-plays should be semistructured (Decker & Nathan, 1985). Unstructured role-plays do not provide enough of a framework to elicit specific behaviors, but highly structured role-plays turn into a form of demonstration (participants do not choose how to behave; it is dictated).
- Use realistic scenarios.
- Make sure role-play scenarios are task-specific.
- Develop roles for each participant in the training exercise.
- Allow many opportunities to practice training exercises.
- Provide guidelines for running the role-play.
- Pilot-test role-play exercises on teams similar to those that will receive training to ensure they meet training objectives and will proceed as expected.

Tip 7: The Prepractice Environment Has an Effect on Trainees

Although it is true that guided practice during training is essential to an effective team training system, prepractice conditions may also affect its results. Recently it has been argued that a number of factors prior to the actual training and practice sessions can affect the utility of practice opportunities during training (Cannon-Bowers, Rhodenizer, Salas, & Bowers, 1998). Specifically, training developers should not neglect the impact that tools, such as advance organizers (outlines, diagrams, graphic organizers), preparatory information, prepractice briefs, goal orientation, and metacognitive strategies may have on practice opportunities during training. Some prepractice tools help improve actual practice time by providing a framework for the shared knowledge that drives teamwork and the requisite coordination requirements. For example, advance organizers may be used to help trainees develop a basic structure for the information that will be provided in the practice environment. Preparatory information may help trainees form expectations about the events that will occur during training, and their consequences. The trainer may use prepractice briefs to clarify team performance expectations and set team member roles and responsibilities. This serves to develop shared knowledge and increase coordination.

Other prepractice conditions affect motivation to practice and try out new strategies during training (goal orientation) or the ability to self-correct during practice (metacognitive strategies). For example, the goal orientation that the trainer sets in the learning environment can affect motivation, attention, and self-efficacy during training. It has been argued that if trainers set goals that reflect the promotion of understanding the task and task strategies, as opposed to stressing a certain outcome, participants will be more motivated during practice (Kozlowski, Gully, McHugh, Salas, & Cannon-Bowers, 1996). In other words, telling trainees to focus on understanding the characteristics of the best decision (mastery) is different from telling them that the goal is to make as many correct decisions as possible during training (performance). See Exhibit 8.1 for guidelines.

Tip 8: Training Can Be Delivered Through Various Proven Strategies

As shown in Figure 8.2, tools, methods, content, and objectives combine to form a team training strategy. Several strategies have proven to be effective in the team training environment: team coordination training, cross-training, guided self-correction, and event-based training. A thorough review of these strategies is beyond the scope of this chapter; see the following sources for a more complete review: Weiner, Kanki, and Helmreich (1993), Swezey and Salas (1992a), and Cannon-Bowers and Salas (1998).

Perhaps the broadest team training strategy is team coordination training (see Wiener, Kanki, & Helmreich, 1993; Swezey & Salas, 1992a), which has been used in many domains, and especially aviation, where it is called crew resource management training. This strategy focuses on team training in general—fostering team competencies. It usually does not narrow training down to one competency but targets several, as needed by a particular environment. Team coordination training may be delivered through a variety of mechanisms; it may be lecture-, demonstration-, or simulation-based, as well as offering practice and feedback opportunities.

Cross-training, the second strategy, is based on shared mental model theory. The goal is to provide exposure to and practice with other teammates' tasks, roles, responsibilities (Volpe, Cannon-Bowers, Salas, & Spector, 1996) in an effort to increase shared knowledge among team members. As already noted, this is believed to promote and enhance teamwork by guiding team members' expectations and behaviors. This strategy is delivered through lectures, role-plays, multimedia, and simulations (see Marks, Sabella, Burke, & Zaccaro, forthcoming). Guided practice and corresponding feedback play a large role in this strategy.

Guided team self-correction, the third strategy, seeks to profit from a team's natural tendency to review team action—similar to recapping a sports event in a bar (see Cannon-Bowers & Salas, 1998). This process is driven by the team itself, and training involves illustrating how to conduct a team debriefing in an effective manner without the help of outside facilitators or an instructor. In essence, in guided team self-correction there is an event review or recap, error identification and feedback exchange, statement of expectations, and based on revelations during this self-correction event, development of plans for the future (Smith-Jentsch, Zeisig, Acton, & McPherson, 1998). Team members are highly involved in this process, and positive as well as negative examples of teamwork are discussed. Finally, this training strategy combines several of the delivery methods already mentioned (training via lecture, demonstration, practice, and feedback).

The final strategy, event-based training (Dwyer, Oser, Salas, & Fowlkes, 1999), is usually used in complex environments where decision making and coordination are essential. Trigger events, or cues, are embedded in scripted scenarios. They trigger the competencies that have been identified through team-based needs analyses and reflect the training curriculum. By embedding predetermined events at several moments during a scenario, opportunities to practice the targeted behaviors are guaranteed. This strategy also provides a guide for observers and measurement processes. For guidelines, see Exhibit 8.1. (For more information see Cannon-Bowers & Salas, 1998, and Salas & Cannon-Bowers, 2001.)

Tip 9: Timely Feedback Is Critical, to Allow Team Members to Adjust Their Knowledge Before Incorrect Behaviors Become Deeply Ingrained

The timing of feedback can be critical to an effective training program. The sooner the team and its members get feedback, the sooner they can begin to correct faulty knowledge structures and behavioral patterns. Similarly, the longer teams persist in incorrect cognitive, behavioral, or attitudinal patterns, the harder it is for them to change because these patterns have become ingrained in their way of thinking. Effective feedback in a team environment should enable each team member to perform his individual task, demonstrate the contribution of his performance to the performance of other members, and demonstrate the contribution of his performance to the performance of the team as a whole.

Although both the timing and the delivery of feedback are known to be important, several questions remain unanswered. First, should the feedback focus on the team as a whole or on the individual? Second, what type of feedback should be collected: process (that is, team interaction) or outcome? Finally, how are the answers to these two questions affected by stage of training? For example, it has been suggested that early in training individual feedback should be given, whereas later on team-level feedback is more appropriate (Klaus & Glaser, 1970, as cited in Salas et al., 1993). So although most team researchers would agree that feedback needs to change focus at different points in team training, the most effective uses of team feedback in team training tasks are not entirely understood (Salas et al., 1993).

Guidelines for Practice: Feedback Delivery

Despite the remaining questions, some general guidance on feedback can be offered:

- Give both process (feedback related to team interaction) and outcome (feedback related to the team's end goal) feedback.
- Make sure feedback is clear, concise, and constructive (focus on task, not person).
- Use checklists and benchmarks to evaluate team performance; they provide the basis of feedback.

- Provide feedback on all important aspects of team functioning—individuals tend to perform best in the areas in which they receive positive feedback.
- Use team self-correction techniques; peer involvement during this process helps to develop a team member's ability to provide accurate feedback.
- Base feedback on training objectives.
- Before practice, make clear the relationship between teamwork processes and outcomes that will be used as a basis for feedback.
- Give trainees feedback that is specific to their skill performance.

Tip 10: Team Performance Measurement Is a Critical Part of a Successful Team Training System

In order to assess whether a training program is effective in its content, delivery method, and implementation, a systematic evaluation of team training needs to be done at its conclusion. Program evaluation can also provide insights into the appropriateness of the training content, the methods used, and how to ensure transfer. It may also serve as the basis of feedback for program participants.

Several guidelines have been developed on team performance measurement. For example, measurement needs to assess relevant team competencies (Cannon-Bowers & Salas, 1997) that are tied to initial training objectives. Second, measurement needs to assess the performance of the team as a whole as well as performance at the individual level. Third, measurement tools should capture team process (interactions among team members) as well as outcome measures. Team performance measurement systems need to be diagnostic in order to aid in performance feedback. Although outcome measures are important, because they provide a picture of how the team as a whole did in completing the training or the task, process measures are also important, because they provide diagnostic information. Process measures tell practitioners how the team completed the assigned task or goal by capturing the moment-to-moment behaviors and allowing for diagnosis of the strengths and weaknesses of the team's interactions (Dwyer & Salas, 2000). Finally, team performance measurement systems should facilitate observation. Because process measures are a necessary component of team measurement, many have argued that there is no avoiding observation (Baker & Salas, 1997). Here are a few recommendations to help facilitate observation: train the observers, use event-based measurement when possible (it lets observers know a range of time when targeted competencies should occur), choose measurement tools that are practical and easy to use, and measure at multiple points.

Guidelines are shown in Exhibit 8.1. For more information on team performance measurement and training evaluation in general, see Brannick, Salas, and Prince (1997), Kraiger, Ford, and Salas (1993), Kraiger, Salas, and Cannon-Bowers (1995), and Kirkpatrick (1976).

Conclusion

Because the use of teams remains a dominant organizational strategy, it becomes increasingly important to create guidelines to help practitioners develop and implement successful team training programs. A successful program is the result of both theory and practical constraints. From a theoretical standpoint the essential components are that members master both the task skills associated with the project and the teamwork skills needed to work in a team. Furthermore, although transportable competencies are applicable across many tasks and teams, some competencies are specific to the task or the team (Cannon-Bowers et al., 1995). To decide what type of competencies to teach in a training program, practitioners should conduct a team-based needs analysis (organizational, team task analysis, cognitive task analysis, and person analysis). Although some components of the needs analysis process used with individuals can be adapted fairly easily to teams, others, such as team-based task and cognitive analyses, need further research that can be translated into more practical guidelines.

The team-based needs analysis then drives the actual development and implementation of the training program by providing its foundation. Once training goals are clarified, there are many team training strategies that may be used (see Salas & Cannon-Bowers, 2000a). However, in designing the program, practitioners need to make sure that the conditions for practice during training—and perhaps prepractice—are at their best, and prepare trainees for the transfer process. Finally, once the program has been implemented, a longitudinal systematic evaluation should be conducted to determine whether the training is successful. This measurement system should be tied to training objectives, assess both process and outcome, and collect information at the team and individual levels. Information gathered through team performance measurement is then used as a basis for constructive feedback to team members.

Although there exists a fair amount of work on the design and development of team training programs, there still remains a lack of translation of this knowledge into practical guidance and tips that can be used by human resource personnel. It is our hope that this chapter will fuel further efforts in this area.

References

Baker, D. P., & Salas, E. (1997). Principles for measuring teamwork: A summary and look toward the future. In M. T. Brannick, E. Salas, & C. Prince (Eds.), *Team performance, assessment, and measurement: Theory, methods, and applications* (pp. 331–355). Mahwah, NJ: Lawrence Erlbaum Associates.

Beard, R. L., Salas, E., & Prince, C. (1995). Enhancing transfer of training: Using role-play to foster teamwork in the cockpit. *International Journal of Aviation Psychology, 5*(2), 131–143.

Blickensderfer, E., Cannon-Bowers, J. A., Salas, E., & Baker, D. P. (2000). Analyzing knowledge requirements in team tasks. In J. M. Schraagen, S. F. Chipman, & V. L. Shalin (Eds.), *Cognitive task analysis* (pp. 431–447). Mahwah, NJ: Lawrence Erlbaum Associates.

Bowers, C. A., Baker, D. P., & Salas, E. (1994). Measuring the importance of teamwork: The reliability and validity of job/task analysis indices for team-training design. *Military Psychology, 6*(4), 205–214.

Brannick, M .T., Salas, E., & Prince, C. (Eds.). (1997). *Team performance assessment and measurement: Theory, methods, and applications.* Mahwah, NJ: Lawrence Erlbaum Associates.

Cannon-Bowers, J. A., Burns, J. J., Salas, E., & Pruitt, J. (1998). In J. A. Cannon-Bowers & E. Salas (Eds.). *Making decisions under stress: Implications for individual and team training* (pp. 365–374). Washington, DC: American Psychological Association.

Cannon-Bowers, J. A., Rhodenizer, L., Salas, E., & Bowers, C. (1998). A framework for understanding prepractice conditions and their impact on learning. *Personnel Psychology, 51,* 291–320.

Cannon-Bowers, J. A., & Salas, E. (1997). A framework for developing team performance measures in training. In M. T. Brannick, E. Salas, & C. Prince (Eds.), *Team performance, assessment, and measurement: Theory, methods, and applications* (pp. 45–62). Mahwah, NJ: Lawrence Erlbaum Associates.

Cannon-Bowers, J. A., & Salas, E. (Eds.). (1998). *Making decisions under stress: Implications for individual and team training.* Washington, DC: American Psychological Association.

Cannon-Bowers, J. A., Tannenbaum, S. I., Salas, E., & Volpe, C. E. (1995). Defining team competencies and establishing team training requirements. In R. Guzzo, E. Salas, & Associates (Eds.), *Team effectiveness and decision making in organizations* (pp. 333–380). San Francisco: Jossey-Bass.

Decker, P. J., & Nathan, B. R. (1985). *Behavior modeling training.* New York: Praeger.

Driskell, J. E., Salas, E., & Johnston, J. H. (1999). Does stress lead to a loss of team performance? *Group Dynamics, 3*(4), 291–302.

Dwyer, D. J., Oser, R. L., Salas, E., & Fowlkes, J. E. (1999). Performance measurement in distributed environments: Initial results and implications for training. *Military Psychology, 11*(2), 189–215.

Dwyer, D. J., & Salas, E. (2000). Principles of performance measurement for ensuring aircrew training effectiveness. In H. F. O'Neil, Jr. & D. H. Andrews (Eds.), *Aircrew training and assessment* (pp. 223–244). Mahwah, NJ: Lawrence Erlbaum Associates.

Goldstein, I. L. (1993). *Training in organizations: Needs assessment, development, and evaluation* (3rd ed.). Pacific Grove, CA: Brooks/Cole.

Guzzo, R. A., & Dickson, M. W. (1996). Teams in organizations: Recent research on performance and effectiveness. *Annual Review of Psychology, 47,* 307–338.

Guzzo, R. A., & Salas, E. (Eds.). (1995). *Team effectiveness and decision making in organizations.* San Francisco: Jossey-Bass.

Hall, J. K., Dwyer, D. J, Cannon-Bowers, J. A., Salas, E., & Volpe, C. E. (1993). Toward assessing team tactical decision making under stress: The development of a methodology for structuring team training scenarios. *Proceedings of the 15th Annual Interservice/Industry Training Systems and Education Conference* (pp. 87–98). Washington, DC: National Security Industrial Association.

Kirkpatrick, D. L. (1976). Evaluation of training. In R. L. Craig (Ed.), *Training and development handbook: A guide to human resource development* (2nd ed., pp. 18.1–18.27). New York: McGraw-Hill.

Kozlowski, S.W.J., Gully, S. M., McHugh, P. P., Salas, E., & Cannon-Bowers, J. A. (1996). A dynamic theory of leadership and team effectiveness: Developmental and task contingent leader roles. In G. Ferris (Ed.), *Research in personnel and human resource management* (Vol. 15, pp. 253–305). Greenwich, CT: JAI Press.

Kraiger, K., Ford, J. K., & Salas, E. (1993). Application of cognitive, skill-based, and affective theories of learning outcomes to new methods of training evaluation. *Journal of Applied Psychology, 78,* 311–328.

Kraiger, K., Salas, E., & Cannon-Bowers, J. A. (1995). Measuring knowledge organization as a method for assessing learning during training. *Human Performance, 37,* 804–816.

Levine, E., Penner, L. A., Brannick, M. T., Coovert, M. D., & Llobet, J. M. (1988). *Analysis of job/task analysis methodologies for team training design* (Technical Report No. TCN 87–117). Orlando: Naval Training Systems Center.

Marks, M. A., Sabella, M. J., Burke, C. S., & Zaccaro, S. J. (forthcoming). The impact of cross-training on team effectiveness. *Journal of Applied Psychology.*

Morgan, B. B., Jr., Glickman, A. S., Woodard, E. A., Blaiwes, A. S., & Salas, E. (1986). *Measurement of team behaviors in a Navy environment* (Technical Report No. 86–014). Orlando: Naval Training Systems Center.

Oser, R. L, Cannon-Bowers, J. A., Salas, E., & Dwyer, D. J. (1999). Enhancing human performance in technology-rich environments: Guidelines for scenario-based training. *Human/Technology Interaction in Complex Systems, 9,* 175–202.

Prince, C., Oser, R., Salas, E., & Woodruff, W. (1993). Increasing hits and reducing misses in CRM/LOS scenarios: Guidelines for simulator scenario development. *International Journal of Aviation Psychology, 3*(1), 69–82.

Salas, E., & Cannon-Bowers, J. A. (2000a). Designing training systems systematically. In E. A. Locke (Ed.), *The Blackwell handbook of principles of organizational behavior* (pp. 43–59). Cambridge, MA: Blackwell.

Salas, E., & Cannon-Bowers, J. A. (2000b). The anatomy of team training. In S. Tobias & J. D. Fletcher (Eds.), *Training and retraining: A handbook for business, industry, government, and the military* (pp. 312–335). New York: Macmillan.

Salas, E., & Cannon-Bowers, J. A. (2001). The science of training: A decade of progress. *Annual Review of Psychology, 52,* 471–499.

Salas, E., Cannon-Bowers, J. A., & Blickensderfer, E. L. (1993). Team performance and training research: Emerging principles. *Journal of the Washington Academy of Sciences, 83*(2), 81–106.

Schraagen, J. M., Chipman, S. F., & Shalin, V. L. (2000). *Cognitive task analysis.* Mahwah, NJ: Lawrence Erlbaum Associates

Smith-Jentsch, K. A., Zeisig, R. L., Acton, B., & McPherson, J. A. (1998). Team dimensional training: A strategy for guided team self-correction. In J. A. Cannon-Bowers & E. Salas (Eds.), *Making decisions under stress: Implications for individual and team training* (pp. 271–297). Washington, DC: American Psychological Association.

Sundstrom, E. (1999) (Ed.). *Supporting work team effectiveness: Best management practices for fostering high performance.* San Francisco: Jossey-Bass.

Sundstrom, E., McIntyre, M., Halfhill, T., & Richards, H. (2000). Work groups: From the Hawthorne studies to work teams of the 1990s and beyond. *Group Dynamics, 4*(1), 44–67.

Swezey, R. W., & Salas, E. (Eds.). (1992a). *Teams: Their training and performance.* Norwood, NJ: Ablex.

Swezey, R. W., & Salas, E. (1992b). Guidelines for use in team-training development. In R. W. Swezey & E. Salas (Eds.), *Teams: Their training and performance* (pp. 219–245). Norwood, NJ: Ablex.

Volpe, C. E., Cannon-Bowers, J. A., Salas, E., & Spector, P. E. (1996). The impact of cross-training on team functioning: An empirical investigation. *Human Factors, 38,* 87–100.

Wiener, E. L., Kanki, B. G., & Helmreich, R. L. (Eds.). (1993). *Cockpit resource management.* Orlando: Academic Press.

PART 3

Evaluating and Institutionalizing Training

CHAPTER 9

Planning, Managing, and Optimizing Transfer of Training

M. Anthony Machin

Broad and Newstrom (1992) defined the transfer of training to the workplace as "the effective and continuing application, by trainees to their jobs, of the knowledge and skills gained in training—both on and off the job" (p. 6). The authors also stated that, in their experience with a wide range of organizations, transfer problems nearly always occurred when training employees. Other authors have suggested that as little as 10 percent of training is transferred to the workplace (Georgenson, 1982), although this level may be higher immediately after training and decline over time (Newstrom, 1986).

When training does not transfer it is likely that employees will perceive training to be a waste of their time and employers will continue to question the benefit of their investment in it. A number of authors have addressed the problem of how best to optimize the transfer of training. Although the focus of this chapter is on specific strategies for improving transfer of training, there are several important theoretical models of the transfer process that form the foundation of these strategies. Therefore, some of these models will be outlined, an integrated model will be described, and then the specific strategies for optimizing the transfer of training will be presented.

Broad and Newstrom (1992) outlined a series of strategies for managing the transfer of training that focused on three time periods—before, during, and after training—and on the responsibilities of three separate organizational roles—the role of the manager, the role of the trainer, and the role of the trainee. Milheim (1994) also presented a model for the transfer of training that included pretraining strategies, strategies to use during training, and posttraining strategies. The strategies suggested by these authors highlighted the importance of viewing the transfer of training as a process rather than an outcome. This chapter will divide the transfer process into the same three time frames and describe strategies that can be implemented at each stage.

Other authors have developed theoretical models that examine the impact of different training input variables, such as trainee characteristics, training design variables, and work environment factors, on the transfer process (Baldwin & Ford, 1988). Successful transfer of training to the workplace is not solely determined by any one factor—such as performance in the training program. The employee's level of motivation and ability to understand and benefit from training are important determinants of the learning outcomes. There are also organizational and contextual requirements for the effective transfer of training. Kozlowski and Salas (1997) proposed a three-level model incorporating the individual level, the team or unit level, and the organizational level, which expanded how the transfer process was conceptualized. They suggested that at each level there are complex processes involved in transfer of training and also processes by which outcomes at one level combine to emerge as higher-level (that is, unit or team, or organizational) outcomes. Therefore, it is proposed that an integrated model of the transfer process should examine strategies that can be applied before, during, and after training at the individual, unit or team, and organizational levels.

Thayer and Teachout's (1995) Transfer Training Model (see Figure 9.1) focused on several aspects of the training process that affect transfer outcomes. In particular, Thayer and Teachout highlighted the climate for transfer of training and the transfer-enhancing activities that occurred during the program as important determinants of transfer. The model also includes individual variables such as ability, self-efficacy, previous knowledge and skill,

Figure 9.1. The Transfer Training Model.

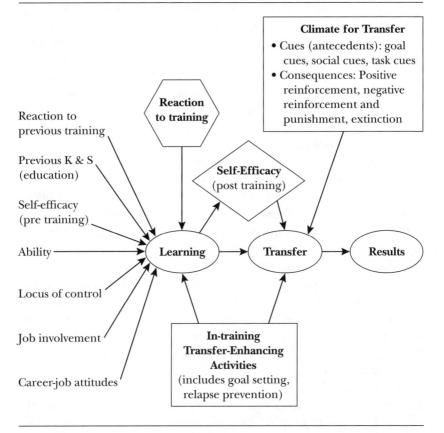

Source: Thayer, P. W., & Teachout, M. S. (1995). *A climate for transfer model.* AL/HR-TP-1995 0035. Armstrong Laboratory, Brooks AFB, Texas.

reactions to training, and the level of understanding. Locus of control, job involvement, and career attitudes were also possible influences on the learning process. The main advantage of this model is that it identifies influences at the organizational level (climate for transfer) that influence individual-level outcomes.

Holton (1996) suggested a similar framework that includes three primary outcomes of training—individual learning, individual performance, and organizational results—that are influenced by a combination of motivational, environmental, and enabling factors. In this model, the outcome of individual learning is influenced by the trainee's motivation to learn, reaction to the training climate, and experience and ability. The outcome of individual performance (after training) is influenced by the trainee's motivation for transfer, the transfer climate, and the design of the training program. Finally, the organizational results achieved are determined by the expected utility of training or return on investment of time and resources, the external events that constrain or amplify productivity, and the link between training and the strategic objectives of the organization. The advantage of Holton's model is that it specifies the kinds of intervening variables that influence each of the outcomes and indicates the directions of causal effects.

Thayer and Teachout's (1995) model and Holton's (1996) model share similar elements, such as specifying the trainee characteristics, training design variables, and work environment factors that affect the transfer of training. However, these models emphasize the *horizontal* transfer of training and do not identify strategies or outcomes at the individual, unit or team, and organizational levels that operate at each of the three stages mentioned earlier to produce *vertical* transfer of training. An integrated model of transfer of training needs to provide a description of the events before, during, and after training that affect both individual and team learning outcomes during training and individual and team performance after training, and the way in which individual and team outcomes subsequently become transformed into organizational outcomes. One way of graphically representing this model is to specify for a particular training program the training inputs, the training outcomes, and the transfer outcomes that would be applicable at each of the three levels. Machin (2000) presented this kind of model in a paper that focused on strategies for enhancing the transfer of training in an aviation team setting (see Figure 9.2). It is included here as an example of the integrated, multilevel approach that has been described.

The rest of this chapter will describe a model of the transfer of training process that is based on the three training stages mentioned in Broad and Newstrom (1992), the multilevel model for training implementation and transfer presented in Kozlowski and Salas (1997), and the models of training transfer presented in Thayer and Teachout (1995) and in Holton (1996). It will describe strate-

Figure 9.2. An Integrated Transfer of Training Model.

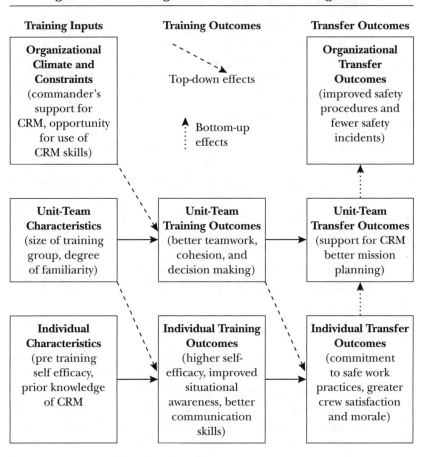

Training Inputs	Training Outcomes	Transfer Outcomes
Organizational Climate and Constraints (commander's support for CRM, opportunity for use of CRM skills)	Top-down effects ⋮ Bottom-up effects	**Organizational Transfer Outcomes** (improved safety procedures and fewer safety incidents)
Unit-Team Characteristics (size of training group, degree of familiarity)	**Unit-Team Training Outcomes** (better teamwork, cohesion, and decision making)	**Unit-Team Transfer Outcomes** (support for CRM better mission planning)
Individual Characteristics (pre training self efficacy, prior knowledge of CRM	**Individual Training Outcomes** (higher self-efficacy, improved situational awareness, better communication skills)	**Individual Transfer Outcomes** (commitment to safe work practices, greater crew satisfaction and morale)

Source: Machin, 2000.

gies that may be applied at each of the three stages, across different levels, taking into account the primary motivational, environmental, and enabling factors that influence the outcomes at each stage.

Pretraining Interventions

This section highlights important pretraining interventions.

Interventions to Improve Motivation

Baldwin and Ford (1988) identified three types of individual-level variables that could influence training and transfer outcomes: ability, personality characteristics, and motivation. Although motivation has received the most attention by researchers in this field and is regarded as one of the key influences on the transfer of training process, it is not specifically mentioned in Thayer and Teachout's (1995) Transfer Training Model. Therefore, an integrated model of transfer of training would include the trainees' pretraining level of motivation (an individual-level training input) as a determinant of their level of learning (an individual-level training outcome). Also, improving motivation and readiness to benefit from training would be one of the main pretraining interventions aimed at the individual trainee. Examples of interventions that improve motivation and readiness include goal setting, participating in decision making, and reviewing information on the purpose and intended outcomes of training. Each of these will now be described in greater detail.

Goal Setting

Goal setting is a powerful technique that has been found to improve performance in many different areas (Locke & Latham, 1990). Goal setting may assist trainees to increase transfer of training by focusing on the steps required to achieve their longer-term career outcomes (Hesketh, 1997a). However, goals that emphasize higher levels of work performance may in fact lower motivation if participating in training is subsequently perceived as a sign that work performance is substandard and if the training program initially involves publicly demonstrating poorer task performance and receiving negative feedback from others (Farr & Middlebrooks, 1990). Therefore, the kinds of goals that might increase motivation would relate to the trainee's level of participation and acquisition of new skills. Supervisors should assist prospective trainees to establish the following kinds of goals:

- Participate actively in all aspects of training (for example, ask questions when uncertain about a concept).

- Master each component skill taught in the training program (to achieve a high level of expertise).
- Practice actively new skills at the first opportunity (keep looking for opportunities to apply the skills across a range of settings).

Participating in Decision Making

When possible, trainees should be consulted about attending training courses, discussing whether they need to attend, when they need to attend, and what mode of attendance would be most suitable for them. However, participating in decision making may not have a positive impact on motivation unless the trainee's input is reflected in the training that is given. Baldwin, Magjuka, and Loher (1991) found that when trainees' input was not reflected in the training they received, their level of pretraining motivation decreased, as did their performance during training. Steps that supervisors may take to increase trainees' participation in decision making include these:

- Ask trainees what kind of training they wish to take, when they wish to receive it, how they would like to attend (full time versus part time, in person versus on-line), and what they expect the benefits to be for their work performance.
- Find out their reactions to previous training programs they have attended, and especially reasons for negative reactions.
- Allow them to develop their own training programs for specific job-related skills.

Receiving Information About Training

Trainees need to be given accurate information about the nature of the training program to help them form realistic expectations of it. Cannon-Bowers, Salas, Tannenbaum, and Mathieu (1995) found that subsequent fulfillment of these expectations creates higher levels of motivation, self-efficacy, and organizational commitment. Organizations should ensure that trainees receive positive messages about the benefits of each training program in a particular organizational setting, as long as the expected benefits are relevant to the trainee and are likely to be realized. For example, a sales manager may explain to a sales representative how attending an upcoming training program would prepare her to sell a new product that will be released later in the year. Specific statements that supervisors could make to trainees would include explaining

- How training will enhance their personal skills, especially those that are essential to their performance at work
- How training will lead to further positive experiences, such as opportunities to undertake a wider range of work tasks or be given more responsibility
- How training will increase their control over their work demands or give them greater flexibility in how they perform their main tasks
- How training will help prepare them for expected future changes in the workplace, such as new technology

Other Factors

Several researchers have examined the relationship between attitudes toward work and pretraining motivation. Noe (1986) suggested that career- and job-related attitudes such as career exploration and job involvement were important influences on pretraining motivation. Although there is little evidence to support these proposed relationships, career exploration and career planning may indirectly affect pretraining motivation through the kind of career plans and goals the trainee develops.

Organizational commitment may also have a positive link to pretraining motivation. This is the individual's sense of attachment to the organization and the actions that she takes as a result of this attachment (Meyer, Allen, & Smith, 1993). Facteau, Dobbins, Russell, Ladd, and Kudisch (1995) found that individuals who were committed to organizational values and goals had higher levels of pretraining motivation. Cannon-Bowers et al. (1995) found that organizational commitment was positively related to pretraining performance expectations and training desires, and that all three were positively related to pretraining motivation. Therefore, organizational commitment may be an indicator of readiness to undertake and benefit from training. Low levels of organizational commitment may reflect the climate in the workplace and the need for improvements to occur at this level. Strategies for improving organizational climate will be discussed in a later section.

Interventions to Improve Trainee Self-Efficacy

A great deal of research has focused on the role of trainee self-efficacy. Self-efficacy—that is, the judgment of one's own capability to organize and execute courses of action required to attain a specified level of performance (Bandura, 1997)—plays a powerful role in determining the choices people make, the effort they put in, how long they will persevere in the face of challenge, and the degree of anxiety they experience. Self-efficacy is regarded as a stronger influence on behavior than knowledge and skills, and strong feelings of self-efficacy can motivate intensified effort an persistence in the face of setbacks. Haccoun and Saks (1998) concluded that level of self-efficacy is one of the main determinants of whether individuals will benefit from training and transfer their training to the workplace. Pretraining self-efficacy (another individual-level training input) is included in Thayer and Teachout's (1995) Transfer Training Model as a determinant of individual learning outcomes.

Haccoun and Saks (1998) presented a self-efficacy intervention framework that described how the four important sources of self-efficacy information may be integrated into the three stages of training to demonstrate how and when to intervene to improve self-efficacy. They proposed that interventions prior to and subsequent to training that would be most beneficial should focus on verbal persuasion and physiological states of arousal. Trainees most likely to benefit from these interventions are those with low levels of pretraining self-efficacy or higher levels of pretraining anxiety. Supervisors should focus their assistance on employees who have experienced a series of difficulties, such as poor performance or failure to transfer skills from previous training, or who express strong reservations about their ability to master the training. Some strategies that might be useful in improving pretraining self-efficacy include these:

- Reduce any perceived threat to the trainee by initially emphasizing the learning outcomes and deemphasizing performance
  outcomes (although the performance outcomes are extremely
  important after training).
- Help the trainee develop better learning strategies to use during training, such as summarizing the main points, using
  mnemonics to aid retention, and planning for frequent revision of material.
- Develop a plan for how the trainee will use the skills learned
  during training. This last point is explained further in the
  next section.

Interventions to Improve Organizational Climate

Thayer and Teachout's (1995) model portrays climate for transfer
as influencing transfer outcomes only after training. However, the
organizational climate for transfer of training (an organizational-
level training input) may also influence pretraining motivation and
self-efficacy (Baldwin & Magjuka, 1997). The transfer climate includes situations and actions that convey the support of management for the transfer of training as well as the value that the
organization places on successful transfer of training (Rouiller &
Goldstein, 1993). Other aspects of the workplace transfer climate
include specific situational constraints on the use of skills and the
opportunities that exist for use of skills. Where there is a perceived
lack of management support for the transfer of training or a perception that the transfer of training is of little value to the organization, there is little incentive for trainees to invest the effort
required to succeed in training. Therefore, before commencing
training, it is important to ascertain trainees' perceptions of management support for the training they will receive and their expectations that correct use of skills learned will be rewarded. Supervisors
can assist trainees before training by doing the following:

- Work with trainees to identify external factors that may restrict their ability to use their new skills in the workplace.
  (For example, will the correct equipment be available after
  training?)

- Help trainees identify organizationally valuable outcomes from training. (For example, will training help them improve the quality of their work or be more competitive when applying for a promotion?)
- Contract with trainees to provide positive reinforcement and desirable rewards that should be contingent on correct use of skills learned during training. This may be a difficult outcome for a supervisor to monitor, but specific criteria should be established against which transfer can be assessed.

Haccoun and Saks (1998) argued that training that is not supported by organizational change efforts is likely to be ineffective. Training managers will have to consider all the environmental constraints in which training operates and focus on providing the kinds of training that are aligned with their organization's strategic direction.

Summary of Pretraining Interventions

Pretraining interventions focus on improving the individual and organizational readiness to benefit from training in three main areas: trainees' pretraining motivation, pretraining self-efficacy, and perceptions of organizational support for training. These goals and strategies are summarized in the first column of Exhibit 9.1. The next section will describe some of the learning principles derived from experimental psychology and how they have been applied to the design of training programs to optimize transfer of training. There are also strategies aimed at improving trainees' transfer intentions and reactions to team or unit training.

Interventions During Training

Important interventions during training itself are highlighted here.

Interventions to Improve Learning and Expertise

Baldwin and Ford (1988) reviewed the organizational training literature to determine basic principles that affect individual training outcomes or transfer of training. Although individual learning

Exhibit 9.1. Summary of Goals and Strategies: Before, During, and After Training.

Pretraining	Within-Training	Posttraining
Goals	*Goals*	*Goals*
1. Improve trainees' motivation to learn.	1. Improve trainees' understanding and adaptive expertise.	1. Improve the climate for the transfer of training.
2. Improve trainees' pretraining self-efficacy or knowledge.	2. Improve trainees' intentions to transfer.	2. Improve the *vertical* transfer of training.
3. Demonstrate organizational support for training.	3. Improve trainees' reactions to training.	
		Strategies
Strategies	*Strategies*	1. Provide trainees with specific goals for improved performance resulting from transfer of training.
1. Use goal setting.	1. Use procedures in training that are similar to those in the workplace.	
2. Allow trainees to participate in decision making.	2. Use real-life problems that the trainee is familiar with.	2. Ensure supervisors and coworkers are supportive of attempts to transfer training.
3. Provide information on the purpose and intended outcomes of training.	3. Provide different examples during training and highlight the important features of each.	3. Ensure trainees have access to equipment or resources that are essential to transfer of training.
4. Reduce any perceived threat to the trainee.		

5. Help the trainee develop better learning strategies.
6. Develop a plan for using the training.
7. Identify external factors that may restrict the trainees' ability to use their training.
8. Assist trainees in identifying organizationally valuable outcomes from training.

4. Help trainees develop detailed, well-integrated knowledge structures and self-regulatory skills such as planning, monitoring, and evaluation.
5. Set short-term goals for the immediate transfer of training.
6. Set longer-term goals that focus on mastery of the training.
7. Help trainees develop and commit to specific implementation plans.
8. Use relapse prevention as a tool to identify specific situations where trainees may be at risk of failing to use their training.
9. Create a positive training climate.

4. Positively reinforce better performance.
5. Reduce barriers such as lack of time or opportunity to perform the tasks learned during training.
6. Train all members of a work unit at the same time.
7. Monitor posttraining performance.
8. Align training with organizational goals and directions.

is incorporated in Thayer and Teachout's (1995) model as an individual-level outcome of training, expertise is a newer concept that is receiving a great deal of attention. The research on enhancement of individual learning will be discussed first, followed by a description of research into enhancement of adaptive expertise.

Baldwin and Ford cited the work of McGehee and Thayer (1961), who found that most of the empirical research linking learning principles to the design of training could be summarized into four basic principles: the use of identical elements (that is, making the training setting similar to the work setting), the teaching of general principles (that is, outlining a principle that can be applied across a range of problems or situations), the provision of stimulus variability (that is, using a variety of examples to illustrate a principle), and the conditions of practice (that is, how often trainees practice the tasks, what kind of feedback is provided, and how complex tasks are simplified). Although these principles have been extensively researched from a behaviorist perspective, recent research from a cognitive, information-processing perspective has highlighted a number of areas in which the impact on transfer of learning is markedly different from that predicted earlier (Druckman & Bjork, 1991, 1994). Strategies derived from each of the four principles will be described, followed by strategies that focus on the development of adaptive expertise that is not confined to a particular setting.

Identical Elements

Many studies have demonstrated that transfer of learning occurs most often between very similar situations but that there is little positive evidence of transfer generalizing to different situations (Singley & Anderson, 1989). When the *physical* characteristics of the transfer environment match the learning environment, the actual stimuli may be identical—for example, when equipment used in training is identical to that used in the workplace. However, this view of identical elements may be too narrow. Holding (1991) suggested that functional fidelity may be achieved when the *psychological* meaning attached to two situations is identical, even without a lot of physical similarity. For example, studying flight simulators used to train novice pilots to fly, Lintern (1991) concluded that the level of detail only needs to be sufficient to provide the most relevant information (such as speed, direction, and altitude), and not identical in every detail. Therefore, it is likely that a greater level of physical fidelity would not enhance the overall transfer of skills, provided that the appropriate level of psychological or functional fidelity is achieved in the training setting. In order to increase psychological fidelity, trainers need to ensure the following:

- Trainees are given an explanation of any dissimilarity between the tasks performed during training and work tasks that will be performed after training.
- Trainees are encouraged to focus only on important differences between training tasks and transfer tasks (such as the speed with which the training tasks are performed), rather than nonessential differences (such as equipment that is not the same model but has the same features).
- The procedures used in training are similar to those used in the workplace, and when they differ trainees can make the necessary adjustments to accommodate the differences.

General Principles

Teaching general principles or problem-solving strategies that can be applied across a range of problems or situations has been seen to have a limited beneficial effect, even though many studies have been conducted (see Detterman, 1993). Essentially, the teaching of general principles is an example of a "high-road" approach to transfer (Salomon & Perkins, 1989) that focuses on assisting learners to develop abstract schemas that can be applied across a number of different types of situations. The "low-road" approach involves developing context-specific skills that after a great deal of practice become fairly automatic. The development of abstract schemas has yet to be shown to benefit the transfer of learning in a general sense. It also may be harder for the learner to grasp the principle in the early stages of learning new material. Therefore, the potential benefits of using general principles must be weighed against the possible reduction in motivation during training. Ivancic and Hesketh (1995–96) suggested that in order to enhance understanding of a principle, training should incorporate strategies designed to do the following:

- Capture the trainee's attention, such as presenting a real-life problem that the trainee is familiar with.
- Provide feedback about the accuracy of the trainee's knowledge structures (thus providing the trainee with an awareness of her training needs).
- Direct the trainee's attention to similar examples from her own experiences, so that she can make connections between strategies that have been effective in different situations.

Stimulus Variability

Using a variety of examples during training to illustrate a principle may help trainees develop an understanding of general rules that may be transferred to other situations. Trainees do this by learning to recognize the common features of the examples. Gick and Holyoak (1987) identified the need for trainees to differentiate between the structural and surface components of situations. Although the surface components may be varied to help trainees develop general rules, the structural components need to be consistent for transfer of learning to occur. For example, consider a training program in how to provide performance feedback to subordinates. Surface components of the examples could be varied: a male supervisor with both male and female employees and then a female supervisor with both male and female employees, supervisors providing both positive and negative feedback with different employees who either accept or reject the feedback, and a supervisor who is very formal and keeps a distance from employees versus a supervisor who is informal and chooses to sit closer to employees. In contrast, the structural components that would need to remain consistent include using specific behavioral examples of both good and poor performance, providing an opportunity for employees to ask questions or disagree with comments made by their supervisor, and including the employees in developing strategies to improve areas of poor performance.

Baldwin (1992) reported that including both positive and negative models in a behavioral modeling program had a significant negative effect on initial learning but a significant positive effect on transfer to a different task. Other research has confirmed that using a variety of examples does benefit the transfer of skills but may have a negative effect on initial skill acquisition (Schmidt &

Bjork, 1992). Therefore, evaluations of the effectiveness of training should be based on the immediate training outcomes as well as longer-term transfer outcomes, as displayed in Figure 9.2. Trainers may incorporate stimulus variability into training by doing the following:

- Provide different examples during training and highlight the important features of each example.
- Provide both positive (what to do) and negative (what not to do) examples.
- Be aware that trainees may experience initial confusion but that this that does not translate into poorer performance on transfer unless they fail to demonstrate mastery of the training content.

Conditions of Practice

Some of the issues that Baldwin and Ford (1988) included in conditions of practice were the degree of overlearning (that is, how long trainees continue to practice their tasks), the frequency and type of feedback, the distribution of practice (that is, how often the trainees practice their tasks), and whole-task versus part-task training (that is, how complex tasks are simplified during training).

Overlearning involves continuing practice well beyond the point of being able to perform a task successfully, and it is related to the likelihood that material learned during training will be retained after training. Although there is an initial positive effect on transfer, the benefits of overlearning appear to weaken with time (Driskell, Willis, & Cooper, 1992). Also, trainees only need to overlearn those task components that are consistent across a range of transfer conditions (Proctor & Dutta, 1995). Therefore, overlearning is suggested as a strategy best used for tasks that are routine and whose structure remains consistent after training, such as with standard pieces of equipment. The military has enshrined this principle in its weapons training; trainees are drilled to the point where weapons assembly is done automatically.

Feedback is considered to be one of the most important strategies for improving learning. When feedback is gradually reduced during skill acquisition, the individual learner is encouraged to develop self-regulatory skills that enhance his ability to generalize the learning beyond the original task. Kluger and DeNisi (1996) warned that if feedback focuses the individual's attention away from the task and toward more general processes, it may promote a superficial level of understanding and have a negative effect on transfer. Hesketh (1997a) noted that a distinguishing feature of experts is the accuracy of their own self-assessments. Therefore, providing feedback cues may enhance learning and transfer if the feedback initially specifies how task performance may be improved and if the trainee learns to recognize his own weaknesses and correct his own performance. This procedure is also discussed in the following section that examines self-management strategies.

Spacing training over a number of sessions, so that sessions are separated by other activities, has been found to benefit the long-term retention of learning (Schmidt & Bjork, 1992). However, there is a strong tendency in many organizations for training sessions to be grouped—that is, conducted all in one period with no other activities between sessions. Although trainees receiving massed practice may appear to demonstrate satisfactory learning outcomes, this is usually only the case when short-term results are considered (Druckman & Bjork, 1991). Hesketh (1997a, 1997b) recommended several ways to overcome this reliance on strategies that promote short-term training outcomes, such as focusing on the measurement of different types of training outcomes, including cognitive (what I know), behavioral (what I do), and affective (what I feel or value) outcomes over longer periods (for example, six months later, one year later, two years later, and so on). Trainers are starting to incorporate these practices into their training evaluations.

Finally, the issue of whole-task versus part-task training concerns how complex tasks are simplified during training. In many cases, students are trained to perform the components of a task separately before being required to integrate the components. For example, surgeons make incisions, tie sutures, and clamp blood vessels many times as individual tasks before actually performing an operation. Although some authors have suggested that part-task training can be effective, particularly when the task is easily decomposed into unrelated subtasks, others have questioned these findings (Schmidt & Young, 1987). Another factor that influences the effectiveness of part-task training are the strategies employed to decompose the task during training and then reconstruct the whole task at transfer. Druckman and Bjork (1991) outlined a number of difficulties encountered in recombining part-tasks, especially the need to integrate task components and generate new responses to the same stimuli. Therefore, the research on part-task training suggests that this strategy may only improve learning and transfer outcomes when the tasks are easily decomposed into separate *and* unrelated components. Part-task training may not be suitable for many of the complex, highly integrated tasks that are commonplace today.

To summarize the section on conditions of practice, there is a growing need to design training that does not concentrate only on short-term, behavioral outcomes but promotes longer-term skill development. The solution involves in part a new understanding of the importance of cognitive processes in training and transfer. The next section will describe specific strategies that focus on the development of adaptive expertise, where the emphasis is on skills and knowledge that can be applied across a range of situations.

Adaptive Expertise

Training researchers are increasingly focusing on the development of adaptive expertise as one of the most important outcomes of training (see Hesketh, 1997a, 1997b; Smith, Ford, & Kozlowski, 1997). Traditionally, many training courses were designed to promote *routine expertise*—that is, where trainees reproduced specific behaviors in similar settings with an emphasis on short-term retention, rather than *adaptive expertise,* which can be applied across a range of complex tasks and settings. Training that has the goal of developing adaptive expertise may require some radical changes in design and focus on evaluating different types of learning outcomes (Smith et al., 1997). Ford and Weissbein (1997) identified three training strategies that have the potential to improve adaptability and effectiveness of training transfer: discovery learning, error-based learning, and development of metacognitive skills. These will be briefly described and illustrated with examples. It is more difficult to provide specific strategies that enhance adaptive expertise because this is a much newer area of research.

Discovery learning occurs when trainees are given the opportunity to explore and experiment with aspects of the training material and thereby infer general rules and strategies. Guidance is provided by answering questions, asking leading questions, or providing prompts without giving specific answers (Kamouri, Kamouri, & Smith, 1986). Discovery learning allows trainees to be more involved and actively engaged in the learning activity (Singer & Pease, 1976), while the trainer can help them acquire several learning strategies that involve greater levels of conscious attention in their application (McDaniel & Schlager, 1990). Individual learners may also become more aware of which strategies are most effective in novel situations. Frese and Zapf (1994) pointed out that self-generated knowledge is more easily integrated into existing knowledge and also can be applied more flexibly in different situations. Discovery learning could be incorporated into training by using case studies of real situations that require participants to identify appropriate responses that were effective in more than one situation. For example, trainees may be asked to think of real situations and then describe several different ways of responding. In the process of producing different responses, they learn to differentiate between those that are more effective and those that are less effective.

The second approach to enhancing adaptability is *error-based learning* (Ivancic & Hesketh, 1995–96). Error-based learning differs from guided discovery learning in that learners develop specific error-management strategies that help them improve their learning and deal with the motivational consequences of errors. Hesketh (1997a) emphasized the important role that errors play in testing hypotheses about underlying knowledge structures. Frese and Altman (1989) also linked the active processing of errors to the refinement of a trainee's mental model. Error-based learning could be used to assist trainees in developing their own mental database of the different kinds of errors that are possible and the steps that can be taken to prevent each kind. This may be particularly effective in training for expertise in fault-finding procedures, where the initial stimulus is a breakdown in a system (such as a process control system in manufacturing) or a piece of machinery (such as a photocopier).

The third approach focuses on *developing metacognitive skills*. Metacognitive skills enable learners to be consciously aware of and in control of their cognitive processes, including their learning and

application of new knowledge and skills (Butterfield & Nelson, 1989). Hesketh (1997a) suggested that metacognitive skills promote adaptability of expertise by allowing strategic use of various components of expertise, such as processes involving planning, monitoring, and evaluating one's own performance. Smith et al. (1997) outlined two avenues by which metacognitive skills may be developed: increasing the degree of control that learners exert over the learning process and cultivating a mastery orientation toward the learning task. Volet (1991) has shown that students who were given metacognitive skills training had better grades in their course and were better able to apply their knowledge to solving new problems. Examples of metacognitive skills training include training in the way the trainees think about their learning (see Downs & Perry, 1984, for a learning-to-learn training program), solve different kinds of problems (see De Bono, 1985, for a description of a course in lateral thinking), and transfer their training (see the following section for a description of relapse prevention training).

Smith et al. (1997) concluded that using adaptive expertise training strategies such as the three described here may help trainees develop detailed, well-integrated knowledge structures and self-regulatory skills such as planning, monitoring, and self-evaluation. Other interventions can be used during training to focus on improving the trainees' transfer intentions. These will be discussed in the next section.

Interventions to Improve Transfer Intentions

Foxon's (1993, 1994) model of the transfer of training process begins with the trainee's *intention* to transfer and subsequent attempts at initiation, followed by partial transfer, conscious maintenance, and finally unconscious maintenance of new skills. This model incorporates the multilevel aspects already mentioned, such as components of organizational climate, and also highlights the importance of the trainees' transfer intentions. Interventions designed to improve motivation to transfer and level of self-efficacy will assist in the development of stronger transfer intentions—one of the preconditions for effective transfer of training. Transfer intention is not specifically mentioned in Thayer and Teachout's (1995) model but would be a separate individual-level outcome

that precedes actual transfer of training and would be influenced by the same three factors—that is, posttraining self-efficacy, learning, and transfer-enhancing activities that occur during training. The most direct strategy for improving transfer intentions is to use in-training transfer-enhancing activities such as goal setting (that is, to set goals for transfer), followed by planning how to achieve these transfer goals, and then to use relapse prevention, which is a strategy for preparing trainees to deal with the problematic situations they may face after training. All three of these strategies will be described in more detail here.

Goal Setting

When trainees set specific goals for the transfer of training, it has been found to assist them with transfer, although goal setting may be most effective for those trainees with higher levels of self-efficacy (Stevens & Gist, 1997; Murtada & Haccoun, 1996). Latham and Seijts (1999) recommended that trainees set short-term goals as well as long-term goals because short-term goals provide them with more immediate opportunities for successful outcomes that will lead to higher levels of self-efficacy and further goal attainment. Latham and Seijts suggested that short-term goals should be set both for knowledge and skill acquisition during training, and then for maintenance and generalization of the knowledge and skills learned after training. Hesketh (1997a) stated that goal setting might also help trainees strive for longer-term outcomes (such as career goals) that appear less attractive because there is a delay in achieving them. Therefore, trainers should ensure that all trainees have the following:

- Clear, short-term learning goals for the training program. For example, "I will complete all of the required modules in the allocated time."
- Short-term goals for the immediate transfer of their training. For example, "I will begin to use my new skills at the first opportunity."
- Longer-term goals that focus on the continued mastery of the training content. For example, "I will seek feedback from my supervisor and peers after one month and continue to review my progress each month."

Implementation Intentions

Gollwitzer (1999) proposed that two kinds of intentions affect goal achievement: goal intentions and implementation intentions. He defined goal intentions as specifying a desired end state as well as some level of commitment to achieving it. He defined implementation intentions as specifying the situational cues or conditions that trigger goal-directed actions. In other words, this kind of intention is a commitment to act in a certain way whenever certain conditions are fulfilled. Therefore, implementation intentions can help individuals to know when it is important to use their new skills.

The kinds of implementation intentions that are relevant to the transfer of training are likely to be intentions to use transfer enhancement procedures such as goal setting, self-management, and relapse prevention, which are effective in promoting the transfer process (Machin & Fogarty, 1998). Other activities that might promote transfer include seeking support from supervisors and peers, practicing skills learned in training, and looking for opportunities to demonstrate those skills. Trainers can encourage trainees to examine the various situations in which they will use their training and commit to specific implementation plans, such as those described in the following paragraphs. The crucial step is that trainees decide before finishing training what they will attempt afterward. Trainers could ask them: What is the first thing you are going to do when you get back to your job? When is the best time and under what specific conditions should you initiate use of the skills learned during training? What specific goals do you have for the maintenance of your skills? (This might include a plan to establish specific levels of mastery at certain key points.) What kind of positive reinforcement do you expect from your supervisor or peers? (Of course, trainers should recognize that supervisors and peers may have limited time and few opportunities to observe directly the trainees performance after training.)

Relapse Prevention

Relapse prevention (RP) training has been recommended as a key strategy for enhancing transfer (Marx, 1982). It is designed to help trainees during the period immediately after training, regarded by some researchers as the most crucial period in facilitating positive transfer (Tannenbaum & Yukl, 1992). Relapse prevention training originated in the field of clinical psychology and was developed to improve the likelihood that people recovering from addictive behaviors could anticipate and effectively deal with difficult situations without relapsing into their former behaviors (Marlatt & Gordon, 1985). The focus of RP training was to develop high levels of self-efficacy for identifying problematic situations and exercising control over one's behavior by using appropriate coping strategies. For a trainee, it will not be exposure to alcoholic beverages that constitutes a high-risk situation but rather criticism from the supervisor or peers, for example, or coping with pressures to meet several deadlines.

Tziner, Haccoun, and Kadish (1991) demonstrated that training that incorporated an RP module was found to be more effective because trainees reported greater use of the transfer strategies they had learned and supervisors judged those trainees as demonstrating greater use of their new skills. The trainees who were given RP training also demonstrated higher levels of mastery of the content, although the reason for this is unclear. The RP module was not equally effective for all trainees in all situations, with transfer being influenced by personal and situational elements extraneous to the training intervention. Trainers should encourage trainees to identify specific situations where they may be at risk of failing to use their training and ask them to develop an action plan that includes the following:

- A description of the specific challenging situation in which they will be required to use their skills (such as when an aircraft crew faces a series of delays, extra demands, and bad weather conditions)
- An explanation of what skills they will apply (such as situational awareness, communication, and decision-making techniques appropriate for an aircraft crew that have been learned in crew resource management training)
- The results they expect from an improvement in their performance (such as greater aircraft safety through maintenance of safety margins, and less disruption of passengers' plans)
- A description of any potential obstacles to the implementation of their plan (such as unpredictability of weather conditions and subsequent delays)

- A description of how they would deal with those obstacles (such as using standard operating procedures that emphasize safety and communicating relevant information about delays to passengers to enable them to make alternative plans)

Haccoun (1997) described RP as a strategy that focuses on "the development of proactive, strategic actions that take into account work level constraints" (p. 342) and therefore may have an impact on trainees' expectations that the training can be successfully transferred. The action plans may be crucial in the period immediately after training when they are most susceptible to the influence of barriers to transfer in the workplace. Also, these procedures help trainees attribute failure to transfer their training to a deficit in their use of transfer strategies, rather than a deficit in their motivation or ability. Haccoun and Saks (1998) recommended that trainers use a contingency approach to the implementation of strategies like RP, taking into account the characteristics of the trainee, the task being learned, and the training and transfer environment.

Interventions to Improve Reactions to Training

Thayer and Teachout's (1995) model portrays trainees' reactions to the current and previous training courses as an individual-level training outcome that is a determinant of individual learning. However, there may be a contextual influence of the training environment on individual reactions to training, as well as individual learning outcomes. Contextual factors that may influence individual reactions to training include characteristics of the training cohort (Baldwin & Magjuka, 1997) and aspects of the training climate (Choi, Price, & Vinokur, 2000), which are both group-level training inputs.

Training Cohort

Training cohort variables include the size and composition of the training group and norms for the degree of cooperative learning required. Baldwin and Magjuka (1997) proposed that trainees do take careful note of the other participants in training, the degree of cooperation that is expected from the group, and which trainees are rewarded. Depending on the type and purpose of the training, arguments can be made for having relatively homogeneous or heterogeneous training groups. However, trainees will not necessarily understand these choices in the same way as the managers responsible for making them. Baldwin and Magjuka concluded that there is currently little evidence to support the notion that small, relatively homogeneous groups will result in better training outcomes.

There is, however, growing evidence to support the value of cooperative learning as a means of enhancing training performance (Latham & Crandall, 1991). The main reason to promote cooperative learning is to develop supportive group norms. When the group's success depends on all members improving their performance, it is expected that they will encourage each other and support cooperative learning (Slavin, 1983). Therefore, trainers need to analyze carefully the extent to which transfer of training will depend on the cooperation and support of other employees and ensure that the same level of support and cooperation is provided during training. Specific ways in which trainers can encourage trainees to support one another include establishing ground rules that do not permit trainees to criticize one another (the trainer models the kind of support and encouragement that is expected) and using team-building exercises to create a climate of acceptance in the group as well as an increased awareness of intragroup processes.

Training Climate

Numerous studies involving assessments of school and tertiary classroom settings have been carried out to determine the impact of the learning environment on student achievement (Fraser, 1981). There is also evidence that supportive and encouraging relationships between trainer and trainee are associated with better levels of well-being in unemployed trainees and with improvements in well-being over time (Creed, Hicks & Machin, 1996).

Choi, Price, and Vinokur (2000) identified several group-level effects that have the potential to influence individual-level outcomes, including a safe group-learning environment, a positive group atmosphere, mutual support among group members, and trainers with strong referent power. They found that leadership processes, such as leader behavior and social attractiveness, influenced trainees' mastery of the training content when measured at the individual level. However, group processes, such as group climate and social attractiveness of the group, influenced individual-level outcomes as well as showing an additional contextual effect for the whole group. In other words, although trainees who had positive group experiences reported more positive outcomes, those who were surrounded by others who shared their positive group perceptions were able to achieve even greater positive outcomes. Therefore, trainers need to ensure not only that individuals have positive experiences with the group but also that these perceptions are widespread. This is an important contribution to understanding the multilevel nature of the processes involved in transfer of training and in particular the way in which individual-level outcomes are embedded in higher-level (that is, group and organizational) processes.

Summary of Interventions Used During Training

Interventions applied during training have been described that focus on three main areas: improving trainees' learning outcomes (including their level of adaptive expertise), transfer intentions, and reactions to training. The key concepts underlying these interventions are the individual's readiness to transfer the training, the identification of potential barriers to doing so, and the understanding of contextual effects on individual learning outcomes. These goals and strategies are summarized in the second column of Exhibit 9.1.

Posttraining Interventions

This section will describe posttraining strategies that can be used to optimize transfer of training and will further elaborate on the importance of considering contextual processes.

Interventions to Improve the Transfer Climate

Baldwin and Ford (1988) proposed that characteristics of the work environment influenced training and transfer outcomes. Characteristics that may affect transfer include situational constraints, support from supervisor and peers, and opportunity to use new knowledge and skills on the job. Specific climate for transfer factors will be described in greater detail and illustrated with examples.

Peters, O'Connor, and Eulberg (1985) identified specific groups of situational constraints that may affect work performance. They suggested that there are eleven basic categories of constraints: job-related information, tools and equipment, materials and supplies, budgetary support, required services and help from others, task preparation, time available, work environment, scheduling of activities, transportation, and job-relevant authority. Although not all are relevant to the transfer of knowledge and skills acquired during training, some are relevant to training design. For example, are the tools and equipment the same as those used in training? Other constraints may affect the actual transfer of training—for example, the work environment and scheduling of activities (which is similar to opportunity to perform). Therefore, constraints in all areas of the work environment can be barriers to transfer of training.

Building on the earlier work on situational constraints, Rouiller and Goldstein (1993) developed a model of the transfer climate based on social learning theory (see Luthans & Kreitner, 1985). Their model included situational cues (for example, goal, social, task, and self-control cues) and several types of consequences (for example, positive feedback, negative feedback, punishment, and no feedback). Situational cues served to remind trainees of their training or provided them with opportunities to use their training, and consequences affected the likelihood that trainees would continue to use their skills. Rouiller and Goldstein found that both factors were important in predicting transfer of training. Where a more positive transfer climate existed, trainees demonstrated significantly more trained behaviors, even after controlling for learning and unit performance.

Tracey, Tannenbaum, and Kavanagh (1995) attempted to replicate and expand on Rouiller and Goldstein's work by evaluating transfer of training among supermarket managers using separate measures of transfer climate and a continuous learning culture. Both transfer climate and continuous learning culture were directly related to posttraining behaviors, even after accounting for pretraining performance and knowledge gained during training.

The authors found that the social support components in both the climate and culture measured had the strongest relationships with the underlying constructs being measured. This indicated that the extent to which supervisors and coworkers encouraged the learning and use of trained skills on the job might be *the* crucial elements in the transfer environment.

Another line of research has focused on factors that influence opportunity to perform trained tasks on the job (Ford, Quiñones, Sego, & Sorra, 1992; Quiñones, Sego, Ford, & Smith, 1995–96). These studies, which involved graduates from United States Air Force (USAF) training courses, found that supervisor attitudes and work group support both affected the opportunity that trainees were given to transfer training. Other determinants of opportunity to perform included individual characteristics such as trainee self-efficacy and career motivation, even after the organizational and work context factors were taken into account.

Therefore, in order for trainees to transfer their training effectively, the transfer climate must contain the antecedents necessary and ensure that trainees experience suitable consequences such as positive reinforcement. Machin and Fogarty (2000) offered different strategies that trainers and supervisors could use to enhance the positive aspects of the climate for transfer and reduce the negative aspects. Strategies to improve the positive aspects include these:

- Provide trainees with specific goal cues that target improved performance resulting from transfer of training (these may be self-determined or assigned).
- Provide trainees with social cues where supervisors and fellow workers are supportive of the attempts to transfer training.
- Provide trainees with appropriate task (or structural cues), such as access to equipment or resources that are essential to the transfer of training.
- Provide positive reinforcement (such as recognition in a company newsletter or staff-member-of-the-month scheme) to those trainees who demonstrate better performance through the transfer of their training.
- Make a link between trainees' transfer of training and their access to further training, as well as their future job success.

Strategies to reduce the negative aspects include these:

- Reduce the situational constraints that may prevent trainees from transferring training, such as lack of time or opportunity to perform the tasks learned during training.
- Reduce the likelihood of trainees being criticized by their supervisors or peers by using an approach where all members of a work unit are trained at the same time.
- Reduce the likelihood of continued poor performance after training by improving monitoring of posttraining performance.

Interventions to Improve the Vertical Transfer of Training

The term *vertical transfer* has been coined to describe the process whereby individual-level performance outcomes combine to determine higher-level outcomes such as unit or team outcomes, or organizational performance (Brown, Weissbein, & Kozlowski, 1998). Where individual performance is combined across individuals, such as in a typing pool, the process is known as *composition* (Rousseau, 1985). In this situation, any one individual has a small impact on the group's overall performance. But when the performance of the team depends on a minimum contribution from one or more members, such as with an aircraft crew, the process is know as *compilation*. In this situation, transfer of each individual team member's training is critical for the team's performance. Cannon-Bowers and Salas (1998) described how transfer of training to team settings may require a better understanding in several areas. They suggested that further research was required to identify and establish techniques for analyzing team tasks. Also needed was further research on team cognition. A final research area was to develop a better understanding of ways to foster a continuous learning environment in teams. The Transfer Training Model (Thayer & Teachout, 1995) includes organizational results as an outcome of transfer of training but does not distinguish between the different processes (composition versus compilation) that operate to determine group-level outcomes.

Therefore, when transfer of training occurs in a team environment, particular attention must be paid to the mechanisms by which an individual's knowledge and skills are transformed into a team's overall performance. Kozlowski and Salas (1997) offered a number of suggestions for improving the vertical transfer of training (that is, where group-level outcomes are mainly dependent on compilation processes), including these:

- Training should be delivered at the unit or team level (that is, to intact units or teams) whenever the role of each member is critical to the group's performance and there are no redundant group members.
- Teams or units need to receive training that specifically develops the shared knowledge and understanding of members rather than simply focusing on individual knowledge and skill development.
- Training for teams or units may need to include all group members simultaneously in order to achieve the same level of reciprocity in training that occurs in the work environment.

As for the effect of the organizational context on the vertical transfer of training, Kozlowski and Salas (1997) proposed the following:

- The aspects of the climate for transfer of training that are relevant in any particular situation depend on the nature of the training provided, with only those aspects that are aligned with the training content having an influence on the transfer process.
- Training that is inconsistent with the defining values and culture of the organization is less likely to be supported.
- Organizations that promote a culture of continuous learning and align their human resource practices with the strategic direction of the organization will create a positive climate for the transfer of all types of training.

Summary of Posttraining Interventions

The posttraining interventions described here focus on improving the climate for the transfer of training and improving the vertical transfer of training. The key concepts underlying these interventions are the effect of the organizational context on trainees' implementation of their training, the need to understand the compilation processes that operate when training unit or team members, and the importance of aligning training with organizational goals and directions. These goals and strategies are summarized in the third column of Exhibit 9.1.

The next, concluding section of the chapter will discuss the difficulties and challenges that trainers, supervisors, and trainees face when they attempt to implement the pretraining, during training, and posttraining interventions outlined previously.

Difficulties and Challenges

Pretraining interventions focus on improving trainee motivation, enhancing self-efficacy, and improving perceptions of organizational support for training. Interventions during training focus on improving trainees' learning outcomes, improving transfer intentions, and improving reactions to training. Finally, posttraining interventions focus on improving the climate for the transfer of training and improving the vertical transfer of training. These strategies are the results of synthesizing the most up-to-date research in the area and can be applied by trainers, supervisors, and in some cases, the trainees themselves.

There has not been any consideration so far of the costs of each of the interventions or the relative difficulty of the different strategies. For example, when there is very little opportunity for the trainer to control the composition of the training group or the expectations that trainees have before the program begins, it is important that soon after commencement he or she give them an opportunity to set appropriate learning goals, participate in making decisions about the training course, and start planning how they will implement their training in their workplace. The trainer also needs to identify very early on those who may be threatened by the type of training that is being provided or who are at risk of not being able to participate fully in the training program. This may happen if a trainee does not attend all sessions, which is common when training takes place over a number of weeks.

Trainers also have little control over what happens after training and whether trainees will be rewarded for implementing the skills they have learned. One strategy is to prepare them to deal with the worst scenario they may face—that is, a totally negative climate for transfer—so that they do not become discouraged after their first attempts to use their new skills. However, this may have the effect of reducing their motivation to learn and transfer their training. The key to managing the transfer process is to make contingency plans specifying all the barriers and setbacks that can be anticipated and the appropriate course of action to follow. Training that does not prepare trainees to deal with the posttraining environment is quite likely to be ineffective.

Trainers may also struggle to assess the extent to which training develops in trainees adaptive expertise, because the core attributes (a detailed, well-organized knowledge structure and metacognitive skills) are difficult to measure. Simple behavioral measures of training outcomes are usually preferred (for example, a behavioral checklist) and these are usually administered at the end of training or shortly afterward. However, this practice may focus the attention on short-term behavioral outcomes rather than long-term development of expertise. Although trainers need to make use of a greater variety of assessment instruments that capture some of the core elements of adaptive expertise, these are not yet readily available.

The organizational climate for transfer of training has been shown to have a strong impact on training and transfer. First, there is an indirect impact through the trainees' pretraining motivation and expectations of being able to implement their training. Second, there is a direct impact on the opportunities for trainees to perform according to their training and the degree of support and encouragement they get from supervisors and coworkers. Training needs to go hand in hand with efforts to improve the organizational climate for transfer, although this is not usually attempted during training and development programs. One proposal is to replace the traditional training needs analysis with a transfer of training needs analysis (TTNA; Hesketh, 1997b) that identifies organizational constraints to the transfer of training. In some cases, the TTNA may conclude that transfer is very unlikely to occur and therefore that training should be delayed or abandoned.

Finally, the focus of training needs to shift from the purely individual level to include the unit or team and organizational levels. Many employees work in self-managing teams, and in some situations these teams cannot operate effectively unless each team member fulfills a particular role. But training courses have often focused on the individual team members' knowledge and skill, rather than the shared understanding of the team, and have been delivered to team members at different times, rather than incorporating intact teams. A better methodology is needed (such as better ways to analyze team tasks) to help trainers determine when training is required at the team level.

Conclusion

The reality is that training will sometimes be delivered in an organizational context that is not supportive, with trainees who have little motivation or interest, and with a focus on short-term outcomes that do not contribute to desirable team or organizational outcomes. However, the growing body of research and range of interventions that are now available will help ensure that when organizations do invest scarce resources in training their employees, there will be a much greater likelihood that the transfer of this training will be successful.

References

Baldwin, T. T. (1992). Effects of alternative modeling strategies on outcomes of interpersonal training. *Journal of Applied Psychology, 77,* 147–154.

Baldwin, T. T., & Ford, J. K. (1988). Transfer of training: A review and directions for future research. *Personnel Psychology, 41,* 63–105.

Baldwin, T. T., & Magjuka, R. J. (1997). Organizational context and training effectiveness. In J. K. Ford, S.W.J. Kozlowski, K. Kraiger, E. Salas, & M. S. Teachout (Eds.), *Improving training effectiveness in work organizations* (pp. 99–127). Hillsdale, NJ: Erlbaum.

Baldwin, T. T., Magjuka, R. J., & Loher, B. T. (1991). The perils of participation: Effects of choice of training on trainee motivation and learning. *Personnel Psychology, 44,* 51–65.

Bandura, A. (1997). *Self-efficacy: The exercise of control.* New York: Freeman.

Broad, M. L., & Newstrom, J. W. (1992). *Transfer of training: Action-packed strategies to ensure high payoff from training investments.* Reading, MA: Addison-Wesley.

Brown, K. G., Weissbein, D. A., & Kozlowski, S.W.J. (1998). *Linking training to organizational results: Research and practice on vertical transfer.* Unpublished manuscript, Henry B. Tippie College of Business, University of Iowa, Iowa City, IA.

Butterfield, E. C., & Nelson, G. D. (1989). Theory and practice of teaching for transfer. *Educational Technology Research and Development, 37*(3), 5–38.

Cannon-Bowers, J. A., & Salas, E. (1998). Team performance and training in complex environments: Recent findings from applied research. *Current Directions in Psychological Science, 7*(3), 83–87.

Cannon-Bowers, J. A., Salas, E., Tannenbaum, S. I., & Mathieu, J. E. (1995). Toward theoretically based principles of training effectiveness: A model and initial empirical investigation. *Military Psychology, 7*, 141–164.

Choi, J. N., Price, R. H., & Vinokur, A. D. (2000). *How context works in groups: The influence of group processes on individual coping outcomes.* Unpublished manuscript, Institute for Social Research, University of Michigan, Ann Arbor, MI.

Creed, P. A., Hicks, R., & Machin, T. (1996). The effects of psychosocial training climate on mental health outcomes for long-term unemployed individuals. *Australian & New Zealand Journal of Vocational Education Research, 4*(2), 26–41.

De Bono, E. (1985). *Six thinking hats.* Harmondsworth, UK: Penguin Books.

Detterman, D. K. (1993). The case for the prosecution: Transfer as an epiphenomenon. In D. K. Detterman & R. J. Sternberg (Eds.), *Transfer on trial: Intelligence, cognition, and instruction.* Norwood, NJ: Ablex.

Downs, S., & Perry, P. (1984). Developing learning skills. *Journal of European Industrial Training, 8*, 21–26.

Driskell, J. E., Willis, R. P., & Cooper, C. (1992). Effects of overlearning on retention. *Journal of Applied Psychology, 77*, 615–692.

Druckman, D., & Bjork, R. A. (Eds.). (1991). *In the mind's eye: Enhancing human performance.* Washington, DC: National Academy Press.

Druckman, D., & Bjork, R. A. (Eds.). (1994). *Learning, remembering, believing: Enhancing human performance.* Washington, DC: National Academy Press.

Facteau, J. D., Dobbins, G. H., Russell, J.E.A., Ladd, R. T., & Kudisch, J. D. (1995). The influence of general perceptions of the training environment on pretraining motivation and perceived training transfer. *Journal of Management, 21*, 1–25.

Farr, J. L., & Middlebrooks, C. L. (1990). Enhancing motivation to participate in professional development. In S. L. Willis & S. S. Dubin, (Eds.), *Maintaining professional competence: Approaches to career enhancement vitality, and success throughout a work life* (pp. 195–213). San Francisco: Jossey-Bass.

Ford, J. K., Quiñones, M. A., Sego, D. J. & Sorra, J. S. (1992). Factors affecting the opportunity to perform trained tasks on the job. *Personnel Psychology, 45,* 511–527.

Ford, J. K., & Weissbein, D. A. (1997). Transfer of training: An updated review and analysis. *Performance Improvement Quarterly, 10*(2), 22–41.

Foxon, M. J. (1993). A process approach to the transfer of training. Part 1: The impact of motivation and supervisor support on transfer maintenance. *Australian Journal of Educational Technology, 9*(2), 130–143.

Foxon, M. J. (1994). A process approach to the transfer of training. Part 2: Using action planning to facilitate the transfer of training. *Australian Journal of Educational Technology, 10*(1), 1–18.

Fraser, B. J. (1981). Predictive validity of an individualised classroom environment questionnaire. *Alberta Journal of Educational Research, 29,* 240–251.

Frese, M., & Altmann, A. (1989). The treatment of errors in learning and training. In L. Bainbridge & S.A.R. Quintanilla (Eds.), *Developing skills with new technology* (pp. 65–86). New York: Wiley.

Frese, M., & Zapf, D. (1994). Action as the core of work psychology: A German approach. In H. C. Triandis, M. D. Dunnette, & L. M. Hough (Eds.), *Handbook of industrial and organizational psychology* (Vol. 4, 2nd ed., pp. 271–340). Palo Alto, CA: Consulting Psychologists Press.

Georgenson, D. L. (1982). The problem of transfer calls for partnerships. *Training and Development Journal, 36*(10), 75–78.

Gick, M. L., & Holyoak, K. J. (1987). The cognitive basis of knowledge transfer. In S. M. Cormier & J. D. Hagman (Eds.), *Transfer of learning: Contemporary research and applications* (pp. 9–46). Orlando: Academic Press.

Gollwitzer, P. M. (1999). Implementation intentions: Strong effects of simple plans. *American Psychologist, 54,* 493–503.

Haccoun, R. R. (1997). Transfer and retention: Let's do both and avoid dilemmas. *Applied Psychology: An International Review, 46,* 340–344.

Haccoun, R. R., & Saks, A. M. (1998). Training in the 21st century: Some lessons from the last one. *Canadian Psychology, 39*(1–2), 33–51.

Hesketh, B. (1997a). Dilemmas in training for transfer and retention. *Applied Psychology: An International Review, 46,* 317–339.

Hesketh, B. (1997b). W(h)ither dilemmas in training for transfer. *Applied Psychology: An International Review, 46,* 380–386.

Holding, D. H. (1991). Transfer of training. In J. E. Morrison (Ed.), *Training for performance: Principles of applied human learning* (pp. 93–125). New York: Wiley.

Holton, E. F. III. (1996). The flawed four-level evaluation model. *Human Resource Development Quarterly, 7,* 5–21.

Ivancic, K., & Hesketh, B. (1995–96). Making the best of errors during training. *Training Research Journal, 1,* 103–126.

Kamouri, A. L., Kamouri, J., & Smith, K. H. (1986). Training by exploration: Facilitating transfer of procedural knowledge through analogical reasoning. *International Journal of Man-Machine Studies, 24,* 171–190.

Kluger, A. N., & DeNisi, A. (1996). Effects of feedback intervention on performance: A historical review, a meta-analysis, and a preliminary feedback intervention theory. *Psychological Bulletin, 119,* 254–284.

Kozlowski, S.W.J., & Salas, E. (1997). An organizational systems approach for the implementation and transfer of training. In J. K. Ford, S.W.J. Kozlowski, K. Kraiger, E. Salas, & M. S. Teachout (Eds.), *Improving training effectiveness in work organizations* (pp. 247–287). Hillsdale, NJ: Erlbaum.

Latham, G. P., & Crandall, S. R. (1991). Organizational and social factors. In J. E. Morrison (Ed.), *Training for performance: Principles of applied human learning* (pp. 259–285). New York: Wiley.

Latham, G. P., & Seijts, G. H. (1999). The effects of proximal and distal goals on performance of a complex task. *Journal of Organizational Behavior, 20,* 421–429.

Lintern, G. (1991). An informational perspective on skill transfer in human-machine systems. Special Issue: Training theory, methods, and technology. *Human Factors, 33,* 251–266.

Locke, E. A., & Latham, G. P. (1990). *A theory of goal setting and task performance.* Englewood Cliffs, NJ: Prentice Hall.

Luthans, F., & Kreitner, R. (1985). *Organizational behavior modification and beyond: An operant and social learning approach* (rev. ed.). Glenview, IL: Scott, Foresman.

Machin, M. A. (2000, November). *Enhancing the transfer of aviation team training.* Paper presented at the Fifth Australian Aviation Psychology Symposium, Manly, Australia.

Machin, M. A., & Fogarty, G. J. (1998, August). *The role of transfer climate and implementation activities in the transfer of training to the workplace.* Paper presented at the 24th International Congress of Applied Psychology, San Francisco.

Machin, M. A., & Fogarty, G. J. (2000). *The structure of transfer climate and its role in the transfer of training to the workplace.* Unpublished manuscript, Department of Psychology, University of Southern Queensland, Toowoomba, Australia.

Marlatt, G. A., & Gordon, J. R. (1985). *Relapse prevention: Maintaining strategies in the treatment of addictive behaviors.* New York: Guilford Press.

Marx, R. D. (1982). Relapse prevention for managerial training: A model of maintenance of behavior change. *Academy of Management Review, 7,* 433–441.

McDaniel, M. A., & Schlager, M. S. (1990). Discovery learning and transfer of problem-solving skills. *Cognition and Instruction, 7*(2), 129–159.

McGehee, W., & Thayer, P. W. (1961). *Training in business and industry.* New York: Wiley.

Meyer, J. P., Allen, N. J., & Smith, K. A. (1993). Commitment to organizations and occupations: Extension and test of a three-component conceptualization. *Journal of Applied Psychology, 78,* 538–551.

Milheim, W. D. (1994). A comprehensive model for the transfer of training. *Performance Improvement Quarterly, 7*(2), 95–104.

Murtada, N., & Haccoun, R. R. (1996). Self monitoring and goal setting as determinants of transfer of training in real settings. *Canadian Journal of Behavioural Science, 28*(2), 92–101.

Newstrom, J. W. (1986). Leveraging management development through the management of transfer. *Journal of Management Development, 5*(5), 33–45.

Noe, R. A. (1986). Trainee attributes and attitudes: Neglected influences in training effectiveness. *Academy of Management Review, 11,* 736–749.

Peters, L. H., O'Connor, E. J., & Eulberg, J. R. (1985). Situational constraints: Sources, consequences and future considerations. *Research in Personnel and Human Resource Management, 3,* 79–114.

Proctor, R. W., & Dutta, A. (1995). *Skill acquisition and human performance.* Thousand Oaks, CA: Sage.

Quiñones, M. A., Sego, D. J., Ford, J. K., & Smith, E. M. (1995–96). The effects of individual and transfer environment characteristics on the opportunity to perform trained tasks. *Training Research Journal, 1,* 29–48.

Rouiller, J. Z., & Goldstein, I. L. (1993). The relationship between organizational transfer climate and positive transfer of training. *Human Resource Development Quarterly, 4,* 377–390.

Rousseau, D. M. (1985). Issues of level in organizational research: Multilevel and cross-level perspectives. In L. L. Cummings & B. Staw (Eds.), *Research in organizational behavior* (Vol. 7; pp. 1–38). Greenwich, CT: JAI Press.

Salomon, G., & Perkins, D. N. (1989). Rocky roads to transfer: Rethinking mechanisms of a neglected phenomenon. *Educational Psychologist, 24,* 113–142.

Schmidt, R. A., & Bjork, R. A. (1992). New conceptualizations of practice: common principles in three paradigms suggest new concepts for training. *Psychological Science, 3,* 207–217.

Schmidt, R. A., & Young, D. E. (1987). Transfer of movement control in motor skill learning. In S. M. Cormier & J. D. Hagman (Eds.), *Transfer of learning: Contemporary research and applications. The educational technology series* (pp. 47–79). Orlando: Academic Press.

Singer, R. N., & Pease, D. (1976). A comparison of discovery learning and guided instructional strategies on motor skill learning, retention, and transfer. *Research Quarterly, 47,* 788–796.

Singley, M. K., & Anderson, J. R. (1989). *The transfer of cognitive skill.* Cambridge, MA: Harvard University Press.

Slavin, R. E. (1983). When does cooperative learning increase student achievement? *Psychological Bulletin, 94,* 429–445.

Smith, E. M., Ford, J. K., & Kozlowski, S.W.J. (1997). Building adaptive expertise: Implications for training design strategies. In M. A. Quiñones & A. Ehrenstein (Eds.), *Training for a rapidly changing workforce* (pp. 89–118). Washington, DC: American Psychological Association.

Stevens, C. K., & Gist, M. E. (1997). Effects of self-efficacy and goal orientation training on negotiation skill maintenance: What are the mechanisms? *Personnel Psychology, 50,* 955–978.

Tannenbaum, S. I., & Yukl, G. (1992). Training and development in work organizations. *Annual Review of Psychology, 43,* 399–441.

Thayer, P. W., & Teachout, M. S. (1995). *A climate for transfer model* (AL/HR-TP-1995–0035). Brooks Air Force Base, TX: Technical Training Research Division, Armstrong Laboratory.

Tracey, J. B., Tannenbaum, S. I., & Kavanagh, M. J. (1995). Applying trained skills on the job: The importance of the work environment. *Journal of Applied Psychology, 80,* 239–252.

Tziner, A., Haccoun, R. R., & Kadish, A. (1991). Personal and situational characteristics influencing the effectiveness of transfer of training improvement strategies. *Journal of Occupational Psychology, 64,* 167–177.

Volet, S. E. (1991). Modeling and coaching of relevant metacognitive strategies for enhancing university students' learning. *Learning and Instruction, 1,* 319–336.

CHAPTER 10

Creating and Maintaining the Learning Organization

John C. Jeppesen

For the purposes of this chapter, learning organizations are defined as companies that deliberately design employee development and support continuous learning systems to deliver "future-ready" operational capacity and competitive performance. This definition incorporates the features and benefits that leaders usually want to get from a learning organization.

- *Desired features:* Design and development of systems to integrate organizational, team, and individual learning for combined (synergistic) effects
- *Desired benefits:* Deliberate or intentional development of learning systems that enhance the future readiness of the organization or its competitive performance

Since 1990, when Peter Senge's book *The Fifth Discipline* popularized the concept of learning organizations, writers have offered a wide variety of definitions. They generally address the value of knowledge and learning for the purpose of business success and survival. Common themes in the actions, processes, and purposes of learning organizations are summarized in Exhibit 10.1.

This chapter looks at research on the characteristics of and outcomes for learning organizations. Advances in research in cognitive science (the way adults learn) and knowledge engineering (system designs for knowledge acquisition and application) sug-

Exhibit 10.1. Fundamentals of the Learning Organization.

Actions (What)	Processes (How)	Processes (How)
Align: Define a shared business vision (Senge et al., 1994), a perception of performance gaps (DiBella & Nevis, 1998), and the role of learning in business success (Guns, 1996). *Invest:* "Better manage knowledge, utilize technology, empower people, and expand learning" (Marquardt, 1996, p. 2).	*Purposefully:* Consciously and intentionally create effective learning systems (Morris, 1997). *Systemically:* Integrate business process with learning (DeGeus, 1997; Raelin, 2000).	*Prepare:* Anticipate and make ready for future business scenarios (DeGeus, 1997). *Respond:* Adapt and change (Marquardt, 1996). *Change:* Make changes in behavior based on learning (Garvin, 1993).

gest practical design principles and processes for learning organizations. Much of the applied research (Ford, Kozlowski, Kraiger, Salas, & Teachout, 1997) also supports certain design features to produce desirable business outcomes. These findings suggest that a systemic or integrated—that is, organization-team-individual—approach to improvement of training transfer in turn supports the capacity-building and performance objectives of learning organizations.

Although the theory behind learning organizations is maturing, the criteria for assessing an organization, creating key components, monitoring its progress, and measuring business outcomes are less well defined. This chapter provides the business case for learning organizations, a review of their key characteristics, and evidence of their benefits and performance outcomes. Then, a new tool for designing and measuring learning systems is described, and practical guidelines are offered for developing and maintaining learning organizations. Finally, key roles for leaders at all levels and facilitators, such as human resource and OD practitioners, are presented.

The Need for Learning Organizations

Training and development of employees are only one kind of investment that organizations must make to enhance business capacity and performance. To create a learning organization, development of teams and processes for organizational change is also required.

What is driving the need for learning organizations and enhanced business capacity and performance? Several issues come to mind: the shift from a capital-intensive economy to a knowledge-intensive one; rapid advances in technology, especially in communications and e-commerce; the "de-jobbing" (adaptable project assignments and roles) of organizations; changing motivations of the workforce; changing definitions of and competencies for leadership; and global competition (Bachman, 2000; Chandler & Tang, 2000).

Faced with these challenges, organizations are considering the advantages of learning organization design and strategies. Business leadership and continuous learning strategies are also being redefined and integrated for a more sustainable business advantage. At the same time, organizations are viewing their employees as individual contributors (value-added roles) and independent contractors (outsourced specialty models). In other words, employees are expected to perform at a level above the conventional job title and task assignments. They are expected to bring more knowledge and learning to the business challenge. They may also expect more of themselves and other team members. Here are some of the personnel issues involved: more emphasis placed on the value an individual adds by integrating knowledge (for example, creating a business solution that is both technically sound and culturally appropriate to the organization); fast, demanding work cycles (bringing products to market in a shorter time frame or working collaboratively in a way that requires developing working relationships in addition to delivering a work product); a premium on applied knowledge of leading-edge technologies (for example, ways to use the Internet for integrated marketing or creating Web links to multiple products and services); expectation of cross-functional and generative skills (technical with sales support, team leadership roles, personal management, codevelopment, and so on); and personal investment in changing jobs, assignments, and business partnerships as situations change (actively looking for client engagements that build new performance capacities).

Because of these issues, the relationship between the company and the employee has changed; increasingly, the employee is considered a "learning customer" with personal preferences and motivations. The learning organization provides an environment for growing the individual's capabilities and experience while also growing its own collective capacity and business performance.

Characteristics of Learning Organizations: Current Models

In many ways, learning organization theory is a now a melting pot of organizational and learning theory and practice. This is understandable, because developing and maintaining a learning organization is a major change management or organizational development initiative. To get the greatest business benefits it is necessary to involve the members of the organization, as follows:

- Design with the end in mind—focus on performance or capacity goals.
- Leverage learning (or knowledge) assets.
- Build an integrated approach that includes key organizational characteristics.

This section of the chapter discusses all three areas and gives examples. The following section discusses business outcomes (that is, performance and capacity achievements).

Eight characteristics are common to current learning organization theories: systems thinking, leadership requirements, focus and framework, learning and work integration, multiplicity-diversity, continuous learning and knowledge use, external-internal connection, and learning in teams. The value, function, and common criteria for each characteristic are presented.

Systems Thinking

Peter Senge defined systems thinking as "a conceptual framework . . . to make the full patterns clearer, and help us see how to change them effectively" (Senge, Kleiner, Roberts, Ross, & Smith, 1994,

p. 7). By seeing, discussing, and taking action on the patterns in the internal and external events and processes that affect organizations, organizations can make informed business decisions.

As the concepts, practices of, and research on learning organizations have matured, it has become clear that leaders and facilitators of learning organization development benefit from viewing training and learning as interventions that are part of the larger systems that influence training transfer. In fact, training transfer is only one influence on the typical learning organization goals of increased business capacity and performance. For example, Stolovitch and Keeps (1998) observe that a learning organization intervention would include both learning and nonlearning (environmental, motivational, performance supports). Also, *systems* are defined from multiple perspectives, both individual and organizational.

Systems thinking may be defined in part by the integration of its tangible products. For example, in a global pharmaceutical company, the brand and product management department measures systems thinking by the quality of the brand plan, the extent to which it addresses the value proposition (exactly what is offered to the customer) of each pharmaceutical product relative to the diseases that it addresses, and its position against competitive drugs.

Processes that are typical of systems thinking also define it. From a management perspective, systems thinking is operationalized in terms of the extent to which needs assessment includes multiple levels of analysis and multiple domains (individual, team, and organizational) (Kozlowski & Salas, 1997) and of the extent to which learning systems design has congruent technical structure and business skills. Obviously, design and development should be guided by multilevel assessment and revised based on measurement and evaluation. It is also important to consider the fit between the organizational culture (Schneider, 1994) and the change initiatives. This approach defines how organizational goals can be met.

From the organizational perspective, systems thinking includes consideration of potential barriers to learning. Barriers are identified and removed. These situational constraints (Mathieu & Martineau, 1997), including information about the job, tools, equipment, and supplies needed for learning, have an effect on learner motivation.

In addition, an assessment to confirm and explore the specifications, availability, timing, and learning media preferences of the learners serves two functions: it helps identify learning barriers and it provides data against which assumptions about these important learning systems design factors can be checked and modified. Once the learning systems are deployed, it may also be useful to confirm that the barriers are in fact removed from the learners' perspective. If learners are aware of these efforts, it may positively influence their motivation.

Organizational support for learning is consistently shown to have a positive impact on training transfer (Machin, Chapter Nine, this volume; Mathieu & Martineau, 1997). For example, senior executives were involved in the design of a business simulation for top managers in a petroleum products corporation. Participants were told to leave their cell phones and their work at home. The executive team facilitated the simulation and also was directly involved in debriefing and meaning-making sessions during the simulation. At the end of the simulation, which lasted several days, participants were asked to write a letter to themselves indicating their specific intentions to apply the learning. Overall, participants not only gave the simulation high marks but in-process measures of decision-making quality (a desired outcome) improved for all teams.

From an individual perspective, important motivational aspects of systems thinking are defined in terms of social cognitive theory (Bandura, 1986) and valence-instrumentality-expectancy theory (Vroom, 1964). Research on social cognitive theory (Baldwin & Magjuka, 1997) indicates that individual behavior is influenced by and affects the environment. Individuals' behavior is influenced by the degree to which they think they can do something (self-efficacy) and their expectations of what will happen if they do (outcome expectancies). For example, in a global research project that I did for a high-technology company on learning preferences, infrastructure status, and learner motivations, learners consistently ranked the motivations of "being challenged" and "making a difference" higher than monetary compensation. Research also shows that setting difficult goals is often related to high performance outcomes (Locke & Latham, 1990). When individuals have information that training or learning is an opportunity, training effects can be enhanced (Martocchio, 1992). It is reasoned that measurement of perceived self-efficacy and expected outcomes provides a focus for part of the pretraining assessment (Baldwin & Magjuka, 1997) and can guide the organizational change design needed to develop the learning organization. This approach examines how organizational needs can be met by better understanding what the individuals and teams in the organization need.

The framework of valence-instrumentality-expectancy (VIE) theory is useful for understanding how individual motivation is related to postlearning outcomes (Mathieu & Martineau, 1997). *Expectancy* refers to a person's belief that he can learn a skill, *instrumentality* refers to his beliefs about whether the skill will be useful for certain outcomes, and *valence* refers to his judgment of the desirability of those outcomes. As with social cognitive theory, assessment of these learner motivation factors suggests a systematic and practical approach to training focus, design, and organizational support. If the organization views its members as learning customers, then these considerations are simply a way to design customer-focused training or learning systems. This customer focus should include communications to influence learners' beliefs about the learning content, application, and personal outcomes.

Together, organizational and individual- or team-level assessment with systematic design and development of the learning organization are measurable evidence of systems thinking at the organizational level. Research strongly recommends that learning interventions involve "domains" that influence transferability to work and the goals of growth in organizational capacity and performance. However, systems affecting the organization are not just internal; measures that involve the larger business environment are addressed in the following discussion of the external connection.

Leadership Requirements

Developing and maintaining a learning organization is a huge undertaking. The guidance of leadership must be observable and continuous. Furthermore, leadership need not be defined only at the top of an organization's hierarchy; many organizations today include explicit leadership competency requirements for most job positions. For one electrical instrument firm, teams (called "adhocracies") including formal leadership, subject matter experts, and strategy-minded employees from many areas of the organization make strategic, visionary decisions affecting the organization's future. These adhocracies are also a primary means by which the organization shares its vision and sets strategic goals. In essence, decision making is a learning activity, and the process of developing business strategy refines the organization's ability to learn (DeGeus, 1997). By including diverse participants, the organization may identify and leverage influences for business success.

The role of leadership in the learning organization may also include facilitation and even internal performance consulting. To start with the fundamentals, Thompson notes that it is necessary for the organization's executives to remove their own blocks to learning and demonstrate commitment to it by providing a clear vision, a specific blueprint (basic structure), investments, and milestones for change (DeGeus, 1997).

Bob Guns (1996) in his book *The Faster Learning Organization* asserts that the executive must provide direction for the organization by defining the "value constellation" for the business. This value constellation provides the rest of the organization with a clear direction for individual and team contributions. For example, the president of a small consulting firm, who was seeking investment capital, urged business unit leaders to "productize" services so that they had tangible features, reusable tools, benefits, a quality assurance process, and proven marketability. This focus not only provided guidance for demonstrating business valuation but also provided concise information for sales and standards and tools for training new hires.

Focus and Framework

With the support of leadership, a basic focus on becoming and maintaining a learning organization can motivate individual employees and teams to build a shared framework for building capacity and business performance. This framework may include a shared vision (Senge et al., 1994), a clear idea of the company's direction (Catalanello, 1994), a focus on or clarification of the business purpose (DeGeus, 1997), agreement on how business success is defined (Handy, 1997), and a shared perception of a performance gap (DiBella & Nevis, 1998).

The framework also includes decision and measurement tools. For example, the organization might learn what the key leading indicators of the business or a functional area are and teams may be allowed to determine the success criteria and measures that will be included in a routine summary measurement report, like the balanced scorecard popularized by Kaplan (Kaplan & Norton, 1992). The balanced scorecard is also a means to monitor multiple business processes, influences, and outcomes, and this in turn supports other essential learning organization characteristics, such as systems thinking and external connection. It also provides a simple medium for vertical and horizontal organizational communications and dialogue.

For example, a balanced scorecard framework for a large petrochemical business included industry standards for environmental responsibility and community involvement along with financial performance indicators. Leadership training simulations were designed to include experience in balancing resources to achieve financial goals but not at the cost of environmental responsibility (prevention of and response to accidents) and active community involvement. Because this simulation was required of all upper management employees, the message that all three goals were important for business success was delivered consistently.

Catalanello (1994) recommends that measurement tools should emphasize progress and improvement rather than control and accountability. When measurement focuses on control and accountability, this may lessen the motivation of individuals and teams to continue with change initiatives.

Learning and Work Integration

The tradition in organizations has often been to consider training as an isolated, necessary event for employees to gain knowledge and skills that they will apply someday. But increasingly organizations are asking for a return on the training investment, and ultimately they need to know that these investments will support business goals in both the short and long term. Current learning organization theory and practice consistently endorses efforts to use what is known about adult learning, cognitive science, and knowledge management practices to make a strong link between learning and actual performance requirements.

Byrd (1997) and Marquardt (1996) both state that in learning organizations learning and operations must be linked, and learning must be viewed as an essential investment in business success. In his groundbreaking work *Work-Based Learning* (2000), Joseph Raelin recommends several types of initiatives, including action learning, which enhances learning-work integration and dramatically improves the training transfer to on-the-job challenges. Similarly, Estee Solomon Gray, chief e-learning officer at Interwise, states that when the Internet is integrated successfully, learning happens automatically and becomes completely integrated with "doing"; in other words, learning changes from knowledge as matter to knowledge as practice.

At one of the world's premier luxury hotels, providing reliable and superior customer service is paramount. To guarantee transfer of best-in-company practices, any unique practice refined by a hotel employee must be simple, process-specific, and of reliable quality and cost. The employee then takes the role of internal consultant to other hotels in the same chain. He or she is given the opportunity to provide the information and follow up with a site visit necessary to duplicate the innovation in these other hotels; if successful, he or she is assisted with his or her next career move in the company. This policy on transferring best-in-company practices clearly serves the needs of both the hotels and the innovative employees. Integration of the training aspects with work is also a good example of the motivating power of social cognitive theory and VIE theory in action.

Multiplicity-Diversity

Learning organizations need many sources of learning in order to detect the need for, anticipate, and build for change. Several sources are needed because single or traditional sources may not allow for detecting or understanding changes in the marketplace, translating an idea into action, or adopting successful solutions. For example, in the luxury hotel business just mentioned, ideas and sources for process improvement were taken from an entirely separate business—manufacturing. The organization needed to manage flawlessly the conferences and meetings held at its hotels, so it borrowed lessons learned from job shop industries that also customize processes to meet each unique customer need. If a business is overcommitted to business strategies and tactics that are not tested by diverse applications and points of view, it may not get what it needs to adapt and change successfully. To survive and thrive, learning organizations need to support multiple, diverse inputs and analysis.

Thompson (1997) refers to the benefit of multiple feedback structures. Many organizations have embraced the practical value of cross-functional teams. By inviting input from team participants with different functional responsibilities, business solutions can be improved and process costs can be reduced. Jack Stack's (1992) case study of a dramatic turnaround in a remanufacturing business shows the value of having all employees work from the same open book for success (income statement, cash flow statement, and balance sheet) and find ways to improve continually. Annual sales increased by a factor of five and stock value skyrocketed. Arie DeGeus (1997) asserts that a learning organization can measure its tolerance for the necessary diversity through an index of the openness of the system.

Continuous Learning and Knowledge Use

First, let us revisit the basics. *Data* are transformed into *information* when people organize the data, and information is transformed into *knowledge* when people attach meaning to it. Each step in the process brings more meaning and potential value for the learning to individuals and the organization. The hallmark of learning organization processes is continuous learning and practical application of knowledge gained. Continuous learning is supported because it promotes the acquisition, testing, and application of knowledge gained in the learning cycle and applied to the adaptability and readiness of the organization to inevitable internal and external changes. Both adaptive and anticipatory learning have been seen to be characteristics of learning organizations. Argyris and Schon (1978) identify different types of adaptive learning; in increasing order of value for breadth and depth of application, they include *single-loop learning* (gaining information to maintain or solve immediate problems), *double-loop learning* (reflecting and questioning the system or process), and *deutero learning* (learning about learning, to invent new ways to learn and improve the learning process itself). DeGeus (1997), of Royal Dutch/Shell, refers to planning and business scenario testing as learning in anticipation and in preparation for the future (*anticipatory learning*). *Action learning* is the fifth type of learning that is relevant for learning organizations. It is learning designed to solve real business problems. As we have indicated, Raelin (2000) presents this type of learning as one of the most effective tools for addressing the training-learning transfer to the job.

Leaders of learning organization development and research all refer to one or more cycles of learning, each with specific stages. When operational definitions are applied to the specific parts of a learning cycle, there is the potential for measurable evidence that learning happened and the knowledge gained was used. Also, like the progression of data to information to knowledge, each stage adds value. The cyclical aspect of learning is simply that the last step feeds back information that influences the next iteration; this is the continuous part of continuous learning. Each step of the learning cycle must be supported or the full value will be lost. Exhibit 10.2 shows three different taxonomies for learning cycles.

What the models have in common is this: information is recognized for its value, structured or synthesized into knowledge, and then stored, transferred, or used. These learning processes, of course, may have higher-order value if questioning the system or process (double-loop learning) or even reinventing the learning

Exhibit 10.2. Comparison of Learning Cycle Models.

Strategic Learning Cycle[a]	Knowledge Subsystem[b]	Organizational Learning[c]
• Continuous planning • Improvised implementation • Deep reflection on the results	• Acquisition (data and information) • Creation of new knowledge through problem solving and insights • Storage • Transfer-utilization	• Knowledge creation or acquisition • Knowledge dissemination • Knowledge use

[a]Catalanello, 1994, p. 23.
[b]Marquardt, 1996, p. 26.
[c]DiBella & Nevis, 1998, p. 28.

process (deutero learning) is promoted by the organization, its teams, or its members.

Evidence of double-loop learning suggests that the organization is truly on the continuous learning path, because this type of learning (and deutero learning) can change the organization's future. According to the American Society of Training and Development's Learning Organization Network, the presence of double-loop learning is an important criterion for characterizing a true learning organization (Catalanello, 1994).

The minimum criterion for continuous learning is that both individuals and the organization support all steps of a learning cycle. The maximum criterion is that the organization continually explores and encourages higher-order learning while maintaining learning cycles at other levels.

Another criterion for continuous learning is the degree to which the organizational infrastructure reinforces knowledge and practice needed for behavioral readiness (Raelin, 2000). This infrastructure can include multiple media choices (for example, e-mail, brown bag lunches, and Web-based learning), hardware (computers and other learning tools), and varied methods of learning (different ways to access content, both technological and interpersonal). Marquardt (1996) adds use of technology as a learning organization characteristic.

Continuous learning and systems for knowledge use usually involve support of many strategies that may include people, processes, technology, or all three. For example, one high-growth consulting firm has "people managers" who help individual consultants with both personal development plans and resources and capture reusable contributions to business products and processes. Content assets from the process of meeting particular client needs are managed and retrieved by corporate "cybrarians." They also use brown bag sessions with staff to convey lessons learned and discuss applications. This process progressed from the goal of equipping participants to be fluent in discussing it later to the goal of preparing them actually to demonstrate the new behaviors after the session. Similarly, one of the top three automakers in the United States uses a knowledge management system (KMS)—a searchable database—to manage intellectual capital. The company captures lessons learned in an electronically accessible "book of knowledge" that employees can access whenever they need to. This has helped the company retain the knowledge gained by people who have left or changed locations. The leadership believes that this KMS, combined with cross-functional team learning, is a big contributor to cycle time reduction (time from product concept to building the car) from sixty to thirty months, as well as billions of dollars in cost.

External-Internal Connection

To be in touch with the marketplace, customers, employees, and other departments, learning organizations need to use external connections. David Schwandt's (1997) organizational learning model of the environmental interface is the main source for information. It is the raw material for the continuous learning–knowledge use characteristic of learning organizations. Although Schwandt refers only to the external source, the model applies equally well to connections inside an organization. Internal connections are clearly relevant when other individuals, teams, or departments are considered as sources for useful information, data, or knowledge.

In general, external-internal connections should provide what DiBella and Nevis (1998) call the learning organization's "scanning imperative" (p. 63). The learning organization must have many ways of looking outside, and many perspectives at the organizational, team, and individual levels. Sanford (1997) identifies improved communication and interaction in the organization and connecting individuals to the marketplace as an improvement target.

What are some of the types of internal and external connections that are characteristic of learning organizations? The list is expansive. Specific examples of external connections include partnering (Byrd, 1997) as a way of amplifying, leveraging, and exchanging knowledge. Chandler and Tang (2000), in their investment report on the e-learning industry, also note that the extended knowledge distribution enterprise can integrate and include players in the whole value chain (internal employees, direct sales, value-added resellers, distributors, wholesalers, retailers, and end users). To this internal and downstream list, the upstream players (business partners and suppliers) may be added. Whether external connections are informal (personal contacts) or formal (direct training and collaboration), consideration should be given to their advantages and disadvantages. Criteria for the effectiveness of these learning and information connections vary, depending on the players in the exchange and their respective roles and objectives.

One example of external-internal connections comes from a large pharmaceutical company's market research team. Brand and product managers, as well as the sales team, are updated on the changing industry structure, trends, and tactics through internal cross-functional meetings. Those who attend the meetings maintain active participation in professional associations, supplier forums, and their contacts with key industry watchers and customers. Collectively and individually they scan competitive trends, specific techniques, and lessons learned.

In another example, an electronic components firm has institutionalized external scanning. Like many organizations, it conducts external benchmarking but also specifically encourages an expanded focus that includes what it calls "the state of the art in service businesses." By casting the net widely in its niche, the company establishes relationships and gains knowledge from unconventional sources. It also offers paid sabbaticals during which its employees can get exposure to new learning experiences.

Learning in Teams

Teams are a cohesive group assembled for a purpose. They are key to the learning organization because they are a forum for dialogue and support the reflective learning (Senge et al., 1994) necessary to advance the value of lessons learned and meaning attributed to team experiences. For leaders and facilitators, teams are the crucible for developing the group learning skills of the organization. For its members, the team is a place to work on business needs, issues, and problems and to improve personal competencies— listening, balancing advocacy of a point of view with the inquiry and exploration of other points of view, and conducting postmortems on decisions or conclusions, developing relationships and trust, and valuing diversity (Senge et al., 1994). Depending on the company culture and situation, teams may even run the company, as we have already seen. DeGeus (1997) asserts that this may be a good strategy for the most innovative companies.

When group motivation to learn is considered, research indicates that the structure for learning should be a group context, and rewards should be based on collaborative effort (Baldwin & Magjuka, 1997). This requires congruence between assignment, process, and compensation systems. Johnson and Johnson (1984) find that creative solutions and better decision making often result from cooperative learning.

For one large office technology company, organizational reflection is a core value. When the company invests in important change initiatives, an executive team collectively reviews what went well and what might be improved. Knowledge gained from the process is used to improve the project and other initiatives.

Another example is a financial corporation that has won the Baldrige National Quality Award. This company reviews each product during a semiannual performance appraisal. The process includes a team review of job design, necessary competencies, and training priorities. Subject matter experts (SMEs) from each product group make detailed presentations. Product groups also share lessons learned with all the other product groups. Both of these examples illustrate double-loop learning.

Evidence of Business Outcomes

Learning organizations systematically invest in business initiatives that are designed for a purpose. For Royal Dutch/Shell Oil, the purpose was to survive anticipated changes in the energy marketplace. The organization wanted the organizational capacity and readiness to change with the marketplace. Business scenario building (determining most likely future business conditions) was used to inform the leadership about the investments that would be necessary and the contingencies that would need to be practiced before the need was imminent. As a result of its investments in developing as a learning organization, the company diversified its business model to weather the dramatic changes in the energy market during the Arab oil embargo. Shell has given increasing autonomy to its operating divisions, pioneered scenario planning, and practiced processes for healthy peer review of business plans and operations. This process of linking learning to changes in business definition and process appears to be working. These factors seem relevant to Shell's business success: it exceeded Exxon in revenue in 1990, and from 1972 to 1992 the market value of its stock rose from twelfth to fourth worldwide (Catalanello, 1994).

Other organizations purposefully invest in the features of a learning organization that best meet their specific performance goals. For example, for the financial corporation with Baldrige honors, an innovative approach to customer relationships is to collaborate with customers to identify their goals and then work backward to determine how to realize them. The group completes a thorough "process mapping" that includes determining what needs to be done both upstream (before the internal process) and downstream (after the internal process) to achieve the customer goal. Measurement criteria for the goal are determined first, then a process is designed to make it possible. Overall, the company formally recognizes that knowledge is the key to customer relationships, and all departments are expected to learn about the customer relationships. The company has been able to double its sales volume with a major customer while holding costs stable. With this kind of performance, the financial corporation can state that they are meeting all of their financial goals while planning for the future."

Another common performance goal is improved cycle time. For example, a large office technology company with a core value of organizational reflection considers time to market the critical factor for its business success; leaders say a new technology is only successful if they get there first. To compete on a global level, they frequently find that they must look for alliances with competitors. Scanning for these external connections has paid off. Alliances make it possible to provide the customer solutions required by a rapidly changing market.

A prestigious business research firm offers another example. Its leaders recognize that the speed of business is driven by technology. New technologies are changing customer expectations about how fast they can get answers to research questions. Understandably, cycle time reduction is a competitive advantage. Accordingly, the company has invested in processes to learn customer relationships (through client books that record reflections on what works and what does not) and then design the business process for speed. In fact, it has used anticipatory learning to deliver not only what customers asked for but also things they did not know they needed. Through anticipation and planning for technological changes, the group builds capacity to deliver in parallel with actual information technology releases. Investing in a learning organization includes a focus on information technologies and the customer relationship; both are external connections that are vital to the business. Learning is intertwined with the business process and structured so that the whole team is well informed. Knowledge is obtained from client engagements, recorded in client books, and used to improve individual projects. The result is that cycle time for research production has decreased dramatically. The company now handles more business with the same number of staff.

A high-growth consulting firm that provides customized e-learning solutions has found that a redefinition of cycle time has helped identify a competitive advantage. This firm defines cycle time not from project start to delivered training product but rather from initial contact with the client to the realized performance change desired by the client. By taking a systems thinking approach to the cycle time issue, the sales partners are fully integrated in the cycle and advance the design and performance elements to make all links in the end-to-end process faster and better. This process includes a team learning approach with better external connection and continuous learning that is integrated into the work. With this approach, the consulting firm has realized a 30 percent reduction in cycle time over three years. Most of the improvement has come in the last year and a half.

A New Tool for Creating and Maintaining a Learning Organization

As we have seen, to be successful, creating and maintaining a learning organization must be a purposeful and continuous endeavor. Much as product and brand management are about the care and feeding of long-run market share and profitability, and Total Quality Management (TQM) is about the care and feeding of the quality process, leading or facilitating the learning organization is about the care and feeding of the systems, infrastructure, and learning processes that serve capacity building and performance goals. In essence, leaders and facilitators frequently need to take on an expanded role of internal performance consultant. With the right tools, they can design and support integrated learning systems with the end results of capacity and business performance in mind.

In the last five years, authors like DiBella and Nevis (1998) and Kozlowski and Salas (1997) have proposed a framework for multi-level, integrated models for learning organizations. Leaders and facilitators in organizations may have the components for learning organization development in place, but many lack a framework for integrating existing assets and investing in improvements. Practitioners often lack tools for examining and designing interventions in multiple domains that together support the link between learning systems and performance outcomes.

A recommended new tool for learning organizations uses the basic dynamic pattern found in all the characteristics of the effective and efficient learning organization: short-loop interaction (SLI) technology. It is a conceptual tool for organizing, supporting, and measuring the exchange of value and opportunity between critical domains in the learning organization. Again, in Peter Senge's words, systems thinking is "a conceptual framework . . . to make the full patterns clearer, and help us see how to change them effectively" (Senge et al., 1994, p. 7). SLI is a systems-thinking technology that helps identify the patterns between domains, plan for desirable effects, and diagnose problems. It is a companion tool to the more complex causal loop diagramming that is a specific learning tool for examining organizational processes and challenging the mental models associated with them (Senge et al., 1994). SLI is a tool for a top-level look at the many domains of the learning system. It helps identify the design features that may need additional or more detailed consideration. It is a practitioner's tool that applies to designing, diagnosing, and maintaining the characteristics and vital processes of the learning organization. The basic tool for SLI is depicted in Figure 10.1.

Consistent with the learning cycle models presented in the current literature (see Exhibit 10.2), this model represents a cycle. The difference is that it highlights the choices and benefits of *interactions,* which are key to the success of the learning organization.

Domains may be individuals, teams, or organizations. The SLI loop structure depicts a generic process with separate entities (organizations, teams, individuals) in Domains A and B that can choose to observe, assess, and interact with each other and with

Figure 10.1. Short-Loop Interaction (SLI) Technology Tool.

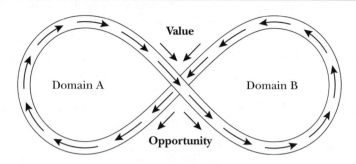

others for the purpose of adapting, changing, and preparing for future needs.

Interactions are viable when value and opportunity are exchanged between domains. Thus models of learning interactions may be considered building blocks of a systems-thinking framework. For example, let us say an individual in Domain A gains information or knowledge (an opportunity), expands on it to develop potential value to others in the organization or team, and then shares it with an individual in Domain B. In turn, that individual may perceive this as an opportunity (organizational, team, or individual) to learn and build value (again for the organization, team, or self), perhaps through reflective or action learning, and then share a new insight or solution with the same or several entities in one or several domains. The interaction is mutually beneficial to the extent that value and opportunity are perceived, tested, and acted on. The SLI model also incorporates the motivational features of Bandura's (1986) social cognitive theory (self-efficacy, outcome expectancies) and Vroom's (1964) VIE theory, here translated into beliefs about learning from the other domain, usefulness of creating value, and desirability of the potential opportunities.

Learning organization characteristics, such as the leadership requirements, focus and framework, and learning and work integration discussed earlier, are simply areas that can be supported and maintained so that interactions among individuals, teams, and organizations (the domains) build the learning that delivers business capacity and performance. For leaders and practitioners, these are the areas in which to consider interventions. The goal is to support the kinds of interactions and relationships among people in separate domains that further business capacity and performance. The SLI framework offers a simplified view of individual building blocks that can combine for the desired synergistic effects.

Let us examine some of these considerations in a practical business example that illustrates SLI building block combinations. In this example, leaders (leadership characteristic, Domain A) present to development teams (people, in Domain B) the "strategic leverage opportunity" (Guns, 1996, p. 46) of some key proprietary knowledge. Let us further say that the development teams are product management teams and that the value of proprietary knowledge will cause them to rethink how they can offer customer value. The leader (the company president) has provided the proprietary knowledge as a valued piece of information that can help the teams consider the variety of products or product extensions (multiplicity-diversity characteristic) that may succeed in the changing marketplace. The Domain B teams might well consider the business case for R&D investments needed to make the shift. This process is part of continuous learning–knowledge used. Let us say that learning in teams requires that all members bring their own experience and external connections with other domains, such as professional associations and routine scanning of the marketplace. The team leaders might coach them, or they might be guided by their own motivation to succeed personally; therefore, they would bring value to their interactions in these domains by knowing generally what they are looking for in the external connections. Learning-work integration also occurs when individual contributors in teams see the connection between learning more about the external factors that support or disagree with the business meaning of the proprietary knowledge. If leaders wish to maintain the benefits of their own learning, they might also remove the perceived barriers for individual contributors to provide a short-loop interaction of feedback on both the successes and failures of the focus or framework they provided in the form of the specific proprietary knowledge. This is an opportunity to examine the mental models and pursue a dialogue that both the company president and the team members or individual contributors used to form the learning content that they shared or did not share. If properly examined, these exchanges could serve the benefit of examining the process of the exchange (double-loop learning) or even reconsider the content domains used by each participant and how the learning process could be improved (deutero learning).

Typical SLI domain interactions that provide planning and diagnostic value include, but are not limited, to organization–individual contributor, management–individual contributor, individual contributor–outside sources, team–individual contributor, training–desired business benefits (capacity and performance). And because all are considered true interactions, each side of the loop affects the other side. For the leader or facilitator, the task is to conduct a multilevel assessment that will inform the decisions about where to start and to consider which investments in learning systems will promote the interactions that build the learning organization. Leaders need to identify the types of SLI domain interactions that are needed for successful learning organization initiatives.

In looking at SLI domain interactions that may be part of initial or ongoing initiatives, considerations may include leadership (for example, direction, structure, focus, motivation), barriers to performance, training and nontraining issues, knowledge development and learning cycles, learner motivation and supporting systems, consistency and congruence of organizational supports for learning (for example, use of multilevel needs assessment, compensation, coaching), learning content and business goals alignment, situational factors, external connections, and ways to operationalize and measure the inputs and outputs. The SLI framework illustrates the importance and process of making decisions about which interactions are well-suited to the learning and the performance goals of the organization. Because developing a learning organization involves change initiatives at several levels, it is important to have a consistent model for planning the change, anticipating needs, and diagnosing problems with mutually supporting systems. SLI offers a way to look at many levels and domains of interactions that can affect learning and business outcomes. As a tool, it is also neutral in cultures and situations; it works with all considerations of interest to the practitioner.

The short-loop part of the SLI technology is an objective that is analogous to the speed, efficiency, and effectiveness needs of the dynamic process. "Shorter is better" because adaptation, adjustment, and future readiness can happen sooner, with less effort, and with better outcomes. When the interaction involves entities that communicate directly and when they understand, appreciate, and use the value brought by their counterpart entities in the other domain, the interaction loop is shorter. Alternatively, when the interaction is initially indirect or less effective—such as when an individual gathers market intelligence without dialogue with the source—then understanding the reliability, frequency, and predictive value of the source may motivate the individual contributor to refine and improve the speed, efficiency, and effectiveness of using that source. The loop can be shortened.

The SLI tool also helps structure questions about how people in distinct but related domains can improve the value they bring to the interaction and how they can adapt to recognize, reframe, and respond to potential opportunities. In other words, the SLI tool can help those in a learning organization learn how to make useful contributions that invite critical interactions and increase overall learning capacity.

Practical Guidelines

Based on the research and case studies, the following guidelines are suggested for the development and maintenance of a learning organization.

• *Assess business strategy and links to learning initiatives.* First determine the strategic organizational goals and how learning may have a part in achieving them. For example, if long-term survival of the corporation is paramount, then building operational flexibility and capacity for change will be the priority. In contrast, if goals are more immediate and tied to short-term financial performance and specific business investments, then building capacity may be less important than continuing to muster resources that help realize the performance objectives. This will determine key priorities and therefore the types of investments in learning that will be needed. Development of a learning organization is a change initiative; where you need to go will determine how you get there.

• *Support necessary roles.* Key to a successful strategy is involving people at multiple levels of the organization. As Guns (1996) notes, the critical roles include leaders, key people who will develop others, and people who will transform the strategy. For long-term business advantage, consider and include diverse individual contributors. The combined roles of individual, group, and organizational interactions (as demonstrated by the SLI model) will be part of the key to success.

- *Invest in learning organization characteristics that match strategic needs.* To realize the best benefits from investment in learning organization initiatives, the organization needs to develop on multiple fronts. This approach simply applies the logic of investing for synergistic effects. Initiatives should be selected and designed for sustainable business advantage. For example, clear organizational focus and framework tools for learning help target support for continuous learning and knowledge use, multiple external and internal scanning for ideas and solutions, and reflective learning.
- *Test and adapt.* Effective learning involves discovering and testing assumptions, expectancies, and beliefs against experience. If objective, measurable criteria for determining what works are used, that will improve the cycle of learning. Suggestions on the types of criteria that may be considered were noted in the discussion and examples in the section on learning organization characteristics. Usually, measurement and monitoring of these criteria (for example, consistent reflective learning by teams) will serve as the leading indicators of the desired business outcomes (for example, doubled sales volume). Most learning organizations measure key processes but cannot prove that investment in each initiative directly caused the business outcome. As one benchmark company contact noted, "We strongly believe that investment in these areas is logical and related, but it is one of many reasons for the good results." The investments are viewed as necessary to get the results.

Roles for Leaders and Facilitators

The roles of leadership and of human resources are also changing in the evolving learning organization. In organizations where the stakes are high for business payoffs in faster, more productive learning, the process of developing the learning organization requires a paradigm shift in multiple domains. This paradigm shift may require new or expanded roles for the organization's leaders and facilitators. Exhibit 10.3 shows the paradigm shift needed for a systems approach to learning, and the associated leader or facilitator roles.

Overall, the conditions depicted in the "from" column of the exhibit reflect a conventional definition of training and learning with only indirect connections to business benefits. By contrast, the "to" column—and associated learning organization roles—reflects direct connections between learning and business benefits. Instead of directing or requiring employees to take training, the systems approach to building the learning organization's capacity and

Exhibit 10.3. Taking a Systems Approach to Learning.

Shift	From	To	Roles
Purpose of learning	To provide learning material on designated content	To build future-readiness capacity and competitive performance	Act as internal performance consultant, including learning and knowledge management systems
Scope of training and learning	Departmentalized expense	Systemic investment	Integrate learning systems with work operations and the larger business environment (internally and externally)
Learning occurs as . . .	An event	A process, embedded in organizational change context	Support varied formal and informal learning at organizational, team, and individual levels
Learning structure	Content-based university model	Performance- and capacity-based model	Build and support learning systems that build performance and capacity
Needs assessment	Focus on individual learning gaps	Focus on learning system needs	Use multilevel, systemic needs assessment tools to define and diagnose integrated learning system needs

Relationship to job design	Training as an add-on activity	Learning is an essential part of the job	Promote training and learning as an opportunity for employees to build skills, improve performance, and make a stronger contribution
Application on the job	Little consideration to transferring skills to the job	Focus on pretraining and posttraining supports for transfer to work assignments	Identify obstacles, supports in the work environment before designing learning systems
Learner's motivation	Employees required to participate	Employees want to learn; learning systems aligned with their needs and those of the organization	Assess needs at multiple levels and provide learning systems that support capacity and performance potential of the organization
Learner's role	Employee as student (directed and taught)	Employee as learning customer; has access to formal and informal learning resources to get results	Inform employees about business objectives and specific roles of learning and shared benefits
Company role	Deliverer of training	Integrator-learning facilitator	Departments-employees are ultimately responsible for addressing their learning needs

performance focuses on the learners as customers. Leaders provide the basic framework around the core business process, a vision for contributions of individual and group learning, and investments that "walk the talk." Leadership forms the foundation for commitment, action, and continuity for the learning organization.

In the exhibit, the first four items describe roles for supporting the necessary infrastructure of the learning organization. The last six items are the most common technical roles, including consulting with departments and teams on learning systems design and facilitation, and measuring and monitoring progress. Again, the leader and facilitator roles are about the care and feeding of the systems, infrastructure, and learning processes that serve capacity building and performance goals. When learners are considered the learning organization's internal customers, leaders and facilitators become business partners in the formal and informal learning systems that serve individuals, teams, and the organization as a whole. From the learner's perspective, the learning process should be indistinguishable from the challenge of the work. As a leading microcomputer business executive said: "Our learners do not resist learning because they do not see the difference between learning and doing their job."

References

Argyris, C., & Schon, D. (1978). *Organizational learning: A theory of action perspective.* Reading, MA: Addison-Wesley, 1978.

Ayas, K. (1997). *Design for learning for innovation: Project management for new product development.* Rotterdam, Netherlands: Eburon.

Bachman, K. (2000). *Corporate e-learning: Exploring a new frontier* (Investment Report). New York: W. R. Hambrecht & Co.

Baldwin, T., & Magjuka, R. (1997). Training as an organizational episode: Pretraining influences on trainee motivation. In J. K. Ford, S.W.J. Kozlowski, K. Kraiger, E. Salas, & M. S. Teachout (Eds.), *Improving training effectiveness in work organizations* (pp. 99–127). Hillsdale, NJ: Erlbaum.

Bandura, A. (1986). *Social foundations of thought and action.* Englewood Cliffs, NJ: Prentice Hall.

Byrd, M. (1997). Creating a learning organization by accident. In S. Chawla & J. Renesch (Eds.), *Learning organizations: Developing cultures for tomorrow's workplace* (pp. 477–487). Portland, OR: Productivity Press.

Catalanello, R. F. (1994). *Strategic readiness: The making of the learning organization.* San Francisco: Jossey-Bass.

Chandler, D. L., & Tang, M. Y. (2000). *Education and e-learning: The next revolution* (Investment Report). New York: Needham & Co.

DeGeus, A. (1997). *The living company.* Boston: Harvard Business School Press.

DiBella, A. J., & Nevis, E. C. (1998). *How organizations learn: An integrated strategy for building learning capability.* San Francisco: Jossey-Bass.

Ford, J. K., Kozlowski, S.W.J., Kraiger, K., Salas, E., & Teachout, M. S. (Eds.). (1997). *Improving training effectiveness in work organizations.* Hillsdale, NJ: Erlbaum.

Garvin, D. (1993). Building a learning organization. *Harvard Business Review, 71*(4), 78–91.

Guns, B. (1996). *The faster learning organization: Gain and sustain the competitive advantage.* San Francisco: Jossey-Bass.

Handy, C. (1997). Managing the dream. In S. Chawla & J. Renesch (Eds.), *Learning organizations: Developing cultures for tomorrow's workplace* (pp. 45–55). Portland, OR: Productivity Press.

Johnson, D. W., & Johnson, R. (1984). *Cooperative learning.* New Brighton, MN: Interaction.

Kaplan, R. S., & Norton, D. P. (1992, January-February). The balanced scorecard: Measures that drive performance. *Harvard Business Review,* 71–79.

Kozlowski, S.W.J., & Salas, E. (1997). An organizational systems approach for the implementation and transfer of training. In J. K. Ford, S.W.J. Kozlowski, K. Kraiger, E. Salas, & M. S. Teachout (Eds.), *Improving training effectiveness in work organizations* (pp. 247–287). Hillsdale, NJ: Erlbaum.

Locke, E. A., & Latham G. B., (1990). *A theory of goal setting and task performance.* Englewood Cliffs, NJ: Prentice Hall.

Marquardt, M. J. (1996). *Building the learning organization: A systems approach to quantum improvement and global success.* New York: McGraw-Hill.

Martocchio, J. J. (1992). Microcomputer usage as an opportunity: The influence of context in employee training. *Personnel Psychology, 45,* 529–552.

Mathieu, J. E., & Martineau, J. W. (1997). Individual and situational influences on training motivation. In J. K. Ford, S.W.J. Kozlowski, K. Kraiger, E. Salas, & M. S. Teachout (Eds.), *Improving training effectiveness in work organizations* (pp. 193–221). Hillsdale, NJ: Erlbaum.

Morris, L. E. (1997). Development strategies for the knowledge era. In S. Chawla & J. Renesch (Eds.), *Learning organizations: Developing cultures for tomorrow's workplace* (pp. 323–335). Portland, OR: Productivity Press.

Raelin, J. A. (2000). *Work-based learning: The new frontier of management development*. Englewood Cliffs, NJ: Prentice Hall.

Sanford, C. (1997). Vitalizing work design: Implementing a developmental philosophy. In S. Chawla & J. Renesch (Eds.), *Learning organizations: Developing cultures for tomorrow's workplace* (pp. 305–321). Portland, OR: Productivity Press.

Schnieder, W. E. (1994). *The reengineering alternative: A plan for making your current culture work*. Burr Ridge, IL: Irwin.

Schwandt, D. (1997). Learning as an organization: A journey into chaos. In S. Chawla & J. Renesch (Eds.), *Learning organizations: Developing cultures for tomorrow's workplace* (pp. 365–379). Portland, OR: Productivity Press.

Senge, P. M. (1990). *The fifth discipline: The art and practice of the learning organization*. New York: Doubleday.

Senge, P. M., Kleiner, A., Roberts, C., Ross, R., & Smith, B. (1994). *The fifth discipline fieldbook: Strategies and tools for building a learning organization*. New York: Doubleday.

Stack, J. (1992). *The great game of business*. New York: Doubleday.

Stolovitch, H., & Keeps, E. (1998). Implementation phase: Performance improvement interventions. In D. G. Robinson & J. C. Robinson (Eds.), *Moving from training to performance* (pp. 95–133). San Francisco: Berrett-Koehler.

Thompson, J. W. (1997). The renaissance of learning in business. In S. Chawla & J. Renesch (Eds.), *Learning organizations: Developing cultures for tomorrow's workplace.* (pp. 85–99). Portland, OR: Productivity Press.

Vroom, V. H. (1964). *Work and motivation*. New York: Wiley.

CHAPTER 11

Decision-Based Evaluation

Kurt Kraiger

The technology of effective training evaluation is built largely on the knowledge of what and how to measure. The art of training evaluation springs from knowing why. There are a limited number of ways in which to address questions of training success. This fact sometimes leaves training practitioners feeling frustrated with both the state of evaluation research and the lack of guidance for implementing evaluation programs. This chapter looks at what to measure but puts that issue into a broader framework in which success indicators and the reasons why the evaluation is being conducted are also considered. Thus, the purpose of the chapter is to advance both the technology and the art of training evaluation by proposing a comprehensive, decision-based approach to measurement.

Consider a recent measurement report (Bassi & Ahlstrand, 2000) published by the American Society of Training and Development (ASTD). Data are reported on a set of standardized evaluation measures distributed to over two thousand organizations in thirty-four countries. The purpose of the ongoing study was to create standardized, outcome-based measures for assessing the impact of investment in training and to understand relationships among training outcomes and training or organizational contexts.

Despite the state-of-the-art feel to the project and the report itself, many of the measures do not look different from those that might have been used thirty or forty years ago. Perceived impact of the training was assessed by questions such as these: "The knowledge and skills gained through this course are directly applicable to my job" and "Overall, I was satisfied with this course." One year later, participants were asked: "To what extent have you actually used the knowledge and/or skills presented in this course after completing the course?" and "As a result of this course, my overall job performance has changed by _____ percent."

Reviewing these questions, we may conclude that there really is nothing new under the sun. The types of questions used to evaluate training, apparently unchanged over four decades, seem drawn from some finite domain. This may in fact be a valid conclusion; progress in evaluation may come not from thinking of new ways to ask questions but from choosing questions based on a new decision-based framework. A careful review of the evaluation instruments in Bassi and Ahlstrand (2000) reveals that their post-training evaluation measure includes not only questions on training impact but also questions on training context—questions on opportunity to perform new skills, self-efficacy regarding new skills, and perceived barriers and enablers of transfer. As discussed later in this chapter (and in other chapters throughout this volume), these latter questions provide critical insights for addressing questions of training system effectiveness.

The Baseline for Training Evaluation

It is important to contrast new ways of thinking about evaluation with traditional standards. For over forty years, the predominant approach to training evaluation has been Kirkpatrick's (1959a, 1959b, 1960a, 1960b) four-level hierarchy. Although often referred to as an evaluation model, the origin of the hierarchy lay in a set of practical suggestions Kirkpatrick made to members of the American Society of Training Development at a time when few guidelines were available in the professional or scholarly literature. Since then, the hierarchical approach has risen to model-like status, becoming part of the everyday vernacular of training practitioners. Generally, alternatives proposed have been mere extensions of the reactions-learning-behavior taxonomy—for example, splitting one level into two (Mathieu, Tannenbaum, & Salas, 1992), or adding a fifth level (Hamblin, 1974; Phillips, 1997). It was only in the last decade that serious criticisms of Kirkpatrick's hierarchy emerged (Alliger & Janak, 1989; Holton, 1996). Given the widespread acceptance of the Kirkpatrick hierarchy, any reasoned discussion of training evaluation must start there. The goal of this discussion, however, is to consider seriously the practical bases and implications of the Kirkpatrick hierarchy before presenting an alternative approach grounded in the purpose and context of evaluation.

Origins of a Hierarchy

As Kirkpatrick (1959a) noted, the impetus for his evaluation guidelines came during his tenure as ASTD president, when members continually asked him for suggestions on how to evaluate their training programs. Drawing primarily on personal experience, he responded with a series of four papers, published in the association's training journal, prescribing the assessment of the following:

> Step 1: *Reaction.* How well did the conferees like the program?
> Step 2: *Learning.* What principles, facts, and techniques were learned?
> Step 3: *Behavior.* What changes in job behavior resulted from the program?
> Step 4: *Results.* What were the tangible results of the program in terms of reduced cost, improved quality, improved quantity, etc.? [Kirkpatrick, 1976, 18.2]

The hierarchical nature of the approach indicates that "higher" levels should not be assessed unless satisfactory results are achieved at lower levels. That is, if trainees do not like the course, there is little reason to measure learning; if trainees show no learning during training, changes in on-the-job-behavior are not likely. The notion of hierarchy also implies that changes at higher levels are better, or more beneficial, to the organization than changes at lower levels.

Kirkpatrick's recommendations were published more formally in the ASTD *Training and Development Handbook* (for example, Kirkpatrick, 1976), and have been offered up, with little change, ever since (Kirkpatrick, 1994). As noted earlier, the approach has enjoyed great popularity over the years. This popularity is due in part to the hierarchy's simplicity (although, as discussed later, it is perhaps deceptively simple). It is always clear what needs to be done next; I have spoken to any number of training managers who say things like, "We have always measured reactions, so now we need to do a better job of measuring learning," or "We are doing a pretty good job of measuring reactions and learning, so we need to move to behaviors." It should be noted, however, that this causal linking of levels is an assumption of the approach (Alliger & Janak, 1989) rather than a requirement of effective evaluation.

Criticisms of the Hierarchy

Despite the popularity and widespread application of Kirkpatrick's hierarchy, there have emerged in recent years several important critiques of it. First, Alliger and Janak (1989) criticized three assumptions of the approach: that each succeeding level is more important than the prior, that each level is caused by the previous level (for example, positive reactions causes learning), and that changes in levels are correlated with each other. Holton (1996), referring to the "flawed four-level model," took exception to references to the approach as a model, arguing that it lacked the rigor of a true scientific model and instead is more of a taxonomy of learning outcomes. (As I will clarify later, characterizing Kirkpatrick's measures of reactions or results as learning outcomes may be inappropriate. For example, typical reaction measures are better viewed as evaluations of training processes than as indicators of learning.)

In general, there are five important concerns with Kirkpatrick's approach. First, it has little grounding in theory, and to whatever extent it may be theory-based it is rooted in a 1950s behavioral perspective that predates (and ignores) cognitively based information-processing theories of the 1970s and 1980s. Although a methodology does not have to be theory-based to be useful, evaluation techniques rooted in an understanding of how individuals actually learn would potentially be more valid than techniques that are not (Kraiger, Ford, & Salas, 1993).

Second, there is a lack of clarity about the constructs at most of the levels. For example, the approach treats reaction and learning constructs as unidimensional. As discussed later, emerging research suggests that trainee reactions are multidimensional (for example, Alliger, Tannenbaum, & Bennett, Traver, & Shortland, 1997; Morgan & Casper, 2000). Learning theory extending back to the 1960s supports the multidimensional nature of learning (for example, Krathwohl, Bloom, & Masia, 1964). Lack of clarity in the approach is also evident in confusion in Kirkpatrick's writings about other levels. For example, employee performance is sometimes used as a synonym for behavior and at other times for results.

Third, strict application of the approach leads to illogical actions. For example, Kirkpatrick recommends that learning not be measured until there is evidence of positive reactions, yet by the time reaction data are tabulated, attendees may not be available to assess learning. Fourth, the approach makes assumptions about relationships between training outcomes that are either not supported by research (for example, Alliger et al., 1997) or do not make sense intuitively. Most of us can easily recall classes that we did not like but from which we learned a lot, yet Kirkpatrick argued that learning will not occur without positive reactions to training. Also, training may be structured so that learning is not evident at the time of acquisition but may become evident sometime later when certain situational cues are present. (Similarly, parents usually teach values to their children to affect choices made much later in life.)

Finally, the approach does not take into account the purposes for evaluation. When training managers state, "We've always done Level 2, and now we need to do Level 3," I ask them why they need to measure behaviors, or how that information benefits them. In nearly all cases, they cannot give a reason other than "Because that's what comes next." If I ask how the information will be useful to them, or what they hope to gain from an evaluation, they are usually better able to provide reasons. Frequently, these reasons may or may not necessitate Level 3 evaluation, and the evaluation plan we develop will be rooted in what they hope to accomplish rather than what number comes next.

A Guide to Decision-Based Evaluation

Although the Kirkpatrick approach provides a useful heuristic for thinking about what can be measured, it provides insufficient direction about what should be measured. Accordingly, the purpose of this chapter is to present an alternative framework for thinking about evaluation. The title "Decision-Based Evaluation" suggests that the intent is to encourage those associated with training to make better choices of why, what, and when to evaluate training.

Why Evaluate?

When initiating a new evaluation effort, the first question to ask is why it is being done. As will be seen, several specific questions can be answered by evaluation planners. Whether it is training, selection, or performance measurement, when it comes to human resource systems, too often reasons for doing things a certain way are because it has always been done that way, because someone else is doing it that way, or because someone told us we should do it that way. Thus, the first step toward better decision making about evaluation is to specify why the evaluation is to be done. Specifically, two issues need to be addressed:

- *What is the purpose for evaluation?* How will the results be used to make decisions affecting training courses or the training function?
- *What are the obstacles to evaluation?* In other words, why not evaluate? What have been the characteristics of the organization, the training function, or the training programs that have prevented thorough, constructive evaluation in the past?

Purpose for Evaluation

Clarifying the purpose for evaluation is crucial to making efficient decisions about what to measure. If the purpose for evaluation is to defend training expenditures, measures of trainee satisfaction may be irrelevant, just as bottom-line return-on-investment indicators may be meaningless for shaping instructor behavior during training. Despite the critical nature of evaluation purpose, it is infrequently discussed in prior evaluation models.

In the most general sense, evaluation may be done for either formative or summative purposes (Worthen & Sanders, 1987). Formative evaluation is done so that results are used to modify a program or redesign presentations, materials, or training content. Summative evaluation results are used to make judgments about a program's effectiveness or worth. Specific to training evaluation, Kirkpatrick (1994) offered three possible purposes: to justify the existence of the training function, to decide whether to discontinue existing training programs, and to improve future training programs. Sackett and Mullin (1993) suggested four reasons: to make decisions about the future use of a training program or instructional technique, to make decisions about trainees (for example, to certify workers), to contribute to the scientific understanding of training effectiveness, and for political or public relations purposes. Finally, Twitchell, Holden, and Trott (2001) examined the evaluation of technical training programs and collected perceptions of the value of evaluation in improving training, demonstrating impact on job performance, demonstrating value of training to upper management, and demonstrating impact on organizational outcomes. Summarizing these discussions, it appears that there are three purposes for conducting training evaluation: *decision making, feedback,* and *marketing.*

The first purpose for evaluation is to provide input for decision making about training. I/O psychology as a whole can be characterized as a science of generating data that help organizations make informed decisions about the efficient use of human resources (Kraiger, 2001). Specific to training, organizations may use the outcomes of an evaluation to make decisions about aspects of training such as course retention (for example, with diminishing resources for training, is there enough evidence of training impact or cost effectiveness to argue that a given course should be offered again?); course revision (Is the course in its current format sufficiently long to cover the material? Could it be shortened? Is there enough time allocated for practice? Is it still relevant to job requirements?); and personnel decisions (Is the instructor effective in covering the intended material? Should he or she be retained? Are trainees sufficiently proficient at the trained tasks to do their jobs? Is additional on-the-job training required? Can trainees be certified or licensed in their jobs?). Note that as the decisions to make about the use of the data are clarified, the kind of information that must be collected also becomes clearer.

The second purpose for evaluation is to provide feedback to course designers, trainers, or the trainees themselves. In a recent survey of evaluation practices for technical training, frequency of Level 1, 2, or 3 evaluation was significantly correlated with the perceived value of evaluation for improving training (Twitchell et al.,

2001). If an evaluation of the relevancy of the training material reveals that some topics are overemphasized and others are underemphasized, course designers can make appropriate revisions and perhaps reconsider the processes that led to faulty design (Ford & Wroten, 1984). A safety program for donning protective gear may reveal to trainees that although the gear was put on properly and within safety limits, the total time they took would be too long during certain emergencies. Finally, feedback to trainers may encourage them to provide more (or fewer) real-world examples (or "war stories") in subsequent sessions.

Data collected for decision-making purposes may also be useful for feedback purposes. Reaction data on dimensions of instructor competency may be used not only to aid instructor retention decisions but also to provide constructive feedback to those retained.

The final use for training evaluation data is for purposes of marketing the training program. The target audience may be other organizations, other departments or units in the same organization, or future trainees. In a recent survey of evaluation practices for technical training, frequency of Level 4 evaluation (but not 1, 2, or 3) was significantly correlated with the perceived value of evaluation for demonstrating achievement of organizational outcomes and marginally correlated with demonstrating the value of training to upper management (Twitchell et al., 2001). Again, information used for either decision making or feedback purposes may be used for marketing purposes as well. More often, though, data collected for marketing purposes may be anecdotal or visual, helping future sponsors or trainees to understand the changes initiated through training. An everyday example is an infomercial for fitness or diet plans that exposes viewers to fit models who supposedly completed the program.

The benefits of collecting impact data to market training to future sponsors are obvious. Organizations considering a new sales training program or organizational units considering implementing a supervisory training program rolled out in another department will seek evidence of effectiveness before they adopt it. For training practitioners, thinking about the types of data that will be most persuasive to outside agencies can often be helpful when choosing the types of impact data that will be the most persuasive to the agency sponsoring the training.

Research has shown that before training, trainees form perceptions of the usefulness and relevancy of the program based on prior experience, hearsay, or the experience of others. These perceptions become powerful determinants of their motivation for learning upon entry into the program (see Baldwin, Magjuka, & Loher, 1991; Noe & Colquitt, Chapter Three, this volume). Sales representatives who see data showing that past participants in the same training program increased their sales volume by 40 percent will be more motivated to attend.

Obstacles to Evaluation

A second issue to consider in planning an evaluation is why training programs in that organization have not been evaluated more extensively in the past. Kirkpatrick (1994) noted that many training departments will think about "doing more" but will not do so for several reasons, including these: more thorough evaluation is not considered important or urgent, they do not know how to do it, or there is no pressure from upper management to do it. In their survey of evaluation practices for technical training, Twitchell et al. (2001) collected data on perceived impediments to evaluation. The top reason offered for not conducting evaluation was that it was not required by the organization. Additional costs associated with evaluation and lack of training in evaluation methods were also primary reasons. Finally, lack of time was an important reason for not conducting evaluations of learning; a similar finding for on-the-job measures was reported in a survey of performance improvement specialists by Moller and Mallin (1996). Twitchell et al. (2001) suggest that the results indicate that evaluation models may not be sufficiently clear or simple for typical practitioners (even though the most frequently cited strength of the Kirkpatrick approach is its simplicity).

In considering the difficulty of implementing an evaluation program, it is important to differentiate evaluation content from evaluation context. The Kirkpatrick approach, as well as other evaluation taxonomies, have traditionally addressed what to evaluate. The perceived difficulty of evaluation may lie in deciding when to evaluate and how to isolate the effects of training. As discussed later, there have been several recent discussions of evaluation design that greatly demystify and simplify the evaluation context.

Although generally not openly discussed, yet another reason for not conducting more rigorous evaluations is that the training function may have everything to lose and nothing to gain from the data. If there is an ongoing commitment to employee training and development by the organization, no news may be good news when it comes to documenting training impact. Decisions to implement new or maintain existing training programs may be characterized as "nature versus nurture" decisions. "Nature" decisions are made out of habit or by following popular fads; they require no data or input to make. Despite well-established instructional systems models, "nurture" decisions driven by needs assessment or evaluating training effectiveness may be the exception, not the norm. Given the cost and perceived difficulty of conducting training evaluation, training departments may understandably be prone not to evaluate existing programs.

The problem with this logic, however, is that it addresses only one of three purposes for evaluation. Although an absence of data may prolong course offerings, it may also mean there is a lack of information to use for revising courses, retaining trainers, preparing trainees, and selling the training to new constituents. In the end, failure to evaluate may result in ineffective courses or a failure to open new markets for good courses, and each of these results puts more stress on the training function.

Guidelines for Practice

- Be clear about the purposes for evaluation. Ask questions of trainers, training function managers, and key organizational stakeholders to determine how the results are likely to be used; examine how training results have been used in the past.
- Use the purpose for evaluation as a guide for all subsequent decision making about evaluation. Be certain that what is measured and how data are collected is consistent with the stated purpose for evaluation.
- Understand and plan for ongoing obstacles to evaluation. Elicit input and feedback from key stakeholders early in the evaluation design process both as a mechanism for detecting existing obstacles and to reduce the probability of future obstacles.
- Identify the impetus for moving forward on evaluation at this point in time. Organizations or training departments often think about evaluation for a long time before doing something about it; understanding what finally triggered the decision to move forward is a valuable resource for understanding political forces that may hinder or facilitate evaluation efforts.

What to Evaluate: Decisions About Content

Questions of what to evaluate concern what data should be collected to address one or more of the stated purposes for evaluation. As discussed in the previous section, different purposes may require different types of data. Training departments that conduct some evaluation but want to do more often believe that other organizations are conducting multifaceted evaluation more frequently than they are. Available data suggest that most training programs are evaluated in some way, but few are evaluated in multiple ways, particularly with respect to measures of transfer of training, performance improvement, or return on investment.

Only recently has the American Society of Training and Development begun formally tracking evaluation practices of its members. In its 2001 report, the frequency of evaluation practices are reported for 365 companies reporting to its benchmarking service and for a subset of these companies designated as training investment leaders (Van Buren, 2001). (The latter companies have made a commitment to training as indicated by their training expenditures, training hours per employee, percentage of eligible employees receiving training, and application of learning technologies.) The results are reproduced in Figure 11.1. It is interesting to note that ASTD's depiction of evaluation practices confounds content (for example, Level 3 behavior) with methods (for example, observation). It is also interesting to note that regardless of type of evaluation, there is very little difference in frequency between all responding organizations and designated training leaders. Finally, it is both interesting and important to note that although most organizations measure trainee reactions, less than half measure whether instructional outcomes were achieved and less than a fifth measure whether learning was applied on the job.

Similar results were reported in Twitchell et al.'s (2001) survey of technical training programs: 73 percent of those surveyed used reaction measures, 47 percent used learning measures, 31 percent used behavior measures, and 21 percent used results-performance measures. Noting past surveys (Catalanello & Kirkpatrick, 1968; "Industry report," 1996), the authors concluded that "it would appear that evaluation practices today are not much more widespread than thirty years ago, except at Level 2" (Twitchell et al., 2001, p. 96).

Figure 11.1. ASTD Survey of Evaluation.

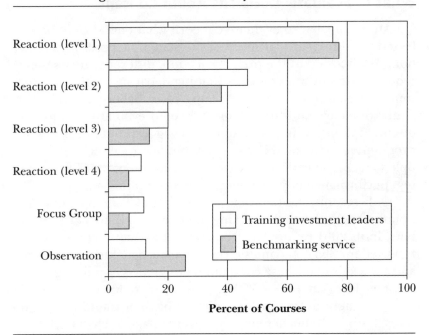

Source: Adapted from Van Buren, 2001.

As already noted, there are limited measurement targets amenable to evaluation. Where guidance and insight may be provided is in conceptualizing how these targets may be assessed. For example, it is valuable to assess the relevance and instructional effectiveness of the training content and delivery. Such data may be useful for revising future training courses. Traditionally, data for training content and delivery have been collected through trainee reactions at the end of the program. Consequently, the data collection method—trainee reactions—has been confounded with the measurement target, such as instructor empathy or whether there were sufficient opportunities for practice. What gets lost is rational decision making about issues such as whether novice learners are always the best judges of the relevancy of training content or the adequacy of instruction.

Figure 11.2. Targets of Evaluation.

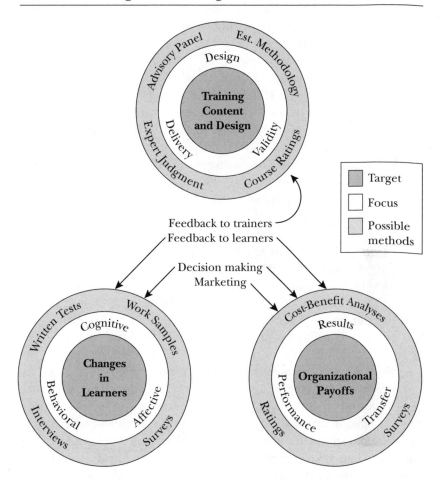

Figure 11.2 presents an alternative measurement model that clearly distinguishes evaluation targets from collection methods. Targets and methods are linked through mediating foci, and targets, focus, and methods are linked to evaluation purpose. Thus, the approach overcomes some of the ambiguities of the traditional Kirkpatrick approach by linking evaluation purpose to evaluation target, separating method from target, and clarifying the options (foci) available for measurement given desired change. Each target is discussed in more detail in the following paragraphs.

Training Content and Design

Evaluations of the training content and design are usually carried out primarily for formative purposes, but they may also be done to evaluate the effectiveness of the training itself (Lee & Pershing, 1999). In addition, traditional reaction criteria may serve a public relations role ("They care enough to ask the very best") or indicate potential problems in transfer of training (Morgan & Casper, 2000). Because the purpose of evaluation is rarely articulated, common reaction data more suited to providing feedback to trainers or course designers may mistakenly be used to make decisions about program retention or promote the effectiveness of the training to other organizational units. For example, trainees' responses to the question "Was there sufficient opportunity to ask questions?" can provide useful input into revising the agenda for future course offerings but may not persuade other organizations to implement the program locally. Thus, clarity of purpose will drive the development of measures of training content and design.

As shown in Figure 11.2, questions about training content and design can address focal issues of design, delivery, and content validity. The dimensionality of participant reactions to training has been a topic of research interest in recent years. Warr and Bunce (1995) suggested that participant reactions are not a unitary construct but one that includes reactions on affect or satisfaction, perceived utility, and perceived difficulty. Alliger et al. (1997) concurred but suggested that reactions usually include two dimensions: affect and utility. Finally, Morgan and Casper (2000) administered thirty-two common reaction questions to a sample of more than nine thousand government workers taking at least one of about four hundred different courses. Respondents' answers were factor-analyzed, uncovering six factors underlying participant reactions to training: satisfaction with the instructor, satisfaction with the training or administration process, satisfaction with the testing or evaluation process, utility of training, satisfaction with materials, and course structure.

A useful taxonomy of content and design dimensions for assessment was provided by Lee and Pershing (1999), and is shown in Exhibit 11.1. The exhibit lists ten potential assessment dimensions, along with the specific purpose for the dimension (what is to be learned, and how that information is useful), and sample questions. Additional information about the dimensions and additional sample questions are available in Lee and Pershing (1999).

ibit 11.1. Dimensions and Examples of Training
Content and Delivery Evaluations, Cont'd.

	Purpose or Examples
ent	To evaluate the adequacy of the physical training environment, including classroom, dining room, lodging, and leisure facilities • Was the training environment appropriate for the subject matter? • Were environmental conditions—comfort, heating, noise, visibility—conducive to learning?
ed action or er expectation	To evaluate the participants' plans-expectations and anticipated barriers for applying training content on the job • Was the training content relevant to your job? • Do you expect the organization to support your use of the skills learned in this program?
gistics ministration	To evaluate the smoothness and effectiveness of the scheduling, registration, and other logistical and administrative matters • Was the scheduling of the course efficient? • Was the registration process for this course easy?
Overall evaluation	To determine overall participant satisfaction and feelings about the training program • Did the training program meet your needs? • Would you recommend this training program to others?
Recommendations for program improvement	To receive suggestions-recommendations for improving similar or future training programs • What would you suggest to improve the training program?

Source: Adapted from Lee & Pershing, 1999.

Exhibit 11.1. Dimensions a
Content and Delive

Dimension	Pu
Program objectives or content	To evaluate prograı participants' expecta appropriateness, stru of the program conter • Did the content mee • Was the content up-to
Program materials	To determine effectivenes usefulness of written mater • Were the materials consis objectives? • Was the content of the hanı understand?
Delivery methods or technologies	To judge the appropriateness anı of delivery methods, including me • Were the presentation technolo class effective? • Were the visual aids helpful?
Instructor or facilitator	To rate the ability, preparation, and effectiveness of the trainer or facilitator leading the program • Did the instructor present material cle • Was the instructor responsive to particip questions?
Instructional activities	To evaluate the appropriateness and helpfulness of in-class and out-of-class activities • Were the course exercises relevant to the program objectives? • Were the group discussions helpful to participants in exchanging ideas with each other?
Program time or length	To assess the length of the session or entire training program for schedule change and considerations of program length • Was the length of program appropriate for the stated objectives? • Was there enough time to practice course content?

Exh

Dimensio
Training environm
Plann trans
Lo ac

Training evaluators who wish to evaluate training content and design *and* use participant reactions as a primary measurement method will find Exhibit 11.1 a useful taxonomy for thinking about the types of questions to ask. If the evaluation purpose is to provide feedback, dimensions such as program objectives-content, delivery methods-technologies, instructor-facilitator, and recommendations for program improvement may be particularly useful. If the purpose is to make decisions about program effectiveness or if training should be made shorter or longer, dimensions such as overall evaluation, planned action–transfer expectation, and program time-length may be useful.

Referring back to Figure 11.2, it should be noted that participant reactions are only one methodology for making decisions about training content and design. It is worth considering whether novice training participants are always the best source of information about the instructor's knowledge in the area of study or if sufficient practice time was allowed. For example, in academia, student course evaluations rarely serve as the only input for judgments on teaching effectiveness during tenure deliberations.

As suggested in Figure 11.2, there are alternative methods available for evaluating training content and design. In many instances, these methods are easier or require less time or fewer resources than participant reactions, and they may provide more valid assessments. One reason why these methods have not been widely used in the past may be that they appear less objective, or more inbred than participant ratings. This may be a concern if the purpose of evaluation is to aid decision making or promote training effectiveness. However, if the purpose is to facilitate continuous improvement (as it usually is), then methods should be chosen based on their potential for providing useful feedback, not for their appearance of objectivity.

The relevancy of course content and handouts can be easily assessed through expert review panels or advisory boards, with members including training or subject matter experts drawn from inside the organization (for example, high performers or supervisors) or outside of it (professional colleagues). General strategies for documenting content validity are well known (Lawshe, 1975), and these strategies have been adapted for review of training domains (Ford & Wroten, 1984).

The use of established methodologies suggests that when training departments have a sound process (that is, thorough needs assessment leading to effective course design and the selection of effective instructors) that has resulted in successful training programs in the past, there should be confidence throughout the organization that future programs using the same development process will prove similarly effective. This is more than false confidence on the part of the trainers. Organizational decision makers form impressions of the general effectiveness of multiple units in organizations, so that as long as there is periodic evidence of training impact, the argument that training is being effectively designed to address agreed-upon needs should be sufficient in many instances.

Guidelines for Practice

- Use a taxonomy such as that in Exhibit 11.1 to identify a comprehensive set of dimensions and questions for evaluating training content and design.
- Be clear on the purpose of evaluation in choosing content and design dimensions and questions.
- Consider alternatives to asking training participants to make judgments on all content and design dimensions of interest.

Changes in the Learner

As suggested in Figure 11.2, measures of changes in learners can be used for any of the common purposes for evaluation. The focus of evaluation may be changes in the knowledge, skills, or affective states of learners, and these changes may be assessed through a variety of methods including (but not limited to) questionnaires, role-plays, ratings, work samples, and written tests. This information may be useful primarily when the purpose of the training is to provide feedback or to make decisions about training.

It should be noted that through links to different targets for evaluation, the model in Figure 11.2 separates changes in behavior from changes in performance that result from training. This corrects one of the ambiguities inherent in the Kirkpatrick approach. As a result of training, employees may change their behaviors but not improve job performance. Or training may improve job performance but without any apparent change in job behaviors. By linking behavioral change to changes in the learner and performance change to organizational payoffs, the target model reinforces the notion that the objective of training is to create permanent changes in trainees' knowledge, skills, and affective states. But whether those changes are transferred effectively to the job depends on a host of interpersonal and organizational variables (Machin, Chapter Nine, this volume; Noe & Colquitt, Chapter Three, this volume).

A taxonomy of potential changes in the learner is shown in Exhibit 11.2, which is based on taxonomies of learning outcomes published by Kraiger et al. (1993), and more heavily, by Jonassen and Tessmer (1996–97). Those taxonomies are rooted in learning outcome taxonomies in the field of education dating back to the 1950s and 1960s (for example, Bloom, 1956; Krathwohl et al., 1964). Many readers may be surprised to see measures of affective or attitudinal change included as measures of learning. This may be in part because of the ubiquitous use of the Kirkpatrick approach, which characterizes attitudes and feelings as reactions to training. Their surprise may also be a result of the ongoing influence of the behavioral paradigm that dominated most of psychology and much of instructional design through the 1960s and 1970s. Training theorists such as Robert Mager taught us that the only good (or measurable) learning objective was a behavioral one (for example, Mager & Beach, 1967). Thus, training practitioners dutifully translated legitimate cognitive or affective outcomes into behavioral ones.

The learning outcomes in the exhibit are organized into three broad categories: affective, behavioral, and cognitive (the ABCs of learning). Each category is broken down into subcategories, with specific outcomes nested within the subcategories. Potential measurement methods and examples are provided for each outcome.

Cognitive Outcomes. For example, the exhibit shows that there are seven subcategories of cognitive outcomes: declarative knowledge, structural knowledge, formation of concepts and procedures, situated problem solving, ampliative skills, self-knowledge, and executive control. There are three specific outcomes under situated problem solving (identifying-defining problems, hypothesizing solutions, evaluating solutions), each with suggested measurement

Exhibit 11.2. Taxonomy of Cognitive, Affective, and Behavioral Outcomes.

Cognitive Outcomes

Declarative Knowledge:

No.	Outcome	Measurement Method	Example
1.1	Propositional knowledge	Recognition, recall	• Recognize questions as examples of a focus of measurement • State uses for measures of training content and delivery
1.2	Acquiring new information	Paraphrase	• List three foci for measurement of changes in learners

Structural Knowledge:

No.	Outcome	Measurement Method	Example
2.1	Knowledge organization (static)	Relationship of similarity judgments with or without representation (for example, Pathfinder) Card sorts	• Given a set of evaluation methods, judge similarity between pairs and submitting to Pathfinder for representation
2.2	Semantic mapping (static with dynamic components)	Concept mapping	• Create a project plan for evaluation given knowledge of evaluation purpose and available measures
2.3	Structural mental models (dynamic)	Pathfinder nets or card sorts	• Rate the appropriateness of a set of potential measures given knowledge of the evaluation purpose, and characterizing possible causal relationships among measured outcomes

Formation of Concepts and Procedures:

No.	Outcome	Measurement Method	Example
3.1	Forming concepts	Identifying and classifying new instances	• Identify examples of statistical problems that can be solved using ANCOVA
3.2	Reasoning from concepts	Drawing conclusions, recognizing obstacles	• Explain why anecdotal stories can be used for ROI
3.3	Using procedures	Performing procedures	• Design a trainee rating form to assess perceived utility of training
3.4	Applying rules	Demonstrating algorithms	• Calculate the sample size necessary to ensure adequate statistical power in a simple training design
3.5	Complex procedures (convergent problem solving)	Selecting and using cognitive components	• Write a set of internal referencing strategy items

Situated Problem Solving:

No.	Outcome	Measurement Method	Example
4.1	Identifying and defining problem	Describing problem space and identifying issues, operations, sub-problems	• Given a case or scenario, describe the obstacles to conducting a comprehensive evaluation of training.
4.2	Hypothesizing solutions	Generating hypotheses and solution options	• Given a case or scenario, suggest one or two strategies to achieve the intended purpose for evaluation without using a quasi-experimental design
4.3	Evaluating solutions	Assessing hypotheses and solution options	• Given a case or scenario and multiple options, choose the best strategy for evaluation without using a quasi-experimental design

Exhibit 11.2. Taxonomy of Cognitive, Affective, and Behavioral Outcomes, Cont'd.

Ampliative Skills:

No.	Outcome	Measurement Method	Example
5.1	Generating new interpretations	Stating, defending, rationalizing	• Given a standard reaction form, write training design evaluation questions for a panel of experts.
5.2	Constructing or applying arguments	Stating, defending, rationalizing	• Defend the use of external judges instead of trainees as a source for evaluating training processes.
5.3	Analogizing	Writing analogies	• Write an analogy comparing evaluation outcomes to a legal evidence in a court case.
5.4	Inferring	Inferring from known information, drawing implications	• State the implications for the need for a control group given changes in training purpose.

Self-Knowledge:

No.	Outcome	Measurement Method	Example
6.1	Articulating awareness	Explaining, differentiating, integrating performance	• Characterize previous evaluations you have done as examples of specific learning outcomes
6.2	Articulating personal strategies (strategic knowledge)	Explaining or thinking aloud	• Describe a plan for involving stakeholders in an evaluation program
6.3	Articulating cognitive prejudices or weaknesses	Explaining, differentiating, integrating performance	• Describe past efforts to translate cognitive or affective outcomes into behaviors

Executive Control:

No.	Outcome	Measurement Method	Example
7.1	Assessing task difficulty	Problem assessment, think aloud	• Provide estimates of return rates for performance surveys mailed to random supervisors
7.2	Goal-setting activity	Self-report, think aloud	• Set goals to conduct new forms of evaluation in the next quarter
7.3	Goal structure complexity	Self-report, think aloud, rated for complexity or quality	• Develop hierarchical goal scheme (master and subgoals), including contingency plans for goal blockage
7.4	Allocating cognitive resources	Self-report, think aloud	• Block out dedicated time for planning evaluation efforts
7.5	Assessing progress, error checking	Self-report, think aloud	• Assess progress toward meeting deadlines

Affective Outcomes

Motivation:

No.	Outcome	Measurement Method	Example
8.1	Exerting effort	Observations, self-report	• Make the time to do an extensive revision of a performance appraisal instrument
8.2	Persisting on a task (tenacity)	Observation, self-report, time-on-task	• Send revised appraisal to peers for review and make multiple revisions to the instrument
8.3	Engaging intentionally (willingness)	Observation, self-report	• Read additional resources or references on evaluation on own time
8.4	Goal difficulty	Self-report, think aloud, rated for difficulty	• Set a goal of convincing upper management to allow a true control group for an evaluation study
8.5	Mastery orientation	Self-report, questionnaire	• Posttest scores on a mastery orientation scale

Exhibit 11.2. Taxonomy of Cognitive, Affective, and Behavioral Outcomes, Cont'd.

Attitude:

No.	Outcome	Measurement Method	Example
9.1	Self-efficacy	Self-report, questionnaire	• Posttest scores on a task-specific self-efficacy scale
9.2	Attitude object	Self-report, questionnaire	• Report a change in affect toward Kirkpatrick framework as universal evaluation model
9.3	Attitude strength	Self-report, questionnaire	• Develop a strong self-reported preference for alternative evaluation models

Behavioral Outcomes

Skill Acquisition:

No.	Outcome	Measurement Method	Example
10.1	Proceduralization	Behavioral checklist on work samples, role-plays	• Generate learning outcomes from instructional objectives given step-by-step directions
10.2	Compilation	Behavioral checklist or performance ratings on works samples, role-plays, transfer to novel stimuli	• Generate learning outcomes from instructional objectives or suggest possible objectives given a learning outcome

Automaticity:

No.	Outcome	Measurement Method	Example
11.1	Automatic processing	Behavioral observation, performance rating, performance on secondary task	• Write quality scenarios to enable trainees to demonstrate learned behaviors while attending to a secondary task (for example, listening to voicemail)
11.2	Tuning	Behavioral observation, performance ratings of individualization	• Write quality scenarios that reflect complexity levels beyond those received in training in scenario writing

Source: Adapted from Kraiger et al., 1993.

strategies and examples. The outcomes listed may not exhaust the list of possible learning outcomes but are sufficiently broad so as to be useful for evaluating most training programs. Readers interested in more detailed information about specific measurement techniques are referred to Jonassen and Tessmer (1996–97), Kraiger et al. (1993), and Royer, Cisero, and Carlo (1993).

Implications for Measurement. How can the outcomes in Exhibit 11.2 be useful for evaluating specific training programs? Kraiger and Jung (1997) provide guidelines for identifying learning outcomes based on knowledge of the training goals, instructional objectives, training content, or the intended performance domain. Kraiger et al. (1993) suggested that given both a broader understanding of how trainees change during training and increased confidence that different forms of learning can be validly measured, training designers should feel free to write instructional objectives to reflect desired changes rather than a restrictive behavioral framework. Objectives that would make traditionalists shudder—such as "see the big picture" or "be aware they are making mistakes"—may actually need little rewording to fit the taxonomy. Following Kraiger and Jung, specific instructional objectives can be classified into broader learning outcomes, at which point specific measures are suggested to capture trainee learning. For example, seeing the big picture consists in part of understanding relationships between one's work activities, position, or organizational unit and the activities of others or the mission of the unit or organization as a whole. Depending on whether this is conceptualized as static or static-dynamic knowledge, an individual's understanding of the big picture can be considered a specific case of either of two learning outcomes: knowledge organization or concept mapping. A set of terms can be created to represent positional responsibilities of the trainee and others, and indicators of unit and organizational missions. The terms can be organized using relationship ratings with a structural representation such as Pathfinder (see Goldsmith & Kraiger, 1997) or a card sort, or represented using concept mapping.

By following the taxonomy, training decision makers may end up developing a broader set of assessment measures than with traditional paper-and-pencil tests. Accordingly, at first glance the taxonomy may appear overwhelming. However, because the outcomes may actually be more reflective of how subject matter experts or stakeholders describe the intended performance domain, applying the taxonomy may require less effort than writing instructional objectives at the front end. Whether training practitioners actually choose to construct multiple outcome-specific measures such as concept maps or behavioral checklists, the primary benefit of applying the taxonomy will come from thinking clearly about intended changes at all phases of the instructional design process.

Affective Outcomes. Because the notion of measuring affective change may be foreign to some readers, as might be some of the specific behavioral outcomes, it is worth providing some commentary on these outcomes. The rationale for measuring affective outcomes is that in many instances they are either direct or indirect outcomes of training programs. They are direct outcomes when the training is intended to increase awareness or appreciation of specific attitudes or values. For example, one of the primary outcomes of job readiness training programs for the chronically unemployed is to increase the value they attach to holding jobs or to increase their willingness to follow rules once they get jobs. Affective changes are often indirect outcomes—when, through exposure to a topic or continued practice, trainees gain greater confidence (self-efficacy) or the desire to learn more to master a skill set (mastery orientation), for example. Research has shown that changes in self-efficacy or mastery orientation are significant predictors of transfer of training and continuous learning on the job (for example, Stevens & Gist, 1997). In most instances, affective change is measured through self-report measures or questionnaires and can be easily integrated into traditional trainee reaction measures. For example, a question about how relevant the training material was may be followed by a question about the extent to which the trainee believes he or she will be able to apply it back on the job.

Behavioral Outcomes. With respect to behaviors, the skill acquisition outcomes refer to evidence that, in the context of training, learners are able to demonstrate behaviors that they have previously not demonstrated or performed effectively. Automaticity outcomes refer to evidence that trainees are able to perform these new behaviors fluidly and without conscious monitoring or that they have begun to individualize the behaviors. Usually, the former set of outcomes is demonstrated under maximal performance conditions (ideal circumstances and minimal distractions designed to elicit the best possible performance), whereas the latter set of outcomes is demonstrated under normal performance conditions (everyday circumstances that elicit more typical performance). There are a number of appropriate data collection methods for assessing behavioral outcomes, including surveys, questionnaires, observation, interviews, action planning, and performance monitoring (Phillips, 1997).

There are two posited skill acquisition outcomes: proceduralization and compilation. Proceduralization refers to the capacity to reproduce trained behaviors, or the extent to which trainees can mimic modeled behavior. In some instances, evidence of proceduralization may be elicited by walk-through demonstrations or by asking trainees what they would do in certain situations. Compilation occurs after continued practice and is characterized by more fluid performance, fewer errors, and the integration of discrete events into a single act. For example, eventually a novice golfer develops to the point where he or she stops attending to discrete elements of a swing (backswing, contact, follow-through) and smoothly strikes the ball in a single movement. The distinction between proceduralization and compilation is evident in a recent charismatic leadership training study by Towler and Dipboye (2001). The authors provided training in charismatic behaviors or interpersonal skills. After training, participants prepared and delivered a recruitment speech that was videotaped and scored. Assessors blind to training condition scored the tapes first for evidence of charismatic communication behaviors (for example, use of metaphors or appeals to values) and then for the quality of communication using a set of bipolar adjectives such as incompetent-competent and unfriendly-friendly. The incorporation of charismatic behaviors into the speech was a desired outcome of training, so that the frequency of these behaviors on a practice trial is evidence of proceduralization. The extent to which assessors perceived the use of multiple strategies as having an impact on overall characteristics of the speech (for example, implied competence) can be interpreted as evidence of compilation.

As suggested by the measurement examples in Exhibit 11.2, automatic processing and tuning may be assessed through scripted scenarios and work samples that allow trainees to demonstrate learned behaviors. To the extent that trainees are unaware of their behaviors or are able to perform secondary tasks as they demonstrate the newly learned skills, there is evidence of automatic processing. To the extent that they perform new behaviors correctly but individualize the acts or adapt them to unique scenario characteristics, they are showing evidence of tuning. Note that most training situations may be too brief for automaticity to occur unless the learned skills are very straightforward.

Guidelines for Practice

- Be clear on the purpose of evaluation when choosing measures related to changes in the learner.
- Write learning objectives in language that is most comfortable to trainees, trainers, or organizational decision makers, rather than forcing objectives to look behavioral for the sake of measurement.
- Remember that training may result in changes in behavior but not improved performance, or that training may improve performance without changing behavior; be clear on what you expect will happen.
- Use a taxonomy such as that in Exhibit 11.2 to identify objectives under different learning outcomes, then choose measures that reflect those outcomes.
- Use awareness of intended learning outcomes to guide decision making during all steps of the instructional design process.
- Design measures that allow trainees to demonstrate knowledge, affect, or behavior consistent with the instructional objectives. Because the goal is to assess learning (and not the trainee), the more straightforward the measure, the better.

Organizational Payoffs

The final target for evaluation is the payoff to the organization. As shown in Figure 11.2, this includes any evidence that trainees are applying learned behaviors or skills back on the job, that these behaviors result in more effective performance, and that the training has some bottom-line impact on unit or organizational effectiveness. This information may be primarily useful when the purpose of the training is decision making (for example, course retention) or marketing.

Indicators of organizational payoffs are shown in Exhibit 11.3, along with examples and references. As can be seen in the exhibit, there are three payoff dimensions. Investments in training are recouped by the organization when trainees transfer learning to the job, perform their jobs more effectively, and carry out activities that have a financial impact on the job. Each dimension is discussed briefly here.

Transfer of Training. Although transfer climate is not actually a characteristic of trainee behavior, it is sometimes valuable to measure it as part of broader assessments of training effectiveness (see Machin, Chapter Nine, this volume; Noe & Colquitt, Chapter Three, this volume). Transfer climate refers to those situations and actions that indicate organizational support for transfer of training as well as situational constraints that restrict the application of trained skills in the workplace. By including a measure of transfer climate along with other indicators of changes in the learner and training impact, training practitioners can identify whether failure to transfer is rooted in initial learning or problems in the broader performance domain.

Before trainees can use their training to perform their jobs better, they must have the opportunity to apply what they learned. Opportunity to perform refers to the extent to which trainees are provided with or actively seek experiences in which they can apply newly learned skills, knowledge, and behavior. As conceptualized by Ford, Quiñones, Sego, and Sorra (1992), opportunity to perform consists of three dimensions: the number of trained tasks (breadth), the frequency with which trained tasks are performed (activity level), and the difficulty or criticality of the trained tasks performed (task type). Somewhat like transfer climate, opportunity to perform is primarily determined by system-level factors rather than trainee volition. Also like transfer climate, including a measure of opportunity to perform can help isolate potential problems in transfer. As evident in the Bassi and Ahlstrand (2000) study, opportunity to perform can be assessed directly through surveys of trainees back on the job (for example, "In the past six months, to what extent have you been able to apply newly learned word processing skills to your job?").

Exhibit 11.3. Indicators of Organizational Payoffs.

Focus of Evaluation	Description	Example (Reference)
Transfer of Training:		
Transfer climate	Measure of trainee perceptions of situations and actions that indicate organizational support for transfer of training	Transfer climate survey (Tracey, Tannenbaum, & Kavanaugh, 1995)
Opportunity to perform	Measure of trainee (or observer) perceptions of whether trainees are provided with or seek experiences to apply new skills, knowledge, and behavior	Opportunity to perform survey (Ford et al., 1992)
On-the-job behavior change	Determination of what specific activities have changed or are performed more frequently as a result of training	Behavioral checklist (Noe, 1999)
Skill maintenance	Determination of whether the application or frequency of new behaviors are maintained over time	Performance on job tasks at two points in time (Simon & Werner, 1996)
Skill generalization	Measure of whether trainee can apply new knowledge or skills to situations not covered in training	Probed protocol analysis (Kraiger et al., 1993)
Results:		
Performance effectiveness	Evaluation of the impact of knowledge and behavior to job performance	Estimated percent increase in performance (Bassi & Ahlstrand, 2000)
Unit impact	Evaluation of whether improved job performance results in tangible outcomes to the work group, office unit, or organization (reduced turnover, higher productivity, greater customer service)	Reduction in driver accidents and injuries following a safe driving course (Phillips, 1996)

Exhibit 11.3. Indicators of Organizational Payoffs, Cont'd.

Focus of Evaluation	Description	Example (Reference)
Financial Impact:		
Cost-benefit analysis–Return on investment	Application of accounting principles to the calculation of the cost and benefits of training; may be expressed as an ROI ratio	Return on investment of training in three operational areas (Robinson & Robinson, 1989)
Utility analysis	Application of economic modeling to estimate the impact of training given knowledge of the effect size for training, costs of training, and value of the job to the organization	Economic modeling of impact of training in dollar terms (Mathieu & Leonard, 1987)

On-the-job behavior change simply refers to whether trainees are doing things differently, as intended by training. Trainees who receive training in presentation software should be demonstrating the skills acquired in training back on the job (for example, using presentation templates, adding animation to slides). However, measuring behavioral change does not imply performance improvement. A self-taught golfer may experience worse scores once he or she starts to apply correct elements of a swing acquired through golfing lessons. The implication is that through continuous practice, effective performance (measured under the results dimension) will follow. Still, evidence that trainees have applied the behaviors learned in training back on the job provides the most straightforward assessment of transfer. Data for on-the-job behavior change may be collected in a number of ways, but the most straightforward are observation or completion of checklists by others who are in the best position to observe trainee behavior (such as customers evaluating the application of customer service skills by newly trained sales associates).

Baldwin and Ford (1988) noted that once there is evidence that training is applied on the job, the organization should still be concerned with whether the new behaviors are maintained over time and whether new skills are generalized to new situations or stimuli. Training is ineffective if trainees try new ways of doing things but after a time go back to old habits. The value of training is compounded to the extent that newly acquired skills are generalized to new applications. For example, a mechanic who attends a training course on a specific mechanical problem may be able to generalize new diagnostic techniques to different types of problems. Assessing skill maintenance requires primarily the same methods as assessing behavioral change, but multiple measurement points and analysis of performance trends over time are needed (see Baldwin & Ford, 1988). Because skill generalization also involves certain cognitive skills, such as cue recognition and problem solving, it may be assessed through self-report techniques, such as structured interviews or probed protocol analysis (see Kraiger et al., 1993). Probed protocol analysis consists of a subject matter expert guiding a learner through a verbal description of the task, asking questions about what she was thinking as she performed the task, what cues she was attending to, what options she considered, and so on.

Results. Measuring the payoffs of training in terms of results requires that data be collected to show that the training had some positive impact on the performance of individual trainees, the immediate work unit, or the organization as a whole. Performance effectiveness is usually measured at the individual level but could be done at the team level in some cases. Unlike on-the-job behavior change, measures of performance effectiveness reflect whether trainees are better at their jobs (as a result of training). Performance effectiveness may be evaluated through traditional performance ratings or 360-degree feedback systems. It may also be evaluated through formal certification programs or assessment centers. In the example given in Exhibit 11.3 and at the beginning of this chapter (Bassi & Ahlstrand, 2000), performance effectiveness was measured simply by asking trainees or their supervisors to estimate the percentage improvement in job performance as a result of training. Regardless of the type of measure, the focus should be aspects of performance that related to training objectives rather than overall job performance.

Measures of unit impact assess whether improved trainee performance translates into outcome measures valued by the organization. Again, choice of outcome indices should be related to the stated objectives of training; a project management course for research scientists should be related to the percentage of projects completed on time but not the creativity of new products. Traditional hard measures of group, office, or organizational impact include production, sales, work backlog, cycle time, equipment downtime, deadlines met, number of grievances, error reduction, number of customer complaints, turnover, and reduced expenses (see Phillips, 1997, for a more extensive list). So-called soft measures of aggregate impact include employee satisfaction or organizational commitment, customer satisfaction or retention, and quality of new ideas. Phillips (1997) suggested a number of ways to collect measures of unit impact, including organizational performance records, participant self-reports, surveys, and evaluations or judgments by supervisors, peers, or external constituents (such as customers).

Financial Impact. Assessing financial impact means determining whether training costs were recouped, whether the investment in training resulted in tangible benefits to the organization, or whether the training function can project positive consequences from improvement in employee performance. Impact estimates may in some cases be based on actual financial data but in many instances are based on economic models that rely on assumptions about the worth of human behavior. The most common and straightforward method involves a cost-benefit analysis of training. Costs are estimated using common accounting methods. Direct costs include training materials, instructor payments, use of space and equipment, and travel expenses for participants. Indirect costs are associated with maintenance of the training function (for example, costs associated with the project linked back to the training director and his or her staff), overhead, and postage, shipping, and so on. Development costs may include payments to external consultants or the costs associated with the project linked back to the training development staff. Finally, costs associated with trainee attendance are calculated, with the assumption being that if trainees are being paid to attend training, then they are being paid not to contribute directly to the production of goods and services by the organization.

After calculating the costs of training, the benefits are estimated. Benefits may be estimated directly from organizational records. For example, in a study by Robinson and Robinson (1989), the researchers identified that the average number of accidents in a wood plant dropped from twenty-four to sixteen after training. At an average cost per accident of $6,000, the financial benefits of the reduction in accidents can be easily estimated. In many instances, training benefits may be calculated indirectly with knowledge of training outcomes. Frequently, training benefits may be expressed in time savings and then translated to dollar metrics given the known cost (including benefits) of an individual's time. For example, I once evaluated the financial impact of a self-directed learning program of twelve municipal managers. Each chose different learning objectives and development activities, so it was impossible to come up with an overall measure of training success. However, each provided anecdotal evidence that could be converted to a measure of financial impact. One manager took a business writing course after realizing that his boss could not understand any of the memos he wrote and frequently asked for the memos to be rewritten (often several times). Working with the manager, I estimated the number of memos he wrote per month, how many had to be rewritten before training, and how many had to be rewritten after training. We estimated that as a result of the course, he was writing about twenty fewer "bad" memos per month (memos that were so unclear that they had to be rewritten). We timed how long it took him to write a memo, how long it took his secretary to type a memo, and how long it took his supervisor to read a memo and write back that it was unclear. Using this information and the salaries of each of the three parties, we estimated the total savings per month from writing better memos. If expressing the savings of time in dollar terms seems a stretch, recall that time spent is considered a cost of training. The objective is not to estimate exactly how much extra money will be available at year's end but to compare training expenditures to benefits using a common metric.

Following a cost-benefit analysis, the results may or may not be expressed as a return-on-investment ratio (ROI). Generally, ROI is simply the ratio of total training benefits (expressed in dollar terms) divided by total training costs (also expressed in dollar terms). For example, in the Robinson and Robinson (1989) study, the researchers estimated the total "operational results" at $220,800 and the total training costs at $32,836. Dividing the former total by the latter, the researchers estimated the ROI of training at 6.7:1. In other words, for every dollar spent on training, the organization can expect to realize $6.70 in greater efficiency or productivity. Phillips (1997) reported that ROI estimates in excess of 100:1 may be common (although it is questionable how credible such estimates are).

Although in one sense ROI estimates are simply numerical transformations of cost-benefit results, they have two advantages. One is that it may be possible to estimate the long-term impact of training and adjust ROI ratios accordingly. For example, if wood plant trainees in Robinson and Robinson's (1989) study estimated that 50 percent of the skills learned in training are still relevant to accident prevention in year two, then a second two-year ROI could be calculated: ROI = ($220,800 + $220,800/2)/$32,836 = 10.1:1. The other advantage is that with ROI there is no reason why benefits have to be expressed in dollar terms. Indeed, this is the part of the process that organizational decision makers often find the most uncomfortable. By examining training outcomes rather than outcomes translated into dollar savings, the training evaluator can express ROI in terms such as "Every $1,000 spent on training will result in two fewer accidents per year" or "Every $100 spent on training will result in five more sales leads a month." Very often, decision makers can better appreciate the value of the change in outcomes expressed in these terms than if the evaluator used a set of assumptions and formulas to translate the outcomes into dollar terms.

The other method of estimating financial impact is to estimate the utility of training. I/O psychologists have traditionally applied utility models to quantify the impact of selection programs, but the same models can be applied to assess the impact of any human resource program for which an effect size measure can be estimated (Cascio, 1982; Mathieu & Leonard, 1987). In its simplest form, the utility (or value added) of a training program can be estimated by subtracting estimated costs from estimated benefits. Estimated costs are calculated with methods similar to those described earlier. Benefits are estimated by multiplying the estimated duration of training impact by a measure of training effect size by the standard deviation of performance in dollar terms (SD_y). The estimated duration of training may be estimated from subject matter experts or based on the number of years until trainees must be retrained. The effect size is the difference between the job performance of a trained group and an untrained group expressed in standard units (for example, divided by a pooled standard deviation term). The standard deviation of performance in dollar terms indicates the relative worth of the job to the organization. It is roughly equivalent to the value added or cost of replacement of the employee at the eighty-fifth percentile compared to the employee at the fiftieth percentile. (See Cascio, 1982, and Mathieu & Leonard, 1987, for recommendations for estimating each of the utility parameters.) When the various utility parameters are combined, the result is an estimate of the economic value of training over time. For example, Mathieu and Leonard estimated that assuming a yearly 25 percent decrease in training effectiveness (in other words, the impact of training diminishes over time), the utility of training twenty-six bank branch managers was $36,107 after one year and $75,879 after three years. Given knowledge of effect sizes, total number of employees, and costs and SD_ys for various jobs, utility analyses can be useful for making informed decisions about where to invest in training or to compare investments in training to other human performance solutions, such as selection or job aids. Unfortunately, utility estimates often suffer from credibility problems because many assumptions need to be made and the final estimates often seem too high to be believable. In addition, many practitioners may be scared off by the practical difficulties of estimating effect sizes and SD_y.

Guidelines for Practice

- Know your audience and ensure that measures of training impact will provide the evidence that is most persuasive based on their preferences for receiving information.
- Use measures of transfer climate and opportunity to perform to isolate whether lack of organizational payoffs are due to problems during training or problems in the transfer environment.

- Distinguish between whether or not trainees apply learned behaviors to the job and whether applying new behaviors make them perform more effectively; measure the outcome that makes the most sense given the purpose for evaluation.
- Distinguish between organizational results and the financial impact of those results; measure the outcome that makes the most sense given the purpose for evaluation.
- Recognize that as the evaluation plan moves from evidence of behavioral change to organizational payoffs in dollar terms, more assumptions are necessary to derive the evaluation data and the results are more likely to be questioned by organizational decision makers.

When to Evaluate: Decisions About Effective Design

The final decisions about evaluation concern creating effective designs for isolating and measuring the impact of training. Many managers with little research background appreciate the difficulty in accomplishing these goals. They ask, for example, "How do we know performance wouldn't have changed even without the training?" or "How do we distinguish the contribution of training on performance from. . . . (seasonal fluctuation in sales, new products, and so on)?" Individuals asked to conduct training evaluation who have a background in research design understand all too well the practical constraints against rigorous evaluation designs with pre- and posttests, control groups, and random assignment to conditions.

Perspectives on Evaluation

Before providing specific design recommendations, it is useful to consider several perspectives on evaluation designs. McLinden (1995) made a valuable contribution when he likened the training evaluator to a lawyer in court. In a criminal case, the prosecuting lawyer does not have to prove, absolutely, that the defendant committed the crime. Rather, he or she must present sufficient evidence that is consistent with a hypothesis (the charge) that the defendant was responsible—that is, that the defendant had the motive, means, and opportunity to commit the alleged act. Similarly, the role of the evaluator is not to prove that the training worked but to present evidence that something happened (the crime of performance improvement), that the training was in the room sometime before or at the same time that something happened (training targeted areas of performance improvement), and that the training had sufficient motives to cause what happened (a needs assessment identified the problem that training tried to fix and the problem has gone away). This perspective stresses the importance of placing training in a sequence of events leading to the observation that something improved and lessens the burden on the training evaluator for proving training works.

A second perspective is provided by Sackett and Mullen (1993), who make two important observations. The first is that training evaluation is sometimes done to assess how much change occurred (for example, is computer-based training better than instructor-led, given the same material?) and at other times to determine whether a target performance level has been achieved (for example, are new customer service representatives sufficiently skilled at their jobs that they can begin taking real calls?). In the latter instances, formal evaluation procedures may not be necessary at all, as long as the evaluator has some confidence in the validity of the measure used to compare trainee performance to the standard. The second observation is that in some instances (situations with small sample sizes), a true experimental design may lack the power to detect changes in learners even if they really occurred and that a weaker preexperimental design (posttest only or no control group) has a better chance of detecting change. Of course, with weaker designs there are more threats to the validity of the conclusion that training worked.

A third perspective comes from my youth. In the mid-1960s I read a book on playing baseball by Sandy Koufax, who was then the dominant pitcher in professional baseball. As a ten-year-old dreaming of becoming a big league baseball player, I was interested in the various chapters on baseball skill development. As a ten-year-old who would one day become an I/O psychologist, I was most interested in Chapter Eight, "The Mental Game." Koufax wrote that when he began each game, he planned to pitch a perfect game—no batters reaching by walks, hits, or errors. If he walked the first batter, he would tell himself, "I can still pitch a no-hitter." If the next batter got a hit, he would tell himself, "A one-hitter is not bad; I can still pitch a one-hitter." If yet the next batter got a hit, he would tell himself, "At least I can still pitch a shutout." If the next batter hit a home run, scoring four runs, he would tell himself, "I can still win the game."

When working with organizations that want to evaluate training, I try to emphasize the difference between pitching the perfect game and still winning the game. It is useful to think of the cleanest design, one that with high internal, external, and statistical conclusion validity. Such a design is a helpful starting point. However, as information becomes available compromising that design ("Oops, it is too late for the pretest"), it is still possible to win the game. Winning comes from accomplishing the purpose of the study—collecting enough data to answer a practical question about training.

Practical Research Designs

A reasonable quasi-experimental design has a control group and one or more trained groups, with a pretest and posttest on the outcome measures (for example, anticipated changed in the learner). Quasi-experimental means that subjects are not randomly assigned to training. For example, managers in one department are sent to diversity training, and managers in a second department are told they must wait two months until they can attend. During the two-month lag period, pre- and posttraining differences between the two groups in, for example, conflict management skills to facilitate collaboration with dissimilar others (see Chrobot-Mason & Quiñones, Chapter Five, this volume) can be used to assess the effectiveness of training in the first department. For those seeking more information, there are several good discussions of research design applied to training (Cascio, 1991; Noe, 1999).

Depending on the use of the evaluation information, high-quality, rigorous evaluation designs may or may not be necessary (Sackett & Mullin, 1993; Tannenbaum & Woods, 1992). More rigorous designs may be necessary if the results are going to be used to evaluate a training program, the training affects important organizational outcomes, or there is a strong measurement culture in the organization (Tannenbaum & Woods, 1992). However, for any number of reasons it may not be reasonable to conduct a pretest or establish a control or comparison group. Both individuals responsible for training and other decision makers in the organization may believe that the absence of these conditions limit, if not eliminate, the possibility of isolating training as the determinant for improved individual performance or organizational effectiveness. One response is to argue with logic, rather than experimental control. Following McLinden (1995), reasonable arguments may be formed that implicate the role of training even without pretests or control groups. For example, archival data may suggest that sales performance has dipped in the second quarter of every year in the past decade, except those when new product training was offered in the first quarter. Similarly, Sackett and Mullin (1993) argued that experimental control is but one strategy for responding to criticisms of the internal or statistical conclusion validity of a research design. Reasoned logic based on knowledge of the measures and intention for evaluation training may be almost as persuasive.

A second, powerful strategy was championed by Haccoun and Hamtiaux (1994). Their internal referencing strategy (IRS) is particularly useful when no control group is available, and even when there is no pretest available. Haccoun and Hamtiaux suggested that when no comparison group is available, items on the evaluation measure themselves can serve as a basis for comparison. Specifically, when creating the measure (which can be knowledge-, behavior-, or performance-based) the evaluator identifies a smaller set of items that are logically related to the training program but in fact were never covered. For example, the IRS items for a training course on performance coaching for managers could include questions on completing appraisal forms or facilitating action planning if those topics are not covered in training. With a pretest-posttest, no-control-group design, the measure is given on two occasions and the researcher looks for a time by relevant-irrelevant interaction, meaning that over the course of training scores on the training-relevant items increased but scores on the training-irrelevant items did not. With no pretest, the researcher can only do a t test on mean scores for relevant versus irrelevant items. Following McLinden's (1995) logic, in either instance the evaluator is in a more powerful position to argue that observed success on posttest is not simply due to subject maturation, history effects, or generally competent trainees, because the success indicators are specific to the content of training.

Finally, there will be times when it may be impossible to conduct pretest scores—there is a fear that the pretest may sensitive trainees, there is not sufficient time before or during training to administer it, or the decision to evaluate training came after training began. When the evaluator faces a posttest-only design with some control group or comparison group, there are several good choices to make in order to isolate training impact. One is to consider other measures readily available by which trainees in the trained group and control group may be compared. For example, members of the two groups may be compared on the basis of a pre-employment cognitive ability test, prior job experience, or prior training courses (on similar content) attended. Any available pretest score that turns out to be correlated with posttest scores (across conditions) can be used as a covariate. Analyses of posttest differences after controlling for potential covariates can strengthen the internal and statistical conclusion validity of the posttest quasi-experimental design. Arvey and Cole (1989) provide an easy-to-follow discussion of analysis strategies for collecting and analyzing covariates.

If pretest data are not available, then the Bassi and Ahlstrand's (2000) strategy of asking trainees to estimate levels of improvement since before training is probably the best way to isolate training impact. Phillips (1997) also suggests asking trainees to estimate how much of the improvement was due to training rather than other factors. The credibility of such data may be questioned by some organizational stakeholders, but those involved in training design should have an idea of whether this will occur from discussions early in the planning process.

In general, it is important to understand the audience and its expectations for quantifying training outcomes. Organizations with a culture of strong measurement may not only be receptive to more field-based measurement but may have stronger expectations of the quality of the design and the job relevance of measures. In many other organizations, any combination of measurement and research design other than end-of-training surveys of trainee satisfaction may be a step forward. When I talk with training departments about evaluation issues, I like to keep in mind what Sandy Koufax would have done. The initial goal is to design the tightest, best controlled study given the purposes for evaluation. However, as aspects of that design become impractical in the organizational culture, timing for training and measurement, or available resources, it is helpful to remember that less formal designs may still lead to evaluation results that meet the intended purpose.

Guidelines for Practice

- Be clear about the expected uses of evaluation data. Evaluation done to certify employees may need less rigorous designs than evaluation done to measure program effectiveness.
- Always start with a plan for a strong, clean design but be willing to compromise at the planning stage. In most instances, some evaluation is better than no evaluation and can still meet the intended purpose for assessment.
- Know your audience and ensure that measures of training impact will provide the evidence that is the most persuasive given their preferences for receiving information.

Conclusion

Training outcomes may be measured in a limited number of ways. The key to effective training evaluation is good decision making at each step of the planning process. The first and most important decision is selecting the purpose for evaluation. Given one or more purposes, subsequent decisions can be made about what to evaluate and how to collect data to isolate the effects of training. At all steps, careful consideration should be given to uses for the information and the preferences of the intended audiences with respect to how data are collected and presented.

References
Alliger, G. M., & Janak, E. A. (1989). Kirkpatrick's levels of training criteria: Thirty years later. *Personnel Psychology, 42*, 331–342.
Alliger, G. M., Tannenbaum, S. I., & Bennett, W., Traver, H., & Shortland, A. (1997). A meta-analysis on the relations among training criteria. *Personnel Psychology, 50*, 341–358.
Baldwin, T. T., & Ford, J. K. (1988). Transfer of training: A review and directions for future research. *Personnel Psychology, 41*, 63–105.

Baldwin, T. T., Magjuka, R. J., & Loher, B. T. (1991). The perils of participation: Effects of choice of training on trainee motivation and learning. *Personnel Psychology, 44,* 260–267.

Bassi, L., & Ahlstrand, A. (2000). *The 2000 ASTD learning outcomes report: Second annual report on ASTD's standards for valuing enterprises' investments.* Washington, DC: American Society for Training and Development.

Bloom, B. (1956). *Taxonomy of educational objectives: The cognitive domain.* New York: McKay.

Cascio, W. F. (1982). *Costing human resources: The financial impact of behavior in organizations.* Boston: Kent.

Cascio, W. F. (1991). *Applied psychology in personnel management* (4th ed.). Englewood Cliffs, NJ: Prentice-Hall.

Catalanello, R., & Kirkpatrick, D. (1968). Evaluating training programs: The state of the art. *Training and Development Journal, 22*(5), 2–9.

Ford, J. K., Quiñones, M. A., Sego, D. J., & Sorra, J. A. (1992). Factors affecting the opportunity to perform trained tasks on the job. *Personnel Psychology, 45,* 511–527.

Ford, J. K., & Wroten, S. P. (1984). Introducing new methods for conducting training evaluation and for linking training evaluation to program redesign. *Personnel Psychology, 37,* 651–665.

Goldsmith, T., & Kraiger, K. (1997). Structural knowledge assessment and training evaluation. In J. Ford, S. Kozlowski, K. Kraiger, E. Salas, & M. Teachout (Eds.), *Improving training effectiveness in work organizations* (pp. 19–46). Hillsdale, NJ: Erlbaum.

Haccoun, R. R., & Hamtiaux, T. (1994). Optimizing knowledge tests for inferring acquisition levels in single group training evaluation designs: The internal referencing strategy. *Personnel Psychology, 47,* 593–604.

Hamblin, A. C. (1974). *The design and evaluation of training.* New York: McGraw-Hill.

Holton, E. F., III. (1996). The flawed four-level evaluation model. *Human Resource Development Quarterly, 7,* 5–21.

Industry report, 1996. (1996, October). *Training, 33*(10), 36–49.

Jonassen, D., & Tessmer, M. (1996–97). An outcomes-based taxonomy for instructional systems design, evaluation, and research. *Training Research Journal, 2,* 11–46.

Kirkpatrick, D. L. (1959a). Techniques for evaluating training programs. *Journal of ASTD, 13*(11), 3–9.

Kirkpatrick, D. L. (1959b). Techniques for evaluating training programs: Part 2—Learning. *Journal of ASTD, 13*(12), 21–26.

Kirkpatrick, D. L. (1960a). Techniques for evaluating training programs: Part 3—Behavior. *Journal of ASTD, 14*(1), 13–18.

Kirkpatrick, D. L. (1960b). Techniques for evaluating training programs: Part 4—Results. *Journal of ASTD, 14*(2), 28–32.

Kirkpatrick, D. L. (1976). Evaluation of training. In R. L Craig (Ed.), *Training and development handbook: A guide to human resource development* (2nd ed., pp. 18.1–18.27). New York: McGraw-Hill.

Kirkpatrick, D. L. (1994). *Evaluating training programs: The four levels.* San Francisco: Berrett-Koehler.

Kraiger, K. (2001). Industrial and organizational psychology: Science and practice. In N. J. Smelser & P. B. Baltes (Eds.), *International encyclopedia of the social and behavioral sciences.*

Kraiger, K., Ford, J. K., Salas, E. (1993). Application of cognitive, skill-based, and affective theories of learning outcomes to new methods of training evaluation. *Journal of Applied Psychology, 78,* 311–328.

Kraiger, K., & Jung, K. M. (1997). Linking training objectives to evaluation criteria. In M. A. Quiñones & A. Dutta (Eds.), *Training for the 21st century technology: Applications of psychological research.* Washington, DC: American Psychological Association.

Krathwohl, D. R., Bloom, B. S., & Masia, B. B. (1964). *Taxonomy of educational objectives: The classification of educational goals.* White Plains, NY: Longman.

Lawshe, C. H. (1975). A quantitative approach to the evaluation of fairness in employee selection procedures. *Personnel Psychology, 28,* 563–575.

Lee, S. H., & Pershing, J. A. (1999). Effective reaction evaluation in evaluating training programs. *Performance Improvement, 38*(8), 32–39.

Mager, R. F., & Beach, K. M., Jr. (1967). *Developing vocational instruction.* Belmont, CA: Fearon, 1967.

Mathieu, J. E., & Leonard, R. L. (1987). Applying utility analysis to a training program in supervisory skills: A time-based approach. *Academy of Management Journal, 30,* 316–335.

Mathieu, J. E., Tannenbaum, S. I., & Salas, E. (1992). Influences on individual and situational characteristics on measures of training effectiveness. *Academy of Management Journal, 35,* 828–847.

McLinden, D. J. (1995). Proof, evidence, and complexity: Understanding the impact of training and development in business. *Performance Improvement Quarterly, 8*(3), 3–18.

Moller, L., & Mallin, P. (1996). Evaluation practices of instructional designers and organizational supports and barriers. *Performance Improvement Quarterly, 9*(4), 82–92.

Morgan, R. B., & Casper, W. (2000). Examining the factor structure of participant reactions to training: A multidimensional approach. *Human Resource Development Quarterly, 11,* 301–317.

Noe, R. A. (1999). *Employee training and development.* Burr Ridge, IL: Irwin.

Phillips, J. J. (1996). Was it the training? *Training and Development Journal, 50*(3), 28–32.

Phillips, J. J. (1997). *Handbook of training evaluation and measurement methods* (3rd ed.). Houston: Gulf Publishing.

Robinson, D. G., & Robinson, J. C. (1989). Training for impact. *Training and Development Journal, 43*(8), 30–42.

Royer, J. M., Cisero, C. A., & Carlo, M. S. (1993). Techniques and procedures for assessing cognitive skills. *Review of Educational Research, 63,* 201–243.

Sackett, P. R., & Mullen, E. J. (1993). Beyond formal experimental design: Towards an expanded view of the training evaluation process. *Personnel Psychology, 46,* 613–627.

Simon, S. J., & Werner, J. M. (1996). Computer training through behavior modeling, self-paced, and instructional approaches: A field experiment. *Journal of Applied Psychology, 81,* 648–659.

Stevens, C. K., & Gist, M. E. (1997). Effects of self-efficacy and goal orientation training on negotiation skills maintenance: What are the mechanisms? *Personnel Psychology, 50,* 955–978.

Tannenbaum, S. I., & Woods, S. B. (1992). Determining a strategy for evaluating training: Operating within organizational constraints. *Human Resource Planning, 15*(2), 63–81.

Towler, A. J., & Dipboye, R. L. (2001, April). *Effects of charismatic communication training on motivation, behavior, and attitudes.* Paper presented at the annual meeting of the Society of Industrial/Organizational Psychology, San Diego.

Tracey, J. B., Tannenbaum, S. I., & Kavanaugh, M. J. (1995). Applying trained skills on the job: The importance of work environment. *Journal of Applied Psychology, 80,* 239–252.

Twitchell, S., Holton, E. F. III, & Trott, J. R., Jr. (2001). Technical training evaluation practices in the United States. *Performance Improvement Quarterly, 13*(3), 84–109.

Van Buren, M. E. (2001). *State of the industry: Report 2001.* Washington, DC: American Society for Training and Development.

Warr, P., & Bunce, D. (1995). Trainee characteristics and the outcomes of open learning. *Personnel Psychology, 48,* 347–376.

Worthen, B. R., & Sanders, J. R. (1987). *Educational evaluation: Alternative approaches and practical guidelines.* White Plains, NY: Longman.

Name Index

Subject Index

M

Maintenance: defined, 57; of diversity training, 150–151; evaluation of, 360, 361–362. *See also* Transfer

Management development, 160–189; coaching for, 160–189; conditions for, 165–167

Management support, 72–73, *xxv;* for diversity training, 126, 144–146; levels of, 72; posttraining, 290–292; pretraining, 272–273; transfer climate and, 290–291, 292; ways to gain, 73

Mapping, of actions to outcomes, in computer-based training, 208

Marketing of training: evaluation for, 338–339, 358; to motivate trainees, 269–270, 339

Mastery orientation, 63; cooperative learning and, 214; evaluation of, 353, 356; feedback and, 215; importance of, for active learning, 200–201; metacognition and, 216; practice guidelines for inducing, 65; in team training, 238, 251

Measures and measurement: of adaptive expertise, 295; of climate, 71, 72; of diversity training, 148–150; of learning, 58; in learning organization, 310, 325; lessons learned about, *xxvi–xxvii;* practice guidelines for, 58; of team performance and training, 239, 254–256; tools needed for, 8; of transfer, 58. *See also* Decision-based evaluation; Evaluation; Outcomes

Mental models, 197, 322; error-based learning and, 282; evaluation of, 350; shared, 252

Mentoring, 160–161, 186–188, *xxi;* coaching *versus,* 161; cognitive task analysis and, 86; conditions suitable for, 174; for continual learning, 26; definition of,

188*n*.1; designing an organizational program for, 186–188; as form of informal learning, 21; indications for, 170–174; mentor selection for, 186; popularity of, 160; reciprocal, 187; relationship in, 187; reverse, 189*n*.5; road maps for, 186; shadowing in, 187–188; topics best suited for, 174

Metacognition and metacognitive skills, 21; for adaptive expertise, 282–283; in computer-based training, 216–217, 219, 220; defined, 216; as learning outcome, 197; practice guidelines for, 219; question-generation strategies for encouraging, 216–217, 219; in team training, 250, 251

Metaphors, in user interface, 208

Method decisions, 87

Method fixation, 87

Military jobs, cognitive task analysis of, 80–81, 86, 88, 94, 95, 101, 102–103, 105–107, 112–113

Mindfulness: defined, 201; importance of, in active learning, 201–202; information structure and, 206; metacognition and, 216; programmed instruction and, 211; user interface and, 207–208

Minnesota Adaptive Instructional System (MAIS), 212

Minorities: expectations and disappointment of, in diversity training, 119, 120, 145; mentoring and coaching, 174, 189*n*.5; as spokespersons, in diversity training, 120

Minority representation, 127, 143, 148

Models, knowledge representation with, 105

Monitoring, self-. *See* Self-monitoring

Motivation, 54, *xvi, xx;* as affective